THEORIES OF DEVELOPMENT

Theories of Development
Contentions, Arguments, Alternatives

SECOND EDITION

RICHARD PEET
ELAINE HARTWICK

THE GUILFORD PRESS
New York   London

© 2009 The Guilford Press
A Division of Guilford Publications, Inc.
72 Spring Street, New York, NY 10012
www.guilford.com

Printed in the United States of America

This book is printed on acid-free paper.

Last digit is print number: 9 8 7 6 5 4 3 2

Library of Congress Cataloging-in-Publication Data

Peet, Richard.
  Theories of development : contentions, arguments, alternatives / Richard Peet,
Elaine Hartwick. — 2nd ed.
      p. cm.
  Includes bibliographical references and index.
  ISBN 978-1-60623-066-4 (hardcover : alk. paper)
  ISBN 978-1-60623-065-7 (pbk. : alk. paper)
  1. Economic development.   2. Dependency.   3. Capitalism.   4. Marxian
economics.   I. Title.
  HD75.P43 2009
  338.9—dc21
                                                      2008050378

For our parents—

Eileen Migala,
Harold Wilfred Peet,
Anna B. Hartwick,
and John A. Hartwick

And our children—

James C. Peet,
Lukas J. Klapatch,
Eric R. Peet,
and Anna E. Peet

My Anna Elaine
It was while sharing a quiet moment together,
when my soft whispering to her
was answered in return
with a wondrous look and a low cooing sound
as her small hand reached out to mine
and her tiny fingers wrapped around my heart
　　　　　　　　　—ABH, August 2002

Preface

This book began as a rewrite of *Global Capitalism*, published by Routledge in 1991, and then of *Theories of Development*, published by Guilford in 1999. But it has become far more than both. Indeed, the final product contains only a few paragraphs entirely intact from the earlier works. This latest version is far more a critical survey of the main theories of development and includes more of the controversies over this vital area of knowledge. We wrote this book during a period of transformation in the global economy, a period when the new international division of labor entered a middle-age crisis, when the certainties of the past 40 years were increasingly viewed as precarious, when the global economy entered financial crisis. During this time, the need for fundamental understanding, for reexamining the great attitudinal paradigms of development, took on new significance. This lent our work an urgency that, we hope, spills onto its pages, imparting to the contents some semblance, at least, of the somberness we felt in composing our words.

The book results from long collaboration between what is now a wife-and-husband partnership. Specifically, Elaine wrote most of Chapter 7, while Richard wrote most of the rest. More generally, the book results from many conversations and collaborations stretching over spaces and times scattered across the past 15 years of our friendship. Yet, authorship should actually include many others, for—as quickly becomes evident—we draw on the works of dozens of writers in presenting anew the finest ideas in the field of development, spanning more than two centuries, from Adam Smith, through Karl Marx, to the contemporary feminist and poststructural thinkers. Most of the ideas that appear in this volume belonged originally to others, and we take responsibility only for the way they are presented in this instance.

Even so, we have not taken a passive attitude toward these ideas, content merely to present them accurately. Instead, each chapter contains a critique, some of which (especially in Part I) even undercut the very foundations on which the key ideas rest. Is this because we feel criticism to be the highest form of appreciation? Or, rather, does it result from a more pragmatic political conclusion that rethinking the essentials of development theory might ultimately result in replacing it with something better? We can only say that our intention has been to survey the past in order to stimulate a new discourse about development, and this approach not only entails negative criticisms but also aims at positive reconstruction.

Both of us have taught courses using the book as the key source material several times. Indeed, as we wrote the new edition, memories of past conversations with our students colored our perceptions. Elaine would like to thank the students at SUNY Albany, Mount Holyoke College, the University of Southern Maine, Central Connecticut State College, Clark University, Keene State College, and, most recently, Framingham State College who participated in her courses dealing with many of the issues in this book. Richard would like to thank his students in Global Society, Political Economy of Development, and Development Policy at Clark University, but also participants in courses taught at the University of Iowa, the University of California at Santa Barbara, and the University of the Witwatersrand in Johannesburg, South Africa. The Guilford Press had an earlier draft read by several reviewers, and their comments proved useful in making revisions. Waquar Ahmed redrew the figures, and we thank him for his generous help.

Our book is dedicated to our parents directly, for making our ideas possible, but also to all working-class people indirectly, for their hard labor that makes existence possible. This edition is also dedicated to our kids—for deepening our joyous lives and for all the great times we have together in the house, in the yard, on the beach, at the river.

As Marx observed some 150 years ago: "The philosophers have only interpreted the world, in various ways; the point, however, is to change it."

RICHARD PEET
ELAINE HARTWICK

Contents

1

Development

Development means making a better life for everyone. In the present context of a highly uneven world, a better life for most people means, essentially, meeting basic needs: sufficient food to maintain good health; a safe, healthy place in which to live; affordable services available to everyone; and being treated with dignity and respect. Beyond meeting these needs, basic to human survival, the course taken by development is subject to the material and cultural visions of different societies. The methods and purposes of development are subject to popular, democratic decision making. Many people might agree that a better life for all is a desirable goal and that development as its theory is time and thought well spent. But not everyone thinks development is universally realizable at the present time ("we are not quite there yet"). And among those who think that the goal of a better life for all is practicable, there are broad disagreements on how to get there. Development understood as a better life is a powerful emotive ideal because it appeals to the best in people. What might be called the "discourse of development" (the system of statements made about development) has the power to move people, to affect and change us forever. Hence, development can be used for many different political purposes, including some, and perhaps most, that conflict with its essentially egalitarian ethic ("a better life for *all*"). Indeed, the idea of development can be used to legitimate what in fact amounts to more money and power for a few. So, putting all this together, development is a contentious issue around which swirl bitter arguments and fierce debates.

Development is a founding belief of modernity. And modernity is that time in Western history when rationality supposed it could change the world for the better. In development, all the modern advances in science and technology, in democracy and social organization, in ratio-

I

nalized ethics and values, fuse into the single humanitarian project of deliberately and cooperatively producing a far better world for all. In this modernist tradition, the radical version of "development" is fundamentally different from the more conventional "economic growth." Economic growth means achieving a more massive economy—producing more goods and services on the one side of the national account (gross domestic product—GDP)—and a larger total income on the other (gross national income—GNI). But economic growth can occur without touching problems like inequality or poverty when all the increase goes to a few people. Indeed, growth has occurred in most Western countries over the past 30 years at the same time that income inequality has widened. In this case, economic growth functions, in the most basic sense, to channel money and power to the already rich and famous. This is fine if you are rich, and even better if you are famous. But for developmentalists this feeding of money to the already wealthy is a travesty of ethics and a tragedy of modern economic practice. The excuses for it, like "trickle down" (eventually everyone benefits from growth as income trickles down from the rich) are not convincing except to those already convinced by their complete adherence to an elite society. Because of social and environmental reasons, growth is justified only when it produces development—when it satisfies essential needs.

As this suggests, development is interested not so much in the growth of an economy but rather the conditions under which production occurs and the results that flow from it. In terms of conditions, development pays attention to the environments affected by economic activity and the labor relations and conditions of the actual producers of wealth—the peasants and workers who produce growth. If growth wrecks the environment, and if growth deadens working life, it is not development. Development looks too at what is produced. If growth merely produces more Wal-Mart junk rather than schools or clinics, it is not development. Development attends to the social consequences of production. If growth merely concentrates wealth in the hands of a few, it is not development. Most contentiously, development analyses who controls production and consumption. If the growth process is controlled by a few powerful people rather than the many people who make it possible, it is not development. If growth means subjecting the world's people to an incessant barrage of consumption inducements that invade every corner of life, it is not development. If growth is the outcome of market processes that no one controls—although a few people benefit—it is not development. Development is optimistic and utopian. Development means changing the world for the better. Development means starting change at the bottom rather than the top.

As an ideal concept, development comes from Enlightenment notions of the intervention of the modern, scientific, and democratic mind into the improvement of human existence. Development entails human emancipation, in two of the senses of the word: liberation from the vicissitudes of nature, through greater understanding of earth processes followed by carefully applied technology; and self-emancipation, control over social relations, conscious control over the conditions under which human nature is formed, rational and democratic control over the cultural production of the human personality. (Is the greatest tragedy of modernity the loosening of social control over the production of subjectivity to people and institutions with the worst of motives—like ad agencies, for instance?) In both senses, external and internal, development entails economic, social, and cultural progress, including, in the latter sense, finer ethical ideals and higher moral values. Development means improvement in a complex of linked natural, economic, social, cultural, and political conditions. Developmentalism is the belief in the viability and desirability of this kind of economic progress. A good example might be Amartya Sen's *Development as Freedom* (2000), concerned with how society grants to individuals the capacity for taking part in creating their own livelihoods, governing their own affairs, and participating in self-government—although we do not find him following this through with a political economics of societal transformation. In brief, development is quite different from growth. Development springs from the most optimistic moment of the modern rational belief, whereas mere growth is practical, technological, but also class-prejudiced thought.

Critics from the poststructuralist end of modern critical social theory say that developmentalism, even when understood in this way (*especially* when understood in this way), monopolizes dreams of progress and destroys alternative conceptions of the future. Modern reason, poststructuralists say, drains experience of emotion so that people become machine-like, air-headed, or both. What appear to be the finest developmental principles at the center of the best of modern existence are subjected by poststructuralists to intense skepticism: modernity, reason, development, consumption cannot be deemed automatically "good." Yet, we respond, development has been laid to rest before, said to be at an impasse, outdated, moribund, morally corrupt, only to rise again. When something is heavily criticized yet persists, it probably has real content. Could it be that development is both the best and worst of human projects—best in terms of potential and worst in terms of its sorry contemporary practice? Either way, as the finest ideal of an enlightened humanity or as a strategy of modern mind control, development is too easily simplified, too quickly dismissed, especially by those who take its real benefits, like modern healthcare or clean water and toilets, for granted. Instead, we argue in this book that development is a complex, contradictory, contentious phenomenon, reflective of the best of human aspirations, and yet, exactly for this reason, subject to the most intense manipulation, liable to be used for purposes that reverse its original intent by people who feign good intentions, the more to gain power. Now, often, when authors use words like "complex," "contradictory," and "contentious," they are preparing to excuse themselves from subsequently writing anything definite—everything is relative, the world is too difficult for precision in thought and statement, and nothing can be done. That will not be the case here. We think the complexities of development can be pierced by rational analysis and its seeming contradictions can be resolved. We think that development, understood in the sense we have used the term, can be achieved. We take sides in the controversy over development.

Thus, developmentalism is a battleground where contention rages among bureaucratic economists, Marxist revolutionaries, environmental activists, feminist critics, postmodern skeptics, and radical democrats. This is an area of profound significance for the interests of the world's most vulnerable people, an area where shifts in emphasis, like the World Bank's switch in focus from basic needs in the 1970s to structural adjustment in the 1990s, can end up killing millions of babies a year and make life far more miserable, desperate, and short for countless others in countries far removed from the "rationality centers" of London, Geneva, or Washington, DC. Theories of development reach deeply into culture for explanatory and persuasive power, while the end products of such deep thinking, together with the dedicated practices of millions of well-meaning people, are political tools with mass appeal. Therefore, we have to make clear the basic theoretical positions in the development debate through effective presentation and thorough critique. We have to assess the fundamental criticisms of the whole development enterprise. And we have to resist the impulse to let these criticisms rest easy on the assumption that, because they are the latest thing, they are necessarily the last and best word on the subject. From the informed critique of development there might arise a new conception of development.

THE GEOGRAPHY OF DEVELOPMENT

Let us take up the issue of social scientific perspective, alluded to briefly earlier. Development can be viewed from a number of perspectives that have come to be identified as "academic disciplines." We happen to be human geographers, and, while we think more as social theorists in general, we often dwell longer than most on the geographic parts. So, we should say what our geographic perspective is. The disciplinary specialization called geography looks at two inter-related aspects, or characteristics, of human life: the aspect of nature—the relations between societies and environments; and the aspect of space—the regional variations in societal type and the relations across space among these regionally differing societal types. The connection between the two aspects of geography is that regional variations in human characteristics are essentially produced by different modes of socially transforming nature. For example, different types of economy, such as agriculture, industry, or services, have different types of relations with natural environments—for example, think of an agricultural landscape as compared to an industrial landscape. In this geographic system, each type of society is spatially related to all others. The most obvious spatial connection is through trade—exchanging goods of different kinds. More significantly, societies with different types and levels of development interact through power relations—societies with high economic growth rates dominate societies trying to achieve better development. Specialized components of society are also bound together through various other kinds of spatial relations, such as commodity chains, the communication of messages, ownership systems, flows of investments and profits, and so on. The entire complex of regional economic forms, tied together by spatial relations, makes up a global totality. This "geographical" approach goes through the regional and local parts to reach an understanding of the global whole of human existence. It is one way of making sense of global complexity in terms of its parts.

Human existence has to be produced. We live now because we worked in the past. The mode of the production of existence (the character of its main social forces, relations, institutions, and thought patterns) varies over space. Most significantly, the degree of material development, particularly the standard of living, is completely different from one place to another. For example, the "average" U.S. citizen spends some $44,000 a year and is responsible for the release of 20 tons of carbon dioxide annually into the local atmosphere (and even more worldwide if exports are considered), while the "average" Rwandan survives on $230 a year and emits only 0.1 ton of carbon dioxide into the atmosphere (World Bank 2007). Different levels of material life entail entirely different life chances for individuals born at various places on the earth's surface—in some places children almost automatically survive their traumatic first months, while in other places death arrives so often as to be treated as normal. Life is experienced as having some fundamental similarities among all people—indeed, among all natural organisms—but there is also a definite version or, in the case of geography, a place-bound type of this entire existence. In other words, existence has universal qualities of life and needs as well as particular qualities or characteristics of livelihood and life chances. Real differences in the modes of life—differences that arise from variations in the types and levels of development—are what geographers try to understand as their specialized task in social science.

MEASURING GROWTH AND DEVELOPMENT

Development is important because it produces an economy, and more broadly a society and culture, that determines how people live—in terms of income, services, life chances, education, and so on. As we have said, "development" is conventionally measured as economic growth, with "level of development" seen in terms of "size of the economy." The size of a nation's economy, under what is called the "income approach" to accounting, is derived from totaling the wages, rents, interest, profits, nonincome charges, and net foreign factor income earned by that country's people—thus, the gross national income (GNI) is basically what everyone earns. Total expenditures on goods and services must, by definition, in this kind of national accounting practice be equal to the value of the goods and services produced, and this must be equal to the total income paid to the factors (workers, shareholders, etc.) that produced these goods and services. Thus, gross national product (GNP) is the total value of final goods and services produced in a year by a country's residents (including profits from capital held abroad). Nominal GNP measures the value of output during a given year using the prices prevailing during that year. Over time, the general level of prices tends to rise due to inflation, leading to an increase in nominal GNP even if the volume of goods and services produced is unchanged. So, real GNP measures the value of output adjusted for inflation. When economic growth over a number of years is measured, change in "real GNP" is the figure usually used to express that growth. Dividing the GNP or GNI by a country's population yields the GNP or GNI per capita. In general, the higher the per capita production or income, the more "developed" a country's people are conventionally said to be, and the higher the annual growth rate per capita, the more rapidly a country is said to be developing.

In 2005 the World Bank (2005: 288–289), the global institution that publishes much of the basic data on such matters, divided countries into three categories depending on their income level: low income, middle income, or high income. As shown in Table 1.1, in 2005 the world had roughly 6.5 billion people, a total income of $45 trillion (a trillion is a thousand billion), and an average per capita income of some $7,000 a year. Just over 1 billion people live in high-income countries, where the total GNI is $35.5 trillion and GNI per capita averages $35,131 a year—in other words, 15.7% of the world's people (those living in rich

TABLE 1.1. Development Indicators, 2005

	Population (millions)	Gross national income $ billions	Gross national income $ per capita	Life expectancy (years) Male	Life expectancy (years) Female	Adult literacy rate (%)
World	6,438	44,983.3	6,987	65	69	80
Low income	2,353	1,363.9	580	58	60	62
Middle income	3,073	8,113.1	2,640	68	73	90
High income	1,011	35,528.8	35,131	76	82	99

Source: World Bank (2007: 289).

countries) get almost 80% of global income. At the other extreme, 2.4 billion people living in low-income countries have only $1.36 trillion in total income and an average GNI per capita of only $580 a year—the 37% of the world's people that live in the poorest countries get just 3% of global income. Moreover, global inequality is increasing. In 1960 the 20% of the world's people living in the richest countries had 30 times the income of the 20% of the world's people living in the poorest countries; in 1973 the figure was 44 to 1; and in 1997 the ratio was 74 to 1 (United Nations Development Program 1999: 36–38). As statisticians find out more about it, the world is turning out to be even more unequal than was previously thought, both in terms of the differences among countries and the differences among groups of the world's people. National poverty rates in the low-income countries lie in the range of 45–70% of the population, while the percentage of people living on less that $2 a day varies from 50% to 90%, depending on the country (Milanovic 2007).

Even so, geographic differences are only the beginning of the inequality story. Class, ethnicity, gender, and regional location distribute incomes extremely unequally *within* each country. Of the almost 80% of global income that ends up in the rich countries, 50% typically goes to the highest-income 20% of their people, while the lowest-income 20% in the rich countries get only 5–9%, depending on the country. In other words, *200 million of the richest people living in the rich countries (3% of the global population) get 40% of total global income.* At the other extreme, in the low-income countries, the richest 20% there typically get 50–85% of national income, depending on the country, while the poorest 20% typically get only 3–5% of the 3% of global income that these poor countries receive (World Bank 2004). In other words, *571 million of the poorest people living in the poorest countries (9% of the world's people) get only 0.12% of global income.* Space and class conspire to produce inequality so severe that one wonders how global society can endure.

One of the great unmentioned facts about global income distribution is this: poverty results from extreme inequalities. Poor people are poor because rich people take so much of the income the economy produces. So, what has been happening to inequality recently? The key factor causing secular changes in class incomes is an even greater divergence in the ownership of wealth, especially financial wealth—that is, bank accounts, ownership of stocks and bonds, and life insurance and mutual fund savings. Particularly important is the ownership of stocks and mutual fund shares. Despite a reported trend in financial markets toward "democratization" (retirement savings invested in mutual funds, etc.), only 27% of U.S. families own stocks. While 78% of the richest families own stocks and mutual funds, only 3% of the poorest families do so. The equalizing trends in wealth ownership of the period between the 1930s and the 1970s reversed sharply during the 1980s so that by 1989 the richest 1% of households owned almost half of the total financial wealth of the United States (Wolf 1995), a concentration of ownership that has only become more extreme since then (Harvey 2005b: 16–17). Within this rich 1%, the super-rich—that one-thousandth of households (145,000 people) making an average of $3 million a year—doubled its share of total national income between 1980 and 2002, to 7.4% (see Figure 1.1), while the share earned by the bottom 90% of the population fell (Johnston 2005: 1).

All this however refers to income and economic growth, conventionally understood—although discussions of inequality are usually left out in conventional accounts. There are many other datasets frequently used, even by such conventional agencies as the World Bank, to measure not only growth but the levels and changes in average age of death, infant mortality, population per physician, secondary education, and use of electricity—for instance, see the right-hand side of Table 1.1. An alternative summary measure that takes these into account is the Human Development Index (HDI) calculated by the United Nations Development Program (UNDP). This measure derives from a different conception of development than that usually presented—what the UNDP calls "enlarging people's choices," especially in terms of access to knowledge, nutrition and health services, security, leisure, and political and cultural freedoms. The HDI measures development in terms of longevity (life expectancy at birth), knowledge (adult literacy and mean years of schooling), and income sufficiency (the proportion of people with sufficient resources for a decent life). In 2007–2008 the countries at the top of this index were, in order, Iceland, Norway, Australia, Canada, Ireland, Sweden, Switzerland, Japan, Netherlands, France, Finland, and the United States—all

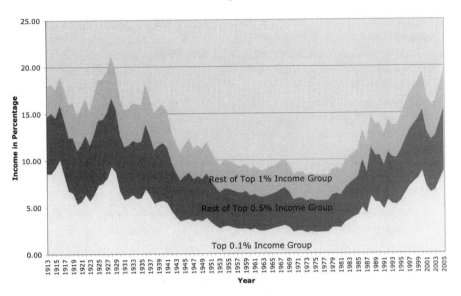

FIGURE I.I. Percentage of income earned by three top brackets, United States, 1913–2005. Source: Piketty, Hess, and Saez (2006).

scoring over 0.9 out of a maximum of 1.0 (the United Kingdom ranked 16th and New Zealand 19th; UNDP 2008). An HDI score below 0.5 represents low development, and 29 of the 31 countries in that category are located in Africa, the others being Haiti and Yeman. The lowest-ranked HDI countries are Sierra Leone, Burkina Faso, Guinea-Bissau, and Niger (UNDP 2008). The idea behind this kind of work is to capture more, and different, aspects of the human condition in a redefinition of development (ul Haq 1995; UNDP 2006). This notion of human development defends the project of intervening to improve conditions in the developing countries. In this light, for the UNDP (1991: 14), development

> has succeeded beyond any reasonable expectation. ... Developing countries have achieved in 30 years what it took industrial countries nearly a century to accomplish. ... The overall policy conclusion is clear. The development process *does* work. International development cooperation *has* made a difference.

However, the UNDP also documents that during roughly this same time span when "development ... succeeded beyond expectation" the gap between rich and poor countries actually *widened* and that the average household in Africa now consumes 20% less than it did about a quarter-century ago (UNDP 2001). Americans spend more on cosmetics than it would cost to provide basic education to the 2 billion people in the world who go without schools. Europeans spend more on ice cream than it would cost to provide basic water and sanitation services to those most desperately in need (UNDP 1998). The UNDP optimistically concludes that human development can be achieved by promoting "more equitable" economic growth and using participatory, democratic political methods. We agree. But we have a different conception of "eqitable" and "participatory democracy," as this book will reveal.

CRITICISMS OF DEVELOPMENT MEASURES

We should immediately note two kinds of deficiencies in the official data on both growth and development. First, not only do these data vary greatly in reliability from country to country but also characteristics such as production, income, or education are, in reality, culturally specific rather than universal. Yet, national and international agencies report only that which can be measured using "conventional" accounting procedures. Whose conventions are used? Those of the First World market economies. Thus, GDP measures that part of production sold for a price in a formal market—but not products consumed within the family nor services exchanged informally. Thus, a major portion of the economic activity in many Third World countries is either ignored completely or simply estimated. Much of this unreported product results from women's work (Rogers 1980: 61); for example, 60–80% of the food is produced in the "informal sector," and 70% of informal entrepreneurs are women (Snyder 1995: xv). All of this informal activity literally does not count when measuring the economy. Even estimates made in France, generally considered to be a highly organized market economy, show informal exchanges of income, such as gifts, amounting to some 75% of the official GNP (Insel 1993). The proportion is much higher in Third World countries, where far more economic activity lies outside the formal market sphere. In other words, the "official" economy, whose measurements serve as the main indicators of growth, may be only a minor part of the *real* economy, whose true measurements are unknown. This has to be remembered when arguments about growth, development, and poverty are made on the basis of existing statistics: these people literally do not know what they are talking about. Similarly, education is officially measured as enrollment in an official school and therefore excludes informal educational institutions, while energy consumption excludes such traditional fuels as firewood and dried animal excrement; and so on.

   In view of these shortcomings, many critics conclude that GNP and GDP measure economic modernization in the prejudiced sense of how closely a country replicates the characteristics of the West rather than development in a whole range of indigenous senses of the term. Increases in GNP per capita, energy use, or education may reflect only an increase in the proportion of activity occurring in the organized, taxed market sector of an economy rather than in the informal sector—total real production can actually decline as GDP increases. So, while GDP may measure quantitative change in market production (economic growth), it is a gross indicator of the qualities of domestic production. Furthermore, as the discussion on inequality suggests, average (mean) figures like GDP per capita, or people per physician, hide enormous differences among groups within countries, as between classes or genders, or between rural and urban populations. Means are meaning*less* in terms of representing the real situation in a society. In summary, the available data give only a poor and often misleading indication of the level and movement of economic development, if by this term we basically mean the level of material standards of living for the majority of the population. In a startling and rare admission of ignorance, the development economist William Easterly (2009) says that manipulating the available data yields no insights into the determinants of economic growth—every time the growth data are revised, or the sample is changed to another equally plausible one, the results vanish: "Goodbye, malaria; hello, democracy."

Second, we move to a more profound criticism of the use of GNP and GDP data to measure development. Even when qualified by the unreliability and insufficiency of the data, conclusions drawn from income figures are increasingly suspect to those theorists intensely skeptical about modernity, development, progress, and many similar notions previously taken for granted in the post-(European) Enlightenment world. The argument is increasingly made that GNP per capita and even more benign statistical devices such as the HDI have *nothing* whatsoever to do with variations in the quality of life. This argument applies not only to peasants on the margins of a supposedly good earth but also to the richest people ensconced in the suburbs of Western cities, whose lives are in truth *impoverished* by an abundance of gadgets and whose aspirations are limited merely to getting more. Take "happiness," for instance. Despite a massive increase in income and wealth in the West over the past 50 years, levels of happiness have not increased. "Standard of living has increased dramatically and happiness has increased not at all, and in some cases has diminished slightly" (Kahneman and Krueger 2006). It is true that people in rich countries say they are happier than people in poor countries. But once people have a home, food, and clothes, any extra income does not seem to make them much happier. It appears that the level of happiness sufficiency is reached at average national incomes of about $20,000 a year (Rudin 2006). So, why not redistribute income from the rich, who don't need it in terms of life happiness, to the poor, who could certainly use it to be a lot better off?

Even so, statistical tables of GNP per capita and even tables of happiness can be seen as instruments of power rather than neutral methods of measurement. This is because their structures, as comparative series, imply a hierarchy—a kind of league table—with a ladder reaching from bottom to top that must be climbed by people and countries aspiring to "development" or even some kind of "universal happiness." High per capita GNP, reached through economic growth, becomes the objective of a society's best efforts, and the economic and political methods used in the past by the rich countries become the development policy for the aspiring poor countries, with "success" measured by change in tabular ranking. Some theorists strangely persist in saying that people are not statistics but living beings. And there is the underlying contradiction that, as GNP increases, resource use and environmental damage increase even faster, with such proven consequences as global warming and climate change, destruction of the protective ozone layer, and El Niño's effects exacerbated by warmer ocean currents. In discourses that transcend developmentalism (discourses in the "postdevelopmentalist" tradition), a high GNP per capita may most accurately signify cultural blindsidedness, environmental degradation, and the capturing of the world's imagination by dreams of American-style consumptive happiness.

THE FACE OF POVERTY

The reader might notice that, while we (the authors of this book) voice various qualifications, we too, sometimes, use statistical data to talk about growth, development, and poverty. We do this because we are part of a scientific tradition that values statistical data as the way of proving statements—showing them to be "true" in the sense of accurately representing reality. But we would like to confess that when we think about unequal development and the poverty it produces, we ourselves do not think primarily in terms of figures. We, the authors of this book, are not numbers people. In fact, we think that too many numbers numb the imagination and make it dead to the real, permitting our minds to contemplate "objectively," as though from a distance, the scarcely imaginable horrors of human existence. Distanced contemplation through the dry data of statistics encourages the institutional manipulation of poverty. So, we use figures but mistrust them, not just in terms of "reliability" but more so in terms of the impoverishment of the statistical or mathematical mind. When *we* think about poverty, graphic images come to mind. Let us tell you about a few of these.

A few years ago, the two of us spent a few months in Johannesburg, South Africa. In that part of the country, illegal migrants cross the border mainly by walking through Krueger National Park, where the lions lie in wait for their nightly feast of human flesh. The migrants then walk a couple of hundred miles further to the city. There are hundreds of thousands of immigrants in the city, but we encountered them dramatically when we got temporarily lost walking near the University of the Witwatersrand. We turned a corner to come across a street filled with a couple of thousand of recent arrivals from all over sub-Saharan Africa. These were dignified people. No one asked for money. No one spoke to us, in fact. They just stared at us in a way that haunts us still—because we had a house to go to, food to eat, a safe bed to sleep in that night, and they did not—in the city of their dreams that they had just risked their lives to reach.

Another quick flash of memory, this time summoning up India. One of us visited New Delhi and Mumbai in late 2007. As the reader may be aware of, both cities have huge slums that stretch for miles—Dharavi (in Mumbai) is in fact the largest slum in Asia. But also the sidewalks along the main streets and the edges to the railroad lines are home to further millions of poor people, who attempt to shelter themselves under blue plastic sheets and eat, wash, and defecate in public—the implications for public health are obvious. Think of a street filled to overflowing with trucks, cars, cabs, and three-wheeled motorcycle rickshaws, all pushing to gain a few yards, with drivers who do not spare the horn, and yet little naked kids tottering a few inches away, their mothers distractedly trying merely to ensure survival for their families that day. No person of conscience can see Mumbai, with its excessive financial wealth, big gated houses, and gracious colonial waterfront, on the one side, and six million people living in "informal settlements" (as the euphemism goes), on the other, and emerge the same person. But from this cataclysmic experience, two images stand out: in Mumbai, two boys flying a homemade kite in the only open space available to them, above the traffic filling the street that is their home; and in New Delhi, a 5-year-old girl singing to herself to relieve the rejection she received a thousand times a day while begging at a traffic light amid the hordes of people going to and fro. Kids desperately trying to experience bits of childhood lost to a life they know will be forever spent in abject poverty. Raw snippets forever seared into memory and learned in "real life," rather than statistical figures read from books, flood our minds as we compose these words.

CONTENTIONS OVER DEVELOPMENT

This volume explores some of the key debates surrounding the leading social and economic theories of development. The basic pattern of affluence and poverty that characterizes the contemporary geography of the world was already obvious by the 19th century, and it immediately stimulated intense social scientific interest. However, scientific interest is hardly separable from the desire for social legitimation—that is, the desire to make a society, usually one's own, appear to be good. Theorists always pursue truth. But "truth" varies, depending on the truth teller's proclivities. And the theorist's logical capacity is located not in a sphere separate from his or her empathy for others, a desire for self-justification, or one's wish to be of service to the dominant social order. The connections among science, values, and development are especially evident when issues like increasing the wealth of some people at the expense of others arise, unavoidably, in one's mind. Theory easily diverges into ideology when the mind tries to comprehend scarcely comprehensible things such as racism, imperialism, sexism, and exploitation—all involved in unequal development.

With notions like these in mind, that is, ideology as only partial and biased "truths," first we survey some system-supporting (politically conventional) theories of uneven growth and development in Part I of this volume, "Conventional Theories," composed of Chapters 2, 3, and 4. (Note that we are summarizing many complex arguments in the next few paragraphs—we suggest reading them to get a rough idea of the structure of the book and then reading them later when this dense jungle of abstractions will make more sense.) Chapter 2 isolates the economic aspect of development, the part designated as economic growth, and separates out the specialized study of this dimension, the discipline called economics, for particularly intensive examination. Anyone wishing to understand development has to know at least the outlines of the leading conventional economic theories. Yet, economic ideas cannot entirely be separated from their material and ideational contexts. So, we delve into the philosophies on which classical economics was founded, especially the concepts underlying the British Enlightenment—like the modern, free individual—that form the basis of Adam Smith and David Ricardo's economics, and then follow the continuing relations with broader social, cultural, and especially political ideas as economics moved through its various phases. The purpose of Chapter 2 is not merely to provide a quick introduction to economics but to demonstrate that the dominant notion of development, as a certain kind of economic growth founded on capitalist efficiency, results from one interpretation of one aspect of one people's history made from the point of view of one class rising to dominance in western Europe. Yet, this biased, particularistic notion is universalized in contemporary neoliberalism as the proven solution to the social and economic problems of the peoples of all countries. Chapter 2 therefore includes fundamental critiques of the philosophical and theoretical bases of conventional (classical and neoclassical) economics.

Chapter 3 covers 20th- and 21st-century conventional economic thought, moving from Keynesian economics through structuralist and developmental economics to neoliberalism. Keynesian economic theory legitimized state intervention into market economies with the aim of achieving growth rates decided on the basis of social policy. Subsequently some degree of state intervention became more or less accepted in mainstream economics and in conventional politics. Similarly, in Latin America a structuralist school of thought emerged that was critical of certain aspects of classical economic doctrine, found conventional economics too abstract, and often urged, as did Keynes, greater state intervention in the growth process. For a while, during the 1950s and 1960s, even quite conventional economists believed in a separate school of development economics. But a "counterrevolution" in development theory, part of a more general neoliberal reaction, opposed Keynesianism, social democracy, state intervention, structuralism, and development economics. We look at this critique and then follow the trajectory of neoliberal economics from its founders in the Austrian school, through "the Chicago boys," to the World Bank and the Washington Consensus. However, all this began to change again during the early 2000s as mass protests erupted against the international financial institutions (IFIs), forcing neoliberal development policies to be reconsidered. A new policy formation within a reshuffled institutional framework arose phoenix-like from the ashes, which we term a "post-Washington benevolent consensus." The chapter concludes critically by arguing that all conventional economic theories of growth and development are hopelessly flawed because economics harbors deeply within its structure an unrealistic and biased view of the world.

Chapter 4 discusses how the first modern (late 19th-century) theories of societal development drew on evolutionary biology for explanatory power, essentially arguing that geographic differences in human achievement were the inevitable consequences of prior variations in natural environments. There were two versions of this idea: the strong (deterministic) thesis that nature creates people with unequal potentials, especially different levels of intelligence; and the weaker thesis that nature provides superior resource environments that are conducive to easier or quicker development in some places than in others. In concluding that the natural environment largely determines levels of development, both versions assert that nature chooses who should be successful and who should not;

this theme is often extended to suggest that the strong naturally exploit the weak in order to survive better or, more benignly, to "bring progress" to the world—"civilize the world" is the phrase often used. These ideas have not disappeared; indeed, they have staged a comeback. A second tradition covered in Chapter 4 sees development as resulting largely from social rather than natural events. In the tradition of Max Weber's sociology, the rationalization of the world, with its utter disenchantment with naturalistic and mystical phenomena, was the original mainspring for the rise of the West. Chapter 4 follows the argument of sociological modernization theory that developed societies carry out their social and economic functions in highly rationalized ways to achieve development. Modernization theory applies this formulation to societal evolution, positing that modern institutional organizations and rational forms of behavior first appeared in 15th- and 16th-century Europe and that subsequent development took the form of the spread of rational action and efficient institutions. Most of these theories take the form of universal stages of growth. Modernization geography thus explains regional variations in development in terms of diffusion, from the originating cores, of modern institutions and rationalized practices. As these innovative cores happened to lie in Euro-America, modernization theory can be seen as continuing the ideological tradition of neoclassical economics. We subject these ideas to considerable criticism. Yet, we see modernization theory as rising again to provide the theoretical backing for recent proposals on the United Nations' "millennium goals" that now are at the focal point of conventional liberal and neoliberal development theory.

From Part I, we next move to nonconventional but highly critical theories of development in Part II of the book, beginning with Marxist and neo-Marxist approaches to societal development in Chapter 5. The most powerful critique of modernization emanated from theorists schooled in the dependency perspective. Dependency theory argues, on a neo-Marxist basis, that contact with Europe may indeed bring modernization to some people in the societies of the Third World, but that modernity arrives bearing the price of exploitation. For dependency theorists, the spread of European "civilization" to the rest of the world was accompanied by the extraction of raw materials, the draining of social resources, and a loss of control over the basic institutions of society—hence arises the notion of "dependency," or at best "dependent development," in what rapidly became the periphery of a world system dominated by the European center. Instead of being developed by their connections with the center of the global capitalist order, peripheral societies were actively *under*developed, and the political and ethical implications were catastrophic for Europe's historical evolution.

Most versions of the dependency perspective draw on Marxism as their main philosophical and theoretical basis. Marxism, covered in Chapter 5, is a materialist explanation of societal structures that sees workers as active agents in transforming nature, through the labor process, into their livelihood. Development amounts to building up the productive forces available for the making of one's livelihood. However, development takes place in class societies in such a way that the material benefits derived from hard work and increased productivity are *unequally* distributed. Class struggle forms the basis of the societal dynamic (including the economic development process). Profits and overconsumption drive environmental destruction. Marxism has a dialectical understanding of history in which change stems from the contradictions and tensions inherent to human groups and between society and the natural world. Marxist structuralism sees new modes of production as, first, emerging from the contradictions in the old, then maturing and spreading in space, and finally bringing different types and levels of development to societies. The idea of articulations (interpenetrations, combinations) between modes of production is a way of understanding intersocietal relations that yields a richer version of the theory of underdevelopment than dependency alone. Critics of Marxism generally emphasize its functional and teleological excesses, linking totalization in theory with totalitarianism in politics. We reply to these criticisms from the perspective of our own socialist politics, which takes the form of radical democracy and critical modernism. We provide examples of socialist development, drawing on the experiences of the Soviet Union (now Russia), Cuba, and Venezuela. We conclude that, by listening to criticism and changing, Marxism still remains capable of providing a coherent and insightful critical theory of societal structures and dynamics as the basis for a politics of liberation.

Marxism comes in for more than its share of criticism—from neoliberalism and conservatism obviously but also from poststructural and postmodern critics, too, who find it to be yet one more (and sometimes the archetypical) modern theory. As we explain in Chapter 6, poststructuralism criticizes all modern theories for their essentializing and totalizing pretensions, while postmodern theorists evidence the most extreme skepticism about the entire modern project of "human emancipation." These criticisms intersect with new examinations of the experiences of the formerly colonial countries by postcolonial critics located often in hybrid positions combining societal types. Then, too, radical and liberal development practice goes through a phase of disillusionment and despair in an age of neoliberal triumphalism. These tendencies come together in the poststructural critique of modern developmentalism. What previously was seen as automatically good is now theorized as a political technique of modern power, effective precisely because it claims to serve the interests of humanity. A number of these positions uneasily cohere in a growing "postdevelopmentalism," entailing the complete rejection of modern development rather than its modification or democratization. Postdevelopmentalism hesitantly proposes some new principles to guide lives lived in poverty, like thinking locally rather than globally, living more simply in material terms, or seeking more spiritual lives rather than worshipping the latest fashions and trends. Yet, the criticisms of the post-developmentalists are so severe, so all-encompassing, that they too must be deconstructed. Perhaps modernism is discarded too readily, without sufficient regard for such modern advances as high-tech machinery and hospitals that admittedly have their beneficial aspects. Perhaps a better, more democratic, more egalitarian modernism is possible. All these issues are extensively explored in Chapter 6, a discourse full of controversy and differences.

Chapter 7 explores feminist attempts at reformulating development theory. Women perform most of the work in many, if not most, societies. So, why have women been excluded from development theory? What differences would result if theory were reformulated to emphasize gender relations? For feminists, new aspects of development are brought into focus—for example, the informal and rural sectors of the economy and the reproductive sphere, that is, the relations between production and reproduction. This change in perspective does not merely change development theory but rather *improves* and *transforms* it. There are several alternative approaches to the interaction between feminist theory and development, which have historically been categorized as Women in Development (WID), Women and Development (WAD), Gender and Development (GAD), Women, Environment, and Development (WED), and Postmodernism and Development (PAD). We discuss in detail, present a brief criticism (brief because we agree with much that is said), and conclude that our own position is closest to the WAD perspective.

Part III of the book, composed of a single chapter (Chapter 8), reconsiders development in light of the many criticisms made of it. For the writers of this book, democracy, emancipation, and development are fine principles of modernity that have been perverted by the capitalist form taken by modernity. For us, the main problem with development is not that it is inherently coercive and controlling but that it has never been achieved in anything like the ways we have characterized it! Our own preferred model, critical modernist developmentalism, gains insights from the many critiques of development theory, but, most importantly, empasizes belief in the radical potential of modernity. Development, in this view, entails significantly increasing the economic capacity of the poorest people. Whereas this conventionally means entrepreneurial skills, here we mean "capacity" literally—that is, control over production and reproduction within a democratic politics quite different from either private ownership or state control. Finally, the authors' belief that theory is not made by the exercise of logic alone but also reflects the theorist's moral reaction to a world in crisis culminates in a discussion of the ethics of development and radical democracy. The book concludes with a radical democratic proposal for guiding development efforts, more to stimulate readers' discussions about alternatives than to act as a universal blueprint for development "planning." Readers who think that democratic socialist development is the dismal politics of social dinosaurs might prefer to peruse this last chapter now rather than wading through all the pages that follow. You should know where we are going and why we are going there before the journey begins. Look, this is not a textbook full of pictures; it is not a PowerPoint presentation translated into "text"; and it is not a collection of generalizations lacking any real substance. You will find portions of this volume difficult to fathom, difficult even to read—bits that seem designed to lull you to sleep right next to bits that test your ire. But there is nothing in this book that you cannot understand if you persist in trying. Just keep reading and rereading, thinking and discussing, until you do understand. We think that everyone can be intelligent, given the chance. We think that everyone has a conscience. Combine the two: read the book with conscientious intelligence.

Part I

CONVENTIONAL
THEORIES
OF DEVELOPMENT

It seems strange that there can be entirely different theories of development. Why can't dedicated intellectuals just make up their minds, agree on the best theory, and then tell the world what policies to pursue? It is because development theories reflect the political positions of their proponents, the places where they developed, their philosophical perspective, and whether they are predominantly economic, sociological, anthropological, historical, geographic, and so on. Probably the most important of these is the *politics* of development theory. On the one side, some theories may be generally designated as "conventional." These conventional theories accept the existing basic capitalist structure as the best kind of society there could ever be—as natural, inevitable, and essentially unchangeable, as the only kind of society that can persist because, for example, capitalism is human nature writ large. Such theories tend to emphasize economic growth over development—or, rather, they see development *as* economic growth. Conventional theories often accept the accumulation of wealth by a few as spurring the entrepreneurship and innovation they see motivating the development effort—social inequality, for them, is the inevitable price of progress. They see poverty as merely an unfortunate consequence of growth that is basically good for most people—poverty as a "challenge" somehow rectifiable "eventually" through faster growth but in the meantime ameliorable through charity, the chief conventional modern instrument of conscience. Conventional theories are centered on the discipline of economics—or at least its "mainstream," its synthesis of bits of Keynesianism and growth theory onto a basically classical and neoclassical framework; this history is covered in Chapters 2 and 3. Modernization theory, derived mainly from sociology, began as a (mild) criticism of neoclassical economics but quickly became its accomplice: this evolution is covered in Chapter 4. Mainstrean economics and modernization theories together see development as a uniform, unilinear, "stage-type" process that was led by the historical example of the rise of the West. In this view, the rest of the world is merely trying to "catch up."

2

Classical and Neoclassical Economics

Development means producing a better life. Development is fundamentally economic. Hence, the discipline of economics has to be integrally involved in the study of development. All theories of development have significant economic aspects, along with other dimensions. So, we have to know economics to understand development. Economics is the most powerful social science, in the sense that economists are constantly consulted by powerful people, while many economists are themselves in positions of power. Yet, economics is also the most committed social science—"committed" meaning devoted to serving an interest, specifically a class interest. Economics has been a highly specialized field of knowledge since at least the mid-19th century. More than any other kind of social knowledge, economics claims the status of "science" in terms of its logical rigor and mathematical sophistication. Economists, more than other academic practitioners, are considered to be professional experts. They are heard with respect because they are thought to speak the scientific truth about issues of vital concern—the economy, growth, employment, and development. Economics is also the most isolated social science. Economic theories of growth, and to a lesser degree theories of development, have their own histories, their own trajectories, their own philosophical basis, their own typical kinds of practice, and their own difficult language, often with only tangential relations to cognate fields. Specialization and intellectual isolation result in a highly formalized discipline with rigorous rules of academic and practical conduct—for example, very specific forms of expression using a closely defined set of terms.

We argue, however, that this highly specialized knowledge rests on a highly precarious philosophical basis, one derived from a particular (class) reaction to the rise of modern market systems.) Yet, this biased, partial, and committed analysis is universalized as a scientifically true discourse valid for all people at all times in every situation. Universalization gives economics a lot of power. The main themes of this chapter, and the next, are universalization, power, commitment, partiality, and superficiality.

We follow the history of conventional economic thought about growth and development in detail because anyone wanting to understand development must be familiar with the discipline. For economics not only represents reality in theoretical terms, but also it has been so powerful that its theories have remade the reality they represent by framing the imaginations of economic actors. We adhere to the convention of dividing mainstream economic theory into historical periods, but slightly altering the usual designation (for example, Dasgupta 1985) to look at development issues during four phases of economic thought: classical and neoclassical economics in this chapter and Keynesian and neoliberal theories in the next one. Let us say from the beginning, these are intended to be critical chapters.

ENLIGHTENMENT ORIGINS OF POLITICAL ECONOMY

Seldom are ideas thought up from scratch—in the sense that theorists suddenly come up with entirely new concepts. Ideas are put together using earlier ideas as the thoughts we think with. So, economic ideas were developed within the philosophical tradition of Western scientific rationalism. But ideas are also reflections on real material processes. Modern economics was developed as a symbolic representation of real events in early capitalism. Yet, neither derivation—ideas developing within an intellectual tradition and ideas as reflections on reality—is scientifically neutral. Thinkers do not divorce themselves from their political beliefs when they think theories into existence. Rather, politics and other beliefs are spurs to the deep thinking involved in high-level theorization. Modern economics was constructed negatively, against the rulers of the previous (precapitalist) feudal order, the landed aristocracy, and against the mercantilist state that acted on behalf of this earlier ruling order. Economics was developed positively by theorists thinking on behalf of a new progressive capitalist class—economics was a theoretical part of their revolutionary effort. As this new class came into dominance, made a lot of money, and became wealthy, economics became conventional. We believe that it should have continued to change—in order to serve the people by recommitting itself to the poor rather than the rich.)

Modern economics seemingly belied the concepts of the old medieval order. These concepts included the feudal-era impulse suggesting that communal economic justice inevitably reflected God's will. Augustinian Christianity (that is, such Catholic doctrines as "original sin," formulated by Saint Augustine during the time of the late Roman Empire) had defined work as a punishment, meted out to everyone because originally Adam had disobeyed God by lusting for Eve. During the late Middle Ages, as European modernity was first dawning, a new notion began to emerge that upended this notion of work being the payment humans had to make for Adam's sin. Work began to be thought of not as a sacrifice but as a virtue—as the source of wealth. The most radical version of this protracted changeover came with the 16th-century Protestant belief in glorifying God actively rather than just meditatively—please God... by working hard! So, Protestants of a Puritanical, and especially Calvinist, persuasion pursued their "calling" (the occupation to which God had summoned male individuals, taking their talents into account) with rigorous discipline, despising idleness or shoddy craftsmanship as a dishonor to God. Additionally, under early modern Protestantism, human acquisitiveness and selfishness changed from being sinful forms of behavior, to being a service to the community (Innes 1995: Chapters 1, 3; see also the section on Weber in Chapter 4 of this book).

These new beliefs and attitudes were developed by the artisans, craftsmen, small (working) masters, and journeymen of early modern capitalism, especially those working in the most important manufacture, the cloth industry of western Europe generally, and England in particular (where the production of woolen cloth employed 8% of the population as late as 1823—Gregory 1982: 27). The new Protestant attitudes toward labor, wealth, and productive life were developed by working craftspeople, who could not avoid knowing that their work produced value—every throw of the shuttle, every inch of cloth passing through the weaving machine, proved that the weaver's labor time was adding value—more time, more cloth, more value, the repetition created the labor theory of value. Classical economists merely translated such beliefs, based in real work experience, into the more abstract realm of theory.

Classical economics also developed in conflict with an earlier set of ideas called mercantilism. Lasting from the 15th century to the early to mid-19th century, mercantilism was a system of ideas, institutions, politics, and economic practices that supported the absolutist (all-powerful) state and the ruling monarchical and aristocratic classes of the early capitalist period. Mercantilist political policy aimed at increasing national power, symbolized by the might of the state. National power, it was realized, rested on economic means rather than the bravery of a country's citizenry or the spirit of its people. Production was understood in the modern way, as the application of labor to natural resources. And this involved a new valuation of small producers—not laborers as much as tenant farmers and artisans—the very people who eventually became the industrial capitalist class. While valued, however, they were included in powerful institutions only reluctantly. Power was still held by the king and the landlords. The period 1600–1850 can be seen as one long class struggle between the landed nobility and the new bourgeoisie for control of the state, control over ideas, and control over the economy and its products. Classical economics was one element in this struggle.

Under mercantilism, a country was considered prosperous when it had a favorable balance of trade (exported more than it imported), resulting in an increased inflow of gold and silver (payments from other countries made to cover trade deficits). To achieve this favorable balance, trade was controlled by the state, and manufacturing was protected, regulated, and encouraged as a source of trading power—and, we might add, exploited as a source of monarchical/state revenue. Mercantilism had already broken with medieval precedent. It was an amoral system, in terms of ends and means, in which the political welfare of the state replaced the spiritual welfare of the people. Mercantilism was, as far as possible, rationalist rather than mystical, believing in the application of science to the solution of practical problems (Newman 1952; Hecksher 1935). Classical economics drew from such mercantilist positions in a critical way—retaining the rationalism but orienting it in a different direction, in the interests of a new class.

THE BRITISH ENLIGHTENMENT

Basically the word "Enlightenment" is used to refer to any period in a civilization when thought goes through a revolutionary change that later is deemed to have been beneficial—that is, thought gets better. "*The Enlightenment*" is a Eurocentric term referring to the revolution in philosophy and theory that occurred during the 17th and 18th centuries in western Europe. "Enlightenment" in this European context refected the growing belief that human reason could be used to combat ignorance, superstition, and tyranny in making a better world—the main opponents being religion (especially the Catholic Church) and the domination of society by a hereditary aristocracy that used force and conservative traditions to have its way. But, as we have stressed, revolutions in thought are not politically neutral—they serve interests. So, the task of the great political-economic philosophers of 17th- and 18th-century Protestant Britain—Thomas Hobbes (1588–1679), John Locke (1632–1704), David Hume (1711–1776)—was to propound political-economic ideas that might serve the new modern capitalist class in its struggle with feudalism and the landed nobility. More specifically, their political-economic philosophy supported the cause of the class of small producers, the tenant farmers, mechanics, and artisans whose hard work formed the basis of mercantilist state power, but who supported the Protestant cause and as Roundheads in the English Civil War showed their disdain for the Catholic monarchy and the "divine right of kings" by beheading Charles I in 1649.

Briefly, Thomas Hobbes reconceptualized society as a calculus of power relations, with power, in effect, traded as a commodity, and the value of the individual measured by the deference accorded him or her by others. People were bound together through moral obligations, he admitted. Yet, rather than invoking imagined deities as the basis of morality, as with the medieval Christian theologians, Hobbes thought that rational self-interestedness was as moral an obligation as could realistically be found. Rational self-interestedness (selfishness that was thought-out) was thus legitimated philosophically as the morality of the new capitalist system.

John Locke, the most important philosopher of early capitalist modernity, began by accepting the medieval Christian view that God originally gave the earth and its products to all people in common. Yet, Locke contended, human individuals had the right to preserve their own lives and, therefore, had rights to the subsistence (food, drink) derived from the earth. Such products had to be appropriated from the earth through labor by individuals with natural rights over their own persons. By mixing labor, encased in natural individual rights, with earth, the individual made stretches of the natural environment into private property—provided, Locke added, in deference to earlier ways of thinking, that enough was left for others. Thus, property rights extended to the commodities people produced from natural materials but also extended to the land people improved through the labor used in clearing, cultivating, and so on. Later in life, Locke added that the invention of money, together with a tacit agreement to place value on it, removed the previous limitations on the extent of property ownership. And, as labor was unquestionably the individual's property, it could be sold for a wage, with the buyer of labor (the employer) entitled to appropriate the product of the sellers of labor (the workers). The first argument on small private property earned through work was particularly important in the founding of the United States and the allocation of "free land" to farmers willing to improve it. The second set of arguments (rights to the products of employed others) not only justified unequal property relations but also legitimated unlimited individual property appropriation (Macpherson 1962: 221) and, we might add, legitimated employer–employee wage relations in the capitalist society forming at the time. It would be difficult to overstress the importance of Locke to early modern capitalist thought.

Finally, the Scottish philosopher David Hume saw human beings as compelled by a consuming passion—avidity (greed) for goods and possessions, a drive that he found directly destructive of society. Yet, people also reasoned that socialization was to their advantage; that is, "Passion is much better satisfied by its restraint, than by its liberty, and by preserving society, we make much greater advances in the acquiring of possessions than by running into the solitary and forlorn condition which must follow upon violence and universal license" (Hume 1987 ed.: 492). In other words, the greater interest of the self-interested individual lay in the preservation of society. Thus, self-interestedness and social responsibility could be reconciled—although selfishness was the more basic part. This reconciliation was actively achieved by the new "middle class" (that is, the small entrepreneurs, between lords and laborers—hence, the "middle" class) who formed the best and firmest social basis for public liberty. Hume supported free trade against mercantilist restrictions and yet found a need still for governmental intervention to preserve national economic advantage (Skinner 1992: 223).

Hence, the philosophers and political economists of the Enlightenment of 17th- and 18th-century Britain theorized on behalf of the new class of small proprietors, who worked hard all day and schemed until late in the night to make good-quality products in order that they might prosper and accumulate possessions—modestly at first. The early modern theorists decried against traditional beliefs, like divine rights (granted by God), or ascriptive social positions (inherited at birth) held by the traditional aristocracy. Increasingly, during the 18th century, as the industrial revolution transformed society, they argued against the entrenched power of the nobility and the absolutist mercantilist state. Their main task in this fight was to rationalize a new set of ideas about selfish individualism and private property accumulation that came to be held at a deep level of belief by modern people. They came up with a system of principles founded on the freedom of the individual, a system that was at first revolutionary but that became normalized in the sense of being unquestioned within polite, conventional discourse about economic and political development.

Their main quandary lay in reconciling individual selfishness with the common good. Increasingly, reconciliation between competitive individualism and communal morality was reached not on the moral basis of religion (by appealing to God), nor on the armed force of the state (by forcing people to obey), but by seeing the freedom of the self-seeking, enlightened individual as disciplined (ordered and restrained) by modern social institutions, principally exchanges among them through markets.

This complex of beliefs forms the basis of modern *liberalism*—that is, the belief in individual natural rights, equality of opportunity, civil liberties, and so on. We use the principled liberal concepts derived from this belief system—freedom, progress, democracy—to think optimistically, talk about the good society, and conceptualize political-economic alternatives even today. Especially in the United States and United Kingdom, we are the descendants, the human products, of the British Enlightenment. These concepts have captured our imagination and our lexicon. They endowed us with our most appealing and inspirational ideas. But, remember that the Enlightenment philosophers were thinking on behalf of early capitalist white men—*their* rights and liberties—not the rights of the workers, nor the peasants, and definitely not women, nor black or brown people (Locke was a shareholder in the Royal African Company, whose most profitable "commodity" was slaves). Putting this critically, our optimism is constrained by their class-committed vision of liberal modernity. If we add that Hume's Scottish confidant was Adam Smith, father of classical economics, we can see a direct line of descent from the political philosophy of the early modern era, through liberal classical economics, to present-day neoliberalism.

THE CLASSICAL ECONOMISTS

"Classical economics" refers to a period of mainly British economic thought stretching from the publication of Adam Smith's book *The Wealth of Nations* in the year of rebellion 1776, to the publication of John Stuart Mill's *Principles of Political Economy* in the equally rebellious 1848, a year marked by liberal revolutions throughout western Europe. Classical economics was part of a larger intellectual system of political economy contained within the even broader liberal philosophy of the British and European Enlightenments that we just discussed. Classical economics originated modern theories of growth and development.

What kind of real-life events did the classical economists represent in theory—as economic growth theory? At the time, in the late 18th and early 19th centuries, the economic landscape of Britain was changing with the agricultural and industrial revolutions. Under the agricultural revolution, technical change was occurring in terms of innovations in crop rotations and production techniques. Social changes were happening, mostly in terms of the "enclosure" of the feudal common lands by the noble landowners. Rather than farming the land themselves (preferring to hunt foxes and build castles) the lords of the land divided their estates among tenant farmers who paid them rent. This new class of tenant farmers employed farm laborers to produce food and raw materials sold in markets to earn money so they could pay rents to landowners. Here was the capitalist class system and modern production in formation.

The industrial revolution was even more complex. England had been an industrial country dominated by the woolen cloth manufacture since the 13th century—the wool from its many sheep was spun and woven by hundreds of thousands of craftsmen employed in textile manufacturing. However, the cloth manufacture was controlled by master clothiers putting work out to hundreds of small producers in specialized districts like Devonshire, East Anglia, the West Country, and the West Riding of Yorkshire. Technological innovations, as with improved spinning machines driven by water power and a shift toward wearing cotton rather than wool, transformed the dispersed textile manufacture into a concentrated factory-type industry during the 18th and early 19th centuries. The factory owners, emerging from the ranks of craftsmen, small masters, and clothiers, were the first industrial bourgeoisie. They were rational men convinced of the benefits of technology and by the efficiencies of modern forms of bureaucratic organization. They were commercially oriented and competitive profit makers, decision makers who were capable still of running a power loom. They were producing not only cloth but also a new economy and society in Western modernity.

The classical economists thought on behalf of these new men. Classical economists thought against the previous ruling class, the noble landowners, whose right to property rested on the force of conquest, as when the Normans conquered Britain and divided it up, and the force of outdated religious ideas, like divine (rather than earned) rights to property (hence the "radical" Lockean notion of labor creating property rights rather than property coming from conquest). Classical economists thought against earlier conceptions of economics, as with the French Physiocrats, who believed that God originally put value into land, from which agricultural labor merely liberated it. The classicals were radical— in that they dared to dismiss God from the value-creating equation.

ADAM SMITH: BEGINNINGS

In economics, the great break from the past was made by a Scottish moral philosopher with a fortuitous name for the founder of a new project, Adam Smith (1723–1790). As is the case with most transformational statements, Smith simply said what he believed to be true, namely, that all humans share certain characteristics—whether innate or resulting from the faculties of reason and speech—that Smith went on to describe as a "propensity in human nature ... to truck, barter and exchange one thing for another" (Smith 1937 ed.: 13). By this he meant that human beings possessed an inherent urge to trade. As traders, humans were also inherently "self-interested" (in the sense of rational selfishness, discussed earlier, including "interested in rationally knowing oneself"), with this interest focused on (naturally) making money. So, it was futile to expect cooperation and assistance from people acting out of their own self-interest—that is, one should not expect people to be good or kind. Instead, the individual should prevail on the other's "self-love," appeal to the other's own advantage, to get the other to do what he or she required: "give me that which I want, and you shall have this which you want." Smith (1937 ed.: 14) added: "It is not from the benevolence of the butcher, brewer or baker that we expect our dinner, but from regard to their own interest." So, a modern economy worked best through the interaction of inherently self-interested individuals. As an Enlightenment philosopher, Smith wanted to harness the incessant rage of human selfishness as an economic motive, a ceaseless drive to produce wealth and create growth. But as a good Protestant he also thought that "self-love" should be self-regulated by the disciplined, rational modern individual, and should that prove insufficient, selfishness (in the form of greed) should be limited by laws made by the state. Smith himself preferred "self-interest"—self-love mitigated (controlled) by "virtue" (understood in the Greco-Roman stoic sense of a set of moral principles that the individual adhered to by force of his or her own will)—as the behavioral motive driving economic behavior. In this way, he said, justice rather than pure selfishness should be the basis of society—with "justice" basically meaning regulated, principled self-interestedness (Smith 1976; Fitzgibbons 1995).

Smith retained medieval arguments that the natural prices of commodities derive from their real costs. But the cost of something was made up from the labor that went into making it. For Smith, the utility (usefulness) of a thing did not determine its price. Rather, "labour ... is the real measure of the exchangeable value of all commodities" (Smith 1937 ed.: 30). In early societies, Smith thought, the amount of (direct physical) labor used to produce commodities (products exchanged in markets) determined their values, with the whole amount of money from the sale of the product belonging to the laborer. Capital originated in savings from these revenues. Capital could then be used to hire additional workers, who also produced value. Yet, when capital accumulated in the hands of capitalists and "they naturally employ it in setting to work industrious people" (Smith 1937 ed.: 42), profit had to be given to the risk taker, the capitalist employer rather than the employed worker—notice that Smith is only restating Locke in this regard. Similarly when common land became private property (during enclosure), landlords demanded rent, for "like others they love to reap what they never sowed" (there is an edge of criticism here) and, what is more, were able to get away with it (Smith 1937 ed.: 49). Hence, the price, or exchangeable value, of a commodity in more advanced societies came to be made up of three parts: wages, profits, and rents, going to workers, factory owners, and landowners. "Natural prices" determined in this way (wages plus profits plus rent) were brought into their proper relation with market prices by the pressure of competition. That is, where market prices exceeded natural prices, landlords and capitalists shifted land and capital into more profitable employment, with the reverse happening when market prices were below natural prices. Also, while the accumulation of capital and its employment in mechanized production might eventually be stalled by a scarcity of workers and high wages, Smith thought that overall population growth too responded to market incentives, with more children born when wages were high, so that over the long term economic growth could continue without labor shortages.

Thus, economic growth, for Smith, depended on capital accumulation, which in turn depended on savings from the revenues derived from working hard—all this grounded in the Protestant virtues of frugality and self-discipline. Economic growth also supposed a culture rooted in morality, a system of natural liberty that respected the "higher virtues" (Fitzgibbons 1995: 145–148). This system of natural liberty meant, for Smith, that there should be no artificial (that is, mercantilist) impediments to trade, markets, and exchange. Based in this set of typical British Enlightenment ideas, Smith's economics tried to explain why some nations prospered, became wealthy, or, in present-day parlance, experienced economic growth. Smith found the technical answer in what he called the "division of labor"—that is, breaking the total labor effort of society into specialized components. Through specializing each kind of work involved in a production process, dexterity (skillfulness) could be increased, labor time saved, and labor-saving machinery invented by persons familiar with the minute tasks they performed over and over again every day—Smith was thinking about the discoveries made by master craftsmen-turned-capitalists in the early British textile, iron, and engineering industries. The products made by specialized producers in specialized industrial districts (Lancashire for cotton spinning and weaving, woolens in Yorkshire, hardware in the British Midlands, etc.) were exchanged, through trade and markets, for agricultural products made elsewhere (East Anglia for grains, Devon and Cheshire for dairy products, etc.). The extent and complexity of the division of labor were limited only by the extent and intricacy of the market system. With improvements in transport, the market system increased in (spatial) size, labor became even more specialized, money came to be used to mediate exchange, instead of bartering, and productivity was increased. In this way, specialization, the division of labor, markets, and trade (along with rational acquisitiveness) were, for Smith, the bases of modern economic growth. Countries that produced in this modern way prospered and became wealthy—that is, achieved economic growth.

Smith thought that relatively free trade organized through networks of markets, as opposed to mercantilism and state intervention, would lead to an efficient allocation of productive resources (land, labor, capital) but thought too that a just (fair, equitable) economy also had to encourage high wages for workers. A society activated by self-interest (in the enlightened sense Smith used the term) needed a regulating (controlling, organizing) medium. Regulation was to be provided *not* by the state, which in Smith's day was still committed to the interests of the noble landowners. Rather, regulation came from competition among free individuals acting as buyers and sellers in the marketplace. Any producer motivated only by greed who charged too much for a product on the commodity market found himself without buyers—because cheaper products would be supplied by others. Over the long run, markets and free competition within them would force prices toward their natural, or "socially just," levels. The web of self-regulating markets was an "invisible hand" organizing the economy efficiently and yet also transforming private self-interest into public virtue. Hence, an automatic mechanism, competition in the market, led to productivity and growth without state interference. Self-interested competitive behavior directed resources to where they could best and most profitably be used. And all classes, Smith believed, shared in the benefits of progress. "Natural liberty implied free competition, free movement of workers, free shifts of capital, and freedom from government intervention" (Lekachman 1959: 89). For Smith, markets were virtuous institutions of social efficiency and the key drivers of invention, innovation, and risk taking. This set of ideas was Smith's magnificent contribution to the Enlightenment. We live by Smith's ideas today—benefiting from their veracity, yet suffering (as we will argue later) from their mistakes in assumptions and logic.

UTILITARIANISM

During the early 19th century, political economy changed in style, if not in essential substance. Earlier moral notions about human nature were elaborated in a more quantifiable and predictable way by the British Enlightenment philosopher and political economist, Jeremy Bentham (1748–1832). Bentham thought that the social problems of late 18th- and early 19th-century England were due to an antiquated system typified by control of the economy by an hereditary landed gentry opposed to modern capitalist institutions. Bentham was specifically critical of the British legal system. He thought that English law had no objective basis and that its underlying morality rested on many irreconcilable foundations (the Bible, tradition, conscience, etc.). In correcting this, Bentham wanted to find some criteria for validating ethical behavior that could serve as the basis for a modern democratic system of law and government.

In his *An Introduction to the Principles of Morals and Legislation* (1996 ed.), first published in 1780, Bentham declared simply that nature had placed humans under the governance of two sovereign "masters": pleasure, which made all people happy, and pain, which everyone hated. Therefore, he believed that morality (and the laws derived from it), could be grounded in a fundamental objective truth about human nature: the maximization of pleasure and minimization of pain. Bentham's "principle of utility" judged every human action by its effect on either augmenting or diminishing the happiness of the individual. Amounts of utility could, in effect, be measured by degrees of happiness. The objective of government should be to enable the greatest possible happiness of the community governed. The happiness of the individual was increased in proportion as the person's sufferings were lighter and fewer and enjoyments greater and more numerous. The care of enjoyments ought to be left almost entirely to the individual.

The principal function of government was to guard against pain. Governments did this by creating rights that are conferred on individuals: rights of personal security, rights of protection for honor, rights of property, rights of receiving aid in case of need. Human liberty meant freedom from external restraint or compulsion. Liberty was the absence of restraint, and to the extent that individuals were not hindered by others they had liberty and were free. (This argument contradicted the French revolutionary position that liberty was "natural" in the sense of existing prior to social life.) Law that restricts liberty was evil. Yet, law was also necessary for social order, and good laws essential to good government. To the extent that law advanced and protected people's economic and personal goods, it reflected the interests of the individual. Similarly, Bentham thought that the government's social policies should be evaluated in terms of their effects on the well-being of the people they affected. Punishing criminals was an effective way of deterring crime because it increased the likelihood that future pain would outweigh the apparent gain of committing the crime. Thus, punishment must fit the crime by changing the likely perception of the value of committing it. Bentham's utilitarianism became the philosophical basis of the "reform movement" in 19th-century Britain. The philosophy was developed by the "philosophical radicals," a group of intellectuals active from London in the 1810s through the 1830s. Utilitarianism was the basis for reform acts legislated into English law such as the Factory Act of 1833, the Poor Law

Amendment Act of 1834, the Prison Act of 1835, the Municipal Corporations Act of 1835, the Lunacy Act of 1845, and the Public Health Act of 1845, as well as for the formation of the Committee on Education in 1839 (Long 1977).

RICARDIAN CALCULATIONS

One member of the "philosophical radicals" was David Ricardo (1772–1823). A British millionaire trader in securities during the day, Ricardo devoted his spare time to intellectual pursuits, eventually writing a rigorous theoretical treatise on political economics, *Principles of Political Economy and Taxation* (1911 ed.), first published in 1817. In this work, Ricardo accepted Smith's labor theory of commodity value with some modifications (a commodity's value was also determined by scarcity) and Benthamite elaborations (labor was the universal measure of value because it always involved exertion and was painful, whereas consuming labor's products was always pleasurable) but also with greater critical emphasis on the distribution of value, especially the part going to rents (the portion of commodity value paid to landlords for use of the original powers of the soil). Like Smith, Ricardo saw the economic world as tending to expand, with capitalists accumulating capital that originated in profits, building factories, and employing more workers while increasing wages. From the French economist Jean-Baptiste Say (1767–1832) Ricardo derived the idea that "supply created its own demand" as producers employed and paid workers who, by spending, generated consumption and formed demand. However, Ricardo added a critical dimension to the theory of economic growth. With an expanding population and increased demand for food, the margins of agricultural production would expand, bringing into cultivation land of lesser fertility, increasing the cost of grain (wheat, the food staple in Britain), yet increasing returns to landlords owning the better lands, earning them differential rents (above the minimum earned on the marginal lands). In turn, the capitalist would be faced by the higher wage costs necessary for buying more expensive grain to sustain workers, while the landlords got more revenues even though, Ricardo concluded (critically again), they themselves contributed little to the wealth-creating process (because they owned land and yet did not work).

In common with Smith, Ricardo was against the land-owning class. In the early 19th century British landlords were protected from foreign agricultural competition by a system of Corn Laws (imposed in 1815) that represented the last remnants of the mercantilist system. These laws imposed a sliding scale of duties (tariffs, that is, state taxes) on imported grains, with the amount of the tariff dependent on the foreign price.

These tariffs kept grain (and bread) prices high, ensuring that landowners benefited from the industrial revolution with its increased demand for food and raw materials. The philosophical radicals opposed these Corn Laws. They argued for freeing trade of all state restrictions—"free trade" would result in lower grain costs that benefited industrial capitalists through lower wages (that is, less money could be paid to workers to buy bread and other food staples).

Ricardo's main contribution to classical economics, which eventually contributed to Parliament's repeal of the Corn Laws in 1846, was a theory of free trade based on the principle of comparative advantage. For this, Ricardo used trade between England and Portugal as a model case. Following the example of Smith in Chapter 6 of *The Wealth of Nations,* Ricardo took the position that trade and the progressive extension of the market increased the rate of profits in a country and led to a more efficient international division of labor. This process was effectuated through "each country producing those commodities for which by its situation, its climate, and its other natural or artificial advantages it is adapted, and by their exchanging them for the commodities of other countries" (Ricardo 1911: 80). International specialization and free trade among countries produced universal benefits. In a statement expanding on Smith's insights, Ricardo declared:

> Under a system of perfectly free commerce, each country naturally devotes its capital and labour to such employments as are most beneficial to each. This pursuit of individual advantage is admirably connected with the universal good of the whole. By stimulating industry, by rewarding ingenuity, and by using most efficaciously the peculiar powers bestowed by nature, it distributes labour most effectively and most economically: while, by increasing the general mass of productions, it diffuses general benefit, and binds together, by one common tie of interest and intercourse, the universal society of nations throughout the civilised world. It is this principle which determines that wine shall be made in France and Portugal, that corn shall be grown in America and Poland, and that hardware and other goods shall be manufactured in England. (Ricardo 1911: 81)

Ricardo's case example was Portugal. Were Portugal to have no commercial connections with other countries, it would have to divert capital from the wine it produced to manufactured goods that it imported from England, while the quality of the cloth, hardware, and other products would probably diminish. The quantity of wine that Portugal gave in exchange for the cloth of England was determined not by the respective quantities of labor used to produce these commodities, as it would be were both to be produced in each respective country. Instead:

England may be so circumscribed that to produce the cloth may require the labour of 100 men for one year; and if she attempted to make the wine, it might require the labour of 120 men for the same time. England would therefore find it her interest to import wine, and to purchase it by the exportation of cloth. To produce the wine in Portugal might require only the labour of 80 men for one year, and to produce the cloth in the same country might require the labour of 90 men for the same time. It would therefore be advantageous for her to export wine in exchange for cloth. This exchange might even take place notwithstanding that the commodity imported could be produced there with less labour than in England. Though she could make the cloth with the labour of 90 men, she would import it from a country where it required the labour of 100 men to produce it, because it would be advantageous to her rather to employ her capital in the production of wine, for which she would obtain more cloth from England, than she could produce by diverting a portion of her capital from the cultivation of vines to the manufacture of cloth. (Ricardo 1911: 82–83)

(See Table 2.1 for a numerical version of this argument.)

Ricardo added that it might seem that all production (of wine and cloth) might best take place in Portugal by moving capital and labor there, but experience showed that "men of property" (British capitalists) were unwilling to move their capital to other countries. The theory assumed that all partners in trade benefited from an increase in total production in accordance with their comparative advantage. Producing in accordance with comparative advantage and trading freely across borders generated economic growth. This insight was Ricardo's contribution to the Enlightenment and to its most important branch, classical economics. Ricardo's liberal principle of free trade is reproduced in contemporary economics textbooks and is a basic geographic component of contemporary economic growth theory. Paul Samuelson, a Nobel prize winner and author of the most popular contemporary economics textbook, concluded that the principle of comparative advantage makes real incomes higher in all places, while ill-designed tariffs or quotas reduce efficiency and incomes. He calls this principle the "unshakable basis for international trade" (Samuelson 1980: 630; 2001).

MILL'S ETHICAL ECONOMICS

Late classical economics combined the arithmetical "precision" of Ricardo with a more socially critical and ethical liberalism that responded to the vicissitudes of the industrial revolution. John Stuart Mill (1806–1873) agreed with Bentham's greatest happiness principle as the basic statement

TABLE 2.1. Theory of Comparative Advantage: Ricardo's Numerical Example

Without specialization

England
  Cloth—100 man hours (mh) produces 100 yards.
  Wine—120 man hours produces 100 barrels.
  [Labor productivities: cloth—1 mh = 1 yard; wine—1mh = 0.83 barrels]

Portugal
  Cloth—90 man hours produces 100 yards.
  Wine—80 man hours produces 100 barrels.
  [Labor productivities: cloth—1 mh = 1.1 yards; wine 1 mh = 1.25 barrels]

Total production in England and Portugal combined
  200 yards cloth and 200 barrels of wine

With specialization

England (specializing in cloth for which it has the least comparative disadvantage)
  Cloth—220 man hours produces 220 yards.

Portugal (specializing in wine for which it has the greatest comparative advantage)
  Wine—170 man hours produces 212.5 barrels.

Total production in England and Portugal combined
  220 yards cloth and 212.5 barrels of wine

Specialization increases total output of cloth by 10% and wine by 6.25%.

Note. Based on Ricardo (1911: 82–83), with 100 yards of cloth and 100 barrels of wine substituted for each country's annual production.

of utilitarian value: "Actions are right in proportion as they tend to promote happiness, wrong as they tend to produce the reverse of happiness. By happiness is meant pleasure, and the absence of pain; by unhappiness, pain, and the privation of pleasure" (Mill 1863: 2). But he did not agree that differences among pleasures could always be quantified. Some types of pleasure experienced by human beings differ *qualitatively* from others. With this latter insight, Mill wanted to promote the moral worth of "higher" (intellectual, sensual) pleasures among sentient beings, even when their momentary intensity might be less than alternative "lower" (bodily) pleasures. Because people cannot calculate accurately the relation between pleasure and pain in every instance, he supposed that humans properly allowed their actions to be guided by moral rules most of the time. In addition to acknowledging Bentham's socially imposed external sanctions of punishment and blame, Mill believed that human beings were also motivated by internal sanctions like self-esteem, guilt, and conscience—that is, the unselfish wish for the good of all could move people to act morally.

Mill's *On Liberty* (1859) defended the view that governmental encroachment upon the freedom of individuals was almost never warranted. A genuinely civil society, he maintained, must always guarantee the civil liberty of its citizens—their protection against interference by abusive authority—even when the government relies on the democratic participation of the people (Mill 1859: 1). The only purpose for which power can be rightfully exercised over any member of a civilized community against his will is to prevent harm to others. Society was responsible for protecting its citizens from one another, but it should not interfere with the rest of what they did. This meant, in particular, that the government was never justified in trying to control, limit, or restrain (1) private thoughts and feelings, along with their public expression; (2) individual tastes and pursuits, as expressed through efforts to live happily; (3) the association of like-minded individuals with one another. No society was truly free unless its individual citizens were permitted to take care of themselves. Human action should arise freely from the character of individual human beings, not from the despotic influence of public opinion, customs, or expectations. Each person must choose his or her own path in life, even if it differs significantly from what other people would recommend. Thus, for Mill individual citizens were responsible for themselves, their thoughts and feelings, tastes and pursuits, while society was properly concerned only with social interests. In particular, the state was justified in limiting or controlling the conduct of individuals only when doing so was the only way to prevent them from doing harm to others by violating their rights. As economic life involved the social interest, it might be subject to regulation, even though free trade was often more effective. Mill was in favor of liberty: governmental action was legitimate only when it was demonstrably necessary for the protection of other citizens from direct harm caused by any human conduct. In every other case, the liberty of the individual should remain inviolate.

In *Principles of Political Economy,* published in 1848, Mill (1909 ed.) argued that the principles of competition were the bases of economic laws that could be outlined with precision and given universal validity by an abstract science of economics. Mill argued that the economic law of diminishing returns—in which additions to the labor working agricultural land were not met by equal additions to product, restricting productivity and growth—could in part be transcended in manufacturing, where productivity could be increased almost without limit. Hence, economic growth was naturally led by industry rather than agriculture. The pessimism that was typified by the writings of Thomas Malthus (1766–1834)—to the effect that economic growth would be restricted by populations increasing faster than production—Mills believed could be avoided by workers voluntarily restricting their numbers (Malthus 1933). With Say and Ricardo, Mill believed that there was no chance of general overproduction (and thus no long-term depressions) as growth proceeded, although specific commodities might temporarily come into oversupply (so there might be *short-term* economic fluctuations). So, capitalism and growth were viewed as proceeding together in relative harmony.

However, Mill's most significant contribution to classical political economy, and to growth theory, lay in his ideas about values. Mill differented science from values. That is, he said, while the "scientific laws" of economics applied to production as though they were natural truths, the distribution of wealth was a different matter entirely, being more a question of values, laws, and customs. Based on their value systems, societies could decide to redistribute wealth through state intervention, said Mill. So, there could be an ethical economic growth—similar to development in the sense that we defined it in Chapter 1. Further still, Mill found notions of competition and the "struggle for existence" as ideals for economic life to be merely disagreeable symptoms of an early, crude phase of industrial progress. When more refined minds took over the reins of power, such coarse stimuli to economic action would be replaced by superior economic principles spread through education. Mill saw the existing relations between workers and capitalists as characterized by mutual suspicion. But he thought that such antagonism could be relieved by profit sharing and eventually avoided through worker–capitalist partnerships and even workers' ownership of factories. Mill thought that laissez faire (the practice of governments not intervening in the economy) should be the general rule, but he found room for many exceptions, as with poor relief (welfare) or factory legislation (state regulations on child labor, hours, and conditions of work, etc.). Mill was a radical liberal who believed that capitalism would eventually give way to cooperativism. His contribution to the Enlightenment took the ethical form of a compassionate developmentalism. More extreme socialist versions of these ideas were worked out by Karl Marx and Frederich Engels (see Chapter 5), who were in many ways the last (and very critical) members of the classical school of political economy.

LIST'S SKEPTICISM

Most accounts of classical economics end with Mill. There was, however, another important alternative economic perspective in the classical tradition, presented by Friedrich List (1789–1846). List was a journalist who lived in the United States and France after being repeatedly imprisoned for writing about liberal ideas in his native Germany. List agreed with the principle of free trade proposed by all the classical economists; but he was importantly influenced by the ideas of Alexander Hamilton, the first U.S. Secretary of the Treasury, who advocated protecting "infant industries" (against British competition) while achieving self-sufficiency. Following this line of thought, List argued that free trade of the Ricardian type presupposed a condition of eternal peace and a single set of laws for humanity that had yet to come into existence. Under the actually existing conditions, in which Britain dominated the world's manufacturing industry in the early 19th century, free trade would bring about not a "universal republic" of equal countries but "universal subjection of the less advanced nations to the supremacy of the predominant manufacturing, commercial and naval power" (List 1909: 103). A universal republic of national powers recognizing one another's rights, and a situation in which free trade could confer the same advantages to all participants, could only come about when a large number of nationalities had reached the same level of development. In the meantime, List proposed a "national economics" in which the state promoted the welfare of all its citizens with tariffs, protecting the national economy, especially infant industries (that is, new economic activities just starting up), until such industries could compete on equal terms with the dominant industrial powers, like Britain (Roussakis 1968; Tribe 1988).

In Mill and List we read the beginnings of a critique of classical economics. Let us now elaborate this critique ourselves.

CRITIQUE OF CLASSICAL ECONOMICS

We have presented here a clear, straightforward summary of the main ideas of classical political economy. These ideas fit together as a sophisticated, believable explanation for the economic growth of modern industrial societies. The overall theory they present is logical and coherent, understandable and persuasive. It basically combines Smithian notions of self-interested, rational, and competitive behavior by capitalists with a technical apparatus of specialization based on comparative advantage, interlocking markets, expanding trade, and innovation specifically in industry. This theory of economic growth has lasted pretty much intact up to the present. Even so, classical economics rests on assumptions that are made up rather than proven. Smith, Ricardo, Bentham, and the others simply assume that all people are innately self-interested competitive traders—that is, "selling things and making money is human nature." But if this is "human nature," then why, under the social systems prevailing for 99% of human history—gathering and hunting, tribal and agricultural systems, the state societies of China, Egypt, and Rome—was it so conspicuously absent? The classical economists legitimated selfish, competitive profit making as "natural." This makes "unnatural" *other* motives for economic practice, such as cooperativeness, the desire to work for the common good, and the desire to organize production to meet the needs of everyone. Human beings are not selfish brats; they are, as Mill recognized, capable of living and acting in accordance with finer ideals.

Then too the classical economists simply assumed that profits and rent are legitimate shares of national income—profits being earned by capitalists' competitive risk taking, rent being payment for the use of land and resources (the classical position was skeptical about this latter share), and wages being the reward for working. But why are profits and rents seemingly so much higher than wages? Or, putting it differently, why is an hour of risk taking worth thousands of times more than an hour of hard physical work? Why do owners and management make so much more than workers? These are not class-neutral assumptions lying at the heart of economics, but rather *class-committed* assumptions.

The classical economists were committed to the interests of the British industrial bourgeoisie, particularly in its fight against the (noble) landlord class but also (not mentioned as much) in its fight against the workers. The classical economists saw the industrial bourgeoisie as the agents of progress and the bearers of rationality. The classical economists believed that these modern men should control the economy for the good of all. They were committed to the market as organizational mechanism and against the mercantilist state, especially in that it represented the monarchy and the nobles—although not when the state served their own interests (as with imperialism). All this is clear. The classical economists did not hide their class commitments. They were proud to support their bourgeois friends. And who could blame them? Given a choice between kings, lords, dukes, and other assorted aristocrats, on the one side, and the early self-made working bourgeoisie, on the other, as the ruling economic class, the new self-made men were obviously preferable—though the questionable part came with Locke's shift from admiring self-made working men to admiring men putting others to work for them and taking their product.

The question for economics is: Why translate a theory that was obviously in favor of the capitalist class as it rose to power into an economic theory that is supposedly good for all people at all times? Why transfer antagonism to the mercantilist state into later opposition to the welfare state? The chief problem is that economic theory eternalizes and universalizes these early class commitments under the rubric of "scientific neutrality."

We raise these issues again later, in more detail, when dealing with neoclassical economics. For the moment, let us take the critique of classical economics in another direction by examining the logic and empirical validity of its theory. Is classical economics logical in the sense that components of the argument fit together as a coherent whole? Is classical economics empirically based, in that it is founded on generalizations that represent reality with some degree of accuracy? Or are its logic and empirical support hopelessly biased by class and national commitments? In answering these questions, let us go to the heart of the classical regime, to a theory that has lasted virtually intact until the present, and to a theory that forms the basis of conventional thinking about economic growth. Ricardo's theory of comparative advantage is such a foundational theory.

Ricardo presented two main arguments in his simple model of comparative advantage. First, he said that specialization based on national comparative advantage that, in turn, is based on "natural or artificial" factors increases the total production of all countries involved in an international trading system freed from tariff restrictions. Within its highly restricted, unrealistic assumptions, the notion of national specializations increasing global production is uncontestable. The main question about this first argument turns on the "natural" (that is, environmental) and "artificial" (that is, socially and historically constructed) bases for comparative advantage—that is, how can specialization be somehow naturally based when institutions, states, and historical and cultural forces always intervene? And if this is the case, trade must always be as much socially and politically determined as naturally based. To give a brief illustration, drawing on the history of cloth manufacture that Ricardo used in his case example: the British cloth industry was state-supported, protected, and regulated from the Tudor monarchs (1585–1603) onward. When the British woolen textile industry made a crucial shift from making broadcloth to producing light worsteds during the 17th century, Dutch and Flemish artisans had to be brought in to teach West Country weavers the requisite new skills (Bowden 1971). So much for natural determination—this was a politically constructed industry. Similarly, the importance of the wine industry in Portugal resulted from the domination of Portuguese society by an agrarian nobility allied with the monarchical Braganza family. Indeed, so powerful was this social and political constructivism that, had Ricardo made a statement about "comparative advantage" that actually represented real economic history, it would have read: "England specialized in cloth, which its powerful mercantilist state supported, while Portugal specialized in wine, which its weaker agrarian state had to accept." So, a position in a trading system, such as Britain's specialization in cloth production, results from state intervention and various other forms of institutional construction rather than from anything resembling "natural" advantage (List was referring to this). Recognizing this conclusion shifts the emphasis in economic theory. Economies are socially constructed, not natural entities. And an economy that is socially constructed can be socially instructed to do better for poor people. Had this been recognized by the classicals, economics would have evolved as an entirely different, and far better, socially concerned discipline—more along the ethical lines of Mills than Smith's misguided trust in the morality of the market.

Second, and more interestingly: according to Ricardo, an increase in total production by all countries combined into an international trading system resulting from specialization "diffuses general benefit" and binds together by common ties of interest all civilized countries that make up the universal society of nations. The main problem is that this argument is not supported by the numerical example used by Ricardo. Whosoever gets the benefits from increased total production depends on the terms of trade (that is, the exchange ratios between cloth and wine in the model case) together with many other equally powerful social and political forces. All the increase in total production coming from international specialization and trade could go to one country, particularly under conditions of unequal power relations (as List suggested). Indeed, that was exactly what *had already happened* in the England–Portugal cloth–wine exchange. This relatively "free" trade (in the narrow sense of tariffs decreased by interstate agreement) had already resulted not in mutual advantage, nor the diffusion of general benefit, but almost exclusively, and over a very long time period, in the concentrated advantage of Britain to the disadvantage of Portugal. The cloth–wine exchange had resulted over a long period of time in a consistent balance of payments deficit for Portugal and surplus for Britain. Portugal had to settle the deficit by reexporting the gold and diamonds it extracted, with not a little force, from its colony Brazil, impoverishing Portugal and enriching Britain (Fisher 1971; Sideri 1970). The conclusion is inescapable: Ricardo claimed universal advantage from a trade relation that he *already knew* favored one country at the expense of another. But, further, this utter bias in Ricardo's mind has been replicated virtually intact by generations of economists ever since, who claim that free trade based on comparative advantage is good for all concerned, in the long run, without investigating whether it was good for Portugal in the long-run model case that underlies their Ricardian belief system. Britain exported cloth to Portugal ... and took it to the cleaners! And ever since, one or a few countries have reaped most of the benefits from "free" trade—Britain during the 18th and 19th centuries, the United States after World War II, Japan and the newly industrialized countries (NICs) during the 1960s and 1970s, and China today.

This was, and remains, a theory replete with lapses in logic, especially in terms of who gets the benefits of trade, and empirically unjustified—empirically wrong, in fact, in that the theory is the exact opposite of the reality it pretends to describe. Given the centrality of the theory of comparative advantage to modern economics, we have to consider the possibility that the economics of growth has been fundamentally mistaken ever since its classical beginnings. We have to consider that economics has, from the beginning, been utterly biased in class and national terms. The implications for the direction taken by economic growth are catastrophic for most of the world's people. What classical economics legitimated and, given its role in policymaking, helped to construct was an unequal world that has kept billions of people in poverty by concentrating wealth in a few places and in the hands of a few people.

NEOCLASSICAL ECONOMICS

During the last half of the 19th century economics changed from being "political economy," part of Enlightenment moral philosophy critically involved with social issues, to being "economic science," part of the scientific revolution of the 19th century. Economics became a specialized scientific discipline fascinated by calculus, algebra, and plane geometry and increasingly removed from social concerns. The central theme of economics changed from the growth of national wealth to the role of margins in the efficient allocation of resources. The marginalist movement in economics began in earnest when three theorists—W. S. Jevons (1835–1882), Carl Menger (1840–1921), and Léon Walras (1837–1910)—independently and almost simultaneously developed the idea of "marginal utility." Jevons (1911) emphasized not the total utility (usefulness, or Benthamite "pleasure") induced by consuming all of a commodity but the final (marginal) degree of utility induced by a very small increment in consuming something—the last bit of chocolate you eat after several pieces, for instance. The idea is that the utility of each bit of consumption eventually goes down: the 20th piece of chocolate is not as pleasurable as the first or second. He saw commodities distributed over several alternative uses so that the final (marginal) degree of utility was equal in each case—hence, the utility of consuming all commodities could be maximized by a rational consumer balancing the consumption of one with that of another (Kauder 1965).

With partial exceptions (Walras), this early version of neoclassical economics did not extend the marginal principle to the "factors of production" (resources, labor, capital, etc.) used in the manufacture of the exchanged commodities. A second generation of marginalist neoclassical economists created the concept of marginal productivity to cover the substitution of one productive resource (labor) for another (capital) in a theory of rational production. The basic idea is that production is efficient if a given quantity of outputs cannot be produced with less inputs. And inputs are substitutable, one for the other—capital (machinery) is substituted for labor (human workers), for instance. This extended the marginal principle to cover all aspects of production and consumption and, for some, all aspects of life in general. Three main schools of thought emerged in England, Austria, and Switzerland (to which we add an important American contribution).

In England, Alfred Marshall (1842–1924) saw the producer allocating saved investment funds (capital) among the factors of production, substituting one for another, an extra machine for two more workers for example, so that the marginal product of each factor was proportional to its price—that is, it was just worth buying. Basically Marshall was working out a model of efficient production based on the minimization of the costs of production. From this formulation Marshall elaborated the conditions of supply and demand, using a simple "static model" based on the "representative firm" (with all other factors being equal, or hypothetically held constant) and three typical time periods, the market (where supplies were fixed and demand determined price), the short run (where the forces of supply had a larger role), and the long run (where again supply was the more important). In long-run partial equilibrium the earnings of each factor of production would equal its marginal real cost. That is, no more substitutions (machines for labor) were worth making, and production was optimal—occurring at the lowest total cost.

Marshall thought that there were increasing returns to the scale of production (that is, more production entails lower per unit costs). He thought that firms reaped external economies of scale: the concentration of several firms in a single location offered a pooled market for workers with industry-specific skills, ensuring both a lower probability of unemployment and a lower probability of labor shortage; localized industries could support the production of specialized inputs; and informational spillovers could improve the efficiency of clustered firms as compared with isolated producers. He also thought that capitalism could raise the standard of living for ordinary people. As was true with Mills, Marshall was an ethical economist. He wanted to know whether it was possible for all people to start in the world with a fair chance of leading a cultured life, free from the pains of poverty and the stagnating influences of excessive mechanical toil. He thought that this question could not be fully answered by economic science, for the answer depended partly on the moral and political capabilities of human nature, and on these matters the economist had no special means of information. But the answer depended to a great extent upon facts and inferences that were within the province of economics, and that gave to economic studies their chief and highest interest (Marshall 1920). The conventional economic view summarized by Marshall was one of the economy as a well-balanced system always tending toward equilibrium. All the forces acting on the economy generated signals or reactions that tended, over time, to push the economy toward an optimal state. A shortage of any good or service brought a rise in its price that in turn called forth additional resources to produce it, creating a greater supply and a reduction in its price. Economic change occurred through smooth and continuous adjustments.

The Austrian school of economics, personified principally by Menger's students Friedrich von Wieser (1851–1926) and Eugen von Bohm-Bawerk (1851–1914), was abstract and antihistorical in method. Wieser's notion of "opportunity costs" abandoned the classical search for the original values of factors of production and saw value as a circular process in which various factors were employed so that their alternative uses produced the same earnings. Bohm-Bawerk concentrated on the roundabout nature of modern production, that is, the large number of stages intermediate between original factors of production and final consumption that created a demand for capital and justified the charging of interest on capital in any kind of economy, socialist or capitalist. Essentially these theorists were working out a theory of efficient supply. At Lausanne, Vilfredo Pareto (1848–1923) set out the mathematical conditions of Walras's general equilibrium in the achievement of an optimal economy ("Pareto optimality") where supply met demand in productive harmony organized through markets.

All together this second generation of marginalists formed the core of the neoclassical school of economics, espousing a science shorn of sociological and historical material, abstract in conception, supposedly nonnormative (that is, neutral, not taking sides, not particularly making prescriptions on how the economy should change except to say it should be more efficient), universal in application, and technical and mathematical in its methodology. Dynamics and questions of economic growth and development took a backseat to statics and partial and general equilibrium. Neoclassical economics leads to the conclusion that markets are generally competitive, do not tend toward monopolies, and that, left unimpeded, market processes usually result in optimum levels of production and allocation. This school of thought also implies that there are relatively limited instances when government should intervene to promote economic ends, other than encouraging market competition, providing adequate schooling, and encouraging savings and investment.

Finally, the U.S. economist J. B. Clark (1847–1938) justified the distribution of incomes under capitalism as in accord with the "laws of marginal productivity," suggesting that capitalists and workers received what they were worth, even though one might be worth hundreds of times more than the other. "To each agent a distinguishable share in production, and to each a corresponding reward—such is the natural law of distribution," he averred, and on this question, he added, "The right of society to exist in its present form … is at stake" (Clark 1988: 5–6). We find, with Clark, the picture of the enlightened maximizing individual, acting within generally competitive conditions in an overall state of static harmony (Hutchison 1953: 260–261). But with Clark we also find neoclassical economics abandoning its veneer of class neutrality—U.S. economics, in the tradition of Clark, was foresquare *for* the entrepreneurial class.

All together, neoclassical economic theory asserted that, under conditions of perfect competition, price-making markets yield a long-run set of prices that balance, or equilibrate, the supplies and demands for all commodities in production and consumption. Given certain conditions, such as the preferences of consumers, productive techniques, and the mobility of productive factors, the market forces of supply and demand allocate resources efficiently, in the sense of minimizing costs and maximizing consumer utilities, in the long run. Finally, all the participants in production receive incomes commensurate with their efforts. Under these assumptions, capitalism was therefore the best of all possible economic worlds—efficient, want-satisfying, and full of social justice (everyone gets what he or she deserves). And, while this was not the main objective, economic growth results from the efficiencies produced by rational producers and consumers meeting in self-regulating markets.

CRITIQUE OF NEOCLASSICAL ECONOMICS

Neoclassical economics is based on a theory of the economic actor derived from Bentham that is often termed *Homo economicus*. It assumes that, when behaving economically, people are "rational": in the limited sense that they act as atomistic individuals seeking to maximize utility as consumers, or profit as entrepreneurs, with commodities produced at the least possible cost under conditions of perfect knowledge. These simplifying assumptions transform human subjects—analyzable using psychology, sociology, anthropology, and the like—into mechanical objects, understandable through mathematics. This shift enabled economics to resemble physics, the leading science of objects. Neoclassical economics appeals to the scientific mind. It presents itself as an objective *science* of society, and its methodology is mathematically elegant. The aim is to represent an economy in the abstract terms of a single equation—not quite Einstein's $E = mc^2$, but similar. Yet, scientific elegance comes at a price. To produce this elegant model, neoclassical economists had to simplify complex subjectivities into objective modes of behavior and strip away the environments of economic action so that the economic world became a sterile plain populated by clockwork "people." Even within conventional economics, and related areas of social science, this has produced criticism—particularly in the area of the rationality of the economic actor (the marginalist calculation mentioned earlier).

Herbert Simon (Simon and Newell 1972), for example, says that people are only partially rational, or that rationality is limited, or bounded by people's ability to formulate and solve complex problems and process information (quoted in Williamson 1985: 553). Daniel Kahneman stresses the role of intuitions—thoughts and preferences that come to mind quickly and without much reflection—in economic decision making. That is, intuitive judgments occupy a position between the automatic operations of perception and the deliberate operations of reasoning. He calls intuition "System 1" and deliberation "System 2," arguing that the explicit judgments people make are endorsed, at least passively, by System 2 but that the monitoring is normally quite lax and allows many intuitive judgments to be expressed, including some that are erroneous (Kahneman 2003). The famous economist Joseph Stiglitz (1943–) originally made a reputation by arguing that asymmetric information is a key feature of the world. In most situations, the two sides of a market have vastly different information about the good or service transacted, sellers typically knowing more about what they are selling than buyers know of what they buy, so that adverse selection occurs. That is, low-quality products drive out high-quality products unless other actions are taken—signaling and screening—so that the economic transactions that occur are different from those that would emerge in a world of perfect information (Arnott, Greenwald, Kanbur, and Nalebuff 2003).

Arguments like these, which earned Kahneman and Stiglitz Nobel prizes in economics, verge on criticizing the notion of *Homo economicus,* the rational, perfectly informed automaton occupying the central position in the whole marginal-market-competitive system of the neoclassical economic imaginary. Even so, these criticisms are limited. They seek merely to qualify a neoclassical economics that they too assume to be essentially valid—Stiglitz (2002) for instance, has written a major textbook that lies within the conventional mainstream. But we believe that more basic criticisms should be raised about this dominant discourse.

A discipline that erects an elaborate logic on insecure foundations is prone to fundamental error. Such error is self-sustaining in the sense that the mathematical logic rather than the empirical accuracy of the theoretical structure becomes all-important. So, we have to ask: Where did the central neoclassical notion of rational choice at the margin among perfectly known alternatives come from? It was not based on empirical observation of the actual behaviors of the main economic agents—not the consumers, nor the entrepreneurs, and certainly not the workers who hardly trouble the conventional economic imagination at all except as "factors." On the consumption side, while poor consumers may choose carefully among competing products when spending scarce money, nothing like "choice at the margin" occurs—it is more a case of simply buying the same necessities that keep families alive, with an occasional splurge on something that is intensely desired but not necessary. Indeed, reducing the consumption of poor people to marginal utility misses the daily drama of a life in poverty. With richer consumers, conspicuous consumption—a matter of taste, status, and aspiration—is the norm, not anything like marginal utility. At the center of the contemporary global capitalist system, consumption comes as waves of desire for particular products—an iPod yesterday, a cellphone that does everything tomorrow—which is more a matter of advertising, crazes, whims, peer pressure, pop idols, cultural trends, and so on. Marginal utility tells us next to nothing about the bursts of demand that have driven the growth surges in economies. On the other side, the supply side, the notion of marginal productivity was not derived from asking entrepreneurs how they made decisions. The conception of choice at the margin is not based on the inspection of economic reality or even a simplification of that reality. Instead, it is what the neoclassical economists "imputed" to behavior in order that it may fulfill their conception of economic rationality. More bluntly, optimizing behavior at the margin was how people "had to act" if equilibrium theory was to work. The contemporary form of this, called "rational choice theory," assumes that individuals have precise information about exactly what will occur under any choice made, that they have the cognitive ability to weigh every choice against every other choice, and that they are aware of all possible choices. The nearest that economics comes to reality is when "buyers" meet "sellers" in "laboratory experiments" in "alternative market mechanisms" (V. Smith 1994). To the neoclassicals, the mathematics of equilibrium theory was more important than the accuracy of representation. And indeed that proved to be the case. It *was* more important, for, with abstraction and mathematical sophistication, economics became *the* science of society. This made economics the most powerful discipline of the social sciences. Economics is to social science what physics is to natural science. But what if it is entirely wrong?

In fact, rather than growing under the impetus of free trade and open markets, most "advanced" countries, at the time that neoclassical economics was being conceived, used tariff protections and subsidies to develop their industries. Britain and the United States, the two countries that are supposed to have reached the very pinnacle of the world economy through their free market, free trade policies, aggressively employed protections and subsidies. For the first half of the 19th century Britain used *dirigiste* (that is, directed by the state) trade and industrial policies involving measures similar to what countries like Japan and Korea used later in order to develop their industries. Between the Civil War and World War II, the United States was the most heavily protected economy in the world (as Alexander Hamilton had presciently advocated). In choosing to protect their industries, Americans went against the advice of Adam Smith, David Ricardo, and Jean Baptiste Say, who saw the country's future in agriculture. However, Americans knew that Britain had succeeded through protection and subsidies and that their nation needed to do the same. And most of the rest of the advanced capitalist countries used tariffs, subsidies, and other means to promote their industries during the earliest stages—Germany, Japan, and Korea are well known in this respect, but also Sweden strategically used tariffs, subsidies, cartels, and state support for research and development to jumpstart its textile, steel, and engineering industries (Chang 2002). In other words, marginalist neoclassical economics, like its classical predecessor, not only misrepresented but also in fact reversed reality, in that it pretended that rational individualism acting through markets was the source of economic growth whereas in reality state policy produced growth.

The most pernicious aspect of all of this was J. B. Clark's leap from marginalist calculation into normative prescription—factors (people) are worth what the market grants them, he claimed, chief executives (CEOs) are worth hundreds of times what workers are, and finance capitalists are worth hundreds of times what CEOs are. Hence, neoclassical economics continues, with Clark, the class prejudices of classical economics—only this time it justifies class inequality in terms of "natural law." This was science for the rich. Hence, when neoclassical economists complain that the state distorts the efficiency of markets, what they are really saying is that the state disturbs the "natural justice" of competitive markets that grants huge rewards to the already rich.

Therefore, neoclassical economics stands indicted on two counts: (1) it is based on unexamined assumptions about human nature and economic behavior and therefore, while mathematically elegant, is a theoretical fantasy subject to gross error; and (2) it is a fantasy theory out of touch with reality, reversing reality, a theory dreamed on behalf of the elite. With minds full of unrealistic, biased theories like these, even sophisticated marginalist economists tended toward the bizarre when they left the abstract world of equilibrium to contemplate turbulent reality. So, Jevons of marginalist fame, seeing that both business and sunspot cycles had average durations of 10.45 years, thought that sunspots caused weather variations that influenced crop yields, which in turn caused business cycles that created depressions! In British and U.S. neoclassical economics most theorists followed Say in reasoning that general overproduction, or massive long-term unemployment, was impossible because "supply creates its own demand." The main weak spot in Say's law, noticed by Marshall, was that a portion of incomes was saved and thus potentially withdrawn from the upward cycle of growth. However, this was easily explained away, for savings were reinvested (by individuals or banks) and contributed to growth. In the marginalist tradition neither growth nor depressions were relevant economic issues. The economy took care of itself. Markets worked.

Then came 1929, when economic reality thumped economic fantasy in the eye. The bodies of "rational speculators" fell like rain from the roofs and windows of New York skyscrapers. Neoclassical economics had nothing to say, nothing that made sense at least. Neoclassical economics failed in the Great Depression of the 1930s. Unfortunately it was not buried in the debris.

3

From Keynesian
Economics to Neoliberalism

Neoclassical economic harmony was disturbed by the critical institutional economist Thorstein Veblen (1857–1929), a Norwegian American from Wisconsin who taught at various universities, usually as an assistant professor (his message was unpopular!). Veblen differentiated between the rational, technical aspects of modern mechanized production and the business and entrepreneurial aspect. The first, technical serviceability, produced useful products that satisfied needs; the second, business enterprise, favored chintzy products that would break or displease quickly, leading to replacement and greater profits for business. Veblen argued that pursuit of gain often caused unemployment, higher prices and costs, and delayed innovation. He thought that borrowing on the basis of anticipated earnings created business cycles of expansion and contraction that enabled large firms to swallow smaller ones. Rather than focusing on class conflicts creating the dynamic of capitalist history (as did Marx), Veblen emphasized conflicts among three cultural tendencies: the machine process, business enterprise, and warlike or predatory beliefs. Business enterprise, he thought, would eventually fail, and the future system would either involve domination by engineers or a reversion to archaic absolutism under military domination (Germany and Japan were cited as examples). Veblen reversed the arguments of neoclassicism.

DYNAMIC ANALYSIS

There were other traditions in economics opposing the neoclassical consensus. In Germany a historical school of economics had long been

critical of the abstract nature of both Ricardian and marginalist economics. The historical school was based in the German philosophical
traditions of idealism and romanticism. Originally formulated by Wilhelm Roscher (1817–1894), Bruno Hildebrand (1812–1878), and Karl
Knies (1821–1898) and developed further by a second generation led by
Gustav Schmoller (1838–1917), the historical school's main themes were
the unity of social and economic life, the plurality of human motives,
and the relativity of history, all regarded from an organicist or holistic
viewpoint (that is, a view that stressed the natural webs of interconnec-
tions among things). The historical school also had an abiding interest in
crisis and development. Roscher and other German economic historians
thought that it was difficult to keep supply and demand "balanced" in
advanced economies and that crises were probable, particularly when
caused by lack of demand, or underconsumption. Other German economists influenced by the historical school stressed the instabilities resulting
from psychological factors in economic processes and the booms caused
by erratic growth in the various sectors of an economy (for example,
steel, shipbuilding, and railroads growing unevenly). The German historical school was empirical, looked at the very long term, and tended to
be more critical of capitalism than neoclassical economics. A bitter debate
between Schmoller and Menger in the 1880s split German-speaking economics into antagonistic camps for decades—Schmoller thought that
classical and neoclassical economics erred in finding universal laws, preferred induction to deduction, and found naive the notion that people
were motivated entirely by self-interest.

Influenced by the German historical school and Marxism but trained
at Vienna in marginalist (Austrian) economics, and an admirer of Walras's
general equilibrium theory, Joseph Schumpeter (1883–1950) combined
methods and theories from all approaches within an overall perspective
derived from advanced natural science. For Schumpeter, neoclassical economics took basic social variables as given and postulated that the play
of self-interests in competitive markets would bring resource allocation
into equilibrium—this was static analysis. Schumpeter argued that eco-

nomic change was exactly the opposite: abrupt and discontinuous rather
than smooth and orderly. His own model saw innumerable exchanges
constituting, in their totality, a circular flow of economic life (Schumpeter 1934: 41). Schumpeter was not interested in small changes, within
the flow, that did not disrupt the existing system. Instead, he was fascinated by the truly dynamic development of economic systems, when the
impetus for change came from within the economy (endogenously), with
effects that displaced the existing equilibrium. These spontaneous and
discontinuous changes, he thought, came not from consumption but from

production, specifically from new combinations of productive materials and forces. Productive innovations could occur in five different ways: the introduction of a new or substantially different good; a new method of production not before tested; the opening of a new market; the conquest of a new system of supply of raw materials or semifinished goods; and a new organization of production, like the creation of a monopoly position. Because such innovations destroyed old channels of production and formed new ones, Schumpeter called the resulting development process "creative destruction."

The economic subjects responsible for innovations were entrepreneurs. Schumpeter thought that relatively few people in any society tried to change customary practices and introduce new things. Entrepreneurs were dynamic, energetic leaders distinguished by will rather than intelligence. And rather than hedonism as the basis of economic rationality (the pursuit of pleasure, the avoidance of pain), Schumpeter thought that dynamic analysis required a fundamentally different kind of entrepreneurial rationalism based on the will to found a new domain, the will to conquer and fight, or the joy of creating new things (there are similarities here with the German philosopher Friedrich Nietzsche's rejection of utilitarianism and advocacy of power and will). Schumpeter thought further that creativity could not be predicted from previous facts, that creativity shaped the course of future events, and yet that creativity was an enigma. Even so, economics had to deal with psychology and human motivation at a different level than everyday utilitarianism.

Innovative investment was financed not by savings but by credit, with interest paid from the profits generated by innovation. Schumpeter saw the development initiated by innovation as uneven, discontinuous, and taking the form of business cycles, rather than causing deviations in a kind of dynamic equilibrium. These business cycles could be short-term (40 months), medium-term (9–10 years), or long-term (for example, the Kondratieff long waves of 50–55 years; Kuznets 1953), which Schumpeter conceptualized as epochs with different values and civilizational characteristics. In this view, economic change is not the result of slow movement from one equilibrium to another but rather is driven by the pursuit of the quasi-monopolistic profits that accrue to innovators. Economic change is propelled by the succession of technologies and practices that destroy old, inefficient arrangements as newer, more efficient, ones are created. New ideas are frequently created by new firms: the business that builds the first railroad is seldom the business that previously operated the stage coaches (Schumpeter 1934). New businesses develop new ideas that displace the old ones. The result is what Schumpeter calls "creative destruction." But for all his praise of the entrepreneur, Schumpeter also thought that an economy satiated with capital and rationalized by entrepreneurial minds would eventually become socialist (Schumpeter 1934; Shionoya 1997).

KEYNESIAN ECONOMICS

Neoclassical theoretical harmony was further disturbed by John Maynard Keynes (1883–1946), a Cambridge economist, admirer of Marshall, and member of the Bloomsbury circle of artists and intellectuals. During the 1920s Keynes began systematically to demolish the postulates of the prevailing neoclassical approach—for example, the neoclassical notion that unemployment was "voluntary." He increasingly came to think that economic systems did not automatically right themselves in reaching "the optimal level of production." But such was the domination of neoclassical theory over economic thought that Keynes's criticism would have been ignored were it not for the Great Depression—when markets proved incapable not only of optimization but also merely keeping workers employed. Keynes's *The General Theory of Employment, Interest and Money* (1936) found that the creation of demand by supply (as with Say's law) could occur at any level of employment or income, including very low levels of employment, so that full employment was but one of many economic possibilities for capitalism. The particular level of employment in an economy, Keynes thought, was determined by the aggregate demand for goods and services. Assuming that the government had a neutral effect, two groups influenced this total demand: consumers buying consumption goods and investors buying production equipment. Consumers increased spending as their incomes rose. But this was not the key to explaining the overall level of employment, for consumption depended on income, which depended on something else. In the Keynesian system, real investment (spending on new factories, tools, machines, and larger inventories of goods) was the crucial variable: changes in real investment fed into the other areas of an economy, expanding the whole economy. Investment resulted from decisions made by entrepreneurs under conditions of risk. Investment could be postponed. The decision to invest, Keynes said, depended on comparisons between the expected profits (from the investment) and the prevailing rate of interest. Here the crucial component was "expectation," or more generally the degree of investor confidence. The cost of the capital used in investment, the interest rate, Keynes explained in terms of speculation about future stock prices, which in turn determined interest rates as savings moved from one fund to another. The decision to invest also depended essentially on expectations about the future. When investors bought machines, they provided income to machine builders (companies and employees), and these spent money, further increasing national income, with the "multiplier effect" (the degree of economic expansion induced by an initial investment) varying with the proportion of additional income that was spent rather than saved (the marginal propensity to consume), and so on; a decrease in real investment had the reverse effects. The government could influence this process through interest rates and other monetary policies, shifting the economy from one equilibrium level to another, generally to higher employment levels (Moggridge 1980).

KEYNESIANISM AND SOCIAL DEMOCRACY

Keynes himself doubted that merely changing interest rates would be sufficient to significantly alter business confidence and thus increase investment to produce a growing economy. The state also had to intervene through monetary and fiscal policies. Subsequently, conservative Keynesian economists have seen monetary policy, especially the manipulation of interest rates, as a relatively nonbureaucratic, non-state-intrusive method by which the central bank of a country tries to influence national income and employment. The basic idea is this: when an economy shows signs of moving into recession, the central bank (Federal Reserve Bank in the United States, Bank of England in Britain, etc.) lowers the rate that it charges for borrowing money—the private banks then follow. Lower interest rates encourage businesses, municipalities, and consumers to borrow money and spend it on new machinery, public works, houses, and consumer goods—the "multiplier effect." Increased demand coming from these sources then restimulates the economy, pulling it out of recession. And business confidence increases, so industry begins investing again—the "accelerator effect."

The other Keynesian device is fiscal policy, as with deficit spending by states—that is, governments deliberately spending more than they take in as revenues through their tax systems, again increasing demand and boosting the economy. The new kind of liberal economists that began to favor state intervention (by comparison with the older school that abhorred state intervention in market systems) also favor this method as a more effective measure, the "liberal" aspect being that deficit spending can be used for social investment, like improving education and social services. While favoring the latter course, Keynes himself thought that simply "government spending" was crucial rather than the social investment part: burying banknotes in old mines, filling these with refuse, and then having private enterprise dig them up was better than nothing if the goal was to increase employment in ending serious recessions like the depression of the 1930s. (In the end, fiscal deficits proved to be structurally necessary just to keep capitalist economies going, with governments regularly having state budgetary deficits on the order of 3–4% of GDP, with this leading to huge and permanent state debts—the U.S. federal government's total debt is $9.5 trillion, or more than $30,000 per person, while that of the U.K. government is about $1.0 trillion, or more than $15,000 per person.) Keynes proved theoretically what actual economic policy and recurring depressions had long shown in practice: free markets do not spontaneously maximize human well-being. Instead, the state has to intervene through demand management, changing the aggregate level of demand of a capitalist economy through monetary and fiscal policies. Keynes also pointed to the chaotic core of market-based decision making, the utter uncertainty that haunts the capitalist imagination, uncertainty as a self-fulfilling prophecy, uncertainty that when spread widely can even cause depression. As Franklin Roosevelt said in 1933 on becoming president of the United States: "The only thing we have to fear is fear itself."

While Keynesian economics was available from 1936 onward, the Depression of the 1930s was ended by pragmatic governmental intervention, as with New Deal employment-generating programs in the United States, and the militarization of all the Western economies involved in World War II. During the postwar period, Keynesian economics became the basis of growth theories promulgated by economists other than Keynes (who died in 1946), particularly in the design of policies that might maintain full employment. Full employment and a better life were promises that all political parties, Republican or Democratic, Conservative or Labor, were forced to make to millions of soldiers returning from a war that saved the West. The question "Whose society did we just risk our lives for?" was too close to the political surface for the previous political-economic platitudes to suffice. Particularly in western Europe, political attitudes turned toward socialism or, more accurately, in a social democratic direction. For example, the British working class ejected Winston Churchill, Conservative party hero of the war, to elect a Labor government committed to full employment, heavily subsidized state-run social services (such as the National Health Service), educational reform (scholarships for university students), and significant income redistribution achieved by taxing the rich and paying the poor (family allowances, etc.). Also, in many countries outside the United States, under social democracy the state directed what remained a basically capitalist economy with key industrial sectors (transportation, mines, steel, chemicals) nationalized—that is, owned and run by state corporations. This (Fabian) socialist version of social democratic politics merged with leftist theoretical interpretations of Keynes to produce a political economics that favored the working class. This was not merely because workers spent any income redistributed to them and therefore kept the economy going in a Keynesian sense. It was also because they deserved higher incomes and free social services, for in the socialist view the people, as workers, are the producers of value and income, while labor creates growth. Most of this view came, for a while, to be taken for granted by popular opinion in the western European countries and the "working-class paradises" of Australia and New Zealand. In Britain, the Beveridge Report of 1942 resulted in a comprehensive system of social security and a National Health Service that provided free health care after the end of World War II. The report was based on the principle of banishing poverty, declaring: "A revolutionary moment in the world's history is a time for revolutions, not for patching" and "The organisation of social insurance should be treated as one part only of a comprehensive policy of social progress" (Beveridge 1942). By comparison, the United States was never fully social democratic. U.S. social legislation, such as the Employment Act of 1946, was far more limited than its European equivalent. When the United States took over the role of guardian of the West from Britain, the resulting political economy is best described as military Keynesianism—that is, the maintenance of high growth rates through "defense" spending by the state (Turgeon 1996)—rather than social Keynesianism, that is, the maintenance of high employment rates through state planning and social progress.

During the postwar period of Keynesian dominance, economics focused much more on economic growth than it had in the past—growth being seen as the source of progress. In the Harrod–Domar model—named for its originators, economists Roy Harrod (1900–1978) and Evsey Domar (1914–1997)—increasing economic growth basically involved increasing the savings rate of a country, in some cases through the state budget, and using the resulting (saved) funds to invest in the growth of the economy. The key to economic growth is to expand the level of investment in terms of fixed capital (factories, machines) and "human capital" (people as workers). To do this, the state needs to encourage savings and generate technological advances that enable firms to produce more output with less capital (that is, lower their capital–output ratio). Harrod used several concepts of economic growth in this analysis: warranted growth, natural growth, and actual growth. The warranted growth rate is the growth rate at which all savings are absorbed into investment. The natural growth rate is the rate required to maintain full employment. In Harrod's model, two kinds of problems could arise with growth rates. First, actual growth was determined by the rate of savings, while natural growth was determined by the growth of the labor force. There was no necessary reason for actual growth to equal natural growth and, therefore, no inherent tendency for the economy to reach full employment. This problem resulted from his overly simple assumptions that the wage rate is fixed and that the economy must use labor and capital in the same proportions. The second problem implied by Harrod's model was unstable growth. If companies adjusted their investment according to their expectations of future demand, and the anticipated demand occurred, warranted growth would equal actual growth. But if actual demand exceeded anticipated demand, they would have under-invested and would respond with further investment. This investment, however, would itself cause growth to rise, requiring even further investment, resulting in explosive growth. But if the reverse happened, with actual demand falling short of anticipated demand, the result would be a deceleration of growth. This became known as Harrod's knife-edge—between too much and too little growth. The "knife-edge" means that the economic growth path is unstable, in that slight shocks to the system lead to instabilities that are self-reinforcing rather than self-correcting (Harrod 1939, 1948; Domar 1947).

In critique, Robert Solow (1956) argued that the real-world economy is not on a "knife-edge" (except for the Great Depression). Solow said that there must be some market mechanism that brings an economy back to equilibrium and the warranted growth rate when it deviates from them. Harrod's model assumed that the labor–capital ratio is constant over time. But "if this assumption is abandoned, the knife-edge notion of unstable balance seems to go with it" (Solow 1956: 65). Solow found this assumption inconsistent with neoclassical economics. When firms have excess capacity (excess investment), they substitute labor for capital—Solow essentially modified the Harrod–Domar model to allow neoclassical factor substitution in production. According to Solow, there can be stable equilibrium growth if the growth model is set up with this correct neoclassical assumption. Solow tried three production functions and picked one (the Cobb–Douglas production function) because it theoretically generated stable equilibrium. Solow argued that there exists a rate of investment—balanced investment—that keeps the growth of the capital stock equal to the growth of the labor force. If actual investment exceeds balanced investment, the amount of capital per worker grows until it reaches a level consistent with full employment—what Solow called the steady-state point. Hence, Solow showed that the neoclassical growth model is stable. It has the self-adjusting mechanism that guarantees a return to equilibrium. Solow's model was an attack on the Keynesian explanation of unstable economic growth.

Solow followed this critique with another article, "Technical Change and the Aggregate Production Function." Economics had believed that the main causes of economic growth were increases in capital and labor.

But Solow (1957) showed that half of economic growth in the United States cannot be accounted for just by increases in capital and labor. The unaccounted-for portion of economic growth—the "Solow residual"— he attributed to technological innovation. Basically, Solow argued that an economy with a higher savings ratio experiences higher per capita production and thus higher real income. But in the absence of technological progress the rate of growth is purely dependent on an increased supply of labor. As a result, technological development has to be the motor of economic growth in the long run. In Solow's model, growth in real incomes is exclusively determined by technological progress. Solow's model pictured technology as a continuous, ever-expanding set of knowledges that simply became evident over time—technological change was "exogenous" rather than something specifically created by economic forces. Solow's model became the mainstay of the economic analysis of growth. Robert Solow is one of the major figures of the neo-Keynesian synthesis in macroeconomics. Together with Paul Samuelson, he formed the core of the Massachusetts Institute of Technology (MIT) economics department, widely viewed as *the* "mainstream" of the postwar period. The Solow model greatly affected the policy recommendations of economists during the 1960s and 1970s.

Let us follow this trajectory in economic thought to the present. In turn, the Solow model has been critiqued by what is termed "new growth theory." As we have said, Solow established the primacy of technological progress in accounting for sustained increases in output per worker. The economist Paul Romer countered this by constructing mathematical representations of economies in which technological change is the result of the intentional actions of people, such as in research and development. New growth theory, of which Romer is the leading figure, has two main characteristics: it is an "endogenous" growth theory because it internalizes technology into a model of how markets function—it views technological progress as a product of economic activity; and it holds that, unlike physical objects, knowledge and technology are characterized by increasing returns that drive the process of growth. Because ideas can be infinitely shared and reused, they can accumulate without limit (that is, they are not subject to the eventual onset of "diminishing returns"). The source of economic progress is ideas. New growth theory tries to make sense of the shift from a resource-based economy to a knowledge-based economy. Higher living standards result from steadily improving knowledge of how to produce more and better goods and services with ever smaller amounts of physical resources. No amount of savings and investment, no policy of macroeconomic fine-tuning, and no set of tax and spending incentives can generate sustained economic growth unless they are accompanied by the countless large and small discoveries that are required to create more value from a fixed set of natural resources (Romer 1993: 345). "As the world becomes more and more closely integrated, the feature that will increasingly differentiate one geographic area (city or country) from another will be the quality of public institutions. The most successful areas will be the ones with the most competent and effective mechanisms for supporting collective interests, especially in the production of new ideas" (Romer 1992: 89).

A view of the space economy of deveopment follows from this approach. Idea creation, new business development, and economic change happen in specific places. Differences among places are particularly important in terms of "knowledge spillovers," meaning that some of the benefits of new ideas flow to persons or economic actors other than those who create the new knowledge. Spillovers also happen in particular places, with the result that the new growth theory has implications for the geography of economic activity. As we saw in Chapter 2, Alfred Marshall made the connection between knowledge spillovers and local economic development. Noting the agglomerations or clusters of industries in particular locations, Marshall observed that, in addition to the advantages of labor force pooling and access to specialized suppliers, a group of firms in a similar activity in a particular location, like Sheffield's (U.K.) steel district, meant that knowledge was in the air (Marshall 1920), meaning that it was part of the local culture. Interest in Marshall's arguments about the external economies of knowledge spillovers increased in the 1980s, following studies of small industrial districts in northern Italy. Dense clusters of small firms, typically located in a single community, competed successfully in international markets by specializing in the production of certain products, like tiles, fashion apparel, and industrial machinery. Studies of the development of these districts stressed the strong networks, social linkages, and information flows among producers (Piore and Sabel 1984). The arrival of sophisticated communications technologies, particularly the Internet, brings the perception that information can be moved instantaneously, without cost, from place to place—hence, the "death of distance" or the "end of geography." But the counterargument to this disappearance of space is that the revolution in technology does not completely erase the importance of distance to knowledge spillovers. There are two types of knowledge: codifiable knowledge, which can be written down; and tacit knowledge, learned from experience and not easily transmittable from one individual to another (M. Polanyi 1967). Because tacit knowledge is embedded in the minds of individuals and the routines of organizations, it does not move easily from place to place. Similarly, a base of tacit knowledge is frequently a prerequisite for making use of any particular bit of codified knowledge. As well, culture and institutional factors influence knowledge flows among firms located close to one another. So, place still matters in development.

New growth theory has implications for economic development policy. It stresses that creating new knowledge is the key driver behind economic growth, for the economy as a whole and for particular areas. It also emphasizes the role that institutions and policies can play in creating conducive circumstances for innovation and the diffusion of knowledge.

New growth theory suggests five broad strategies for governments:

1. Economic strategies should focus on creating new knowledge in universities and laboratories and by businesses.
2. States and communities are not powerless to influence their economic destinies.
3. The path-dependent quality of growth means that the possibilities of future growth depend, in large part, on the current local base of knowledge and expertise, which communities should try to enhance.
4. Ideas of all kinds, large and small, play a role in economic growth: innovation by front-line workers is as important to the knowledge economy as scientific research.
5. Knowledge-based growth can stimulate a self-reinforcing cycle in which faster growth triggers additional knowledge creation and more growth (Cortright 2001).

THE DEVELOPMENTAL STATE

In the Third World, the "developmental state," a parallel conception to Keynesianism, drawing from it but differing in several respects, was employed during the postwar years, following the example of Japan. Since the beginning of Japan's modern period (the "Meiji Restoration of 1868"), the state has been crucial to the country's development. Initially, the Japanese state established state-owned "model factories" in a number of industries—shipbuilding, mining, textile, and armaments—and after these were privatized, the state subsidized their operations, The first modern steel mill was established by the government in 1901. The state was heavily involved in infrastructure development, as with the railroad and telegraph system. Infant industries were protected by tariffs placed on imports of competing products, while raw material imports were subsidized. In the 1920s the Japanese state encouraged the "rationalization" of key industries (through cartels, mergers, etc.) in order to restrain "wasteful competition," achieve economies of scale, and introduce scien-

tific management (Wade 1990; Chang 2002). Thus, Japan's rapid industrial development, it has been argued (Johnson 1982), resulted from the
intervention of a "plan rational" state—that is, a state directly intervening in the development process rather than relying on market forces—
to establish "substantive social and economic goals" that would guide
the processes of development. At the center of the Japanese state system
was a competent bureaucracy staffed by the country's brightest students,
dedicated to devising and implementing a planned process of economic
development. One key element was the "pilot agency," in this case Japan's
Ministry of International Trade and Industry (MITI), charged with
directing the course of development and devising a range of policy tools
to ensure that indigenous business was nurtured in the overall national
interest. MITI and the Ministry of Finance were able to use control over
domestic savings to provide cheap credit for particular industries chosen
for emphasis by the state. Japanese planners were able to guide the initial
industrialization and subsequent industrial upgrading as new, more valuable, industries were supported (engineering, automobiles, electronics),
while older ones (textiles, shoes, toys) were encouraged to move offshore,
remaining under Japanese corporate control (Beeson 2003).

   The economic "miracle" in postwar Japan and the East Asian newly
industrialized countries (NICs—South Korea, Singapore, Taiwan) since
the 1970s was fundamentally due to activist industrial, trade, and technology policies introduced by the state. The East Asian developmental
states gave substantial well-designed export subsidies to industries they
favored and granted tariff rebates that cheapened imported raw materials and machinery. States intervened to systematize economies through
indicative (suggestive) planning—that is, planning via subsidies, grants,
and tax inducements rather than state fiat. States regulated the entry of
firms into key industries and restricted intercompany competition. Foreign investment was restricted and regulated. And states were actively
involved in enhancing countries' skill bases and technological capabilities through subsidies and public provision of education, training, and
research and development (Amsden 2001; Chang 2002). Ha-Joon Chang
has argued that state intervention, such as protecting infant industries,
was used by most countries when they were in catch-up positions.

STRUCTURALISM AND IMPORT SUBSTITUTION

Similarly in Latin America, a school of thought emerged that was critical
of certain aspects of classical economic doctrine, that found conventional
economics too abstract, and that often advocated, with Keynes and the
social democrats, state intervention in the growth process. As we have

seen, neoclassical economics assumes that smoothly working market systems and effective price mechanisms organize all economies efficiently. This notion of a universal economic science ("monoeconomics") was contested by a "structuralist approach" to development economics that insisted, instead, on the specificity of Third World economies—their differences—and therefore the inapplicability of universalist neoclassicism. Two main areas of economic practice came into contention, namely, the causes of inflation and trade theory. First, inflation: during the 1940s, 1950s, and 1960s several Latin American countries experienced inflation rates of 80–100% a year. Standard deflationary policies had little effect. Conventional monetarist economists argued that inflation was caused by excessive increases in the supply of money and that price stability could be achieved by decreasing the money supply. Structuralist economists argued conversely that supply and demand operated differently in Latin American countries, with supply being inelastic (that is, requiring a large price change to bring about even small changes in the quantities of goods) because of structural characteristics like the domination of agriculture by *latifundia* (large estates) that did not operate on market principles. The inflation problem could be resolved only by such structural changes as land reform, import substitution (to make countries less dependent on foreign manufactures), education, and improved fiscal systems (Seers 1962, 1983).

Second, trade theory: in Latin American countries early development strategies had favored an outward-oriented economic model in which countries provided primary goods, such as coffee, wheat, or copper, to the European and North American markets in accord with the Ricardian theory of comparative advantage. The depression of the 1930s revealed weaknesses inherent in this position, as demand and prices fell to the point that coffee was burnt as fuel for the Brazilian railroads. After World War II a coherent Latin American perspective on the development process was formulated in the United Nations Economic Commission for Latin America (ECLA). The commission found that conventional (classical and neoclassical) theories were inadequate for understanding the underdeveloped world. Instead, an appreciation of the different historical contexts and natural situations of these countries, their different social structures, types of behavior, and economies, required a new "structuralist" perspective. The main tenets of this theory were outlined by Raul Prebisch (1901–1986), formerly head of the Central Bank of Argentina, and Hans Singer (1910–2006), a U.S. economist, in what became known as the Singer–Prebisch thesis.

Prebisch (1972) saw the world not in monoeconomic terms, as one homogenous system, but as two distinct areas, a center of economic power in Europe and the United States, and a periphery of weaker countries in Latin America, Africa, and Asia. As we have seen, conventional economic theory (comparative advantage) argued that the exchange of central industrial goods for peripheral primary goods was to the peripheral country's advantage. This was because technical progress in the center would lead to lower prices for industrial exports and that ultimately a unit of primary exports would buy more units of industrial imports— hence, over the long term, progress would accrue to the periphery without it having to industrialize. Disagreeing with this conventional argument, Prebisch argued instead that Latin America's peripheral position and primary exports were exactly the causes of its *lack* of progress, specifically because of a long-term decline in the periphery's terms of trade (the ratio between the value of exports and the value of imports). Using Britain as a case study (because it had a long statistical record), Prebisch showed that the terms of trade for center countries had improved with industrialization; from this, he deduced that those of the periphery must have deteriorated. Technical advances benefited the center countries rather than the entire world. This was not a temporary phenomenon, but a structural characteristic of the global system. Conventional economic theory failed to work, he said, because (1) markets in the center were characterized by imperfect competition and price reductions (stemming from technical advances) could be avoided, while competition among primary producers reduced the prices for their goods; and (2) the income elasticity of demand (that is, the degree to which demand changes with a given change in income) is higher for industrial goods (like electronics) than for primary goods (like food), so that the periphery's terms of trade tended to decline from the demand side. Prebisch concluded that Latin America's underdevelopment was due to its emphasis on primary exports. The periphery was underdeveloped because it had to produce more and more food and raw materials for export in order to import a given amount of industrial imports. In effect, the periphery was working for the center.

The solution lay in structural change in peripheral economies: industrialization using an import substitution strategy (that is, replacing industrial imports with domestic production). After World War II, most of the larger countries in Latin America accepted the ECLA analysis of the problems involved in gearing their economies towards the traditional world division of labor (Baer 1972: 97). Many Latin American countries adopted a mix of trade and macroeconomic policies, typically involving trade barriers and exchange rate controls, taxes on export activities, and import substitution. There were complex mechanisms that gave preferences for strategic imports (for example, capital goods and industrial raw materials), the direct participation of the state in the economy (via state-owned enterprises), and cheap credit for "strategic" sectors.

Import substitution industrialization (ISI) led to significant structural changes in the Latin American economies in the post-World War II era, with the manufacturing sector expanding its share of GDP between 1950 (when it was 19.6%) and 1967 (24.1%). Structural change was particularly significant in the case of Brazil, where industry increased its share in the economy from 19.8% in 1947 to 28% by 1968. In the second half of the 1950s, the Brazilian government enacted a series of policies intended to industrialize the economy. The government gave special attention to industries considered basic for economic growth, specifically the automobile, cement, steel, aluminum, cellulose, heavy machinery, and chemical industries. As a result of ISI, the Brazilian economy experienced rapid growth and diversification. Between 1950 and 1961, the average annual rate of growth in the GDP exceeded 7%, with industry having an average annual growth rate of 9% between 1950 and 1961, compared to 4.5% for agriculture (Hudson 1997). In addition, the structure of the manufacturing sector experienced considerable change. Traditional industries, such as textiles, food products, and clothing, declined, while the transport equipment, machinery, electric equipment and appliances, and chemical industries expanded.

ISI was widely adopted in Latin America, as elsewhere in the Third World, with impressive results as industry grew rapidly. The newly industrialized countries (including Latin American countries with large populations, like Brazil, Argentina, and Mexico) collectively had growth rates of 8.4% in 1964–1973 and 5.3% in 1973–1983, with the East Asian countries sustaining growth rates on the order of 10% a year, often for a decade or more (Organization for Economic Cooperation and Development 1988). Import substitution and infant industry protection led to high productivities, particularly in Latin America during the 1960s and 1970s (Bosworth and Collins 2003). More importantly, as industrialization moved from the production of simple products like textiles to more complex products like steel and automobiles, workers who were increasingly unionized were able to demand and get higher wages from employers and better services from Third World states. Over time, however, import substitution industrialization came to have a bad reputation in conventional circles—it was said to produce high-cost, low-quality industrial goods, it neglected agriculture, and it established entrenched positions for foreign capital. The remedy came to be seen as the cause of the illness (Blomstrom and Hettne 1984; Chilcote 1984; Harris 1986). "Bad reputations," however, are often undeserved. ISI served Third World countries well, enabling an industrialization that would never have happened in the classical liberal conditions of free trade, open borders, and no state intervention.

In general, structuralist development economics "attempts to identify specific rigidities, lags, and other characteristics of the structure of developing economies that affect economic adjustments and the choice of development policy" (Meier 1984: 118). The main structuralist point was that neoclassical economics was not a universal science, that the price system varied in effectiveness over space, and that a new type of economics had to be developed for the Third World. In general, structuralist economics argued that developing countries had features that set them apart from the economies theorized by orthodox economics. These features included high levels of rural unemployment, low levels of industrialization, more obstacles to industrialization, and disadvantages in international trade. Structuralist economics in the 1950s and 1960s tried to remedy these problems by removing the obstacles to growth specific to poor countries.

DEVELOPMENT ECONOMICS: BALANCED AND UNBALANCED GROWTH

During the 1950s a "development economics" emerged that was different from neoclassical and Keynesian economics. It focused specifically on developing countries, and it had greater practicality in terms of a more immediate policy orientation. Development economics assumed that economic processes in developing countries were distinct from those of developed countries, as the structuralists argued. But gradually monoeconomics (the position that all economies work in similar ways and that neoclassical economics was universally applicable) came back in, although "getting the prices right" (the standard neoclassical remedy to making an economy efficient) was acknowledged to be more difficult in the developing world. Also while population, technology, institutions, and entrepreneurship were exogenous (assumed to be outside the system) in neoclassical economics, they were endogenous (within the system) for development economics—indeed, these were often the main factors requiring economic explanation. The position of development economics eventually became not that neoclassical economics was inapplicable to Third World development, but that it needed to be extended to problems of income distribution, poverty, and basic needs, or to be modified because the unemployment problem was not of the Keynesian variety (Meier 1984: 145–147). The result was a hybrid development economics, a melange of ideas, part structuralist, part neoclassical, part Keynesian, part pragmatic.

Some of the main positions of structuralist development economics were as follows:

1. *Dualistic development:* the idea that a modern commercial sector developed alongside a traditional subsistence sector, resulting in a dual economy in poor countries. The two sectors differed in terms of the growth process and conditions in labor markets (Lewis 1955; Higgins 1968; Todaro 1971).

2. *Mobilizing domestic resources:* the idea was to find ways of increasing the savings rate and mobilizing domestic savings (through banks and other financial institutions), making domestic funds available for productive investment in poor countries.

3. *Mobilizing foreign resources:* however, there might remain a "savings gap" and a "foreign exchange gap," which could be filled from external sources through public financial aid, loans, private foreign investment, and nonmonetary transfers of managerial and technological knowledge.

4. *Industrialization strategy:* industrialization should produce, often in labor-intensive, capital-saving ways, the simple producer and consumer goods required, particularly by rural people.

5. *Agricultural strategy:* progress in agriculture was thought essential for providing food and raw materials, yielding savings and tax revenues for development elsewhere in an economy, and earning foreign exchange, with farmers forming a market for industrial goods.

6. *Trade strategy:* development economists were originally divided on whether free trade increased international inequalities or could contribute to the development of primary exporting countries. Increasingly they favored export promotion of semimanufactured and manufactured goods and the "liberalization" of trade regimes (that is, low tariffs).

7. *"Human resource" development:* the accumulation of material capital was to be paralleled by investment in "human capital"— that is, improving the quality of people as productive agents, changing abilities and skills, even modifying motivations and values (hence, an interaction with modernization theory—see Chapter 4).

8. *Project appraisal:* with investment resources scarce in developing countries, there was a particular need for the rational allocation of capital and thus for development project appraisals by governments and international agencies like the World Bank (Meier 1984).

9. *Development planning and policymaking:* some development economists voiced criticisms of the market mechanism as ineffective, unreliable, or irrelevant to the problems faced by developing

countries. They found a need to supersede markets with state planning.

Development economics was founded in Britain during, and shortly after, World War II. Its founding economists doubted the usefulness of neoclassical economics, with its presumptions of smoothly operating markets, and saw the state as being key to the development process. Here the seminal work was by Paul Rosenstein-Rodan. He argued that industrialization of the "international depressed areas," like eastern and southeastern Europe, was in the general interest of the world as a whole. It was the way to achieve a more equal distribution of income between different areas of the world by raising incomes in depressed areas at a higher rate than in the rich areas. Rosenstein-Rodan found there to be an "agrarian excess population" amounting to 25% of the population that was totally or partly unemployed—a "waste of labor." This waste could be solved either by transporting workers toward capital (emigration) or bringing capital toward labor (industrialization). Since emigration and resettlement would present special difficulties, industrialization was necessary. This could occur under a Russian model that aimed at self-sufficiency without international investment, and involved all aspects of industry, heavy industry, machine industries, as well as light industry, with the final result being a national economy built like a vertical industrial concern. But this approach entails disadvantages in that it could only proceed slowly, because capital had to be supplied internally at the expense of the standard of living and consumption, and implied heavy and unnecessary sacrifice. The alternative model of industrialization would fit eastern and southeastern Europe into the world economy, preserving the advantages of the international division of labor, and would therefore, in the end, produce more wealth for everybody. It would be based on substantial international investment or capital lending. The first task was to provide for training and the "skilling" of a million new industrial workers a year, a huge task requiring the setting up of a planning board within an "Eastern European Industrial Trust" rather than relying on private entrepreneurship—half the capital would come from domestic sources and half from creditor countries. It would involve large-scale planned industrialization, paying workers more than they previously earned *in natura* (in the rural areas), creating its own additional market and gaining external economies of scale (that is, lower costs of production due to many firms producing in an area). But even a bold, optimistic program of industrialization could not solve the whole problem of surplus population within a decade after the ending of the war—at best 70–80% of the unemployed workers could be employed, and emigration would still have to supplement industrialization (Rosenstein-Rodan 1943). Rosenstein-

Rodan's thesis was seen as applicable to the problems of many Third World countries and came to be known as the "big push" theory, implying the need for a coordinated expansion and the intervention of the state in development planning. The basic idea was that investment was restricted by the small size of the market in poor regions, but a number of projects begun simultaneously in different industries might provide markets for one another. So, there was a need for a broad attack to get an economy out of its vicious cycle of poverty: "A wave of new investments in different branches of production can economically succeed, enlarge the total market and so break the bonds of the stationary equilibrium of underdevelopment" (Nurkse 1953: 15). This was also known as "balanced growth," in the sense that a whole set of complementary investments would be made.

This approach was countered by the theory of unbalanced growth, formulated by Albert Hirschman. For Hirschman, development was a "chain of disequilibria," and the task of development policy was to maintain tensions, disproportions, and disequilibria. Hirschman attacked the balanced growth thesis, arguing that problems of industrialization did not require a simultaneous solution, as claimed by Rosenstein-Rodan, Nurkse, and others. Indeed, new industrialization processes in the underdeveloped countries needed solutions that were essentially different from those undertaken by the older industrial countries. Instead of emphasizing obstacles to economic progress, like land tenure systems, family structure, administrative instability, lack of savings, and so on, Hirschman stressed the need for inducement mechanisms. In his view, the fundamental problem of development consisted in generating and channeling human energies in a desired direction. He found the big-push theory to be unrealistic in that it relied on resources (like investment capital) that poor countries had in short supply. For Hirschman (1958), the greatest shortage in poor counties was entrepreneurship, or the ability to perceive opportunities and make investment decisions. The notion of unbalanced growth was based on creating situations where people were forced to make investment decisions by deliberately unbalancing different sectors of the economy. If certain parts of the economy are made to grow (by state investment, for instance), shortages in other sectors will force investments for their growth. The initial unbalancing should be done in an activity that has strong backward and forward linkages (Ilchman and Bhargava 1966). In Hirschman's conception, backward linkages corresponded to the stimuli going to sectors that supplied the inputs required by a particular activity, whereas forward linkages were the inducement to set up new activities utilizing the output of the proposed activity. The main source of development would be activities with high-potential linkage effects, mainly backward ones. The idea that industrial development should (and in fact would) proceed largely through backward linkages was quite revolutionary at the time: instead of doing things in the conventional way, industrial development would work its way from the "last touches" to intermediate and basic industry. Industrialization of certain leading sectors would pull along the rest of the economy. In this sense, it was not feasible or desirable to suppress the tensions and disequilibria created by the development process, since there was a "creative virtue" in them.

In a related conception, Gunnar Myrdal (1963: 151) thought that orthodox economic theories were "never developed to comprehend the reality of great and growing economic inequalities and of the dynamic processes of under-development and development." This was because conventional economic theories were based on the assumption of stable equilibrium—where equilibrium, once disturbed, is reestablished by secondary changes in the opposite direction. He also thought that development analysis could not be restricted to interactions among purely "economic" variables, ignoring "noneconomic" factors. Instead, Myrdal thought, most processes exhibit characteristics of "circular and cumulative causation" so that a small initial change amplifies over time to become a substantial trend: "In the normal case a change does not call forth contradicting forces but, instead, supporting changes, which move the system in the same direction but much further. Because of such circular causation a social process tends to become cumulative and often to gather speed at an accelerated rate" (Myrdal 1963: 13). Applying circular and cumulative causation to regional growth processes, Myrdal thought that market forces widen interregional differences, causing rich regions to grow richer, and poor ones poorer. This divergence stems from two sources: "backwash effects" that retard growth in poor areas, such as a lack of external economies, a brain drain, and capital flight; and "spread effects" of momentum in a center of economic expansion, again operating through external trade, capital movement, migration, and other favorable changes that weave themselves into the cumulating social process by circular causation. Depending on which set of effects predominates in a region, the cumulative process could evolve upward, as in the "lucky" rich regions, or downward, as in the "unlucky" poor regions (Myrdal 1963: 27). In underdeveloped countries, the spread effects are weak relative to the backwash effects. In such a situation, international trade becomes the medium through which market forces tend to result in increased inequalities. In neoclassical economics, by comparison, with its assumption of diminishing marginal returns, capital would have relatively high returns in a poor region, migrating from rich regions to poor. Myrdal disputed this contention, arguing that capital is attracted to rich regions, where external economies produce increasing returns (Myrdal 1963: 28).

Several of the unbalanced growth theorists drew on Francois Perroux's (1955) notion of "growth poles," referring to investments in propulsive industries (the pole) in strategically located centers that induce growth by firms in technologically related industries through the formation of backward and forward linkages with the propulsive industries. Perroux saw growth in an economy as stemming from the effects of disequilibrium and domination, and necessarily occurring unevenly. To quote Perroux (1955: 309): "Growth does not appear everywhere at the same time; it appears at points or poles of growth with varying intensity; it spreads along various channels and with differing overall effects on the whole economy." The growth pole was described primarily in terms of a complex of industries, using one another's inputs and outputs (for example, the steel and machinery industries) and dominated by a propulsive or stimulant industry, the engine of development by virtue of its capacity to innovate and to stimulate, as well as to dominate, other industries (Parr 1999). This led to an interest in geography and regional planning between 1965 and 1975 in the deliberate formation of propulsive growth centers in poor regions. The growth-pole strategy typically focused investment at a limited number of locations (usually as part of a deliberate effort to modify a regional spatial structure) in an attempt to encourage economic activity and thereby raise levels of income and welfare within a region (for example, Semple, Gauthier, and Youngman 1972). Economic geography also had an interest in cumulative causation as a process that caused uneven development in space. Here the leading work by Allan Pred asked: Why do some cities grow more rapidly than, and at the expense of, other cities? Of several causes, Pred thought, initial advantage was probably most important. By initial advantage he meant processes like inertia and the temporal compounding of advantages and that, once concentration is initiated, it is self-perpetuating. The clustering of economic activity at selected locations created an agglomerative effect (firms get benefits when locating near one another), attracting new economic activity by serving as either national or regional centers for information accumulation or dissemination. Innovations made in cities have a neighborhood effect due to "distance decay" (that is, they affect nearby areas more), and so some places are more innovative than others. The more important the innovative center, the more rapid the economic growth. As the process evolved, a hierarchical structure emerged among the various urban places, essentially linked by the constant interchange of information (Pred 1965, 1973).

Again, let us follow this tendency in economic thought to the present. These ideas were picked up and elaborated in the "new economic geography" and the "new trade theory" of the 1990s outlined by such economists as Paul Krugman, Michael Porter, and Anthony Venables.

For Krugman, economic geography, or uneven regional development, is central to the process by which national economic prosperity and trade are created and maintained. Krugman's theory differs from the Ricardian theory of comparative advantage in that he finds specialization and trade driven by increasing returns and economies of scale rather than by comparative advantage—gains from trade arise because production costs fall as the scale of output increases. In this view, economic specialization is, to some extent, a historical accident. Yet, once a pattern of specialization is established, it gets "locked in" by the cumulative gains from trade. There is thus a strong tendency toward "path dependence" (the tendency for economic outcomes to follow the path of previous outcomes rather than to rely totally on current conditions) in the patterns of specialization and trade between countries—so, history matters. An economy's form is determined by contingency, path dependence, and the initial conditons set by history and accident. Because of forward and backward linkages, once an initial regional advantage is established, it may cumulate over time (as with Pred). However, when change in regional fortunes occurs, it will be sudden and unpredictable (Krugman 1995; Martin and Sunley 1996). Note that the Krugman model differs from that of new growth theory discussed earlier; whereas Krugman thinks that the original cause of growth in a place is relatively unimportant, emphasizing path dependence instead (that is, momentum that keeps on going), Romer stresses the role of ideas in starting and continuing a local growth process.

Development economics was increasingly divided on such crucial issues as the efficacy of the market (neoclassicism) or the need for state planning (Keynesianism). At the same time, development economics was subject to a number of criticisms from the perspective of conventional established economics that undercut its scientific validity and led to its temporary demise.

THE COUNTERREVOLUTION
IN DEVELOPMENT ECONOMICS

The "counterrevolution" in development theory of the 1970s and 1980s was part of a more general neoliberal reaction (in the name of renewed faith in classical and neoclassical economics) that was opposed to Keynesianism, social democracy, state intervention, and structuralism, not to mention radical theories like dependency (see Chapter 5). The story of this counterrevolution has been told by John Toye (1987). For Toye, the counterrevolution in development economics began when University of Chicago economist Harry Johnson (1923–1977) criticized Keynesian economics during the early 1970s. Johnson thought that intellectual movements in economics responded to perceived social needs rather than arising from an autonomous, purely scientific, dynamic. Hence, the secret of Keynesianism's success was its promise to end mass unemployment rather than its scientific veracity. But for Johnson (1971), the depression of the 1930s had resulted from the coincidence of several different factors rather than being a structural crisis. Thus, Johnson found that Keynes's conclusion that capitalism tended to systematically produce massive economic problems (stagnation, unemployment, etc.) to be unjustifiably critical of the entire capitalist system. Economic policies founded on Keynesian theory displayed a similar lack of confidence in capitalism. For Johnson, further, development economists had erred in adopting industrialization and national self-sufficiency as the primary policy objectives with economic planning as their instrument. This had led to unproductive industrial investments in developing countries, especially those of postindependence Africa. It had encouraged corruption, favored import substitution (that in turn led to balance of payments problems), and in general made for misguided (state) interventions into economic life in a futile attempt at achieving social justice. The problems of the developing countries, said Johnson, came not from the legacy of colonial history, nor from global inequalities, but instead from misguided Keynesian development policies. Later Johnson extended this critique to the Harrod–Domar model's "concentration on fixed capital investment as the prime economic mover" (Johnson and Johnson 1978: 232). Johnson thought that Keynesian policy makers' neglect of the possibilities of technical progress and their mesmerization with problems of disguised underemployment, especially in rural areas, led to development policies that merely transferred productive resources into industrial production with no economic gain. In contrast, the viewpoint of the Chicago school of economics regarding the rural sector, propounded by T. W. Schultz (1964), was that even poor farmers were efficient profit maximizers.

A more extended critique came from the British economist P. T. Bauer (1972, 1981; see also Little 1982). Development economics, Bauer said, was not merely wrong—it was intellectually corrupt. Many of the views taken by orthodox development economics conflicted with obvious empirical evidence. Some of the examples cited by Bauer included the thesis of the vicious circle of poverty; the allegation that rich countries have caused the poverty of the poor countries; the allegation of a secular decline in the terms of trade of poor countries; the insistence on the supposed necessity of central planning, and of foreign aid, for the material advancement of poor countries; and the opinion that all men are equally gifted by nature and have equal economic aptitudes (Bauer 1972: 17). A small number of economic theorists who were opposed to the market system, Bauer said, had exercised unwarranted influence on

Western people infused with guilt about the developing countries. Bauer thought that governments (India being the prime example) should stop restricting the energies of their subjects. Reducing poverty in the Third World did not require large-scale capital formation nor even investment in "human capital." Foreign capital aid and technical assistance might also do great harm to developing countries. Bauer particularly insisted that nontotalitarian societies should refrain from governmental participation in the economy.

In Toye's (1987) view the counterrevolution specifically in development economics was extended by Deepak Lal, an economist important in part because he was from the Third World. Lal (1980, 1983) argued that the death of development economics would promote the health of the developing countries. Development economics, Lal said, had perverted standard economic principles, such as the efficiency of price mechanisms or the efficacy of free trade, in the belief that developing countries were special cases rather than being merely further examples of universal rational behavior. For Lal, instead, the fundamental classical and neoclassical ideas about growth in the developed countries applied also to the developing countries (that is, Lal took the position of monoeconomics— one kind of economics for all places). For Lal, in a necessarily imperfect world, imperfect market mechanisms do better, in practice, than imperfect state planning mechanisms. Lal argued against redistributing income from rich to poor people. On standard classical economic grounds, Lal was against all economic controls or governmental interventions and for "liberalizing" financial and trade controls in advocating a return to nearly free trade regimes.

Criticisms like these began to be heard in academic and policy circles during the 1970s, but they were given far greater salience by the coming to power of conservative governments in the United States, Britain, and West Germany during the early 1980s. The news media suddenly discovered the new criticism in 1983 and 1984. By the mid-1980s the whole notion of development economics had been discredited, at least in conventional circles. Yet, this was merely one small part of a sea-level change in economic thought occasioned by a crisis in Keynesian economies and economics, and a revival of the liberal (free trade, laissez faire) economics of the 19th century that came to be called "*neo*liberalism." This profoundly influenced the practice of theory through development policy.

CRISIS IN KEYNESIAN ECONOMICS

Clearly something drastic happened in the core Keynesian economies (the United States, Britain, etc.) during the late 1960s and 1970s. Basically, productivity (the amount of output per working hour) declined while inflation (the money prices charged for that output) increased. Productivity is the basis for economic growth, so this decline in productivity brought about a crisis in economic thought. The decade of the 1970s came to be characterized by "stagflation"—economic stagnation, marked by low growth rates and high unemployment, combined with high inflation. Stagflation is difficult (but not impossible) for Keynesian policies to deal with because boosting the economy through low interest rates or deficit spending causes runaway inflation, whereas damping down inflation reduces growth rates and causes unemployment. But "crisis" can be interpreted in several ways. This particular "interpretive moment" was seized on by neoliberal theorists like Friedrich von Hayek and Milton Friedman (discussed later), who managed to persuade the broader discipline of economics, or at least a good part of it, and through them a significant part of the policymaking elite, that there were fundamental structural deficiencies in Keynesian economics and economic policy. This persuasion was made possible by massive changes in political thinking. Many people, especially in the elite, were disturbed by the revolutionary events of the 1960s and early 1970s—the massive antiwar mobilizations, radical black power movements, and hippies decrying everything that smacked of consumerism. Right-wing and even centrist sections of the elite blamed "all this radicalism" on a soft-hearted Keynsianism manifested in the "nanny state" (that is, a state that looked after people, no matter what their own preferences). They wanted to reestablish law and order and revert to a more conservative political-economic regime. Hence, a movement to the right was manifested in an attack on Keynesianism.

However, the causes of the contradictory nature of change (increased inflation with productivity decline) did not lie entirely, or even mainly, with the internal dynamics of Keynesian economies. One basic cause of "supply-side" inflation was that the Organization of Petroleum Exporting Countries (OPEC) doubled and then redoubled crude oil prices in late 1973 and subsequent months. A basic cause of high unemployment during the same years was the arrival on the labor scene of large numbers of "baby boomers" born just after World War II. These basic causes of stagflation had little to do with the internal economics of Keynesian growth. And, despite much anti-Keynesian rhetoric, the economic crisis of the 1970s was actually "solved" by Keynesian means during the early 1980s—by the largest fiscal deficits (percentage wise) ever, before or since, during the first Reagan administration in the United States. The money was spent on a military buildup to reestablish U.S. political hegemony in the world, and particularly on Reagan's "Star Wars" initiative—a largely unsuccessful attempt to develop the high-tech capacity to shoot down incoming Soviet missiles. Hence, Turgeon's (1996) term "military Keynesianism" for the 1980s, and subsequent times, when economies have been boosted by military spending, like the Gulf War and the invasion of Afghanistan and then Iraq. (Or, we might say "popular Keynesianism" to describe the Bush administration's 2008 stimulus package—putting the Internal Revenue Service into reverse by having it send checks to every family in the United States making less than $165,000 a year!) So, it is true that the economic crisis of the 1970s resulted from real problems in the global capitalist system. But the notion that social Keynesianism was at fault and should be abandoned was only one of several interpretations that could have been made. For example, the economic crisis of the 1970s could far more plausibly be explained as resulting from imperialism—the overstretching of U.S. politico-military and economic might during the Vietnam War. Whatever the facts, the neoliberals won the interpretive debate: Keynesianism retreated, social democracy was ruined, and "New Deal liberalism" became a term of derision. We move now to the economic theorists who made that fatal interpretation that has led to the era of neoliberal dominance since the early 1980s.

NEOLIBERALISM

Neoliberalism originated in political-economic theories formed in the late 19th and early 20th centuries, especially in scholarly debates between German and Austrian economists. In Germany, a historical school of economics had long been critical of the abstract nature of marginalist neoclassical economics, with its unrealistic concepts, especially the notion of economies being in "equilibrium." Economists such as Wilhelm Roscher (1817–1894) and Gustav Schmoller (1838–1917) thought that it was difficult to keep supply and demand "balanced" in advanced capitalist economies. Crises were probable, particularly when caused by lack of demand (underconsumption by underpaid workers). Other German economists influenced by the historical school stressed the instabilities in capitalist development arising from the uneven growth experienced in the various sectors of an economy. The German historical school was empirical rather than abstract, looked at the very long term, and tended to be somewhat critical of capitalism. In the 1880s a bitter debate between the German Schmoller and the Austrian Menger (discussed in Chapter 2) split German-speaking economics into antagonistic camps for decades. Schmoller thought that classical and neoclassical economics erred in postulating universal laws, preferred induction to mathematical deduction, and found naive the notion that people were motivated entirely by self-interest. By comparison, the Austrian school of economics, led by Menger and his students Friedrich von Wieser (1851–1926) and Eugen von Bohm-Bawerk (1851–1914), was abstract (mathematical) and antihistorical in method and more politically conventional than the German historical school. Here the most interesting ideas came from theorists exposed to the broader context of the social theory flourishing in Germany in the late 19th and early 20th centuries—Max Weber's economic sociology, for instance (discussed in Chapter 4). Perhaps the most brilliant of the second-generation Austrian economists was Ludwig von Mises (1881–1973), the true founder of neoliberalism.

Von Mises was able to place his technical ability to make innovative contributions to monetary and banking theory (for example, his *Theory of Money and Credit*, published in 1912) within a broader social philosophy that idealized classical (19th-century) liberalism (see Chapter 2 in this volume). Von Mises believed that socialist ideology was a threat to Western civilization and that classical liberalism alone could uphold freedom (von Mises 1912: 204). As with Hobbes and Hume, society, for von Mises, originated not in some social contract but in the inherent character of the individual: "Egoism is the basic law of society" (von Mises 1922: 402). All social phenomena are spontaneous, unplanned outcomes of choices made by rational individuals. However, in making choices, the individual encounters social necessities, as when the division of labor increases productivity and makes social cooperation more profitable than self-sufficiency. Humans obey the fundamental laws of social cooperation because they are in the person's rightly understood self-interest—obedience to law allows maximum individual freedom, and the pursuit of rightly understood self-interest also assures the highest attainable degree of general welfare. "The point of departure of all liberalism lies in the thesis of the harmony of the rightly understood interests of individuals" (von Mises 1912: 182). For von Mises, the consumer interest counts above all other interests, and all interests are harmonized by market forces, establishing what von Mises called "consumer sovereignty" (this is merely an extension of the marginalist school discussed in the preceding chapter.) A state may be necessary, but liberalism teaches that its power must be minimized and, especially, laissez faire should be left unhampered to work its miracles of development. This sociology is the foundation for von Mises's economic theory of laissez faire, or the free market economy, which basically argues that harmony, not conflict, exists between consumers and entrepreneurs, between entrepreneurs, managers, and employees, and so on. This philosophy of laissez faire, together with theories about the market process, money, interest rates, and cycles, justifies von Mises's conception of freedom. Laissez faire prevails because it is scientifically demonstrated to be the best policy (Gonce 2003).

Von Mises (1922) argued more specifically that socialism could not work in an advanced industrial economy. The basic problem, according to von Mises, is that "economic calculation" is impossible in a socialist community—he meant by this the calculation of costs, profits, losses, and so on. Where there are no markets, there is no price system. And where there is no price system, there can be no economic calculation. The problem of economic calculation, he said, is the fundamental problem of socialism. Proving that economic calculation would be impossible in the socialist community meant proving that socialism was impracticable. Everything brought forward in favor of socialism in thousands of writings and speeches—all the blood that had been spilt by the supporters of socialism—could not make it workable. The masses might ardently long for it. Innumerable revolutions and wars might be fought for it. But socialism would never be realized. And if socialism could not work, neither could specific acts of government intervention into the market—what von Mises called "interventionism." (This line of reasoning was criticized in the 1930s by the Polish Marxist economist Oskar Lange and others—see Roberts 1971). This was the theoretical basis for attacks on state planning and state direction of development.

These ideas were elaborated further by Von Mises's student Friedrich von Hayek (1899–1992). Von Hayek argued that people have little knowledge of the world beyond their immediate surroundings. This is the crucial ingredient that makes the price system work, for prices are not merely "rates of exchange between goods" but also "a mechanism for communicating information" (von Hayek 1945). Von Hayek saw the free price system not as a conscious invention (that is, intentionally designed by humans) but as a spontaneously derived order (that is, coming from thousands of uncoordinated choices). In a complex, uncertain environment, economic agents are not able to predict the consequences of their actions, and only the price system can coordinate the whole economy. For von Hayek the "fatal conceit" of the socialists was that they believed this complex system could be designed by a planning system that "gets the prices right." Von Hayek argued that in centrally planned economies an individual or a select group of individuals must determine the distribution of resources. But these planners can never have enough information to carry out the allocation of productive resources reliably—hence, inefficiency and constant crises. An economy can never be designed by social planning, but rather emerges spontaneously from a complex network of interaction among agents with limited knowledge.

Von Hayek attributed the birth of civilization to private property. In von Hayek's view, the central role of the state should be restricted to maintaining the rule of law, with as little state intervention in the economy as possible. The apparatus of the state should be used solely to secure the peace necessary for the functioning of a market coordinating the activities of free individuals. Hayek saw himself as a liberal in the English Whig tradition—the Whigs being a party in England during the 17th century that advocated popular rights, parliamentary power over the crown, and toleration of dissenters. Classical (18th- and 19th-century) liberalism, or "Manchester school liberalism" as it was often called in the late 19th century (because the Manchester cotton industrialists believed in free trade), supported individual rights of property and freedom of contract. It advocated laissez-faire capitalism, meaning the removal of legal barriers to trade and cessation of government-imposed subsidies and monopolies. Classical economic liberals want little or no government regulation of the market. They accept the economic inequality that arises from unequal bargaining positions as being the natural result of competition, so long as no coercion is used. It is this valuing of liberalism that lends neoliberalism (that is, the resuscitation of liberalism in the late 20th century) much of its appeal. Von Hayek (1984: 365) thought that liberalism of this classical kind "derives from the discovery of a self-generating or spontaneous order in social affairs... an order which made it possible to utilize the knowledge and skill of all members of society to a much greater extent than would be possible in any order created by central direction, and the consequent desire to make as full use of these powerful spontaneous ordering forces as possible."

In his most famous book, *The Road to Serfdom*, published in 1944 von Hayek (1994 ed.) argued that both fascists and socialists believed that economic life should be "consciously directed" and that economic planning should be substituted for the competitive system. But to achieve their ends, planners had to create concentrations and categories of power at magnitudes never known before. Democracy was an obstacle to the suppression of freedom inherent in this concentration of power. Therefore, planning and democracy were antithetical. Von Hayek thought that concentrating power so it can be used in planning not merely transforms, but heightens, power. By uniting in the hands of a single body power formerly exercised independently by many, a degree of power is created that is infinitely greater than any existing before—indeed, power so far-reaching as almost to be different in kind. No one in competitive society can exercise even a fraction of the power possessed by a socialist planning board. The power of a millionaire employer over the individual employee is less than that possessed by the smallest bureaucrat, wielding the coercive power of the state, deciding how people are allowed to live and work. When economic power is centralized as an instrument of political power it creates a degree of dependence scarcely distinguishable from slavery. For von Hayek, in a country where the sole employer is the state, opposition means death by slow starvation. Thus, what was promised as the "road to freedom" (socialist planning) was in fact the "high road to servitude." For von Hayek, any planning, even by social democracies, leads to dictatorship, because dictatorship is the most effective instrument of coercion. Democratic socialism, the great utopia of the past few generations, was simply not achievable. And the further growth of collectivism would mean the end of truth. To make a totalitarian system function efficiently, it is not enough that everybody should be forced to work for the ends selected by those in control; it is essential that the people should come to regard these ends as their own. This is brought about by propaganda and by complete control of all sources of information. Hence, von Hayek concluded, the guiding principle in any attempt to create a world of free men must be this: a policy of freedom for the individual is the only truly progressive policy.

Von Hayek was a professor at the London School of Economics from 1931 to 1950, the University of Chicago between 1950 and 1961, and at Freiburg University in West Germany until his death in 1992. Von Hayek was mentor to the Mont Pelerin Society, begun in 1947 at a hotel in Switzerland, whose annual convocation is attended by the leading lights of neoliberalism. The society is dedicated to the "exchange of ideas about the nature of a free society and... the ways and means of strengthening its intellectual support" (Leube 1984: xxiii). All of this history went relatively unnoticed until the Bank of Sweden awarded the 1974 Nobel prize for economic science to Gunnar Myrdal and Friedrich von Hayek "for their pioneering work in the theory of money and economic fluctuations and for their penetrating analysis of the interdependence of economic, social and institutional phenomena." Von Hayek's ideas became more important during the late 1970s and early 1980s with the rise of conservative governments in the United States and United Kingdom. Margaret Thatcher, Conservative party prime minister of the United Kingdom from 1979 to 1990, was a disciple of von Hayek. Ronald Reagan read von Hayek and took advice from Hayekian economic advisers. Thus, von Hayek completed the rightist revolution begun by his mentor, von Mises.

Even so, Milton Friedman (1912–2006), a colleague of von Hayek's at the University of Chicago, was more important as an immediate influence on Reagan and on the remaking of U.S. and international economic policy in a neoliberal direction during the 1980s. Friedman was the leading theorist of what is called the monetarist school of economic thought. Friedman found a close link between inflation and the money supply. Inflation, he said, can be controlled by limiting the amount of money in the national economy, a function performed in most Western countries by the central bank, as with the Federal Reserve Bank in the United States or the Bank of England in Britain. Friedman rejected government fiscal policy as a tool of demand management and thought that the government's role in guiding the economy should be limited to adjusting interest rates (see our earlier discussion on Keynesianism). Friedman set monetarism within a historical vision that "the two ideas of human freedom and economic freedom working together came to their greatest fruition in the United States" (Friedman and Friedman 1979: 309). He thought that Americans are imbued with freedom as part of the very fabric of their being but that they have strayed from this principle, forgetting that the greatest threat comes from concentration of power in the hands of government. Friedman argued that the Great Depression, or "Great Contraction" as he called it, had not been a failure of the free enterprise system but instead originated in a tragic failure of government. Friedman (1958) thought that "millions of able, active and vigorous people exist in every underdeveloped country" and "require only a favorable environment to transform the face of their countries" within neoliberal policies aimed at creating "more competitive markets with brave, more innovative entrepreneurs." This idealistic right-wing thinking took over from a previously liberal state-interventionist development economics during the 1970s and early 1980s (Straussman 1993; Toye 1987). Friedman lectured in Chile during the military dictatorship of Augusto Pinochet, when thousands of leftists were murdered by the state. Professors from the Chicago School of Economics were advisers to the Chilean government, and Chicago graduates, known as "the Chicago boys," served in the Chilean state ministries. Despite this participation in a murderous regime, the Bank of Sweden awarded Friedman the Nobel Prize in 1976 "for his achievements in the fields of consumption analysis, monetary history and theory and for his demonstration of the complexity of stabilization policy." (All together, five members of the Chicago school have been awarded the Nobel prize in economics—note that the economics prize is awarded by the Bank of Sweden and not by the Nobel Foundation.) Friedman was a member of Reagan's Economic Policy Advisory Board in 1981. After retiring, Friedman went to the Hoover Institute at Stanford University, a think tank closely allied with the Reagan administration.

The neoliberal ideas first propagated by von Mises and von Hayek, and then by Friedman and others in the Chicago school, have become central concepts in mainstream economics. As Palley (2005: 20) points out, the two central principles of neoliberal economics—that "factors of production" (labor and capital) get paid what they are worth and that free markets will not let factors go to waste (that is, markets are efficient)—have been "extraordinarily influential" since 1980. This influence passed through Friedman's monetarism, prevalent during the 1980s, and the "new classical economics" associated with Robert Lucas, also of the Chicago school and also a Nobel prize winner. New classical economics restresses the neoclassical assumption that all economic agents are rational (utility-maximizing) and have rational expectations. Unemployment is the result of governmental intervention into this perfect self-adjusting realm. Hence, the state should restrain from intervening (Lapavistsas 2005). So, mainstream economics "takes competitive markets as the norm" and sees (social) value-driven state interventions, like labor standards (that is, regulating working conditions, pay scales, etc.), "as a distortion which will lead to misallocation and inefficiencies" (Tabb 2004: 335–336). Under the influence of neoliberalism, mainstream economics worships the market as the ultimate arbiter of the trajectory of economic development.

As chief economist of the World Bank and former faculty member at Harvard University, Lawrence Summers once asked what the most important thing was that could be learned from an economics course. He said that he tried to leave his students with the view that the invisible hand is more powerful than the hidden hand of the state—things happen well without direction, controls, and plans. Said Summers: "That's the consensus among economists. That's the Hayek legacy. As for Milton Friedman, he was the devil figure in my youth. Only with time have I come to have... increasingly ungrudging respect" (quoted in Yergin and Stanislaw 1999: 151).

NEOLIBERALISM IN ECONOMIC POLICY

The positions established by these founders of neoliberal theory began to be taken seriously again in a context of economic crisis and political revision during the 1970s and early 1980s. By the end of the 1980s a system of recommendations based in neoliberal ideas became standard in conventional international economic policy circles. One account of these changes, widely referred to, was advanced by John Williamson, senior fellow at the (Washington-based) Institute for International Economics. In 1989 Williamson (1990, 1997) coined the term "Washington Consensus" to refer to the policy reforms imposed when debtor countries in Latin America were called on to "set their houses in order" and "submit to strong conditionality"—what Latin America needed, according to Washington. By "Washington," Williamson meant the political Washington of the U.S. Congress and senior members of the administration and the technocratic Washington of the international financial institutions, the main economic agencies of the U.S. government (the U.S. Treasury and Federal Reserve Board), and the think tanks, such as the one at which he works. By "policy," he meant policy instruments rather than more general objectives of policy or the eventual outcomes of policy. In terms of the institutional formation of recent neoliberal economic policy, the term "Washington Consensus" can be used to refer to ideas pushed by such interest groups as the American Enterprise Institute or the Heritage Foundation that brought right-wing "progressive reform" ideals to Washington during the mid-1970s and early 1980s, for instance, or the bureaucratic-technical interests of economists whose professional training in neoclassical economics proved amenable to Hayekian and Friedmanesque persuasion.

The set of "policy instruments" derived from the Washington Consensus and applied to (mainly Third World) borrowing countries by the World Bank and the IMF was said by Williamson to include:

1. *Fiscal discipline*: Large and sustained fiscal deficits by central and provincial governments are a main source of macroeconomic dislocation in the form of inflation, balance of payments deficits, and capital flight. These deficits result from a lack of political courage in matching public expenditures to the resources available. An operational budgetary deficit in excess of 1–2% of GNP is evidence of policy failure.

2. *Reducing public expenditures*: When government expenditures have to be reduced, the view is that spending on defense, public administration, and subsidies, particularly for state enterprises, should be cut rather than primary education, primary health care, and public infrastructure investment.

3. *Tax reform*: The tax base should be broadened, tax administration improved, and marginal tax rates should be cut to improve incentives.

4. *Interest rates*: Financial deregulation should make interest rates market-determined rather than state-determined, and real interest rates should be positive to discourage capital flight and increase savings.

5. *Competitive exchange rates*: Exchange rates should be sufficiently competitive to nurture rapid growth in nontraditional exports but should not be inflationary—the conviction behind this assessment is that economies should be outward-oriented.

6. *Trade liberalization*: Quantitative restrictions on imports should be eliminated, followed by tariff reductions, until levels of 10–20% are reached—the free trade ideal, however, can be temporarily contradicted by the need for protecting infant industries.

7. *Encouraging foreign direct investment*: Foreign investment brings needed capital, skills, and know-how and can be encouraged through debt–equity swaps—exchanging debt held by

foreign creditors for equity in local firms, such as privatized state enterprises. Barriers impeding the entry of foreign firms should be abolished. Foreign and domestic companies should be allowed to compete on equal terms.

8. *Privatization*: State enterprises should be privatized. Private industry is more efficient.

9. *Deregulation*: All enterprises should be subject to the discipline of competition—this means deregulating economic activity in the sense of reducing state controls over private enterprise.

10. *Securing property rights*: Secure and well-defined property rights should be made available to all at reasonable cost.

In brief, said Williamson (1990: 18), the economic positions that Washington agreed upon in setting growth and development policies for the rest of the world (though did not necessarily follow itself—the federal government heavily subsidizes agriculture, for instance) could be summarized as "prudent macroeconomic policies, outward orientation, and free market capitalism." He thought this group of principles represented a "sea change" in attitudes in Washington. But he also thought that this list of policies making up the Washington Consensus stemmed from classical mainstream economic theory—by "mainstream theory" Williamson meant neoclassical economics with some Keynesianism. From our perspective, the Washington Consensus is mainstream economics greatly influenced by neoliberalism, particularly in its antistate attitudes, as with deregulation, privatization, and so on.

The consensus was subsequently widely interpreted by critics as the essence of a neoliberal development policy package (Williamson 1997). Development policy came to consist in withdrawing state direction and even government intervention in development in favor of the disciplining of economies by market competition and self-interested individuals "efficiently" choosing between alternatives in the allocation of productive resources. In the external arena, neoliberalism entailed the devaluation of currencies (to make exports cheaper), convertible monetary systems (free conversions of currencies into dollars), and the removal of state restrictions on commodity and capital movements into and out of countries—joining economies together through unrestricted globalization. Internally markets were to be deregulated (including deunionizing) while price subsidies on food were reduced and then eliminated. Government spending was reduced and taxes lowered, especially on rich people, so that incomes flowed into private investment, stimulating growth (Brohman 1996b).

This development model was applied to some Latin American countries during the early 1970s, from which it spread to Africa, Asia, and virtually all countries, even a newly liberated South Africa, by the mid-

1990s. Likewise, neoliberalism became the West's model for reshaping the eastern European region in the postcommunist 1990s. A good example was Poland's "return to Europe." Jeffrey Sachs (1991), a Harvard University economist and adviser to Solidarity, the Polish workers' movement, and subsequently to the postcommunist Polish government, saw structural change in the former communist countries occurring through the generalized reintroduction of market forces. Three types of policies were involved in the economic reform program: economic liberalization, the broad rubric for legal and administrative changes needed to create institutions of private property and market competition; macroeconomic stabilization, including measures to limit budgetary deficits, reduce growth of the money supply, and create a convertible currency with stable prices; and privatization, meaning the transfer of ownership of state property to the private sector. However, Sachs also advocated a social safety net, to prevent reforms from injuring the most vulnerable sectors of society, and a public investment program, mainly for infrastructure as a complement to economic restructuring. He thought that measures like these could be introduced virtually overnight (like switching driving practices in Britain from the left side to the right side of the road) in a process that became known as "shock therapy" (Klein 2007; Gowan 1995). The key to economic reform, Sachs said, was that several years had to pass amidst a vale of tears before the fruits of change were fully evident, the amount of time depending on the boldness and consistency of the reforms—if there was wavering, it was easy to get lost in the valley. In one simple statement Sachs summarized the neoliberal approach to development—liberal in the classical (19th-century) sense of lack of state control and reliance on markets and the price mechanism, liberal in the 20th-century sense of concern for victims, but neo in the sense that suffering was accepted as an inevitable consequence of "reform and efficiency."

WORLD BANK POLICY

At an international conference held at Bretton Woods, New Hampshire, in 1944 two agencies were founded that would prove to be of pivotal importance to development during the second half of the 20th century. The International Monetary Fund (IMF) was designed to help countries avoid balance of payments problems by giving short-term loans. The World Bank (or International Bank for Reconstruction and Development) guaranteed private bank loans for long-term investments in productive activities. The two make up the core of the international financial institutions (IFIs). During the 1950s, under Eugene Black (president, 1949–1962), the World Bank mainly loaned capital for the construction of infrastructure (roads, railroads, power facilities, etc.) in the belief that development basically meant economic growth, and this, in turn, depended on public investment. In the mid-1960s, under George Woods (1963–1968), emphasis shifted to education and Third World agriculture. Under Robert McNamara (1968–1981), the World Bank increased rapidly in size and drastically changed its orientation. The immediate priority became enabling decent living conditions (food, clothing, housing, services)—that is, a "basic-needs" approach to development assistance was adopted, in which resources were given directly rather than having to trickle down to the poor. The ultimate goal, McNamara (1981) said, was to raise the productivity of the poor, enabling them to be brought into the economic system. The 1978 *World Development Report* (World Bank 1978) stated that the development effort should be directed toward the twin objectives of rapid growth and reducing the number of people living in absolute poverty as quickly as possible. The idea was to use resources made available by rapid economic growth to expand public services. For a while, supplying basic needs was the development approach of choice among international agencies (Payer 1982). This amounted to a kind of global Keynesianism, but with the investment funds in Third World people and infrastructure coming from international banks as well as domestic savings—the basic idea being to rapidly increase the total productivity of the economies of Third World countries by pouring in foreign investment under IFI supervision.

During the early 1980s, under the leadership of A. W. Clawson, the World Bank shifted emphasis in a neoliberal direction. The first sign of change came with a report on development in sub-Saharan Africa prepared by the bank's African Strategy Review Group, coordinated by Elliot Berg (World Bank 1981). The report concluded that the key problems of the region—low economic growth, sluggish agricultural performance, rapid rates of population increase, and balance of payments and fiscal crises—derived from both internal and external factors exacerbated by "domestic policy inadequacies": trade and exchange rate policies over-protected industry, held back agriculture, and absorbed too much administrative capacity; there were too many administrative constraints, and the public sector was overextended; there was a bias against agriculture in price, tax, and exchange rate policies. These shortcomings had to be addressed, the group concluded, if production was to be given a higher priority. While reluctant to recommend specific measures, the group found that existing state controls over trade were ineffective, expressed the belief that private sector activity should be enlarged and the state sector reduced, and further concluded that agricultural resources should be concentrated on small farmers and human resources should be improved under an export-oriented development strategy. Here we find strong hints of neoliberal development policy.

During the 1970s the elites of many Third World countries had borrowed as much as they could to finance development projects. Third World and eastern European debt tripled (to a total of $626 billion) between 1976 and 1982 (Kojm 1984). As alluded to earlier, in 1973 OPEC raised the price of oil from $3.01 to $5.12 a barrel and shortly thereafter increased the price to more than four times the original level. Many non-oil-producing Third World countries were left without sufficient means of paying for oil imports, on which their economies were heavily dependent. These conditions produced a massive shift in the geography of international payments. Oil-producing states accumulated huge surpluses in their balances of payments, while most non-oil-producing countries, especially in the Third World, went into equally serious deficit. These deficits faced by Third World countries were also an opportunity for private financial institutions to step in, especially commercial and investment banks. Led by Citicorp, a U.S. commercial bank based in New York, First World banks first began to lend large amounts of money to the Third World during the late 1960s. The scale of this lending further increased during the mid-1970s when the commercial banks began recycling "petrodollars," deposited in New York and London banks, as loans to Third World governments. These private institutions were less concerned with the social and political responsibilities attending the loans and were more concerned with the interest earned—on the whole, commercial bank lending was to middle-income industrializing Third World countries, where it was thought that money could be made. The whole process of inflated lending on easy or convoluted terms resulted in even more debt, without much economic growth to service the loans, and in excess, unneeded imports, contributing even further to national deficits. Increasingly, Third World countries accrued new debt merely to repay interest on the old. Then financial institutions in the West suddenly realized that many debtors were not repaying their loans. The major banks panicked and refused to lend more. Third World countries could no longer borrow to cover their balance of payments deficits.

Mexico experienced its first debt crisis in 1982—the peso lost half its value in a week, and the state was unable to meet payments on $20 billion in loans. Along with Argentina, Brazil, and many other countries, Mexico was forced into debt rescheduling (at lower interest rates, with payments over longer time periods) supervised by the IMF. When the IMF and the World Bank intervened, they imposed "structural adjustment" conditions (that is, what a country had to agree to do as a condition for receiving a loan) on the borrowing countries, using a series of policy measures first put into place during the mid-1970s but formalized in 1979 and 1980. By the mid-1980s three-quarters of Latin American countries and two-thirds of African countries were under some kind of IMF or World Bank supervision.

In this context of extreme crisis we find the World Bank's emphasis changing. The 1983 *World Development Report* (World Bank 1983: 29) stated that foreign trade enabled developing countries to specialize in production, exploit economies of scale, and increase foreign exchange earnings. The 1984 *report* (World Bank 1984: Chapter 3) used "growth scenarios" to argue that developing countries could improve their positions by changing their economic policies, specifically by avoiding overvalued exchange rates, reducing public spending commitments, and having an "open trading and payments regime" that encouraged optimal use of investment resources—the case examples at that time were the "outward-oriented" East Asian countries. By the following year (World Bank 1985: 145) the World Bank was warning that a "retreat from liberalization" would slow economic growth. The 1987 *World Development Report* posed the question: What are the ultimate objectives of development? Generally, the answer was "faster growth of national income, alleviation of poverty, and reduction of income inequalities" (World Bank 1987: 1). The bank itself, stressing "efficient industrialization" as the key economic policy, devised a lending program that supported policy reforms and structural changes in a neoliberal direction across the whole spectrum of economic activities in recipient countries. In doing so, the bank drew directly on Adam Smith's argument that industrialization would be retarded by a low ability to trade, and on Ricardo and Mill's perception that trade gave advantages that led to productivity increases. State protection of industry in the past, the bank's annual report concluded, had led to inefficient industries and poor-quality, expensive goods. So, the idea was to reduce trade barriers, switch the economy's focus to exports, and compete vigorously in world markets. The bank suggested policy reform in three main areas: trade reform, specifically the adoption of an outward-oriented trade strategy; macroeconomic policies to reduce government budgetary deficits, lower inflation, and ensure competitive exchange rates; and a domestic "competitive environment," that is, removing price controls, rationalizing investment regulations, and reforming labor market regulations (World Bank 1989, 1990, 1997). These recommendations amounted to essentially a neoliberal Washington Consensus policy regime (Peet 2007).

To give some idea of what was meant by these innocuous-sounding phrases, "reforming" labor market policies meant decreasing minimum wages and ending other regulations that supposedly "distorted" free labor markets. "Reducing government spending" meant reducing antipoverty programs, among other things. Hence, a series of contradictions appears to pervade the political economy of the World Bank's new policy regime; one in which paying workers less increases the poverty the bank claims to be ending, and reducing the interventionary power of the state out of a stronger political commitment to privatization means reducing public power in ending poverty (and so on).

Like most policies based on ideals, structural adjustment was subject to modification. In the late 1980s and early 1990s, the World Bank shifted slightly to a revised neoliberal model that stressed a different version of Keynesianism, "market-friendly state intervention" and "good governance" (political pluralism, accountability, and the rule of law), conditions again found typical in the state interventionist East Asian "miracle economies" (Kiely 1998). The *World Development Report* for 1990 dealt with poverty for the first time since the McNamara era. The bank outlined a two-pronged approach: on the one hand, policies that promoted the use of labor, the poor's most abundant asset, by harnessing market incentives; and, on the other, the provision of basic services to the poor, like primary health care, education, and nutrition. The World Bank has become far more important in setting development policy than its annual $24.7 billion of lending—a mere 2–3% of the capital flows to the Third World—would suggest. As one commentator puts it: "The bank is to economic development theology what the papacy is to Catholicism, complete with yearly encyclicals" (Holland 1998—"yearly encyclicals" referring to the annual *World Development Reports*).

BENEVOLENT CONSENSUS

However, all of this began to change again in the early 2000s. Mass protests erupted against the IFIs, symbolized by the "battle of Seattle" around meetings of the World Trade Organization in 1999. Washington Consensus policies were widely castigated as causing economic decline in Latin America. This perception forced a reconsideration of neoliberal development policies (Born, Feher, Feinstein, and Peet 2003), even within the World Bank and the IMF. One account of these reappraisals was provided by Dani Rodrik of Harvard University. Of Turkish origin, Rodrik occupies a strategic position at the liberal and critical end of the conventional policy spectrum. Rodrik (2006) asserts that the Washington Consensus policies, codified by Williamson, inspired a wave of reforms in Latin America and sub-Saharan Africa that fundamentally transformed the policy landscape in these developing areas. With the fall of the Berlin Wall in 1989 and the collapse of the Soviet Union, former socialist countries similarly made a "bold leap" toward free markets. Indeed, such was the enthusiasm for reform that Williamson's original list came to look tame and innocuous by comparison with what actually happened, as countries scrambled to make themselves look "more competitive" than their neighbors. The reform agenda eventually came to be perceived, at least by its critics, as an overtly ideological effort to impose "neoliberalism" and "market fundamentalism" on developing nations. Yet, one thing is generally agreed upon about the consequences of these reforms, namely, that things have not quite worked out the way that was intended. Indeed, notes Rodrik, it is fair to say that nobody really believes in the Washington Consensus anymore. The question now is not whether the Washington Consensus is dead or alive, but rather: What will replace it? Practitioners of the Washington Consensus have come to think that the standard policy reforms did not produce lasting effects wherever the background institutional conditions were poor. The upshot is that the original Washington Consensus has been augmented by so-called second-generation reforms that are highly institutional in nature. One possible version of these reforms, as summarized by Rodrik, is shown in Table 3.1.

In brief, this amounts to the Washington Consensus provisions plus "institutional reform" in a kind of post-Washington Consensus. Rodrik observes that institutions are deeply embedded in society, and if indeed growth requires major institutional transformation—in the areas of the rule of law, property rights protection, governance, and so on—how can we not be pessimistic about the prospects for growth in poor countries, since typically institutional change rarely happens as the result of major political upheavals?

Rodrik (2006) has his own way of thinking about growth strategies. Step 1, what he calls "diagnostic analysis," involves figuring out where the most significant constraints on economic growth are located in a given setting. In a low-income economy, Rodrik argues, economic activity must be constrained by at least one of two factors: either the cost of finance must be too high, or the private return on investment must be low. Step 2 is creative and imaginative policy design targeted at the identified constraints. The key is to focus on the market failures and distortions associated with the constraint identified in the previous step. The principle of policy targeting offers a simple message: target the policy response as closely as possible on the source of the distortion. Step 3 involves institutionalizing the process of diagnosis and policy response to ensure that the economy remains dynamic and growth does not fizzle out. What is needed to sustain growth? Two types of institutional reform seem to become critical over time. First is the need to maintain productive dynamism. Natural resource discoveries, garment exports from maquilas, or a free trade agreement may spur growth for a limited of time, but policy needs

TABLE 3.1. The Augmented Washington Consensus

Original Washington Consensus

1. Fiscal discipline
2. Reorientation of public expenditures
3. Tax reform
4. Financial liberalization
5. Unified and competitive exchange rates
6. Trade liberalization
7. Openness to direct foreign investment
8. Privatization
9. Deregulation
10. Secure property rights

"Augmented" Washington Consensus—the preceding 10 items plus:

11. Corporate governance
12. Anticorruption measures
13. Flexible labor markets
14. World Trade Organization agreements
15. Financial codes and standards
16. "Prudent" capital-account opening
17. Nonintermediate exchange rate regimes
18. Independent central banks and inflation targeting
19. Social safety nets
20. Targeted poverty reduction

Source: Rodrik (2006: 980).

to ensure that this momentum is maintained with ongoing diversification into new areas of tradable commodities or else growth simply fizzles out. Second is the need to strengthen domestic institutions of conflict management. The most frequent cause for the collapse in growth is an inability to deal with the consequences of external shocks—that is, in terms of trade declines or reversals in capital flows. Endowing the economy with resilience against shocks requires strengthening the rule of law, solidifying (or putting into place) democratic institutions, establishing participatory mechanisms, and erecting social safety nets. When such institutions are in place, the macroeconomic and other adjustments needed to deal with adverse shocks can be undertaken relatively smoothly. What is required to sustain growth should not be confused with what is required to initiate it. Such is Rodrik's alternative proposal.

Let us comment briefly on this. First, it is clear that Washington Consensus policies were widely put in place and just as broadly failed—in their own terms of producing economic growth. Indeed, countries with high sustained growth rates during the 1990s and early 2000s, like China and India, were exactly those *not* using Washington Consensus policies. Second, realizing this, the international financial institutions (or significant components of them) divided, with the World Bank becoming increasingly insecure and uncertain, while the IMF remained steadfast and indeed declared that neoliberal "reform" had not gone far enough! Third, the "augmented Washington Consensus," reflecting lessons supposedly learned from the failure of the first generation of reforms, is in fact a grab bag of miscellaneous policies conceived under various political-economic positions within conventional circles, some from the right ("flexible labor markets" means attacking unions) and some from a kind of renewed liberal concern (social safety nets and "targeted poverty reduction") that to our minds reflects a guilty conscience about the misery inflicted on the world by neoliberal policies—"liberal neoliberalism." Fourth, the liberal, critical wing of neoliberalism, well represented by Rodrik, stays well within policy conventions. Policy is aimed at producing economic growth, and in low-income economies economic activity is constrained predominantly by lack of investment. Basically just the prescription is to get international financial entities to invest more. The problem with the international part is that Third World countries are expected to return interest to foreign investors on the order of 15–25% a year. Thus, within five years the country receiving foreign investment has more than repaid the loan and is effectively "investing" in the lending country. And fifth, there is no hint of social transformation here, no changing power structures, no mention of reducing social inequalities, just a safe prescription for a mild illness.

MILLENNIUM DEVELOPMENT GOALS

The notions of "new reform agenda" and "augmented Washington Consensus" prevailing in the early 21st century as frontiers in hegemonic policy discourse were quite limited in their transformational capacity and their "within the system" lexicon ("targeted poverty alleviation" is our favorite—if only it were that simple!). But the new millennium also brought a more vividly termed approach from a reshuffled institutional framework. The key terms in the new liberal neoliberalism are "Millennium Development Goals" (MDGs) and "debt relief"; the key institutional actors include, besides the United States and the IFIs (the World Bank and IMF), a broader coalition of wealthy countries meeting as the Group of 7 or 8 (G7/G8), the United Nations as a body and as specific development agencies (the United Nations Development Program especially), and one important development economist, Jeffrey D. Sachs (we cover Sachs's most recent ideas in the next chapter). At the Millennium Summit held at the UN in September 2000, the largest gathering of world leaders in history adopted the UN Millennium Declaration, committing their nations to a global partnership that pledged to reduce extreme poverty and setting out a series of time-bound targets, with a deadline of 2015, that became known as the Millennium Development Goals (MDGs). The MDGs outlined in Table 3.2 are said to be "basic human rights—the rights of each person on the planet to health, education, shelter, and security."

The MDGs crystallize commitments made separately at various international conferences and summits during the 1990s. They are said to be innovative in that they explicitly recognize interdependence among growth, poverty reduction, and sustainable development; they acknowledge that development rests on the foundations of democratic governance, the rule of law, respect for human rights, and peace and security; they are based on time-bound and measurable targets accompanied by indicators for monitoring progress; and they bring together, in the eighth goal, the responsibilities of developing countries with those of developed countries, founded on a global partnership endorsed at an International Conference on Financing for Development in Monterrey, Mexico, in March 2002 and a similar conference held at the Johannesburg World Summit on Sustainable Development in August 2002. In 2001, the UN Secretary General presented a *Road Map Towards the Implementation of the United Nations Millennium Declaration* (UN 2001) that is said to be "an integrated and comprehensive overview of the situation, outlining potential strategies for action designed to meet the goals and commitments of the Millennium Declaration." This "road map" has been followed by annual reports on progress toward meeting the goals by the UN Secretary General. The main agency charged with "coordinating global and local efforts" is the United Nations Development Program (UNDP), an organization founded in 1946 that sees itself as "advocating for change and connecting countries to knowledge, experience and resources to help people build a better life" (UNDP 2008). The UNDP has offices in 166 countries and is the largest UN organization. Unlike the World Bank, however, the UNDP has virtually no money to give out as loans or grants. Instead, its methods include campaigning and mobilizing for the MDGs through advocacy; sharing the best strategies for meeting the MDGs in terms of innovative practices, policy and institutional reforms, means of policy implementation, and the evaluation of financing options; monitoring and reporting progress toward attainment of the MDGs; and supporting governments in tailoring the MDGs to local circumstances.

Essentially, however, the MDGs are just a wish list of goals based on fine ideals but lacking means of realization—they are supposed to be realized by each national government, in part using funds made available from debt relief (see below), with "advocacy, monitoring and advice" from the UNDP, the World Bank, and other international agencies. The

TABLE 3.2. Eight UN Millennium Development Goals and 18 Time-Bound Targets

- Goal 1: Eradicate extreme poverty and hunger.
  - Target 1: Reduce by half the proportion of people living on less than a dollar a day.
  - Target 2: Reduce by half the proportion of people who suffer from hunger.
- Goal 2: Achieve universal primary education.
  - Target 3: Ensure that all boys and girls complete a full course of primary schooling.
- Goal 3: Promote gender equality and empower women.
  - Target 4: Eliminate gender disparity in primary and secondary education preferably by 2005, and at all levels by 2015.
- Goal 4: Reduce child mortality.
  - Target 5: Reduce by two-thirds the mortality rate among children under five.
- Goal 5: Improve maternal health.
  - Target 6: Reduce by three-quarters the maternal mortality ratio.
- Goal 6: Combat HIV/AIDS.
  - Target 7: Halt and begin to reverse the spread of HIV/AIDS.
  - Target 8: Halt and begin to reverse the incidence of malaria and other major diseases.
- Goal 7: Ensure environmental sustainability.
  - Target 9: Integrate the principles of sustainable development into country policies and programs; reverse the loss of environmental resources.
  - Target 10: Reduce by half the proportion of people without sustainable access to safe drinking water.
  - Target 11: Achieve significant improvement in the lives of at least 100 million slum dwellers by 2020.
- Goal 8: Achieve a global partnership for development.
  - Target 12: Develop further an open trading and financial system that is rule-based, predictable, and nondiscriminatory and that includes a commitment to good governance, development, and poverty reduction, nationally and internationally.
  - Target 13: Address the least developed countries' special needs. These include tariff- and quota-free access for their exports; enhanced debt relief for heavily indebted poor countries; cancellation of official bilateral debt; and more generous official development assistance for countries committed to poverty reduction.
  - Target 14: Address the special needs of landlocked and small island developing states.
  - Target 15: Deal comprehensively with developing countries' debt problems through national and international measures to make debt sustainable in the long term.
  - Target 16: In cooperation with the developing countries, develop decent and productive work for youth.
  - Target 17: In cooperation with pharmaceutical companies, provide access to affordable essential drugs in developing countries.
  - Target 18: In cooperation with the private sector, make available the benefits of new technologies— especially information and communications technologies.

Source: UN Development Goals (*www.undp.org/mdg/basics.shtml*).

trouble with this kind of proclamation is that it looks like something serious is being done about development when, in fact, governments are just carrying on as before.

DEBT RELIEF

The year 2005, it seemed, marked the onset of an era when the West would finally forgive the debts owed by the world's poorest countries, under mass popular pressure, organized as "Live 8" rock concerts by singers Bono and Bob Geldof. "Debt relief" basically means "writing off" $40 billion owed by very poor countries to foreign lenders by refinancing the IMF and World Bank's Heavily Indebted Poor Countries (HIPC) initiative begun in the 1990s. Under this initiative, countries have to demonstrate, to the economists at the IMF and the World Bank that they have adopted and are carrying out policies judged "sound" by the "international community" in order to get debt relief. That "community" is represented by the IFIs, and behind these the Secretary of the U.S. Treasury Department and the British Chancellor of the Exchequer. And "sound policies" follow the neoliberal prescription—in effect, supplicant countries have to adjust structurally to qualify for debt relief. At their meeting in early June 2005, the finance ministers of the G8 countries agreed to provide additional financial resources, ensuring that the financing capacity of the World Bank, the IMF, and the African Development Bank was not reduced by the HIPC initiative. This will eventually lead to 100% debt cancellation of outstanding obligations of 18 of the poorest countries in the world. The agreement was formalized at the G8 summit meeting in Gleneagles, Scotland, in July 2005. There was a lot of criticism that only a small part of poor country debt would be forgiven, and that debt relief would be long in coming. But whatever its problems of timing and coverage, this commitment to ending the international debt of the poorest countries does show signs of being motivated by genuine benevolence.

But look beneath the headlines, down the list of conclusions from the June 2005 G8 meeting—not too far, only to point 2. This reads as follows:

> We reaffirm our view that in order to make progress on social and economic development, it is essential that developing countries put in place the policies for economic growth, sustainable development and poverty reduction: sound, accountable and transparent institutions and policies; macroeconomic stability; the increased fiscal transparency essential to tackle corruption, boost private sector development,

and attract investment; a credible legal framework; and the elimination
of impediments to private investment, both domestic and foreign. (G8
2005)

The aspect of point 2 seized on by just about all the media at the time was
good government practices, like transparency, anticorruption measures,
and credible legal frameworks. The other aspect of point 2, macroeconomic stability, private-sector development, and removing impediments
to private investment, domestic and foreign, together with bits on free
trade and open markets in later points, went almost unmentioned. Here
we find the G8 countries, or rather their treasury departments, in collu-
sion with the IFIs, telling poor countries how they must run their economies if they want to receive debt relief. Just as the "deserving poor" are
made to do the repentance shuffle to earn a charitable handout, or the
homeless pretend instant arm-waving Christian conversion to get a bed
for the night, now we find the rich countries telling the poor countries of
the world how they must "reform" to get their debt relief.

But it is precisely this type of IFI insistence on neoliberal Washington Consensus policies that brings thousands of demonstrators on to the
streets in protest whenever the World Bank and the IMF try to meet.
Specifically, why? In general, it's the imperialism of economic policy, the
undemocratic notion that a few thousand Western experts steeped in
neoclassical/neoliberal economics know what policy regime works best
for a world of others. More specifically, in the original HIPC proposal,
civil society organizations were supposed to be consulted in preparing a
country's "poverty-reduction and growth strategy." But that turned out
to be a facade for business-as-usual—structural adjustment or, rather,
structural transformation designed in Washington DC. Now we find
fewer references even to "country ownership," the IFI euphemism for
brief consultation with the local finance ministry, home to economists
also trained in American and British universities. Instead, it's prescription by the experts with inspections every 6 months. The G8 version of
structural adjustment disguises an imperialism of expertise in the wondrous garb of world humanity's most generous impulse, the elimination
of global poverty. In the MDGs and debt relief we find business more or
less as usual dressed in the optimistic terms of liberation from poverty.

CRITIQUE OF NEOLIBERAL DEVELOPMENT

It has been difficult to restrain our criticism while outlining the discussion
in this chapter. Let us now comment on the neoliberal school of social
and economic thought and its programs for development. Neoliberalism

is founded on an assumption about the inherent nature of human beings, seen by von Mises as "egotistic and self-interested" and by Friedman as "imbued with freedom." This assumption is elaborated into the further view that social phenomena are spontaneous, unplanned outcomes of choices made by rational, freedom-loving, self-interested individuals. Markets can harmonize these selfish choices. And markets and price systems are not conscious inventions but arise spontaneously. The question is: Does this vision have any basis in historical reality? Take markets, for instance. Karl Polanyi (1944) argues, to the contrary, that there was nothing natural or spontaneous about "free markets"—"The road to the free market was paved with continuous political manipulation, whether the state was involved in removing old restrictive regulations... or building new political administrative bodies." Markets are social and institutional constructions that require rules and regulations to function effectively. The assumption of egotism made in neoliberal thought is pure make-believe. Was the person purely egotistical in feudal society, with its communal social orders and guild allegencies, or in the state societies of India and China, with their long traditions of social obligation and respect for order and ascribed position (as with the caste system in India—imposed by people with freedom in their hearts?)? We are dealing here with a fabrication, a utopian vision, a fantastic dream about an imagined past. The idea is that these natural qualities of the human being and these spontaneous events of history culminated in 19th-century laissez-faire liberal society, when the economy ran itself via self-regulating markets. But, as Polanyi says: "There was nothing natural about laissez-faire; free markets could never have come into being merely by allowing things to take their course.... Laissez-faire itself was enforced by the state." The late 19th century was in fact full of state intervention, as with British imperialism. The countries that grew most powerful had the most state intervention (Chang 2002). As to the notion that markets are populated by autonomous, self-interested actors, economic sociology has argued conversely that actors in markets develop durable moral relationships of trust, with a sense of fairness and responsibility, while abstaining from opportunism (Granovetter 1985).

However, this notion of free individuals meeting freely in markets is not only factually incorrect, it misunderstands the market relation. There is a dense and somewhat obscure passage in Marx's *Grundrisse* (1973 ed.: 243–245) criticizing the supposed elevation of competitive selfishness into a higher order of the common interest (Smith's "invisible hand"). Marx thinks instead that the common interest "proceeds as it were behind the back of these self-reflected particular interests, behind the back of one individual's interest in opposition to that of another." More than this, the "common interest" decided in this selfish way becomes an alienated social force, controlling individuals rather than being controlled by them, so that they are compelled by ruthless competition to do things they know to be socially and environmentally destructive. Spend money on environmentally safe technologies, and you will be driven from the market by producers who do not do so! The idea that markets "harmonize" social relations, as with relations between employers and employees, is contradicted by centuries of struggle and strikes—this is not a history of harmony, it is a record of violence. (Only a member of the elite, like von Hayek—who never worked in a factory or office and was never subject to the arbitrary whim of a boss to deprive the livelihood of the worker and his or her family—could say that employers have less power than the lowest civil servant.) Perhaps the strongest claim made by neoliberal theory is that the price system synchronizes individual knowledge into a higher competitive economic order, producing development, in effect. But prices act as signals only for a limited part of the content of commodities, labor content, and capital investment. Prices do not represent these very well because markets hide more than they reveal. And prices do not represent social and environmental costs and long-term consequences at all. Market systems are environmentally destructive and socially irresponsible as a result. As to prices as signals, the democratic state can signal a higher order of rationality by deliberately increasing prices by adding sales taxes—for example, cigarettes are highly taxed (and should be taxed more) to signal through the price–tax mechanism that smoking kills people. And people smoke because their "innate rationality" is deluded by advertising. The economic calculation problem may have some relevance in state systems like the former Soviet Union, but social democracies use combinations of markets and planning, with planning employed to achieve socially agreed-upon goals—in this sense planning is democratic, while markets are irrational and dictatorial.

We could go on… and on again. But the question recurring as we read this ego philosophy is: Whose interest does it serve? Who are these free individuals, and what does freedom mean in this ideological system? Clearly the neoliberals are not talking about workers in factories, nor women in families, nor peasants on plantations. They mean, by the free individual, the entrepreneur, the capitalist, the boss. And they mean, by freedom, the opportunity to make money, which buys everything (except happiness). These theorists are against the state because it may limit the freedom of the rich to make more money, and it might redistribute existing wealth. These theorists disguise their support for rich people to become even richer, using the lofty terms of "freedom" and "democracy."

Neoliberal economics assumes that privatization, markets, and the right prices can solve all problems. Theories like this can be built only by excluding from consideration most real-world institutions and social processes. Yet, theoretical exclusion of most of reality from model building has to be conducted carefully, in full realization that results derived from highly abstract models are highly tentative. Policy statements derived from partial models must be cast in terms of probabilities rather than certainties. But here we encounter a basic problem of science and scientists. With economics, social science most nearly approaches physics in the natural scientific sense of the term. Economists become fixated on their own image as scientists, obsessed with the formal beauty of their creations, to the degree that the protests of millions hardly reaches their ears—riots against IMF policies, for instance. So, while any statement about the social behavior of human beings must always be cast in self-critical terms, economics is stated instead in terms of scientific mathematical certainty. Versions of economics that break from the fold are either denigrated as mere opinion or disciplined to return—not just by outside critics but by insiders expressing doubts about their legitimacy as science. Thus, in the case of development economics, the notion of a different reality in developing countries, if taken seriously, would have meant formulating a completely different approach with different agents in different—often nonmarket—relations, with different social relations—economics, however, calls this "anthropology." Within the discipline, merely flirting with the possibility of radical difference is dangerous in terms of scholarly respectability. As a result, development economics has remained a mish-mash of basically conventional ideas, with a few precariously stated alternatives (like the possibility of trade favoring the rich countries) dropped, with relief, as soon as possible. Economics is handicapped by its socially restricted vision.

More than any other social science discipline, economics is unified by a dominant theoretical structure, highly developed, mathematically stated, scientifically conceived, thought and taught as truth, and subject only to slight revisions and changes of emphasis within academic and policy circles that reach into the highest echelons of power. Yet, more than other disciplines, economics rests on simplistic assumptions (about human behavior especially) that are taken as given for all time. Economics develops in an intellectual vacuum of high mathematics and unrealistic models, isolates itself from fundamental critiques, and reaches dubious conclusions that, while they affect everyone, are conspicuously lacking in democratic input. These tendencies in contemporary mainstream economics are highly related: it is precisely the policy powerfulness of economics that prevents it from having to take criticism seriously; and it is precisely the mathematical complexity of economics that precludes the whole populace from participating in the construction of economic knowledge. Arguments like these apply with double force to the economics of development, which cries out for participation by those being developed.

Additionally, economics faithfully serves a capitalist system in which a minority owns and controls the means by which existence is collectively reproduced, determining thereby the character and direction of development, the social relations with nature, and the way people are created as kinds of human beings. Production is organized not as a social activity that directly satisfies needs, nor as useful work that employs everyone in satisfying ways, but as a profit-making endeavor in which needs are met and people employed only when profit can be made. Profits are driven by elitist desires for conspicuous consumption (at the extreme, a dress that costs $15,000, made to be worn just once; a string of pearls costing $3 million) but also by the constant need for reinvestment inherent in competitive market relations. In 20th-century capitalism, mass consumption becomes the main source of pleasure; more consumption means a better life. Elitist desires, the competitive need for profit, the substitution of machines for human labor power, the pursuit of the latest style or gadget—all are endlessly expansive: economic growth becomes a necessity rather than a choice. Under its driving force, production is escalated and rapid economic growth occurs, but the natural consequences are depleted resources, energy sources used up, and pollution multiplied, while all the time poor peoples' needs remain tragically unmet amidst landscapes of casual overabundance. But now, after 200 years of plundering the natural world and discharging poisonous effluents and pollutants with reckless abandon, we see signs that natural limitations may impose, at the risk of annihilation, a transformation in social relations, modes of thought, lifestyles, and systems of ethical morality. These relations between economic growth and the natural environment are basic structural contradictions that necessitate fundamental human and societal change.

4

Development as Modernization

The development theories covered in this chapter derive mainly from the discipline of sociology. Rather than covering the entire discipline, we focus on a few themes that have influenced theories of development. One of the main criticisms made of the economics of growth, covered in the last two chapters, is the extremely simple character of its assumptions about economic actors (meaning everyone who acts economically—entrepreneurs, workers, consumers, etc.) and economic behavior (producing, consuming, investing). A couple of examples include Adam Smith's classic declaration that people, as natural traders, are (exclusively self-interested) and the idea in neoclassical economics of *homo economicus*, that is, (consumers as utility maximizers and entrepreneurs as cost minimizers.) These are (simplistic assumptions) that eternalize quick, (subjective) judgments about universal "human nature"—little better than declaring off the top of one's head that "people are naturally selfish ... always out for themselves." Sociology does not make the same mistake, though it may make others.

Economic sociology is derived from theories dealing with the cultural origins and social evolution of the modern human character in the context of the development of equally modern social, cultural, and political institutions. In this viewpoint sociologists draw extensively on anthropology, psychology, history, and geography in building far more sophisticated accounts of people as economic actors. Yet, the (construction of theories of human nature is never politically innocent, even in sophisticated accounts.) This is particularly true for structural, structural-functional, and modernization theories that form the focus of our attention here. While economic sociology might have been theoretically innovative in its reconsideration of the origins of economic behavior, it was politically conservative in its insistence on strong control over the social means of the formation of human character. Structural functionalism sees social control over the production of personality as biologically necessary (we must control the kind of person our institutions produce). Modernization theory, sociology's influential account of development, is (excessively Eurocentric) in terms of its account of the universal supremacy of Western rationalism and Western institutions. Modernization theory basically says: if you want to develop, be like us (the West). So this too will be a controversial chapter. We warn the reader that sociologists like Weber, Durkheim, and Parsons use long words and complex terms in abstruse statements. While we try to simplify to focus on key concepts in the chapter that follows, complex terminology remains in our account. Read the text a couple of times, however, and a lot of this complexity will dissolve.

As in Chapter 2 we begin with the philosophical background to sociological thought. Let us spell out, in advance, the substance of our argument. One theme in this philosophical background is ("naturalism.") Naturalistic theories in sociology (and geography) drew on biology to argue that natural environments create societies and people and that these have different potentials for development—putting this very simply, some people (Europeans) develop earlier and faster than others because of natural superiority. A second theme is rationalism. Weberian sociology looked to the emergence of a certain kind of culture, specifically a form of thinking called rationalism, to explain European progress. Structural functionalism, the leading paradigm in sociology in the post-World War II period, combined naturalism with rationalism in creating a neoevolutionary (part biological, part cultural, part sociological) theory of modernization. Modernization theory spelled out the geography of a global system divided into (1) centers of modern progress and (2) peripheries of traditional backwardness, with the center (us) showing the peripheries (everyone else) their future. All these sociological (and geographic) theories saw development as far more than economic growth. Modernization theory began by criticizing the narrow focus of neoclassical economics (Parsons and Smelser 1956). Yet, like neoliberalism, modernization makes everyone's experience with development copy the approaches and accomplishments of the West. Our point is that development is a form of social imagination. Its theories are as much persuasive ideologies as they are models of deduced understanding. This observation will become clearer as the chapter unfolds.

NATURALISM

Sociology originated in the "positive philosophy" of the early 19th-century philosopher Auguste Comte (1798–1857). Comte's *Introduction to Positive Philosophy* (1988 ed.) was based on earlier attacks on metaphysics (aspects of understanding like cosmology that transcend science) launched by the British and French Enlightenment philosophers. Comte laid out a hierarchy of the sciences differentiated by generality and complexity, with sociology (in the sense of social physics) at the top. Comte thought that scientific understanding progressed through the theological and metaphysical stages to reach the pinnacle of positive knowledge—science studied whatever could be definitely, positively, and physically known. And social science studied society in much the same scientific way that natural science studies nature. So, positivistic social science possessed the same logical forms as the natural sciences (laws, hypotheses, models, etc.). But social science as sociology had to develop some of its own methodologies, for its subject matter (humanity, society) was more complex than the objects of natural science. Even so, human social development, Comte said, might be governed by laws quite similar to the laws of nature. Comte introduced the concept of organicism into sociology—that is, sociology as the study of societies as "social organisms," with the family as the cell, social classes as natural tissue, and so on. However, human deliberation also intervened. Human progress was not blind evolution, but rather it could be rationalized—hence, the main differences between social and natural science arose from human consciousness. That is, humans to some extent direct their own evolution. With this perception, Comte injected a tension between naturalism and rationalism into the positivistic sociological theory (science of society) he was founding.

One solution to the problem of connecting nature with society and natural science with social science was proposed by the 19th-century British evolutionary philosopher and sociologist Herbert Spencer (1820–1903). For Spencer, societies had natural functional characteristics like all living organisms—societies produce, protect, and reproduce. By analogy, therefore, biological principles of organismic evolution (the evolution of plants and animals) applied also to the development of the "social organism," the naturally conceived society. Just as animals derived competitive advantage from their relationships with nature (as with Darwin's theory of adaptation, for instance), so societies occupying different natural environments were differently endowed in their competitive struggle for survival. In Spencer's theory, rich natural environments enabled high population densities that increased the degree of economic specialization and promoted the greater political size and armed might of certain well-endowed societies—he called this process "super-organic" evolution. The reason for this super evolution was that higher natural fertility and therefore greater population density allowed intense social interaction in regions of densely packed populations—that is, people meeting one another more frequently. In turn, for Spencer, social interaction (discussing, exchanging ideas, etc.) was the source of invention, innovation, and the progress these bring—people cannot innovate, he said, unless they meet one another. In Spencer's theory, therefore, the naturally well-endowed areas of the world were areas of innovation, development, progress, and civilization. Also societies went through life cycles, the young conquering the old, with the whole process of survival of the societal fittest leading upward and onward toward an eventual utopian paradise where people could more leisurely pursue high culture (Spencer 1882).

Spencer's ideas were extremely significant in mid- to late 19th-century social thought, especially in the United States (Hofstadter 1955). The Darwinian notion of survival of the fittest, applied to human societies, was used to legitimate laissez-faire economics, market systems, the private ownership of productive resources, and social inequality. This kind of "social Darwinism," combined with the doctrine of Manifest Destiny, excused Euro-American conquest of the American continent from its indigenous inhabitants—the basic argument being that Anglo-Americans used the prodigious natural resources of the continent more productively than the "Indians" and therefore deserved their mastery (Zinn 2005). Additionally, social Darwinism helped explain the transition to an intensely competitive industrial capitalism, and the rise to power of rich and powerful people, who in turn revered Spencer and his many disciples in American sociology because the Spencerian message was that the rich deserve their wealth, for they are the victors in the struggle for existence. As a result of its social and political utility, environmental determinism became the leading school of developmental or evolutionary thought in a number of social scientific disciplines. Let us mention one in passing—the case of geography during the second half of the 19th century.

In the work of geographer Ellen Churchill Semple (1863–1932), the natural environment determined people's racial qualities, especially their levels of consciousness, productivity, and level of economic development (Semple 1903, 1911). As with Spencer and her mentor, the German geopolitician Friedrich Ratzel (1844–1904), Semple believed that Europe's physically articulated yet protected regions were environments conducive to high population densities and the growth of civilizations. In a similar way, confinement of the Anglo-Americans to the eastern seaboard for two centuries, yet their separation from England by the Atlantic Ocean, promoted a strong sense of national cohesion, a sense of being "American." Then too Semple believed that the movement of the pioneers through the Appalachian Mountains and across the prairies had a stimulating effect on the Anglo-Saxon "race" during the 18th and 19th centuries. The great expansion westward fostered democracy and entrepreneurship. Like most environmental determinists, Semple fully supported imperial conquest and economic domination by powerful nations—in the ultimate interest of all humanity, of course (Semple 1903). In brief, environments make innovative people, and these innovators lead development: ergo, environment is the basis of development.

At the turn of the 19th century, the realization grew in sociology, geography, and anthropology that there were great differences between humans and other natural organisms. Humans were self-conscious, aware of what they were doing, and able to choose different courses of action, within limits. Humans could plan or intend their reactions to nature. Humans interposed complex forms of consciousness and culture, intricate systems of social relations, powerful forces of production, and massive buildings and infrastructures between themselves and nature. All these influenced the relations between society and nature—so much so that the organismic analogy, and socio-biological conceptions of causation, came to be highly suspect as bases for the sociological, geographic, and anthropological understanding of development. It was not that environmental determinism was dropped. The mediations between nature and society just became more complicated ... as we shall see.

RATIONALISM

At first sight, the idea of human rationality appears to be contrary to naturalism as a type of social theory—contrary in the sense that through rational processes societies may escape the structuring influences of natural necessity, as just noted in the preceding paragraph. Yet, we find naturalism and rationalism constantly interacting in sociological theories of development. As we have seen, naturalism finds social institutions and human behavior founded on natural bases—for example, people act on the basis of instinct (humans are naturally selfish), or institutions (like the production system) are social forms of natural functions (like working in order to eat). By contrast, rationalism means the capacity for humans to control the world through thought, logic, and calculation. In many ways the two metaphilosophies (great systems of abstract thought), naturalism as a nonreligious understanding of life's origins and rationalism as the celebration of the final victory of the human mind over nature, are among the greatest intellectual achievements of the modern world. They are forms of nonreligious thought that combine into a modern materialist and scientific culture within which there are positivist, structural, Marxist, and other philosophical variants. Combining the two perspectives, naturalism and rationalism, into a powerful theory of societal structure and development was a defining moment in the intellectual history of Western modernity.

The emphasis on rationalism in sociological theory derives from the work of the eminent German economist and sociologist Max Weber (1864–1920). Weber's ideas were descended from the German school of historical economics, mentioned earlier. Weber outlined a historical theory of the stages through which modern rationalism emerged, and Western culture achieved a rationalized development path of what he called "world-historical significance." His theory was based on a comparative sociology of religions—religion being the way people thought deeply in the prescientific age. Weber's position was that the first human societies subscribed to a magical worldview in which there were powers (souls, demons, deities) behind natural events that had intrinsic meaning as wholes (the world was an "enchanted garden"). People contacted the gods through magic, ritual, and taboos. Rather than human conduct, magic determined fate.

A break with natural enchantment began when the belief arose that the gods established rules for human action and watched over the observance of these rules—hence, worship, sin, conscience, and salvation rather than magic and taboos, the beginning of a dualism between humans and God, between this world and a (magical) other world, or the growth of a (quasi-)rationalist metaphysic and religious ethic (that is, people could choose whether to follow God's rules, they had some degree of freedom). Weber focused particularly on the Judeo-Christian tradition, especially the path leading from medieval Catholicism through Lutheranism to Calvinism. Only with Calvinism (the religious doctrine outlined by John Calvin in the 16th century that formed the basis of Puritan belief) was the process of disenchantment complete, in terms of transcending magical means of achieving heavenly salvation.

Two central doctrines, Weber thought, affected the ethical position of the Calvinist faithful. First, Calvinism was distinguished from other kinds of Christianity by its emphasis on God's "transcendence." Calvinists continued to believe that God originally made the world, but it was as though, after the creation, God flung the world away, no longer manifesting an overweening interest in its development. In other words, God did not make everything happen, watch over every event, listen to every thought—because, simply, God was too busy elsewhere in the universe. Therefore, concludes Weber, Calvinists were free to think in terms of natural, physical, and real material causation. Cultures influenced by Calvinism could become scientific rather than remaining religiously mystical.

Second, individuals had their eventual fates (salvation or damnation in the afterlife) predetermined from birth and not revealed until the instant of death. Not even living one's life in total compliance with God's commandments enabled the faithful to be certain of, let alone affect, the fate that a busy God had already assigned them. For Weber these two religious principles, transcendence and predestination, had a momentous impact on the believer's existential posture (that is, attitude toward the world), shaping the ethical principles governing everyday conduct. Calvinists worried constantly whether they were going to heaven or to hell. But, rather than passively resigning themselves to fate or indulging in hedonism (as good or bad behavior did not matter in terms of going to heaven), argued Weber, Calvinists were disciplined in their conduct by a terrible, pressing anxiety to assure themselves that they were "among the elect," among the saints destined for heaven—that is, Calvinists worried all the time about their eventual destination. Weber called this disciplining mental terror "inner-worldly asceticism," with the "inner-worldly" part meaning practice in the public world of mundane (economic and social) reality and "asceticism" meaning strenuous, protracted effort in everyday (economic) life, rather than praying, going to church every day, and so on. Simply put, Calvinists wanted to succeed economically to assure themselves that they were among the elect destined for eternal bliss rather than everlasting pain.

Calvinism shared with Lutheranism a view of each individual's "calling" (occupation) as a center of moral concern. Lutherans kept in touch with God to reassure their souls, but Calvinists found the notion of intimacy with God blasphemous and reduced the significance of religious cult and ritual to a minimum in daily life—Calvinist churches, as is true with Congregational churches in present-day New England, were simple and even austere. With Calvinism, Weber argued, the world was treated as an objective reality separate from God. The world was deprived of mystery, of symbolic significance, and of magical evidences of God's wisdom and lines of access to God's will. Instead, those acting as members of the elect (that is, those who thought they would attain eternal grace by going to heaven) treated the world as a set of resistant objects that tested their mastering and ordering capacities. The doctrine of predestination created an acute sense of separation of one's person from all others because of intense anxiety about the individual's spiritual standing. The individual became motivated by intellect rather than habit, emotion, or feeling—the austere Puritan personality, thoughtful, judgmental, introspective, and nonemotional. Life had a long-term planned direction. People engaged in continuous rather than intermittent work and activity. Responsibility for the outcomes of one's efforts was accepted by the individual rather than blamed on fate or God or other people. Underneath all this, Weber said, was a simple intuition: the individual proved (to him- or herself rather than to other people) that he or she was a member of the elect by acting in a God-like way in the sense of relating to the world (including him- or herself) as God does—that is, through mastery, objectivity, and the long-term perspective. In brief:

> The religious evaluation of relentless, steady, systematic work in one's
> worldly calling is the highest medium of asceticism, and as offering
> at the same time the safest and most visible proof of … a man's faith,
> must have constituted the most powerful instrument for the affirma-
> tion of the conception of life which I have named the "spirit" of capi-
> talism. (Weber 1958 ed.: 172)

In terms of this connection with capitalism, Calvinists considered themselves ethically bound to sustain profitability through relentless, steady,
and systematic activity in business. They strove for maximal returns on
invested assets and yet abstained from immediate enjoyment of the fruits
of their activity. Hence, capital accumulated through continuous investment and the repression of all-too-human feelings of solidarity toward
others—"The entrepreneur is ethically authorised, indeed commanded,
to act individualistically" (Poggi 1983: 73). Or, as Weber (1978 ed.: 164)
said: "The Puritan conception of life … favored the tendency towards a
bourgeois, economically rational, way of life. … It stood by the cradle of
modern 'economic man.'"

Furthermore, through the study of religious cultures other than Calvinism, Weber concluded that only in the West does science reach the
stage of "authenticity" in the forms of mathematics and the exact natural
sciences, with their precise rational foundations. Science was made possible by the Calvinist notion of transcendence—that is, contemplation was
free to find the real, natural origins of things without constantly being
blocked by wondering how and why "God" made things happen. In Calvinism, everyone was expected to read the Bible and was free to interpret
it to some degree in his or her own way—the main regions of Calvinist
dominance, Massachusetts and lowland Scotland, had the highest literacy rates in the world by 1800. Science and technology intersected with
the profit motive to produce economic development following a path of
rationalization unique to the West (Weber 1978 ed.: 338–339). Hence,
for Weber the modern rationalism of world mastery was the product of
an ethical, religious, and institutional development characterized by "disenchantment" (Weber 1958 ed.; Roth and Schluchter 1979; Schluchter
1981). This was a powerful theory, indeed.

CIVILIZED DEVELOPMENT

Let us give an example, cast in the tradition of Weber, of how cultures
of rationality determine paths of development. The English people who
founded Anglo-American New England during the 1620s and 1630s were
extreme Calvinist Protestants. New England's Calvinists (the Puritans)

constructed a moral capitalism complete with networks, norms, and systems of trust. These networks made commercial activity possible. Yet, Puritan individuals were also highly motivated by a religiously based economic culture that fostered industrious and striving behavior. They also had a high savings and investment rate, enforced through proscriptions against conspicuous consumption. Making money was fine, so long as some was given back to the community, especially in the form of libraries, hospitals, schools, and universities—hence, New England now has the greatest concentration of major universities in the world. The Calvinist doctrine of "calling" insisted that everyone should pursue the occupation he chose—following guidance from God—relentlessly and methodically. Thus, work in New England constituted both an economic function and a form of spiritual expression. The region, historian Stephen Innes (1995) has observed, produced a modern personality whose acquisitiveness was disciplined by communal obligation. In creating a culture of development that was metaphysically grounded and socially binding, the Massachusetts settlers fashioned a potent engine of economic and human development.

The litmus test of this new capitalist engine came with industrialization, a phase in the region's economic history that emerged with an intensity that can only be explained by the Calvinist ethic. The New England industrial elite, originating in the merchant class of Boston, Salem, and Newburyport, consciously intended to create a new kind of profitable yet moral economy. During the early decades of the American industrial revolution, in the early 19th century, a socially conscious male elite, overwhelmingly Congregational, Unitarian, or Episcopalian in religious observance, employed a largely female labor force drawn from New England's farms and small towns. They used the farm women to produce an economic system driven hard by profit making and capital accumulation, yet characterized by paternalism, decency, and fairness in the treatment of workers. They conscientiously tried to make a different industrial system compatible with their Calvinist and Unitarian senses of morality. The textile industry was organized during the late 18th and early 19th centuries under a system of mills located eventually near virtually every waterfall in southern New England. This was a region where an exuberant brand of Calvinist entrepreneurship interacted with a copious environment of small rivers, glacial ponds, and waterfalls. In the Waltham–Lowell system—made up of sizable mill complexes situated near large waterfalls that were founded by merchant capitalists (called the Boston Associates) in 1813 and that employed farm women as temporary workers—the moral ideal seems to have been the formation of model communities free of industrial degradation. Around this moral economy was built a political structure that emphasized enlightened public policy, philanthropy, and an educational system second to none. The political and civil authorities continuously debated industrialization and its effects. Massachusetts economic and political liberalism was deeply embedded in Protestant religious culture. It can be concluded from this brief account that an attempt was made to construct an ethical form of capitalist production that combined the aggressive pursuit of profit with the maintenance of religious compassion toward workers from within the New England "civilization."

However, the regional labor supplies became insufficient. Irish and French Canadian (Catholic) workers were encouraged to migrate to the region's burgeoning industrial cities. It proved to be the case that ethical sensitivity was specific to the New England "Anglo-Saxons": one commentator later described the immigrant "invasion" in terms of "masses of non-English speaking foreigners swarming in every industrial center and blotting out the older population [of Yankees], as the contents of a spilled bottle will spoil the written page" (Brewer 1926: 228–229). Increasingly, industrial discipline had to be imposed on a far more reluctant working class who did not share the Calvinist culture. During the second half of the 19th century, the New England moral economy became a class culture of ethnic and gender struggle (Hall 1982). New England frequently erupted into violence during the late 19th and early 20th centuries, as witness the customary battles each year between "Yankee gentlemen" (carrying pistols to "defend their womenfolk") and "Irish mobs" during Boston's Fourth of July parade; and the massive textile workers' strikes led by Italian immigrants in both 1898 and 1912. With such refusal of conscience, workers had to be regulated through Fordist consumptive means (see Chapter 5) that would have been repugnant to the moral sensibilities of the earlier culture. Even so, this epic period in early modern history left its mark on the subsequent trajectory of U.S. economic development. Learning from the past, American capitalism continues to mix individualistic and communal values in very effective ways—"effective" in terms of social control (Peet 1999).

The importance of Weber's argument for development should now be clear. The argument implies that the phenomena we now understand to be "growth" or "development" are not inevitable transhistorical events that were necessarily bound to be realized. Rather, growth occurring through savings and investment is specifically a product of Puritan culture that, in turn, is a product of Calvinist theological contemplation. And the capitalist economic personality is not a product of natural selfishness but rather a social construction created in Puritanical societies, like England and New England. Weber's economics, in other words, is the exact opposite of classical, neoclassical, and neoliberal economics. The pity is that Weber's critical potential has never been realized. Instead,

Weberian thought (as structural-functionalist sociology) has been used to support quite conventional economic and sociological thought.

STRUCTURAL FUNCTIONALISM

Weberian notions of rationalism were integrated with earlier ideas about naturalism into a theory of structural functionalism that became the dominant paradigm of conventional sociology during the post-World War II period. Structural functionalism drew on naturalistic conceptions of society derived from the classical sociological writings of Compte and Spencer, discussed earlier in this chapter. But it drew also on the works of Emile Durkheim (1858–1917) and Ferdinand Tonnies (1855–1936). Let us briefly explain these. The French sociologist Durkheim emphasized such aspects of society as morality, collective conscience, and culture. Durkheim asked: How can societies maintain their integrity and coherence in the modern era when such earlier means of cohesion as shared religious and ethnic backgrounds can no longer be assumed? In answering this question, he focused not on the motivations and actions of individual people ("methodological individualism") but on what he called the "social facts" that have greater and more objective significance than individual actions. In *The Division of Labor in Society*, originally published in 1893, Durkheim (1983 ed.) looked at how social order was maintained in various types of societies. The traditional societies of the past, he said, were "mechanical," held together by everyone being more or less the same, with most communal property held in common, and with the collective consciousness entirely subsuming (dominating and containing) individual consciousnesses. Modern societies, in contrast, have a complex division of labor that results in "organic solidarity." Specialization in economic and social roles creates dependencies that tie people together, since no one could fill all of his or her needs acting alone. Yet, the result of an increasing division of labor is that the individual consciousness emerges, distinct from the collective consciousness and often in conflict with the collective. In societies with mechanical solidarity, the law (imposed by the collective, often in the form of the state) is generally repressive; in societies with organic solidarity, the law is generally "restitutive," aiming less at punishing people than maintaining the normal activity of a complex society.

Durkheim thought that rapid change in society, due to the increasing division of labor, produces confusion regarding social norms, thereby increasing impersonality in social life. This state of affairs leads eventually to relative normlessness—that is, the breakdown of the social norms regulating behavior, or what Durkheim called "anomie" (alienation)—

from which comes deviant behavior, like suicide. Durkheim was interested in the use of education to prevent anomie in modern societies by reinforcing social solidarity. For instance, solidarity can be reinforced through rituals, like pledging allegiance to the flag. With this reinforcement, individuals are made to feel part of a group and therefore are less likely to break rules. Hence arises the theme of economic change accompanied by anomie (or alienation) and the need for social control, which has played a powerful role in conventional sociological thought.

The German sociologist Ferdinand Tönnies (1855–1936) also distinguished between two types of societies: *gemeinschaft,* or community, referring to groups based on family and neighborhood bonds that connote feelings of togetherness; and *gesellschaft,* or society, referring to groups sustained by instrumental goals, as with companies or modern states. This distinction is based on two basic forms of the actor's will: "essential will," where an actor sees him- or herself as a means of serving the goals of the social group in *gemeinschaft;* and "arbitrary will," where an actor sees the social group as a means to further his or her own individual goals—the actor is purposive and future-oriented in *gesellschaft.* Membership in a *gemeinschaft* is self-fulfilling, while participation in a *gesellschaft* is instrumental for its individual members (Tönnies 2001 ed.). Hence arises the theme of development through individual striving in modern societies as contrasted with communal effort in traditional societies.

Similarly, structural functionalism basically posits that society is a system of institutions that fulfills naturalistic functions. In structural functionalism each component of a social system contributes positively to the continued operation of the whole. In more biological versions, the functional need for societies to survive creates urgent necessities to which culture, economy, morality, and even rationality have to respond—people must stick together in societies to survive, must protect themselves, feed themselves, etc. In some versions, the social stratification of people into positions carrying varying degrees of prestige (classes and castes) is also functionally necessary to the survival of the social system—that is, there has to be leadership, otherwise the society disintegrates. Structural functionalism also emphasized the adequacy of a society's methods of dealing with the environment; the differentiation (specialization) of roles (occupations, etc.) and ways of assigning people to them; the communications systems, the shared symbolic systems, the shared values of societies; and, in general, the mutual cognitive orientations (that is, common ways of thinking) that allow people to predict what others are thinking (via some degree of orderliness) in stable social situations where people share similar articulated goals. As structural functionalism developed, the more advanced view was that societies had to regulate the means

of achieving goals through normative ("ought") systems and by placing limits on affective (emotional) expression and disruptive forms of
behavior—societies had to maintain internal discipline, maintain social
order, or, again, they lost out in the struggle for existence. Hence derives
the emphasis in structural functional sociology on the necessity for societies to rigorously socialize their people through common symbols, beliefs,
values, and even emotional structures in the urgent context of presumed
(naturally based) intersociety struggles for survival.

Let us give a quick example of this dynamic. The Harvard political
scientist Samuel P. Huntington in *Political Order in Changing Societies*
(1968) argued that social order, or stability, is the most important characteristic of states. During economic development, political mobilization
(collective attempts at gaining power) can increase faster than the formation of the "appropriate" (containing) institutions, with this leading to
social and political instability. Huntington advocated institution building
during development, most importantly establishing stable political party
systems. He was skeptical about less institutionalized political mobilizations, as with strikes or mass protests. In 1977 and 1978 Huntington
worked at the White House as coordinator of security planning for the
National Security Council. More generally, during the 1970s, he applied
his theoretical insights as an adviser to both democratic and dictatorial
governments. Later Huntington (2000) published an influential essay
titled "The Clash of Civilizations?" that subsequently became important
in explaining the global conflict symbolized by the attacks on the World
Trade Center and the Pentagon on September 11, 2001.

The main hypothesis of Huntington's article is that the fundamental
sources of conflict in a globalizing world are not primarily ideological or
economic. Rather, the great divisions in humankind and the predominant
sources of conflict among human groups are grounded in cultures. Hun- *Terrible*
tington thought that economic modernization and social change separate
people from their previous long-standing local identities (for example,
identifying with the nation-state). In much of the world religion rushes
in to fill the identity gap, often as fundamentalist movements in Western
Christianity, Judaism, and Buddhism as well as Islam. That is, modernization and secularization have been confronted by a growing "unsecu-
larization" and the revival of religions across national boundaries that
re-create older civilizations. Nation-states may remain the most powerful actors in world affairs, but the principal conflicts in global politics
will occur between groups of different civilizations. This "clash of civilizations" will dominate global politics. The fault lines between civilizations will be the battlelines of the future—an example would be between
Islam and the West, with conflict occurring along the "fault line" running
through the Middle East. Western nations might lose their predominance

if they fail to recognize this tension. Note that many critics of Huntington find his "clash of civilizations" theme to be a means of legitimizing U.S. aggression against the Islamic world.

THE PARSONIAN SYNTHESIS

These themes in sociological thought were integrated into one grand theoretical synthesis by the Harvard sociologist Talcott Parsons (1902–1979). Parsons argued that sociology was the study of "meaningful social action" (that is, people doing things)—action that Parsons interpreted as being voluntary and subjective. Yet, action was patterned into a structure, or social order. This social patterning of action occurred through the "normative orientations" of actors—that is, society structuring people's norms, beliefs, and values. This argument was a critique of 19th-century positivist approaches to social science, as with neoclassical economics, that Parsons found unable to account for human consciousness, interpretation, and reflection. From Durkheim came the idea of a collective conscience, or system of common values, that secured social order and solidarity. From Weber came notions of types of rational action, together with an emphasis on ideas and values as driving forces in social change.

Putting these together, for Parsons (1948) the social actor was a selective, perceiving, evaluating agent, or a "personality system." The actor participated in a social system characterized by institutionalization—that is, stable patterns of social interaction controlled by norms that mirrored cultural patterns in such areas as religion and beliefs. Humans were goal-seeking beings active in creating their own lives. Actors made choices within an action system constrained by what Parsons termed "pattern variables." That is, action guided by values was necessarily a matter of choice, each choice conceptualized as a dilemma between two polar opposites. Parsons believed that it was possible to categorize the pattern variables in terms of the following polarities, or extremes: (1) a social actor might judge a physical or social object according to criteria applicable to a range of objects (universalism) or, alternatively, by criteria peculiar to the object itself (particularism); (2) an actor could judge an object by what it did (performance) or in and of itself (quality)—this was also described as the difference between achievement and ascription when referring to people's social roles; (3) an actor could set feelings aside in making judgments (affective neutrality), or he or she could directly express feelings in relation to objects (affectivity); (4) actors might be in contact with one another in specific ways (specificity) or, alternatively, be related through multiple ties (diffuseness); and (5) actors could aim at achieving their own interest (self-orientation) or the aims of the community (collectivity orientation). Note the combination of Weber and Durkheim in this theory of social action. These variables connected norms in the social system with individual decisions in the personality system; here we find sophisticated synthetic notions of socialization, such as Freud's theory of the introjection of normative standards into developing personalities, combined with Durkheim's powerful ideas of the influence of the social context, and equally intricate versions of the idea of social control in which the actor is an autonomous agent and yet reacts to contexts of social constraint.

For Parsons, the study of societies was guided by a (biological) evolutionary perspective, with humans as integral parts of the organic world and human culture analyzable in the general framework of the life process. Parsons saw human action systems (societies) as responding to four social-functional imperatives: adaptation (A), a society's generalized adaptation to the conditions of the external environment—that is, deriving resources and distributing these through the system; goal attainment (G), establishing goals and mobilizing the required social effort; integration (I), maintaining coherence or solidarity, coordinating subsystems, and preventing disruption; and latency (L), or pattern maintenance, storing motivational energy and distributing it through the system, this involving pattern and tension maintenance. These four imperatives made up the functional basis of the social structure (AGIL). Basically Parsons correlated the AGIL with the functional requirements of all social and natural systems. Every society had to have an effective AGIL system to exist, survive, and develop. Moving from top to bottom, in human action systems: cultural systems (L) provided individuals with the norms and values that motivated them; social systems integrated (I) the acting units (human personalities engaged in roles); personality systems defined system goals and mobilized resources around goal attainment (G); and the behavioral organism adapted (A) its functions to transforming the external world. The lower (nonsymbolic) levels provided energy for the higher (symbolic) levels that, in turn, symbolically controlled the lower levels. The AGIL system was thought of as a cybernetic (that is, feedback) hierarchy in which social subsystems high in information but low in energy (culture) regulated social systems high in energy but lower in information (the biological organism).

Also the basic concepts of organic (biological) evolution, like variation, selection, adaptation, differentiation, and integration, Parsons thought, could be used, after adjustment, in social action theory. Thus, social and economic development, like organic evolution, proceeds through variation and differentiation from simple social forms, like gatherer–hunter bands, to progressively more complex social forms, like industrial societies. Advances in the biological sciences, Parsons thought, had generated new conceptions of the fundamental similarity between natural-organic and sociocultural evolution. Biological evolutionary theory enabled the construction of a more sophisticated social development theory scheme than had been possible earlier, in Spencer's time, one with considerable more variability, with societies branching off along different developmental lines (Parsons 1966; Hamilton 1983).

For our purposes, we need to focus more on Parsons's notions of the *development* or, rather, *evolution* of social systems. The most important change process in neoevolutionary theories, like that of Parsons, is the enhancement of a society's adaptive capacity (that is, its adaptation to the environment) either internally (originating new type of structures) or externally through cultural diffusion (importation of new factors from outside). What Parsons called the "adaptive upgrading" of a society basically involves differentiation—subsystems specializing and dividing, as with industry dividing from agriculture and further dividing into types of industrial production (here we find echoes of Adam Smith). As each subsystem becomes better able to perform its primary function, societies become better able to cope with their problems and adapt to their environments. But social differentiation and the proliferation of specialized components of society produce problems of social integration and political coordination. Thus, the other vital component of the evolution of society, for Parsons, is the value system, the cultural pattern that, when institutionalized, establishes and reinforces the continuing desirability of a given social order—culture keeps differentiating societies and keeps them from disintegrating. Adaptation, differentiation, integration—these are the themes of evolutionary social development for Parsons.

At any time in history there exists a fan-like spectrum of different types of society. Some of these variant types favor additional evolution more than others; some variants are so riddled with internal conflicts that they can hardly maintain themselves, and they then deteriorate. Somewhere in the variegated system of societies, a developmental breakthrough occurs, a disturbance that endows a society with a new level of adaptive capacity, increasing the resources available to its system, changing its competitive relations with other societies, and in other ways giving it advantages over them—this is merely an update to social Darwinism. Parsons saw the enhancement of adaptive capacity (particularly in the economy's function of using resources effectively) as the main "advance" projecting "social evolution." Societies could destroy this innovation, adopt the innovation (the drive to modernization among underdeveloped societies being a case in point), confine it to an insulated niche, or lose their social identity through disintegration or absorption by larger societal systems (Parsons 1966: 24). History takes the form of an increasing differentiation between systems of action (for example, between the social and cultural systems) and progressive control over nonhuman factors by purely human (cultural) factors in an evolutionary series of stages in which societies move from primitive to complex, traditional to modern (Parsons 1960, 1961, 1971a; Parsons and Shils 1951; Parsons and Smelser 1956; Roches 1975; Savage 1981; Ritzer 1992).

The reader who has managed to get through all of this dense text has to concede that this is a powerful argument by a very intelligent theorist.

CRITIQUE OF STRUCTURAL FUNCTIONALISM

If we now look back on our earlier chapter on classical and neoclassical economics (Chapter 2), we can see that economic sociology of the structural-functionalist type was an attempt at working out the sociological aspects of the division of labor. On the one side, it was intellectually progressive in that it elaborated far more sophisticated notions of the economic actor and the environments of economic activity than classical or neoclassical economics—*too* sophisticated, in that the language used by these theorists is convoluted, to say the least! On the other side, this is a politically conservative, even repressive, social theory in that it stresses the need for the elites of societies in the process of change ("differentiation" and "evolution") to devise sophisticated mechanisms of social control—that is, keeping dissidents in order. Modernization theory, like conventional economics, has a class commitment—to rich elites—and that is why it merges easily with neoliberalism. It also sees societies as competing for the control of space and resources, competing for survival, an idea that also can be used internally to impose social order and externally to legitimate expansion and the control of other societies (imperialism). Themes such as these have been developed by the many critics of Parsonian structural functionalism.

Thus, the sociologist Alvin Gouldner (1970) regarded such functional theories as Parsons's, to be wholly devoted to maintaining the existing social order with all its inequalities. While stressing the importance of the goals humans pursued or the values they held dear, Parsons never asked *whose* goals and values these were—the focus was always on value transmission rather than value creation, and, as we have seen, functional theories stress the need for elites to maintain social stability. For Gouldner (1970: 218–219) the reason for Parsons's emphasizing value transmission and social malleability was to eliminate the conflicts between the individual and the group—hence, a neglect of things like resistance, power imbalances, and exploitation (Gouldner 1970: 240). Accompanying this perspective was a focus on the sociological equivalent of equilibrium, that is, stable systems of interaction that, once established, tend to remain unchanged over long periods of time. When it did come, change was cyclical or rhythmical rather than transformative. Differentiation was a way for systems to change in an "orderly" manner—not threatening to existing power centers. All of this contributed to a crisis in functional theory and in academic sociology more generally (Gouldner 1970: 351–361). For our purposes, we stress that Gouldner finds structural functionalism unsuited to a theory of social dynamics, like development, because of its bias toward equilibrium, its unidirectionality, and its stress on nonthreatening types of "evolutionary" change. We might also note that many of these criticisms of structural functionalism apply with equal force to its more intellectually deprived cousin, neoclassical economics.

Anthony Giddens (1977) traced modern functionalism (via Comte, Spencer, and Durkheim) to advances in biology during the 19th century. Functionalism borrowed the biological principles of natural systems (by analogy) to explicate the anatomy and psychology of social life. Its intellectual appeal derived from a desire to demonstrate a logical unity between the natural sciences and the social sciences. Giddens found functionalism to be teleological—that is, allowing for only a limited and deficient explication of purposive human action because the end of history is already implicit in the existing historical process. Homeostatic processes (in which change in one element causes change in another, which causes readjustment in the first) have to be seen as fulfilling some "systemic need." In functionalist social theory this need turns out to be a social system's "needs." Yet, Giddens thought, social systems are unlike organisms in that they do not have collective needs; rather, social actors have wants that they act on consciously, and this is different from a society's "needs."

Giddens also found that structural functionalism conflated the notions of "structure" and "system": structure is like anatomy, while system includes how the anatomy functions. For Giddens, structures (patterns) exist in social life only to the degree that they are constantly produced and reproduced by human action—he does not see structures as massive, enduring determinators; rather, structures themselves are made. Furthermore, purposiveness in human affairs cannot be grasped as a homeostatic process, involving merely cybernetic control through feedbacks of information. Rather, human action involves not just self-regulation but also self-consciousness, or (freer) reflexivity: "purpose" in relation to human affairs is related in an integral way to the possessing of reasons for action, or to the rationalization of action during processes of self-reflection (here Giddens is drawing on existential phenomenology that stresses the person's authentic creation of meaning, rather than its discovery or imposition). In this respect, human social purpose is quite different from whatever teleology is involved in self-regulating processes in nature (Giddens 1977: 116). For Giddens, structural functionalism sees change as stimulated by exogenous rather than internally generated factors (internal social struggles, for example); evolution in the animal world operates blindly, whereas there are attempts to consciously control human development; and the relation of human society to its material environment was ill conceived as mere "adaptation"—as Marx said, humans actively transform the nature in which they live (Giddens 1977: 118–121).

This critique led Giddens (1977: 118) to an alternative sociological idea that he terms "structuration," namely, that social systems are produced and reproduced through social interaction. Rather than being natural, repeated social practices involve, for Giddens, reflexive forms of human knowledgeability, "reflexivity" being understood not merely as self-consciousness but as the mental monitoring of the flow of social life (that is, watching and learning from actions). And rather than responding automatically to natural necessities, intentionality characterizes acts that agents believe will have particular forecastable outcomes. For Giddens, actors make things happen, although they take social necessities into account. Action involves power in the sense of transformative capacity—in this sense "power is logically prior to subjectivity" (Giddens 1984: 15). The "duality of structure" in power relations draws on and reproduces resources as structured properties of social systems by knowledgeable agents (see also Cohen 1989; Spybey 1992).

SOCIOLOGICAL MODERNIZATION THEORY

Despite criticisms such as these, structural functionalism informed much of the sociological thinking about social structures and economic development from the 1950s through the 1970s. This influence passed through a conception of development cast in terms of "modernization." According to S. N. Eisenstadt (1923–), a leading sociological exponent, modernization theory refers to whether societies are similar or not to the model of modern industrial society (1973a; 1973b: 12–15). How developed a society was could be measured in terms of indices of similarity with the characteristics of modern industrial society. Modernization theory then asked what factors were impeding a society's "advance" toward this industrial model: What were the conditions and mechanisms of social transition from the traditional to the modern? As with Parsons, traditional societies were viewed as limited by the environments they could master. Also, similarly, modern societies were expansive, able to cope with a wider range of environments and problems. The more the characteristics of structural specialization could be found in a society, the higher its position on an index of modernization. And the more thorough the disintegration of traditional elements, the more a society could absorb change and develop such qualitative characteristics of modern societies as rationality, efficiency, and a predilection toward liberty. Hence, the main structural characteristics of modernization were identified by Eisenstadt (1973b: 23) as follows:

> The development of a high extent of differentiation: the development of free resources which are not committed to any fixed, ascriptive groups; the development of wide non-traditional, "national," or even supernational group identifications; and the concomitant development, in all major institutional spheres, of specialized roles and of special wider regulative or allocative mechanisms and organization, such as market mechanisms in economic life, voting and party activities in politics, and diverse bureaucratic organizations and mechanisms in most institutional spheres.

In other words, a society's resources had to be freely available to the highest bidder rather than locked into a tribal culture; groups had to identify with the nation rather than the clan, tribe, or ethnic group; social actors had to specialize in specific roles, like highly specialized occupations, rather than being "farmers" or "craftsmen." More specifically, in the economic sphere, modernization meant specialization of economic activities and occupational roles and the growth of markets; in terms of socio-spatial organization, modernization meant urbanization, mobility, flexibility, and the spread of education; in the political sphere, modernization meant the spread of democracy and the weakening of traditional elites; in the cultural sphere, modernization meant growing differentiation between the various cultural and value systems (for example, a separation between religion and philosophy), secularization, and the emergence of a new intelligentsia. These developments were closely related to the expansion of modern communications media and the consumption of the culture created by centrally placed elites, manifested as changes in attitudes, especially the emergence of an outlook that stressed individual self-advancement (*gesellschaft*). In general, modern societies were able to absorb change and assure their own continuous growth. Such were the sociocultural differences between traditional societies (low on the evolutionary scale) and modern societies (high on the evolutionary scale).

These ideas were influential in the development of the study of comparative politics in political science. Under the auspices of the U.S. Social Science Research Council's Committee on Comparative Politics (begun in 1954), political science suddenly began to be far more interested in issues of Third World development. At the same time U.S. foreign policy also became interested in issues of development and was looking for a noncommunist theory to counter the influence of the Soviet Union in the Third World. In the pre-Vietnam War period, many scholars saw no problem in linking their interests in development with the foreign policy objectives of the U.S. government. In this context, the Committee on Comparative Politics produced an influential series of studies using a modernization approach within an overall structural-functional framework. Development, these studies concluded, was an evolutionary process in which human capacity increased in terms of initiating new structures, coping with problems, adapting to continuous change, and striving purposefully and creatively to attain new goals. The "development syndrome," they found, increased equality, capacity, and differentiation that produced strains and tensions that might abort or arrest change in traditional societies (Coleman 1971). With the Vietnam War and growing criticism of U.S. foreign policy, this line of work came under attack during the 1970s, and political science looked elsewhere—to dependency theory, for example (see Chapter 5)—for theoretical insight (Wiarda 1998).

ECONOMIC MODERNIZATION THEORY

Parsons's theory of social action was intended, in part, as a reformulation of purely economic theories of growth (as with neoclassicism). In the modernization approach, emphasis was placed on broad social and cultural differences between modern and traditional societies, with an understanding of these differences becoming the basis of development policies. The University of Chicago economist Bert Hoselitz (1913–1995) played a leading role in criticizing economics and proposing a more sociological alternative. Hoselitz emphasized cultural change as a precondition for economic development. In 1952, he founded the journal *Economic Development and Cultural Change* to carry out much of this work. Hoselitz applied the ideas of Parsons and other sociologists to an analysis of the development process under the assumption, drawn from Adam Smith, that increasing productivity was associated with more detailed social divisions of labor:

> A society on a low level of economic development is, therefore, one in which productivity is low because division of labor is little developed, in which the objectives of economic activity are more commonly the maintenance or strengthening of status relations, in which social and geographical mobility is low, and in which the hard cake of custom determines the manner, and often the effects, of economic per-

formance. An economically highly developed society, in contrast, is characterized by a complex division of social labor, a relatively open social structure from which caste barriers are absent and class barriers are surmountable, in which social roles and gains from economic activity are distributed essentially on the basis of achievement, and in which, therefore, innovation, the search for and exploitation of profitable market situations, and the ruthless pursuit of self-interest without regard to the welfare of others is fully sanctioned. (Hoselitz 1960: 60)

As a consequence, a sociological theory of economic growth had to determine the mechanisms by which the social structure of an underdeveloped economy was modernized—that is, altered to take on the features of an economically advanced country. Hoselitz's answer was based on the "theory of social deviance"—that is, that new things were started by people who were different from the norm. So, the capitalist entrepreneur of late medieval and early modern Europe was the prototype of a socially or culturally "marginal" individual who started important new kinds of economic activity. By extension, entrepreneurs or bureaucrats imbued with different modern ideas could do the same for underdeveloped countries today.

Hoselitz thought that small-scale private economic development was the best way of achieving development in Third World economies. This particularly involved revaluing what he called "entrepreneurial performance" so that it provided not only wealth but also social status and political influence. In terms of the place of this new kind of economic behavior, Hoselitz argued that "generative cities" (that is, cities producing innovations) rather than traditional rural areas were the focal points for the introduction of new ideas and social and economic practices (see the discussion of unbalanced growth in Chapter 3). In underdeveloped countries, cities modeled after the Western cities exhibited a "spirit of difference" from the traditionalism of the countryside—westernized cities led the way forward. In terms of development policy, therefore, Hoselitz favored a shift in political power away from traditional leaders and toward control by economic and urban modernizers in undeveloped countries (see also Barnett 1989).

PSYCHOCULTURAL THEORIES
OF MODERNIZATION

Another group of modernization theorists turned their attention more specifically to the psychological, cultural, and behavioral dimensions of modernization, also in an attempt at reformulating purely economic theories of growth (see Chapters 2 and 3). The political scientist and economist Everett Hagen (1906–1993) linked differences in human personalities to technological progress and social change. In traditional societies, he said, people's images of the world included the perception that uncontrollable forces restricted and dominated their lives. Fearing the world and its problems, traditional people were, he thought, uncreative and authoritarian. But this authoritarian personality could change if groups of people experienced a reduction in respect, for example through domestic or external conquest, and they searched for a satisfactory new identity, an innovative personality with a high need to achieve, as part of an effort to reassert themselves. These newly reassertive creative individuals could see technological prowess as a path to the satisfaction of their needs. The values of the new generation might turn in the direction of innovation in production or to institutional reform and economic growth. The deviant group then led the entire society into modernization and development (Hagen 1962).

A similar, if more extreme, position was taken by the Harvard psychologist David McClelland (1917–1998). McClelland thought that human motivation expressed three urgent needs: for achievement (n-Ach), for power (n-Pow), and for affiliation with others (n-Aff). This motivational complex is an important factor in social change and the evolution of societies. Part of the push for economic development, he thought, came from n-Ach, the need for achievement, which made particular individuals suited to entrepreneurial, innovative roles—that is, entrepreneurs have high needs to achieve (McClelland 1961). He thought that some societies (the United States, for example) had high levels of n-Ach and produced lots of energetic entrepreneurs who, in turn, led rapid economic development. The amount of n-Ach could be enhanced through "achievement motivation training," and McClelland recommended this training as a low-cost way of stimulating economic development in what he called "low achievement countries" (McClelland and Winter 1971). Basically, the cure for underdevelopment was to send out retired business executives to conduct achievement motivation seminars.

The sociologist Daniel Lerner (1958) contrasted traditional with modern societies in terms of village versus town, illiteracy versus enlightenment, resignation versus ambition, and piety versus excitement. Modern societies, he thought, encouraged mobility, rationality, and empathy. Similarly, Alex Inkeles and David H. Smith (1974) argued that enlightened modern "man" was characterized by such traits as rationality, abstractness of knowledge, scientific thinking, and urbanity. In a case study of East Pakistan they compared "Ahmadullah," a fictitious traditional man, with "Nuril," a modern urbanite, using the dichotomy of typical characteristics shown in Table 4.1.

TABLE 4.1. Traditional and Modern Man

Traditional	Modern
Not receptive to new ideas	Open to new experiences
Rooted in tradition	Changes orientation
Interested only in immediate things	Interested in the outside world
Denial of different opinions	Acknowledgment of different opinions
Uninterested in new information	Eager to seek out new information
Oriented toward the past	Punctual; oriented toward the present
Concerned with the short term	Values planning
Distrustful of people beyond the family	Calculability; trusts people to meet obligations
Suspicious of technology	Values technical skills
Places high value on religion and the sacred	Places high value on education and science
Traditional patron–client relationships	Respects the dignity of others
Particularistic	Universalistic
Fatalistic	Optimistic

Sources: Inkeles and Smith (1974: 19–34); Scott (1995: 29).

In brief, economic development originated in the growth of the modern personality. People developed high needs to achieve that were satisfied through innovative behavior. Development meant changing the typical social form of personality (from Ahmadullah to Nuril) and changing attitudes toward westernization, education, secularization, exposure to the global media, and so on. We might point out the obvious here: the idea of "changing the typical personality" in the Third World—westernizing it, modernizing it—is full of Eurocentric and imperialistic connotations.

HISTORICAL STAGES OF GROWTH

There is a long history of ideas about the "stages" of growth in various Enlightenment theories of human progress, in the German school of historical economics (covered in Chapter 3), in Marx's theory of modes of production (Chapter 5), and other schools of thought—examples include the theories of Friedrich List, Bruno Hildebrand, Karl Bucher, Gustav Schmoller, Werner Sombart, and Henri Pirenne. An important successor to this long theoretical tradition is the historian W. W. Rostow's *The Stages of Economic Growth: A Non-Communist Manifesto* (1960), clearly proposed as an alternative to Karl Marx's theory of history. Rostow (1916–2003) argued that, in their economic dimensions, all societies lay within one of five historical categories:

1. *Traditional societies* had limited "production functions" (that is, combinations of factors of production) grounded in pre-Newtonian science; primitive technologies; and spiritual attitudes toward the physical world. These placed a ceiling on productivity and limited economies to the agricultural level. A hierarchical social structure, in which political power was held by landowners, gave little scope for social mobility. The value system was derived from long-run fatalism. Rostow admitted that, in placing infinitely various changing societies in a single category (for example, aboriginal Australia was in the same category as classical Rome or China), he was saying little about them. But he justified this historical conflation as necessary for clearing the way to get at his main subject, the posttraditional societies, where each of the major characteristics of the traditional society was altered to permit regular growth (Rostow 1960: 6).

2. *Preconditions for take-off* constituted the second universal historical stage. These preconditions cohered in western Europe during the late 17th and early 18th centuries as the insights of modern science were translated into new production functions in agriculture and industry (for example, more machinery, in contrast to brute labor) in a setting made highly dynamic by international expansion. Favored by geography (its location just off the west European coast), better trading possibilities, and a conducive political structure, Britain was the first country to develop these preconditions. Elsewhere these conditions arose not endogenously (within the society) but exogenously, from intrusions originating in already more advanced societies. These external influences shook traditional society and either began or hastened its undoing. Essentially this involved the spread of the idea of progress not just as a possibility but as a necessary condition for some other purpose judged to be good—like preserving national dignity (for example, the modernization of Turkey after its defeat in World War I) or the making of private profit. During the preconditional phase education expanded, new kinds of people came forward, banks appeared, investment increased, the scope of commerce broadened, and manufacturing plants sprang up—all, however, within societies still characterized predominantly by traditional methods, structures, and values.

3. *Take-off* was the "great watershed in the life of modern societies," when blockages and resistance to steady growth were finally overcome. In Britain and the "well-endowed parts of the world populated substantially from Britain" (the United States, Australia, New Zealand) the proximate stimulus for take-off was mainly technological (railroads, fac-

tories, etc.), but elsewhere a political context favorable to modernization was also necessary. During take-off the rate of effective investment rose from 5% of national income to 10% or more, new industries expanded, profits were ploughed back, urban industrial employment increased, and the class of entrepreneurs expanded. New techniques spread usually from industry to agriculture and, in a decade or two, the social and political structures of society were transformed so that steady economic growth could be sustained. A question immediately arose: If the breakup of traditional societies came exogenously, from demonstration effects from other societies, how could the first take-off in Britain be accounted for? Rostow's general answer (1960: 31) was that the combination of necessary and sufficient conditions for take-off in Britain was "the result of the convergence of a number of quite independent circumstances, a kind of statistical accident of history which, once having occurred was irreversible, like the loss of innocence." Realizing that his stage theory originated in a historical accident, Rostow hastened to add a more complete answer. The first take-off unfolded as a synthesis of two linked features of postmedieval Europe: external (geographic) discoveries (for example, of the Americas) and the internal development of modern science (Newton's physics, steam engines, etc.). Rostow also found crucially significant Britain's toleration of religious nonconformists (that is, Hoselitz's "social deviants"), its relatively open social structure, and the early achievement of a national consciousness in response to threats from abroad. This last factor, Rostow said, placed the first instance of take-off back into the general case of societies modernizing in response to intrusions from abroad.

4. *The drive toward maturity* occurred over a protracted period of time as modern technology spread over the whole spectrum of a country's economic activity, 10–20% of the national income came to be reinvested in the economy, and growth outstripped any increase in population (that is, productivity per capita increased). About 60 years after take-off a society attained "maturity"—that is, a state in which there were sufficient entrepreneurial and technical skills to produce anything the society needed, whether it be machine tools, chemicals, or electrical equipment.

5. *High mass consumption* was the final stage where the leading industrial sectors became durable consumer goods and services (for example, automobiles), real income rose to a level permitting a large number of people to consume at levels far in excess of needs, and the structure of the work force changed toward the urban-skilled and office types of employment. Western societies at this level might choose to allocate increased resources to social welfare and social security. This fifth stage was reached by the United States during the 1920s and more fully during the immediate postwar decade; western Europe and Japan entered this stage during the 1950s; and even as early as 1960 the Soviet Union

had the technical capacity to enter high consumption for the masses, "should its Communist leaders allow" (Rostow 1960: 12).

For Rostow, these are *universal* stages of growth, true for all societies moving from traditional to modern, from backward to advanced, from undeveloped to developed. The basic force propelling a society along the historical path through the stages is technological development in the context of social, cultural, and political conditions suited to modernization. Rostow's stage theory occupied a leading position in conventional development thinking during the 1960s when new liberal attitudes toward the Third World were being established. For example, these ideas formed the "historical basis" for much of the development economics discussed earlier (Meier 1964). Versions of the stages of growth can be found in speeches given by President John F. Kennedy, which is not surprising given that Rostow served at that time as his deputy special assistant for national security affairs (where he was instrumental in getting the United States involved in the Vietnam War). The policy implications of Rostow's stage theory were clear: traditional societies wishing to develop had to copy the already proven example of the West. "Backward and traditional" societies should encourage the diffusion of innovation from the advanced modern societies, should adopt freer markets as the mode of economic integration, and should welcome U.S. aid, investment, and corporate involvement.

MODERNIZATION SURFACES

This kind of historical scheme can also form the basis for geographic models of development. This perspective applies whenever one places the highest stages of growth in one core area (Europe and the United States) and sees the rest of the world as a group of peripheral zones, each zone representing a stage of the past, persisting into the present, and awaiting change through the diffusion, or spread, of innovative changes from the center. Many of these economic and sociological theories implicitly recognized the uneven development of modernization processes in space. But the spatial implications of modernization theory were more explicitly drawn out by geographers. The Swedish geographer Torsten Hagerstrand (1952) saw innovation as waves of change moving across space that gradually lose power due to the friction of distance—like the ripples from a stone (innovation) thrown into a pond (space). Areas close to the origin of innovation were more susceptible to change early, while those at a greater distance felt its effects later. The geographer Peter Gould (1964) concluded that innovations diffused over space in such patterns because people were persuaded to adopt new things through communication with one another and communicative possibilities were constrained by distance—that is, people talk about new things mainly with others living or working near them.

These geographic versions of diffusion theory were then synthesized with ideas from the main body of modernization theory to produce a "geography of modernization." In this view, Third World countries were isolated, parochial, and technically primitive subsistence economies where disease, hunger, and malnutrition were daily problems. Change admidst these oceans of tradition started as islands of progress. Transformation was viewed as a progressive spatial process involving the diffusion of innovations from these islands:

> Unlike former days ... people ... act today in response to the new foci of change, the towns and the cities. Modern transport systems extend the length and breadth of the country [Sierra Leone], bringing new ideas, new methods, new people even to the most remote corners. ... These changes which affect all spheres of life—political, social, economic, and psychological—constitute the modernization process. (Riddell 1970: 43–44)

Modernization was seen as a spatial diffusion process, originating at specific contact points with the West, such as port cities or colonial administration centers, with change moving across the map, cascading down urban hierarchies, and funneling along transport routes. This process could be measured by looking at the spread of modern institutions, like schools or medical facilities, and mapped as a "modernization surface." In keeping with the strongly quantitative temper of the social sciences in the 1960s and early 1970s, many theorists tried to devise statistical indices to measure variations in the level of modernization across space. Typical indices included: (1) the development of transport networks; (2) the expansion of communication and information media; (3) the growth of integrated urban systems; (4) the breakdown of traditional ethnic compartmentalization; (5) the emergence of a money economy; (6) the development of education; (7) participation in nonparochial forms of organization and activity; (8) proximity to, and interaction with, urban cores acting as concentrators, adapters, and distributors of modernization; and (9) physical or geographic mobility. Modernization, however, "is not simply an increase in a set of indices. It involves profound changes in individual and group behavior" (Soja 1968: 4). In many ways this simple statement summarizes the whole modernization approach.

CRITIQUE OF THE MODERNIZATION APPROACH

These modernization theories express an entire system of European attitudes toward the world. Going back to the beginning of this chapter, naturalism in its strong geographic form of environmental determinism asserts that Europe was dominant because the environment endowed Europeans with superior natural characteristics, especially greater natural intelligence. In its weaker sociological versions, such as Spencer's fertility–population density theory, naturalism stresses the superior social systems developed in rich natural environments. With Parsons we find naturalistic theory updated through appeal to the finest intellects of the 19th and early 20th centuries—Weber, Durkheim, Freud—together with the integration of post-World War II developments in systems theory and cybernetics. In the structural-functionalist version of modernization theory the rise of Europe is endowed with natural inevitability so that, with Rostow's stages of growth, global history is reduced to a series of copies made from distilling the experience of the West. And with modernization Europe shows the world its inevitable future. These are more than academic theories—they are cultural attitudes displaying the West's supremacist idea of itself and its masterful relation to the "rest of the world."

The sociological theory of modernization, especially the idea that progress means replicating the experience of the West, underlies most conventional development theories, including contemporary neoliberal economic policy. This notion of societies structured by similar functionally based processes is a political as well as theoretical statement. Structural functionalism, together with its offshoot, modernization theory, came to prominence during the post-World War II period, during the era of Cold War competition between the West and the East, of McCarthyism in the United States, with its political disciplining of social scientists ("Are you now, or have you ever been, a member of the Communist party?"). Basically the West, and especially the newly hegemonic United States, were confronted in the world by communism and socialism. Most of the national revolutions for independence from the colonial powers were led by socialists. The leftist message was: nationalize the colonial plantations—the railroads, electric utilities, and factories—redistribute the land, and use the state to plan an economy imbued with social justice—in sum, let us use our resources and our labor to meet the most basic needs of all our people. What could the United States say in reply? "Let the multinational corporations in, and maybe a few crumbs will fall from their table"? That message had little appeal to newly independent peoples imbued still with the hope for a far better life of their own making.

So, the message from the West had to be deeper and far more subtle—and it was this: "There is an inevitable process leading from tradition to modernity. Follow it and you too can have everything that we Americans have. Your inescapable destiny is to follow our example. Don't resist destiny." So, modernization theory was the West's response to socialism. "Development" came from a society that was assuming its allotted place within a global order already determined by the heroic rise of the West. Development meant assuming the mental models of the West (rationalization), the institutions of the West (the market), the goals of the West (high mass consumption), and the culture of the West (the worship of commodities). Modernization was the early sociocultural equivalent of neoliberalism.

Beginning during the late 1950s but gaining momentum during the mid-1960s, modernization theory was subjected to intense political and intellectual criticism—indeed, criticism was especially ferocious when emanating from dependency theorists (for example, Frank 1969a) or political leftists (for example, Szentes 1976). Attacks were launched on all aspects of the theory, from its original base in structural functionalism to the politics of its policy prescriptions. Modernization theory was criticized for its concept of history or, more exactly, for its ahistoricism, with critical attention focused on Rostow's concept of the universal process of modernization (that is, history does not change but is the same everywhere at all times), his notion of a single fixed end-stage for development ("high mass consumption"), and his ethnocentrism (everyone should copy the English and Americans). The radical dependency theorist Andre Gunder Frank (1929–2005) was particularly effective in exposing the politics of Rostow's theory of history (Frank 1969a; the dependency theory is discussed further in Chapter 5). First, Frank said, Rostow described all "backward" societies in terms of the same uniform traditionalism. So, in his typology, imperial China, aboriginal Australia, Mayan Central America, and the tribal civilizations of southern Africa, along with feudal Europe, were all basically the same. This typology ignored the specific precapitalist histories of diverse Third World societies, reducing them to a common "backwardness," whereas in fact many had been more developed than feudal Europe—the more to disguise the (underdeveloping) effects that initial contact with European capitalism had on the world's civilizations. Second, the developmental history of Euro-America was generalized into a sequence of stages of economic growth that all societies had to follow (Frank [1969a], in contrast, pointedly asked: How could history repeat itself when Europe's development had already altered the context in which historical events occurred?). Specifically, the development of capitalism had already created a powerful center and a dependent periphery, so that progress in the underdeveloped world must contend with an entrenched global structure that Frank found inimical to progress (suggesting that history *cannot* repeat itself). Third, high mass consumption of the U.S. type was propagated as the end point for all development; yet, many people wish to live well without the social and environmental problems associated with overconsuming societies. According to Frank, Rostow subverted people's dreams of a better future and converted them to the worship of the almighty dollar. In short, Frank (1969a: 40) found this entire approach to economic and cultural change—namely, attributing a history to the developed countries but denying it to the underdeveloped countries—woefully inadequate. In Frank's view, an economic policy for the underdeveloped societies had to be based on their specific historical experiences, not on a blueprint for all based on rubber-stamped follow-the-leader prescriptions.

Weberian sociology and structural functionalism can also be criticized as Eurocentric. In his historical-empirical work Parsons (1971b), like most European and North American theorists, traced the origins of European modernization only as far the "seedbed" societies of ancient Israel and Greece. Cultural elements (philosophy, religion) derived from these sources, after undergoing development and combination, made up the main components of modern society. In his own work Parsons failed to see that classical Greece was not the cradle of a distinctively Western civilization, but rather was itself derived from prior African and Asian sources. The Marxist historian Martin Bernal (1987) argued that Bronze Age Greece was heavily influenced by Afro-Asiatic and Semitic cultures and was not an independent invention, a "Greek miracle" that set everything into motion. Bernal's books were part of a concerted attack on Eurocentrism—that is, the portraying of human history from a distinctively European point of view, assuming a sense of European superiority and altogether ignoring the role of non-European civilizations in the development of human culture. Bernal argues that an earlier "ancient model" that had acknowledged the strong Afro-Asian influences on Western civilization was downplayed during the 19th century in favor of an "Aryan model" that conformed better with the racialism and imperialism of the time. The earlier model had cast an entirely different light on the more diverse African and Asian origins of Western modernization, while the later model saw Europe as essentially founding itself. We should note that Bernal's critique initiated intense debate on the origins of Western progress (Lefkowitz 1996; Bernal 2001). One critic, David Gress (1989), suggested that, in titling his book *Black Athena,* Bernal ("son of a Communist fellow-traveler" and "loyal red diaper baby") should have known that it would be used by black activists "as a truncheon in their battle against the place of European thought and history in academic curriculum." Bernal, he added, suffered from a bad case of Third World liberationism and Marxist anti-imperialism. Gress further complained that *Black Athena* was pernicious because it served a political purpose hostile to the culture of scholarship and that it had the same moral and scholarly authority as the Aryan science of Hitler's Third Reich. It is clear that Gress did not care much for Bernal's politics!

In a parallel argument to that of Bernal, the geographer James Blaut (1927–2000) compared Eurocentric ideas about self-directed growth with Third World ethno-scientific models of the world as multicentric (Blaut 1976). A Third Worldist understanding, Blaut said, sees the world as a multicentered complex manifesting relatively equal levels of development. In his view, this multicentered world was disrupted not by the autonomous rise of a rational Europe but by the Europeans as plunderers of the New World (European "discovery" being due solely to the fact that the Iberian centers of expansion were closest to America), the flood of bullion (plundered gold and silver) into Europe, and commercial, industrial, and scientific technological development based on these robbed resources. "Thereafter the dialectic of development and underdevelopment intensified, and the world economy fixed itself in place" (Blaut 1976: 1). Blaut made the following arguments against the notion of the "European miracle": (1) Europe was not superior to other regions prior to 1492; (2) colonialism and the wealth plundered from Third World societies (rather than rationalization) were the basic factors leading to the rise of Europe; and (3) Europe's advantage lay solely in the "mundane realities of location," that is, proximity to the Americas (Blaut 1989, 1993, 1994).

With criticisms like these surfacing, modernization theory seemed to be in doubt.

RETURN OF MODERNIZATION

But modernization theory explains and legitimizes the concentrated power of the West. Thus, despite these sustained criticisms, modernization theory has continued to inform geoeconomic and geopolitical ideas and policies, particularly when these come from elite academic institutions. A good example is the Harvard economic historian David Landes's influential book *The Wealth and Poverty of Nations: Why Some Are So Rich and Some So Poor* (1998). The argument of the book runs as follows: Europe's development success results from a permissive natural environment and European inventiveness. The rich countries lie exclusively in temperate zones, while the poor countries are in tropical and subtropical zones. The simple direct effects of environment (with climate affecting the rhythm of social and economic activity) and the indirect effects (through disease, water scarcity, and disproportionate natural calamities) suggest that the world has never presented itself as a level playing field. Europe, and especially its western regions, had the most favorable conditions for development. Yet, environmental advantages were only the beginning. Growth and development call for enterprise, and this is a quality not to be taken for granted. Grounded in the Greco-Roman concepts of democracy and Judeo-Christian cultural beliefs, such inventions as private property rights and free enterprise made European-based societies different from other civilizations. Landes advocates a "Weberian" thesis of European exceptionalism—the notion that Calvinism promoted the rise of modern capitalism through a secular code of behavior that emphasized hard work, honesty, seriousness, and the thrifty use of money and time. Protestantism produced a different kind of person—rational, ordered, diligent, productive, literate, clock-making, and clock-watching. Europe's development was virtually self-made. And the gains made by the Europeans in knowledge, science, and technology have been good for humanity even though they have been unevenly distributed. Some may claim that Eurocentrism is bad for the world and should be avoided. Landes (1998: xxi) "prefer[s] truth to goodthink" and feels sure of his ground: the rise of Europe has made the rest of the world better.

Another example of the contemporary defense of modernization theory is Jeffrey Sachs's book *The End of Poverty: Economic Possibilities for Our Time* (2005). From his travels throughout the world, Sachs concludes that economic development is a ladder with the rungs representing steps up the path to economic well-being. A billion people still live too ill or hungry to even lift a foot to the first rung. Our generation's "challenge," he asserts, is to help the poorest of the poor escape the misery of extreme poverty so they can begin their ascent to full humanity. Sachs presents a quick history of economic development conceived in Rostow's sense as take-off, transformation, and spread from European centers—so that now 5 billion people live in countries that have at least reached that first vital rung. Why, then, have other countries failed to achieve economic growth? Sachs discusses several categories of problems that cause economies to stagnate or decline. These include such factors as governance failure and lack of innovation, but Sachs tends to rely on a kind of environmental determinism—many poor countries are poor because they are landlocked and situated in high mountain ranges (like Switzerland?), trapped in arid conditions with low agricultural productivity (like Saudi Arabia?), with tropical climates (like Singapore?) that favor killer diseases (as did once the north of England's hills and dales). Sachs dismisses the notion that "geography single-handedly and irrevocably determines the economic outcomes of nations," and yet here, as elsewhere, at crucial points in his argument he takes essentially an environmental determinist stance. Sachs was once special adviser to Kofi Annan, the then secretary general of the UN, charged with laying out an "operational plan" whereby the UN, participating governments, and civil society could fulfill the Millennium Development Goals that focus on the eradication of extreme poverty and hunger.

Sachs's main argument in his book runs as follows. Briefly, "the key to ending extreme poverty is to enable the poorest of the poor to get their foot on the ladder of development." The extreme poor lack six major kinds of capital: enough human capital, as health, nutrition, and skills, to be economically productive; business capital, as machinery and transport, to increase productivity; infrastructure that forms critical inputs into business productivity; natural capital that provides the environmental services needed by human society; public institutional capital that underpins peaceful and prosperous division of labor; and knowledge capital that raises productivity and promotes physical and natural capital. Breaking the poverty trap involves donor-based investments that raise the level of capital per person, producing a capital stock high enough that the economy is sufficiently productive to meet basic needs. Without outside donor funds the necessary investments simply cannot be financed. Ending global poverty by 2025 requires a global compact between rich and poor countries, as with the UN Millennium Project, whereby the rich countries follow through on their previous pledge (made long ago in a similar spasm of optimism) to provide 0.7% of GNP as aid. Indeed, the bottom line is about $135–$195 billion a year in assistance, significantly less than the 0.7% figure. As Sachs (2005: 299) says: "The point is that the Millennium Development Goals can be financed within the bounds of the official development assistance that the donor countries have already promised." Hence, our generation, heir to two-and-a-half centuries of economic progress, can realistically envision a world without extreme poverty. But why should "we" (the people of the rich countries of the world) follow through and actually accomplish the task?

With Sachs, the why is usually answered in terms of "Why not?" That is, why should we not end poverty when it costs a mere half of a percent of GNP to do so? But this answer creates moral difficulties for Sachs, and others, for it suggests a heartless world that could have saved billions of dying babies long ago and not even noticed the cost. So, why *now*? The answer is: because "hard evidence has established strong linkages between extreme poverty abroad and the threats to national security" (Sachs 2005: 331). An economy stuck in the poverty trap often leads to a state's demise, and failed states are seedbeds for violence, terrorism, drug trafficking, and disease. If the United States and western Europe want to spend less time responding to failed states in the post-9/11 era, they will have to reduce the number of failed economies. It has been done before, with the Marshall Plan, meant to ensure Europe's economic stability and strategic security during the postwar era. At the Rio Summit on Sustainable Development and with the Monterrey Consensus, the developed countries committed to doing so again. The richest of the rich should therefore come through with their contribution as a "profound and meaningful demonstration of our generation's unique moment to secure global well-being" (Sachs 2005: 346). Sachs is for an enlightened globalization, in the tradition of Thomas Jefferson, Adam Smith, Immanuel Kant, and Marie-Jean-Antione Condorcet, that would direct criticism at the rich governments of the world, encourage the antiglobalization movement to change to a more procorporate position, encourage trade by removing barriers and agricultural subsidies, and press the United States to end its "reveries of empire."

CRITIQUE OF SACHS

Let us now criticize the Sachs argument and through it the whole notion of stages or ladders of development with us, the Americans and Europeans, at the top. This book by the most prominent development economist in the world derives from a maverick-liberal neoliberalism that represents *the* leading critical edge within the hegemonic policy discourse. Assuming that UN declarations and global compacts among rich countries might make some difference, we are supportive as we are with debt relief. And arguments like this, providing a rationale for what otherwise might instantly dissipate as futile gestures in the general direction of empty promises, are useful indeed. But there are a couple of small points of disagreement concerning Sachs's argument presented in *End of Poverty* that have to be voiced. The first is economic, the second ethical.

As to the first, it is doubtful that foreign assistance can ever "end poverty." This is not solely because not enough aid will be delivered. While that, indeed, will prove to be the case, that particular shortcoming will consume about 95% of the subsequent hand-wringing debate and will allow an easy moralizing excuse for poverty not being eliminated by 2025 ("if only we had given more"). Rather, our more durable skepticism about the Sachs argument, the MDG initiative, liberal neoliberalism, and the whole notion of "modernization" concerns the ability of these theories even to begin to understand the causes of world poverty and thus suggest policies that might indeed spell an end to poverty. Sachs's Fifth Avenue approach—appealing to the rich to help the poor—comes with a hefty price label attached. Most immediately, that price is to cease criticizing the sources of wealth in the present system of global corporate capitalism. Sachs's argument that poverty results not from income transfer, from poor to rich, but entirely from differential national rates of economic growth is historically shallow in a convenient way in that it bends over backwards to protect the capitalist class.

Associated with this mind-boggling dexterity is a lack of criticism of the presently hegemonic policy regime—the neoliberalism that has done so well for the superrich and quietly famous—so that Sachs (2005: 73) blithely asserts that the rich countries have only to enable countries to get to the first rung in the ladder and then "the tremendous dynamism of self-sustaining growth can take hold." In the longer term, the full price tag includes accepting unwittingly a largely conventional economic historical geography replete with take-offs, ladders of development, and successful transformations, as supposedly bits of India and China even currently represent. This largely blind approach to increasing the health and education level of Third World workers through donor investments is, as Sachs suggests, likely to produce a healthier and more educated workforce—but alas, one that is more unemployed. Under all existing aid and debt relief schemes, to get their money poor countries have to agree to open their markets to foreign competition, privatize public enterprises, withdraw the state from service provision, reduce state budgetary deficits, reorient their economies toward exports, add "flexibility" to their labor markets, and so on. This laundry list of requirements reads like a Washington Consensus list written under the belief that markets and free competition can guide any economy into the magic realm of growth, up the ladder of development in Sachs's terms, if only workers are made more employable. To earn "aid," supplicant countries have to restructure their economies neoliberally ("maintain sound macroeconomic policies") so that they reward foreign investment. All of this skullduggery and legerdemain has to be ignored, or merely sniped at, when appeals are made to the rich to open their pockets ... generously.

As for the second criticism, the ethical argument presented by Sachs is abhorrent. After reading an argument on the supposed benefits of foreign aid, all the while assuming that the aim is to make people healthier for their own sake, we are told that the rich countries should invest in poor countries for the sake of their own security, to prevent failed states, to prevent the poor from becoming terrorists! We should invest in them ... because we fear them? Ethics do not spring ready-made from conscience alone but rather rely on interpretations of the human experience that, in late modernism, take the form of theories. In the case of *The End of Poverty,* the cruel pragmatism that passes for moral reasoning is detached from the rest of the argument as an afterthought rather than a moving gesture. This is not just because, having written a book on ending poverty, the author was confronted with the practical question: Why should a Republican administration that just illegally invaded a Third

World country support investing in the Third World poor? It is because the largely conventional economic reasoning of the book itself produces an ethical vacuum from which emerges, by random choice, an ethics of simple morality ("we should just do good things"), or moral utilitarianism ("it will not cost much"), or, at worst, moral pragmatism of fear ("do it to save ourselves"). By "conventional economic reasoning" in this last sentence is meant Sachs's environmental determinism and his Rostovian modernization theory. In terms of the first, we encounter in this book an honorary geographer who has not read any geography, and so does not know the critiques of an environmental determinism that, in blaming nature, leaves little but pity as the basis for morality. In terms of Rostovian modernization theory, we encounter here an author who sees poverty simply, naively, and optimistically as the mere lack of sufficient modernization, the more to disguise its origin in class exploitation. Most seriously, the two deficient ideologies combine to disguise the real culprit behind global poverty—the Western imperialist expansion that ruined the civilizations already existing in these "environmentally deprived" lands—and, thereby, the two ideologies miss too the only viable reason for aid—as reparations for damages done in the past and continuing into the present. The will to assist the Third World has to come from a sense of global justice, from the critical understanding that the extreme wealth of a few has caused the abject poverty of the many.

CRITIQUE OF MODERNIZATION

Structural functionalism and modernization were components of a modern scientific project that involved most of the conventional social sciences—sociology, economics, political science, and geography. Structural functionalism conceived people as products of socialization and acculturation, and only indirectly as the products of nature. Modernization theory saw ladders and stages of development leading from uniform traditionalism toward a singular common future. We can see both philosophical-theoretical devices as lending depth, solidity, and inevitability to the process of development. Why was sociological theory structured this way? The environmental determinism of the late 19th century argued that the Europeans were innately superior to people from elsewhere because their natural environment made them that way—this was at least an advance on earlier notions that God intended people to have innate characteristics. This notion then served to legitimate European imperialism as bringing European civilization to the world, for that was the "white man's burden" (Peet 1985). Structural functionalism, as outlined by Parsons, argued that societies had structures similar to those of all organisms, that there were imperatives that society's functional order had to pursue, and that culture and socialization responded almost automatically to these needs: people were what their society needed them to be, and they did what they had to. In the structural-functionalist conception, too, development was one more instance of the natural (eternal) process of differentiation, in this case focused on the component parts of society, or of the various aspects of an economy, specializing and separating amidst complex divisions of labor.

Again there is a strong sense of inevitability here, but this time the underlying purpose was more to make capitalist development seem natural, inevitable, and necessary in the Cold War against the communist Soviet Union. This formed the naturalistic basis of modernization, the notion that there was a single (universal) process of the evolution of civilization, with Euro-America occupying the eventual position toward which all societies tend. Development for the periphery was reduced to a process of spatial diffusion of innovation from the global center of civilization. The policy conclusion was that societies wishing to develop should open their borders and let change in, should become part of the existing global capitalist system, should welcome and indeed encourage multinational corporations, advanced technology, and export-oriented economic activities, should withdraw state aid and privatize their economies, and should allow the market to discipline their economies. Here modernization theory formed the more general theory of history within which neoliberal economics could be situated, with this difference: the rest of the world should not go through a Keynesian development stage, for that had proven to be a mistake, but should merely copy 19th-century liberalism in its late 20th-century neoliberal incarnation.

The notion that there is a proven path to development that can be read from the experience of the West is so embedded in modern culture that mere academic critique is relatively powerless. Modernization can be countered only through alternatives that are more convincing and persuasive, alternatives summoned up from the perspective of excluded groups or ones based on criticisms of the very concept of development. These alternatives form the nucleus of the second half of this volume.

Part II

NONCONVENTIONAL, CRITICAL THEORIES OF DEVELOPMENT

Some theories may be generally designated as "nonconventional" *and* "critical." These critical theories find the existing structure of capitalist society to be fundamentally flawed, "ethically challenged," morally wrong, and dangerous to people and the planet. Liberal critical theories want to change certain characteristics of the existing society through democratic intervention—for example, states can redistribute income by taxing rich people and spending the resulting revenues on subsidized social services, like free education and healthcare for all. Socialist critical theories agree with this but find it insufficient—how do rich people get the money (that *might* be taxed) in the first place? Leftist critics want to transform the entire structure of society because they see capitalism as inherently unequal, unjust, and nonsustainable. Socialists want to replace private ownership with public control. They want to rein in the market through the exercise of social planning and governmental regulation. Socialists want to go at the heart of social problems in the ownership structure of society.

In general, all critical theories emphasize well-conceived development rather than more growth. Environmental and some poststructural critical theories see further growth as a dire threat to human existence. They posit that global development may have to be achieved *without* growth—by redistributing production, income, and consumption from places where there is now far too much to places where there is far too little. Conventional theorists find ideas like these to be pie-in-the-sky utopianism. Critical theorists respond that such ideas are all too realistic—

because "realism" is all about attacking problems that are severe, lasting, and damaging at their sources—in the social structure. There is some public dialogue between conventional theorists and liberal critical theorists but hardly any with leftist theorists. This is because the media are overwhelmingly privately owned and restrict their coverage to conservative and, at most, liberal variations in conventional thought. Indeed, most people even in the "free democracies" go through life without ever hearing the great critical ideas and the political-economic motives of leftist intellectuals. We believe that free debate between conventional and critical thinkers—supporters and critics—is the essence of democracy.

Here we look at Marxist and neo-Marxist theories (in Chapter 5), poststructural theories (Chapter 6), and feminist theories (Chapter 7).

5

Marxism, Socialism, and Development

Marxism is a philosophy of social existence, called historical materialism; a theory of history, phrased as dialectics; and a politics of socialism, meaning collective social control over the development process. The founders of this school of thought, Karl Marx (1818–1883) and Friedrich Engels (1820–1895), were Enlightenment modernists. As with the Enlightenment philosophers, they believed in social progress and the perfectability of humankind. As with the positivists of their mid-19th-century time, they saw science as having transformative potential. They thought that material plentitude, made possible by technological advances, could make life easier, better, longer, and happier. Yet, they thought differently than most of their contemporary modernists. They saw modern industrial production as emancipatory in the sense that more could be wrested from nature, but they also saw capitalist industrialization as alienated from nature as the environment was destroyed and polluted by uncontrolled overuse. They saw modernity as progress in material life, but they also viewed it as a movement that was directed by a few rich people motivated by profit and capital accumulation and that had unequal results in terms of benefits. So, while modernist in overall commitment, Marx's theoretical analysis was intended as a guide to radical political practice, aimed at changing society, especially its leaders, so that science could directly meet the needs of the poorest people. Marx and Engels came to liberate modernism, not to praise it.

IDEALISM AND MATERIALISM

We should first compare historical materialism, the philosophy of Marxism, with its opposite, Hegelian idealism. "Idealism" basically refers to any explanation of historical events that emphasizes the role of ideas as the leading causes of events—for example, the idea of democracy as a leading theme in creating the political structure of modern societies. Many idealists stress "modern reason" as the source of recent material progress. This "reason" can be human reason, in the form simply of logical thinking; transcendental reason, in the form of some kind of spiritual director; or some combination of the two—spirit informing consciousness. As we have seen, the European Enlightenment of the 18th century is a breaking point when thinking shifted from mystical meditation on the mind of God to thinking about the real material causes of things—revisit Weber's notion about how this shift occurred (in Chapter 4). An important late-Enlightenment German philosopher, G. W. F. Hegel (1770–1831) connected the individual's rational consciousness with a collective and transcendent "World Spirit," or "Absolute Idea," a kind of "Rationality" inherent in the world (Hegel capitalized the first letter of transcendental terms). Hegel thought that, rather than people thinking and then acting in a rational way, movements of the world spirit preceded both human thought and material events, in some way causing both. That is, spirit "thought" first, and human rationality followed (Hegel 1967 ed.).

Hegel postulated that the world spirit (unlike religion) was not all-knowing. Instead, it was conflicted, wondering and searching for a more perfect ("Absolute") idea. The world spirit used human rationality and earthly practice to work out the contradictions in its ever-imperfect thinking. This can be thought of as the spirit proposing a "Thesis" (1a) but also an "Antithesis" (1b) to human rationality—that is, one way of thinking about things and another, alternative way of thinking. Human practice (doing things rationally) then worked out the best combination of the two alternatives as a "Synthesis" (1a-b). This synthesis is then passed back to the world spirit as a solution to its initial quandary. It becomes a new thesis (2a) to which the spirit is forced, out of wondering and quandary, to propose an antithesis (2b), and rationally directed human practice finds a new synthesis (2a-b), passed back through reason to spirit for the whole process to be repeated ... eternally. However, each synthesis (S1, S2, S3 ...) is an advance on the previous one. Hegel thought that spirit progressed through contradiction (between thesis and antithesis) and resolution (synthesis) toward perfection (the "Absolute Idea"), that human rationality became clearer, more complete, and more advanced as a result so that rationally directed material life was improved. This theory of spiritually directed development underlies a lot of subsequent thinking. And note that Hegel's "World Spirit" is variously interpreted as a kind of God force, or as human collective consciousness—that is, the best thoughts we have all had put together as human knowledge or culture. In this kind of idealism, development of the world spirit is the transcendent force behind all things (Hegel 1967 ed.).

In their youthful years (during the 1840s), Marx and Engels adhered to a radical version of German (Hegelian) idealism, for at least Hegel saw the world getting better rather than history repeating itself in reproducing the same miserable existence for the masses of poor people forever. However, the problem with transcendental idealism is its notion of a "World Spirit." Like most sensible people reading Hegel, they wondered about where this spirit was located. (And, like most sensible people, they rejected the idea that spirit is "everywhere in everything" as an excuse for not knowing the answer!) Marx and Engels also did not like attributing the finest thoughts of rational men and women to some spiritual origin—we think up our own ideas and construct our own rationalities, they insisted. As their thinking matured, they developed an alternative—indeed contrary—conception of social existence. In opposition to idealism, they called this conception "historical materialism." As they put it at the time:

> In direct contrast to German philosophy, which descends from heaven to earth, here we ascend from earth to heaven. That is to say, we do not set out from what men say, imagine, conceive, nor from men as narrated, thought of, imagined, conceived, in order to arrive at men in the flesh. We set out from real, active men, and on the basis of their real life-process we demonstrate the development of the ideological reflexes and echoes of this life-process. ... Life is not determined by consciousness but consciousness by life. (Marx and Engels 1981 ed.: 47)

In other words, the real activity ("praxis") of actual women and men is the source of consciousness rather than God, spirit, or some other heavenly force. Or, putting it bluntly, the world was originally without consciousness.

Human rationality is the way the mind thinks, the working of an informed brain, with the brain originating purely through evolution. Human consciousness is the ability to understand in a self-reflexive way—know we exist, be able to think about existence, represent existence through symbols (ideas, paintings, words). So, consciousness, in a materialist understanding, comes from real experience in a material world that preceded thought. Consciousness is the deposit of experience in the memory, interpreted and reinterpreted through beliefs that are passed on through culture. Obviously ideas are important as driving forces in history. But materialism insists that ideas have material (real, natural, social) origins. And that consciousness is a social product resulting from the hard work of deep and sustained thinking, not a gift from the spirit.

DIALECTICS

Thus, Marx and Engels turned spiritual belief back on its material base: for them, consciousness was the *product* of matter rather than its origin. Yet, they retained from Hegel's idealism dialectical ideas like development through contradiction and the notion of individuals and societies transcending their former selves. In a dialectical understanding, the natural and social worlds are not systems eternally the same, but are seen instead as developmental processes capable of rapid change. What brings change about, from a dialectical perspective? Dialectics is a theory of development that sees all things as complex wholes composed of parts. The "inner" relations binding the parts of a thing together have to be complementary and cooperative so that an object has coherence—for example, the mind is in touch with the body within the whole person, or communities have cooperative social relations among one another within the total society. Yet, inner relations are also contradictory, giving an object immanent potential for change—for example, body and mind can move in different directions (the body constantly contradicting the mind's intent), or communities can be riven with conflict, as when one class or gender exploits another.

There is also an "outer" external dimension to dialectical thinking that is especially appealing to theorists fascinated by earth space. In the "spatial" dialectic, an object also develops through "inter" relations with the external environment of other things, and these relations are likewise simultaneously both cooperative (trade, when it actually benefits all partners) and competitive (one society extracting value, resources, and people from another).

Fundamental transformative change occurs when contradictions build to the breaking point—for example, when two people can no longer stand the sight of each other and their relationship disintegrates; or when environments are destroyed by overproduction and too much consumption, the climate changes, and society is transformed by catastrophe; or when one class super-exploits another to the point that the exploited cannot stand it anymore. Changes transmitted from external sources cannot not have transformative effects unless an entity, held precariously together by contradictory internal relations, has already been made highly unstable by inner contradiction and conflict. The developmental process is thus a synthesis between inner and outer dialectics; the two aspects of change (inner and outer) alternate in significance; the types of their interaction are multiple and complex (cf. Ollman 1976).

PRODUCTION AS THE
TRANSFORMATION OF NATURE

In historical materialism, therefore, the origins of human life are sought in the natural evolution of a distinctive kind of eventually conscious social animal. For Marx and Engels, the writing of history began with the natural bases of life and the modification of nature (internal human nature and external natural environment) through human action. As with other animals, the assimilation of natural materials into the body ("metabolism") was "the everlasting nature-imposed condition of human existence ... common to all forms of society in which human beings live" (Marx 1976 ed.: 290; Timpanaro 1975). However, humans distinguished themselves from other animals when they *produced* their means of subsistence—that is, when they consciously, intentionally, and exactly transformed natural resources into materials that satisfied needs:

> Labor is, first of all, a process between man and nature, a process which man, through his own actions, mediates, regulates, and controls the metabolism between himself and nature. He confronts the materials of nature as a force of nature. He sets in motion natural forces which belong to his own body, his arms, legs, head, and hands, in order to appropriate the materials of nature in a form adapted to his own needs. Through this movement he acts upon external nature and changes it, and in this way he simultaneously changes his own nature. He develops the potentialities slumbering within nature, and subjects the play of its forces to his own sovereign power. (Marx 1976 ed.: 283)

For Marx there was no eternal or essential human nature—though humans are a distinct kind of thinking animal. Rather, human nature is actively created under definite natural and social conditions. "Human nature" emerges and changes during the struggle, along with and against others, to gain through labor a livelihood from the rest of the natural world. Human nature is accumulated through experience, particularly in production, in the labor process, but more generally in the reproductive process, in the making of a whole existence.

Originally, human labor was similar to the animal's hunting or gathering—it was the exertion of the body in necessary activities that made further life possible. For Marx (1976 ed.: 228) the transformative moment differentiating distinctively human from natural history came when human beings put consciousness and deliberation into effect as they worked to reproduce themselves. This happened most significantly in the making of "instruments of labor"—tools, implements, machines—which added greatly to the available means of the production of livelihood. Instruments allowed natural materials to be transformed in an intentional way; they also confirmed human effectiveness and reinforced intentionality—people could see that what they intended more readily came about when tools were used. As a result, the forces available for development became labor, physical means like tools, and mental conceptions, intentions, and plans. By applying these productive forces, necessary labor time could be shortened ("necessary" in terms of providing the essentials of life) and more time devoted to conceptualization, science, technology, and the production of more tools—all sources of development in Marx's understanding. Development of the human ability to transform nature through labor gave the possibility of higher material standards of living and thus the potential for a more liberated existence—liberated from the ravages of nature or from eternal back-breaking work.

How did these productive forces advance? Marx had a dialectical understanding of the relations tying the various forces of production together, in the sense that while these formed a unity, they were also riven with conflict. In particular, for Marx, the social relations that combined labor with means of production determined the quality and quantity of productive development. Social relations were therefore Marx's most essential analytical category.

PRODUCTION AS SOCIAL RELATIONS

The analytically distinguishing feature of Marxism resides in the emphasis Marx placed on social relations. Clearly social relations take many forms: relations between individuals within families; relations between people who are friends; relations within communities; and so on. Marx emphasized social relations of reproduction broadly and relations between people in the material production of their existence specifically—"material" in the direct sense of transforming natural materials into the products that make life possible. In examining the social relations of production, one should remember that even relations fundamental to existence—functional relations in structural terms—were characterized in Marxism by a dialectical interplay between cooperation and competition, collaboration and struggle. In Marxism, the productive base of society is inherently conflictive and therefore subject to developmental change.

Human existence is secured by applying productive forces to the extraction and processing of resources from nature in the making of products that satisfy needs and wants. For Marx, the most essential social relations deal with control over the production of human existence—

control over the productive forces and resources available to a society. Social relations are concerned with power in its fundamental guise as control over the possibility of continued existence. In this understanding, a second transformative historical moment (the first being intentionality in production) came when the means of production (land, most fundamentally) came to be controlled by a ruling elite. Occurring some five to six thousand years ago, this original "land grab" created a fundamental social cleavage or class division between owners of the productive forces (land, resources, infrastructure) and the laborers performing the actual work. The aspect of this event crucial for economic development was the extension of the working day beyond necessary labor time: "Wherever a part of society possesses the monopoly of the means of production, the worker, free or unfree, must add to the labor necessary for his own maintenance an extra quantity of labor in order to produce the means of subsistence for the owner of the means of production" (Marx 1976 ed.: 344). Marx's term for the extraction of unrewarded surplus labor time was "exploitation." It basically means performing work for a dominant class under conditions of coercion. Exploitation formed the social relational basis of Marxian economics, lending his version of the classical labor theory of value an entirely different orientation, with a revolutionary political conclusion. To understand this, we must present an outline of the main contents of Marx's economics.

CAPITAL

Marx opened his main work, *Capital: A Critique of Political Economy* (volume 1 was originally published in German in 1867), with an analysis of the commodity form of products, his intention being to uncover the social relations hidden in objects that are made, sold, and bought—that is, commodities are products made for sale in markets. The commodity, for Marx, had three valuable aspects—use value, exchange value, and value—that could be looked at individually and in combinations. First, use value (utility in conventional economics) was the material aspect of the commodity, the qualities of the physical body of the object that satisfied human wants and needs and therefore created demand for it. Rather than emphasizing demand in Benthamite terms of the maximization of individual pleasure (see Chapter 2), Marx's use value concept placed wants and demands in the context of needs, with needs being part of social reproduction; that is, people primarily consumed products so they could gain the energy to work or to feed, house, and raise their families. (Even this construction represents an advance on classical economics, because it says that demand is socially produced rather than being inherent in the individual as some kind of inherent urge to pleasure.) More generally, for Marx, social reproduction was that system of consumptive activities by which the productive resources of a society (human labor, machines, infrastructures) were reproduced from one time period to the next so that they could continue to function. In Marxism, use value thus referred to needs that are far more socialized than in classical, and especially neoclassical, economics.

Second, exchange value was the expression of use value in terms of a commodity chosen to represent value in general (that is, money); exchange value was the basis of market price. Marx agreed with economists that supply and demand set prices in an immediate sense, but he thought that this said little about the inner laws of capitalist production. For one thing, the money commodity itself (gold) had an exchange value, a use value, and a value, while money served various functions—as a measure of value, a medium of the circulation or exchange of commodities, a store of value, and so on—that might conflict one with another. Indeed, by analyzing these functions Marx was able to show how money as a means of payment became capital as a social relation and process. The commodity form of circulation entailed one use value exchanging for another with money as intermediary—that is, C–M–C or Commodity–Money–Commodity (for example, Wheat–Gold–Coat), or, spelling this out, farmers grow wheat that they sell for a money commodity that they use to buy other products they do not make, like coats, with the result that farmers satisfy their needs for clothing by selling and buying in the market. But there was also the possibility of starting with money, buying another commodity, and exchanging this for money again, or M–C–M. The only possible motive for performing this latter exchange, not driven by need, was to have more money at the end of the circulation than at the beginning—or M–C–M', to use Marx's simple notation. Money that was circulated in such a way became capital—that is, money put into circulation to make a profit. For Marx, economic analysis entailed finding the source of profit (the expansion of capital) in a commodity that could create value. What could this value-creating commodity be?

Third, Marx began by following the classical economic position in arguing that the exchange of qualitatively different use values implied some content they had in common, some identical social substance. For both the classical economists and Marx, this common content was human labor. Commodities were congealed quantities of labor, or "crystals of a social substance," and as such were values (Marx 1976 ed.: 128). But Marx differed from the classical economists in distinguishing between concrete useful labor—or labor exercised to produce a specific use value (for example, coat making as a specialized skill)—and human labor in the abstract, labor whose differences have been obliterated by market exchange—the average labor needed to make a piece of clothing, for instance, which Marx termed "socially necessary labor time." For Marx, it was the socially necessary labor time invested in a product—the labor expended under normal conditions at any particular time, with average skill and intensity of effort—that formed the commodity's value (hence economic analysis was historical rather than timeless). Money was the measure of this social substance, necessary labor time. By facilitating exchange, money was also the key for distilling abstract labor out of the many specific types of concrete labors. Money brought thousands of producers into relation (via markets) with one another—hence, the fetishism of commodities, the relation of individual to individual not via direct social relations but via commodities or, more revealingly, via money. From this—social relations among people occurring through money and commodities rather than directly—came Marx's theory of alienation of person from person, worker from work, and commodity fetishism, the inordinate exaggeration of the importance of mere things, under capitalism (Ollman 1976). But this notion of social relations is also the source of an entire sociological analysis of the production of value—its types, relations, and meanings.

The exchange of commodities and the value they contained presupposed, for Marx, the ability of individuals to freely dispose of their labor and the freedom of equals to meet in the market—or the conditions advocated by Hobbes, Locke, Hume, and Smith as the essence of human freedom and equality (see Chapter 2). But Marx saw these conditions of the "freedom of equals" as merely a nice-sounding surface exchange that disguised something entirely different that was going on in real production relations—indeed, he thought that the apparent individuality, equality, and liberty proclaimed by the Enlightenment theorists disappeared in the production process. For Marx, the circulation of money as capital shifted the focus of economic analysis from the sphere of circulation and exchange to the sphere of production. In capitalism, money was expended to buy commodities that functioned as means of production: specifically, money was expended to buy labor on the market. As a commodity, labor already had an exchange value—the socially necessary labor time required for its production at a certain standard of living and with the requisite skills, and this was the price of labor, or its wage. As a commodity, labor also had a use value, its power to produce commodities (coats, wheat, etc.) but, of utmost importance, *labor could also produce more value than it originally contained,* a surplus of value over and above the socially necessary labor already invested in the creation of the laborer—hence, there was a difference, missed by classical economists, between labor and labor *power.* For Marx, labor *power* made surplus value (that is, surplus over the costs of labor reproduction), surplus value was the source of profit, and profit was the expansion of money expended as capital (that is, M–C–M'). When owners of money (capitalists, the bougeoisie) controlled the conditions under which labor made commodities, by controlling factories, surplus value could be expropriated (or taken) from the real producers of value (human workers) as profit that expanded the original stock of money. Used in such a way, money became capital (hence, capital was a "social process"), and the social relation between capitalist and laborer was exploitative (hence, contradictory in the sense of dialectics)—that is, capitalists exploited workers by getting them to produce more value than they were paid in wages to cover their costs of reproduction.

For Marx, natural history had not produced, on the one side, owners of money (capitalists) and, on the other side, owners of labor power (wage workers forced to labor for capitalists because they had no alternative). Nor was this social relation between capital and labor common to all historical periods. Rather, this exploitative relation resulted from the destruction of older social systems and the gradual formation, during historical processes full of class struggles, of the capitalist system—hence, early capitalism witnessed two class struggles, capitalist versus nobility and capitalist versus peasants and workers. In particular, these struggles involved removing peasants from ownership of land or rights to their own means of production, ejecting them into the labor market as owners merely of their own persons and labor ("individual liberty"), and forcing them thereby, by threat of starvation, to sell their value-creating capacity to capital. This lends the sociology of development (as the study of the production of the social conditions for capitalist development) a "somewhat different" critical quality than classical economics or modernization theory! It says that human creativity in the work process, rather than capitalist ingenuity, makes development happen. It says that "inevitability" was socially and historically produced.

As for capitalists and their social relations among themselves via markets, these too were socially produced. In what Marx called the "primitive accumulation" of capital, money comes from surplus made during earlier periods of history, from merchant's capital (in which profits were made by buying cheap and selling dear), from savings and hoarding by small producers, or from raiding other societies for their labor, wealth, and resources. Dealing with the last, Marx said:

> The discovery of gold and silver in America, the extirpation, enslavement and entombment in mines of the indigenous population of that continent, the beginnings of the conquest and plunder of India, and the conversion of Africa into a preserve for the commercial hunting of

blackskins [that is, slavery], are all things which characterize the dawn
of the era of capitalist production. These idyllic proceedings are the
chief moments of primitive accumulation. (Marx 1976 ed.: 915)

Capitalists were originally commercial farmers or small manufactur-
ers (artisans, craftspersons) who put accumulated capital into use by
employing additional wage workers to produce profit—capitalists were
self-made persons rather than nobles or great merchants (compare Locke
earlier). Under market conditions, capitalists had to produce commodities at prices regulated by the average conditions of production. Competition was the precise mechanism of this compulsion: competition was
the external coercive law that directed the capitalist effort. Competition
forced capitalists to extract surplus value from workers in two ways:
absolutely, by extending the working day; relatively, when the productivity of all kinds of labor increased and the costs of reproducing labor
power diminished (hence, a smaller portion of the working day could
be devoted to necessary labor, or paying the worker's wages). Competition propelled capitalism toward perpetual revolution in the productive forces—especially it compelled the substitution of capital invested in
machines ("constant capital" in Marx's parlance, because he did not see
machines as producing surplus value) for capital invested in labor power
("variable capital," because labor was the source of the expansion of
money) in an effort to make the production of any individual capitalist
more efficient than the social average. Competition forced the adoption
of new technologies (more and better machines) and innovative types
of organization (for example, corporations in place of family firms, and
multinational instead of national corporations). Each technological or
organizational change would then have multiplier effects throughout an
economy.

   Rather than seeing this historical process of development as a series
of equilibriums, Marx conceptualized development as uneven (occurring more at some places and some times than at others) and contradictory (some people got a lot more from it than others), and therefore full
of crises periodically necessary for restoring conditions of profitability
destroyed by fierce competition. For the dialectician, "equilibrium" is
a fiction of the economist's imagination. To repeat, for Marx, development was a process of capital accumulation occurring unevenly in terms
of class (the owning class becoming richer) and space (some countries
becoming richer than others). Development was an utterly contradictory
and violent process essentially because of the contradictory nature of its
defining social relations—exploitation and competition (Marx 1976 ed.;
Harvey 1982; Becker 1977; Weeks 1981).

MODE OF PRODUCTION

For Marx, class control over production and development had profound implications for sociocultural and political life as a whole. Marx's own summary of the complex social and economic structures, layers of institutions, and social relations and practices intervening between economic necessity and symbolic consciousness reads as follows:

> In the social production of their existence, [people] inevitably enter into definite relations, which are independent of their will, namely relations of production appropriate to a given stage in the development of their material forces of production. The totality of these relations of production constitutes the economic structure of society, the real foundation, on which arises a legal and political superstructure and to which correspond definite forms of social consciousness. The mode of production of material life conditions the general process of social, political and intellectual life. It is not the consciousness of [humans] that determines their existence, but their social existence that determines their consciousness. (Marx 1970 ed.: 20–21)

Marx did *not* say, in this passage, that the "economic structure" stamps out political and cultural components called "political superstructure" and "consciousness." Dialectical terms for structural relationships like "correspond" and "condition" cannot imply such a mechanical process of determination. Marx *did* argue that the level of development of a society's productive forces—society's ability to transform nature—limited its social and political development and directed its entire cultural mode of existence. Putting it simply, the economic structure (forces and relations of production) determine (influence) the superstructure of society (culture, politics, consciousness) in general. Beyond this general determination, phrased by Marx in terms of influences and pressures, we had to look at the particular historical and geographic conditions to see exactly how economy conditions social and cultural development.

Recalling, that for Marx, societies are exploitative when uncompensated surplus labor or its products are taken from the direct producers by elites and their institutions, be these states or corporations. Surplus is not easily extracted. Particularly at a low level of development of the productive forces, when the margin of survival is narrow, exploitation that takes half of the worker's product means the difference between life and death, especially at times of natural scarcity—exploitation means the death of children and elderly people. So, the exploitation process is seen by Marx as an arena of struggle, the dominant using a combination of economic, political, and ideological force to ensure control over socially

produced surplus and the dominated resisting through overt means such
as labor organizations, strikes, and rebellion and covert means like reluctant compliance, breaking machines, and idling on the job. However,
the exploited might be induced to "volunteer" their own exploitation
with the right persuasion. In such a context, consciousness has to take
ideological forms that rationalize and legitimize exploitation. Organized
religion is one such form—for example, the notion of heaven as a realm
of eventual peace, with a place in paradise gained through good deeds
like hard work and devotion to law and order, as guided by the priest
or as self-disciplined by the Calvinist mind. Yet, even religion is a contradictory ideology, and so oppositional groups have formed alternative
interpretations of spiritual principles—liberation theology, for example,
or humanism as a nondeified admiration of the inherent good in people.
The most sophisticated system-supporting ideologies are ideas like equality of opportunity—meaning that everyone has an equal opportunity to
join the exploiting class, and, if you do not make it, that's your own
fault. So, exploitation is the mechanism hidden by rationalization and
legitimation.

Turning to the political aspects of superstructure, we see that a society characterized by exploitation and conflict has to develop collective
 institutions for ensuring elite domination and for socially reproducing
the conditions and infrastructures of production (Hirsch 1978). Many
of these collective institutions are accumulated in the apparatus of the
state, governed by an appropriate kind of politics ("liberal representative democracy" in advanced capitalism, for instance). In other words,
Marx does not see governments acting on behalf of everyone equally. He
sees the state as made up of rich people, elected by means controlled by
money, pressured by big money to act in the interests of corporations,
and aggressive in its external relations to create wider spheres of influence for capital—in general, the state is the political arm of the economically dominant class. Again, however, while the necessity for a complex
of institutions called "the state" originated in the contradictory nature
of production, its exact character can be found only by examining the
particular empirical circumstances of a given time period (Marx 1976
ed.: 927–928). Hence, for Marx, there are structural connections among
the economy, culture, and politics. The forms of social consciousness and
the kinds of state and politics that come into existence are limited and
directed by the exploitative social relations of production. Within these
structural pressures and constraints, people living in specific times and
places create the more exact historical forms of consciousness and politics. Notice that this means using two kinds of social analysis, structural
and empirical.

In summary, the Marxist concept "mode of production" entails a system of forces of production and social relations that organizes and directs the forces of production in the transformation of nature (see Figure 5.1). The social objectives of economic activity are the production of material goods used to reproduce the conditions of production (necessary labor) and the production of a surplus of values, used partly for investment in new means of production and partly to support the lifestyle of the elite (surplus labor). Development is driven by the exploitation of labor, producing surplus value, and the reinvestment of part of this surplus, under compulsive conditions of competition, in improved technology. Capitalism is the only system in history in which economic growth is compelled to occur through exploitation and competition. The social ability to transform nature, measured by the level of development of the forces of production and guided by exploitative social relations, limits and directs the making of social consciousness into ideological forms, while the state monopolizes collective violence, rationalizes inequality, and guarantees the continued reproduction of the social order in slightly changing but eternally unequal forms. For Marx, this whole process is suffused with social, political, and ideological struggles generated by contradictions at the very heart of society—in the relations that bind social actors together as collectivities of producers.

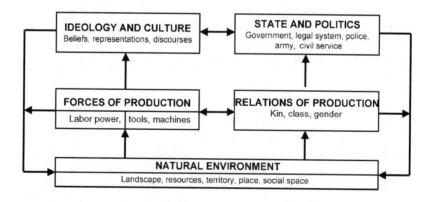

FIGURE 5.1. Mode of production.

DEVELOPMENT AS SOCIAL TRANSFORMATION

Economic development, for Marx, occurs by building up the forces of production, especially adding tools, machines, and infrastructure to human labor power. This process makes production more productive—

that is, the average amount of product made in an hour increases. And higher productivity yields the possibility of a better material life—if some of the extra product can be won by labor through struggle (union strikes, for example). Social transformations involve shifts from modes of production at low levels of the forces of production to modes at higher levels of productive force. Marx envisioned these qualitative changes ("revolutions") as violent episodes undertaken by desperate people only when the productive possibilities of the old social order have been exhausted:

> At a certain stage of development, the material productive forces of society come into conflict with the existing relations of production or— this merely expresses the same thing in legal terms—with the property relations within the framework of which they have operated hitherto. From forms of development of the productive forces these relations turn into their fetters. Then begins an era of social revolution. The changes in the economic foundation lead sooner or later to the transformation of the whole immense superstructure. (Marx 1970 ed.: 21)

In other words, material development is full of crises. These sharpen and intensify the social struggles endemic to class societies. Heightened struggle presents the possibility for structural change. This transformation is led by political and ideological contestations. The new social relations, put into place through struggle, do not materialize out of thin air, nor from utopian thought alone, but are constructed out of embryonic relations already present in the dying body of the old society.

The culminating moment in this line of thought is a reconceptualization of history in terms of temporal sequences of modes of production, and geography in terms of articulations (combinations, interactions) of modes of production. Marx thought it possible to theorize "laws of social transformation"—"laws" being understood dialectically as tendencies or probabilities rather than "iron laws of history" or utter structural necessities (as with functionalist theories). Marx only began to outline the main modes of production that have characterized human history, and he investigated one (capitalism) in detail. Marx's knowledge of noncapitalist modes of production was biased by the (colonial) nature of the available information. However, judging from notes posthumously published as *Grundrisse* (Marx 1973 ed.: 471–514) and subsequent work, we can conclude that Marx seems to have seen societies as passing through the following general types:

• *Primitive communist hunter-gatherer societies:* Recognizably human forms of chimpanzees emerged in eastern Africa some 1.6 million years ago, while *Homo sapiens* came from the same region 130,000 years ago. Based on studies of contemporary hunter-gatherers, mobile groups of foraging and hunting peoples have egalitarian, nonhierarchical "band" social structures, although more sedentary groups have more (but limited) hierarchy (Lee and Daly 1999)—hence the designation "primitive communism." What Marx and others appear to imply by this historical reconstruction is that human beings are thinking apes, all people were originally black, humans lived as communists for 90% or more of their history and, given that hunter-gatherers get most of their protein from plants gathered primarily by women, people are naturally feminist vegetarians (but don't quote us on that).

• *Kin-ordered tribal agricultural societies*: Agriculture was made possible by the domestication of plants and animals some 10,000 years ago in Mesopotamia, the Nile valley, southeast Asia, and central America and the Andes—that is, keeping animals under human control and selectively planting seeds, cuttings, tubers, and so on. This massive increase in the forces of production was accompanied by increased resort to hierarchy in tribal rather than band societies, with the subjugation of women being the main act in forming incipient class society.

• *Tributary or state societies*: Early state formation began to arise in fertile agricultural regions often amenable to irrigation, such as Mesopotamia, the Nile valley, the Indus valley, China, Meso-America, the Andes, and western Africa about 6,000 years ago. In the great "civilizations" of the Middle East, India, and China, social hierarchies were concentrated on emperors and god-kings, with the mass of peasants and artisans supporting the monarchical state through surplus in the form of taxes, tribute, and committed labor. Areas where the central state was less organized had feudal social systems in which the local landed nobility held power and contended for control over the weak central state in incessant interregional and interfamilial wars.

• *Capitalism*: From disintegrating feudal societies, primarily in western Europe, a new social order led not by the landed nobility or the king but by self-made artisans and tenant farmers began to emerge about 500 years ago. Capitalism is characterized by the extension of saved money as capital by an entrepreneurial class intent on making profit by employing waged labor in the making of commodities to be sold in markets (see Marx's account, discussed earlier); by science and the advance of technology; and by the gradual democratization of the state through struggles by the bourgeoisie, workers, and women (Wolf 1982).

In early simple statements Marx tended to see all societies passing through all these historical stages, or modes of production, in a unilinear conception of history. In later statements each mode of production informed several different versions of societal types ("social formations"), and any particular society could move through some modes but not others, might skip a mode or reverse track, in a multilinear and more varied theory of history. What first appears as a simple process of "societal evolution" turns out to be a complex process of uneven development of modes of production, such that capitalism could appear in western Europe while the previously dominant civilizations (China, India, Egypt, Mayan and Incan America) remained societies informed by "Asiatic"-type (that is, centralized) tributary systems, and much of the rest of the world was tribal or communal. In the "articulation of modes of production" approach, spatial relations among societies during any time period took the form of "articulations" (combinations and interactions) among societies with unequal powers, for example: among state formations in Mexico and subsidiaries in southwestern North America; between the Incas and the hunter-gatherer agriculturalists of the Amazon basin; between the Aryan invaders of India and the indigenous forest dwellers; or between European imperialistic capitalists and kin-ordered tribal groups in Africa. Each of these articulations had developmental and underdevelopmental effects, with surplus extracted as value or tribute by the dominant society from the subordinate, further developing the powerful and underdeveloping the less-powerful. Mode of production analysis enables this surplus extraction to be seen as part of an entire structure of economic, cultural, and political relations among societies, each society "informed" by a dominant mode. Hence, the Marxist geographic study of development becomes an analysis of the articulations among modes of production unevenly developing in global space.

STRUCTURAL MARXISM

This notion of articulations of modes of production emerged most strongly in what has been termed "structural Marxism." Modern structuralism of the kind that informed Marxism originated in the structural linguistics of Ferdinand de Saussure (1857–1913) rather than in the naturalistic functionalist ideas of Durkheim, Tönnies, and so on. Structural linguistics emphasizes the supraindividual and social character of language systems. This emphasis has great importance for understanding other aspects of society, culture, and thought in that social and cultural phenomena may be interpreted as signs (Eco 1973). Signs do not have essences, in the sense that there is a direct connection between the object referred to and the symbol used to represent that object. Rather, the meaning of the sign is defined by networks of relations among symbols. If they have meaning, it is the underlying social system of conventions that makes such meaning possible. Thus, the cultural meaning of any particular object or act is determined by the social system of constitutive rules. These rules create the possibility of particular forms of human behavior. In this sense, culture is a symbolic system (Saussure 1986; Lyons 1973; Culler 1973).

Structuralism was particularly important in European social theory during the 1950s and 1960s. A major structural theorist in anthropology, Claude Levi-Strauss (1908–) thought that culture is basically a symbolic system that can be analyzed like any other system of signs—that is, semiotically (semiotics is the study of signs). Within this construct he also hypothesized the existence of an unconscious meaning in culture. To get at this hidden meaning he proposed a "geological" approach drawn from Marx, Freud, and Saussure—geological in the sense of reducing the symbolic surface of reality to its hidden, deeper dimensions ("decoding") and constructing models through which empirical reality could be interpreted to discover its unconscious infrastructure (Levi-Strauss 1966; Rossi 1974).

This notion of structuralism entered Marxism mainly through the work of the French Marxist philosopher Louis Althusser (1918–1990) as a rigorous semiotic analysis, decoding the surface of society by using the analytical concept of mode of production to find hidden relations of power. This process involved elucidating the necessary structural relations among the various "levels" or "instances" of a society (economy, consciousness, and politics) by determining precisely how the method of surplus extraction (the hidden essence) determined the types, relative importance, and general features of the superstructures. This approach has been described thusly: "Economic relations, centrally those between owners and direct producers, are always determinant (in the last instance) but ... this determination by the economic structure takes the rather indirect form of assigning to the other, non-economic levels, their place in a hierarchy of dominance with respect to one another, and the kind of articulation between them" (Benton 1984: 72). In structural Marxism, revolutionary change from one mode of production to another occurs through a "condensation" or "fusion" of several contradictions, occurring unevenly at different levels in a social structure—for example, at the economic level and at the ideological level, as with economic crisis destroying previous ideological faith in the infallibility of capitalism. Structural change is a complex process in which dominance might be displaced from one instance to another—for example, from the political to the economic instance during the transition from feudalism to capitalism (Taylor 1979), or from the productive economy to the mass media in advanced capitalism. In this conception, each mode of production has a characteristic structure, typical contradictions and dynamics, and courses, trajectories, or channels of development. The objective of structuralism was nothing less than a total Marxist structural-semiotic science of society. In this science, a central tendency in a mode (like capital accumulation through profit making) is counterbalanced by other tendencies (like environmental crisis) to produce the complex rhythms of social change that typify any specific historical epoch or region of the earth. Each mode of production is thought of as containing several divergent developmental tendencies in dynamic tension; and several modes of production are present in an actually existing society, or "social formation," as societies are called in the structuralist approach (Althusser 1969; Althusser and Balibar 1970). This was an extremely interesting and even provocative line of thought that vitally affected the thinking of anyone seriously exposed to its depths and subtleties.

Structural Marxism has significant implications for development. Modes of production, characterized most basically by their social relations, have different capacities to expand their productive forces, the basic techno-economic drive behind development. But social formations are formed by the articulation of several modes of production, so the economic dynamic of a specific society has several, often conflicting, developing and underdeveloping tendencies, often located in different regions within a society (geographically uneven development). For example, contemporary India has advanced islands of neoliberal superdevelopment—like Mumbai, with skyscrapers and high-tech connections to global capitalism—in the middle of poor peasant farming regions where oxen pull ploughs and rice is harvested using handheld tools. Surplus is extracted by ruling elites within a given social formation and transferred across space between social formations according to principles of hierarchy and domination that are both social and spatial (geo-economics). Spatial systems of surplus extraction are protected and expanded by state action—imperialism and colonialism, for example—and spatial inequalities and geopolitical aggression legitimized by powerful ideologies—the "white man's burden" or "spreading democracy and freedom in the Middle East." Structural Marxism offered a powerful, deeply theoretical, and complex form of understanding societal structures and intersocietal relations—"offered" in the past tense because structuralism came under attack (from "poststructuralism" among other philosophies) during the early 1980s (see Chapter 6). Its passing represented a tragic loss of understanding at a time when capitalism entered a new structural phase, the neoliberal era of contemporary globalization. However, the great thing about analyses is that they endure in the writings of theorists long gone, and anyone can read them.

IMPERIALISM

From the Marxist perspective, capitalism is a social form of development based on the extraction of surplus value from workers and competition among capitalists. Extraction may be internal to a social formation, as with the exploitation of the working class in the United States or Britain. Or, it might be external—between capitalists in one society, the United States for instance, and the peasants and workers of other societies, like the border regions of Mexico. Marxist theories of imperialism specifically look at the second type of exploitation, capitalist society's external spatial relations. Essentially there have been two main historical phases of Euro-American imperialism, although some Marxists believe we have now entered a third phase of "neoimperialism."

Lasting from the 15th to the 19th centuries, *mercantilist imperialism* saw the European conquest of most of the Americas and significant control over much of southern and southeast Asia. Conquest and control involved the plundering of ancient stockpiles of wealth from precapitalist civilizations, the establishment of unequal trading relations with dominated societies, and the production of bullion and exotic commodities, using coerced (often slave) labor in colonized societies. In Marx's terms, mercantilist imperialism enabled the "primitive accumulation" (primitive in terms of "early" or "first") of stocks of global wealth that were then invested as capital in the western European and North American industrial revolutions.

Mercantilism involved massive state control over society's external relations to the point of declaring war on foreign competitors or heavily regulating trade and commerce to the advantage of the home country (see Chapter 2). Once the forces of production had developed and Britain, for example, as the leading mercantalist country, had a decided economic advantage in industrial production, mercantilist protection was dropped and "free trade" (between unequal partners) was relied on for continued global economic dominance (again, see Chapter 2). Mercantilist theory postulated that a country's level of development depended on its accumulation of gold and silver—hence, external relations with other countries were managed to maximize bullion imports and minimize exports. Mercantilism was the perfect prelude to industrial capitalism in that under mercantilist imperialism the world was raided for its wealth (bullion was the first capital) and slaves were forcibly abducted from western Africa to work in the Caribbean, Brazil, and the United States so that profits from slaving could be reinvested in industrialization even as they also produced essential inputs into industrialization, such as sugar and cotton. Finally, the most "successful" mercantilist countries and regions had Protestant majorities (Britain, the Netherlands, New England) or significant Protestant minorities (the Huguenots in France) who proved better able (had a more modern ideology, Calvinist rationality) to run production and trade than Catholic merchants—for example, the Brazilian sugar plantations were run by Dutch rather than Portuguese managers (see Chapter

4 on Weber). As was noted in the section on English–Portuguese trade in Chapter 2, Britain was by far the main beneficiary from this first mercantilist phase of imperialism.

The wars of independence in the Americas between 1776 and the 1820s are usually seen as marking the end of this period of mercantilist imperialism. We should note, however, that the British conquest of India proceeded while several other imperialistic expansions were going on, such as the U.S. conquest of the American interior from its original inhabitants. The second half of the 19th century saw several large industrial countries competing for global domination and, at times of depression (such as in the 1870s and 1880s), even struggling for economic survival. This framework was the context in which a second *classical imperialism*—even more violent than the first mercantalist version— suddenly emerged (Mommsen 1980). Between 1870 and 1900, European nations added 10 million square miles of territory and 150 million people to their areas of control, roughly one-fifth of the earth's land surface and one-tenth of its people. During this period Britain extended its empire to over one-fifth of the globe controlling one-quarter of the world's people, gaining in the process an empire on which "the sun never sets"—as generations of English school children were taught to repeat proudly. In the meantime, France took possession of much of North and West Africa and Indochina, Germany parts of Africa and the Pacific, Italy and Belgium were active in Africa, the United States finished taking over most of North America and then turned to the Pacific and the Caribbean, while Japan was active in East Asia and the Pacific (Cohen 1973). Why did the Euro-American social formations show a suddenly renewed ferocious appetite for foreign expansion and imperial domination?

Schumpeter (1952) sought explanations in sociopsychological compulsion—instinctive inclinations toward war and conquest rising to the surface as people and nations struggle to avoid competitive extinction. Other theorists have seen imperialism as an act of state power or as a political expression of modern government. And we should remember that the British upper class long thought that they should rule the world to make it a better place, while U.S. neoconservatives explain aggressive warfare in terms of spreading democracy—grand delusions can be "genuinely believed," and ideology has material force. By comparison, Marxists tend to see imperial expansion as systematic, or structural in a more materialistic sense. They identify a relationship between the maturation of industrial capitalism, with its tremendous material demands and competitive pressures, and the redevelopment of imperialism in the latter part of the 19th century (and for a discussion of the relation between oil and U.S. imperialism in the 21st century, see Harvey 2005b). The British journalist John Hobson (1858–1940) linked the internal class relations of industrial capitalism to an external need for territorial control: because underpaid workers had limited purchasing power, capitalist societies tended toward economic stagnation (too much production, not enough demand) and the overaccumulation of capital. Imperialism was therefore a contest between the industrial capitalist powers to control external markets for capital exports (Hobson 1902; Zeitlin 1972). The Austrian socialist economist Rudolph Hilferding (1877–1941) took Marx's idea of monopoly capitalism (competition concentrating capital in fewer hands) a stage further to include capital accumulation by banks (finance capitalism). Under this theory, finance capital needed a strong state, ideally one strong enough to pursue an expansionist policy and acquire colonies. This was given justification by racial ideology but was essentially a matter of economic necessity, since "any faltering of the onward drive reduces the profits of finance capital, weakens its powers of competition and finally turns the smaller economic area into a tributary of the larger" (quoted in Mommsen 1980: 37). The notion of imperialism being related to the export of surplus capital was retained by the Russian Marxist and revolutionary theorist Vladimir Lenin (1870–1924). Lenin (1975 ed.) saw the developing capitalist powers as caught in a struggle to repartition the global system of investment domains, with the latecomer Germany attempting to acquire colonies at the expense of the older imperial powers, Britain and France. Along similar lines, the Polish-German Marxist Rosa Luxembourg (1871–1919) saw the contradictions of capitalism as focused on the inadequate purchasing power of low-paid workers, and followed this thesis through the underconsumption route rather than the surplus capital route—so, for Luxembourg, additional markets for commodities had to be sought in noncapitalist societies. These societies had their own industrial structures. As societies would not submit voluntarily to having their manufacturing industries destroyed, there was a need for state violence and political control (imperialism) to force trade on them on disadvantageous terms (Luxembourg 1951 ed.). Other Marxian theories of imperialism stress the needs of developing capitalist societies for bigger labor supplies or their desperate need for huge external energy and raw material sources as the environment was exhausted in the home countries (Caldwell 1977).

Despite their differences, all radical theories of imperialism have essentially the same dialectical logic—external imperialism serves to relieve internal social and environmental contradictions. Imperialist expansion of all kinds (export of capital, gaining of external markets, opening of new territories, etc.) accelerated the accumulation of capital. Capitalism in spatial expansion was less vulnerable to internal social and political crisis—what the geographer David Harvey (1981) calls the "spatial fix." The dire consequences for the poor soldiers fighting imperial wars on behalf of rich folks who stay home, and the millions of the world's people eradicated by these cruel endeavors, call out for a historical account not written by the victors. And the use of ideologies of patriotism and honor in constructing a mentality of "proud to serve one's country" among troops whose true interests lay more with their victims than with their "leaders" is a topic well worth looking at. As Marx said, material interests underlie the creation of ideologies.

Colonialism was the system of political control forced by imperialism on conquered peoples. It was the system of state administration by the colonial power organized around the extraction of resources from extra-European territories. Beginning with the Spanish conquest of South America in the 1500s, European colonialism lasted until the late 1940s and 1950s, with some countries achieving political independence as late as the 1970s. However, this decline in Euro-American political control occurred only when the economies of Third World societies had already been captured, in structure and orientation, by the capitalist world market. Independence has therefore been termed "neocolonialism" by many radical theorists—that is, control by economic rather than directly political means. From this perspective, the tendency toward globalization entails the increasing homogenization of societies with the incorporation of world space into a single social, economic, and cultural system dominated by the imperial powers.

As suggested above, the question is: Is imperialism a thing of the past, or does it continue as some kind of U.S.-led *neoimperialism* today? "Neo" means new and different, and "imperialism" has long meant geopolitical expansion of national power. By "neoimperialism" is meant something different from, say, the British, French, and other European imperialisms of the 19th and early 20th centuries. In the 19th century, the aim of imperialism was territorial conquest, including permanent physical occupation of foreign spaces, with strict control over the subject people exercised by colonial state authorities directed from London, Paris, and the other capitals in Europe. American neoimperialism of the late 20th and early 21st centuries certainly uses overwhelming physical might to conquer territories and militaristic force to control reluctant peoples, as with the U.S. invasion of Afghanistan in 2001 and the occupation of Iraq in 2003. But the long-term aim of U.S. neoimperialism does not envision long-run direct control by the State Department in quite the same way as the British did through their Colonial Office. Rather, the aim is control of spaces, resources, and specified people indirectly via multinational corporations, international financial institutions, and other global governance mechanisms, and even foreign investment, policy imposition, and charity.

Contemporary U.S. neoimperialism has the confidence to control others in the long term by setting the ideals that people strive for rather than controlling bodies through violent intimidation. Control the way people think—control their economic, political, and cultural objectives—and there is no need for direct control over people physically. The aim of U.S. neoimperialism is to control global space by conquering the political and economic imaginaries of the world's peoples ... by having them "share the American dream." Neoimperialism takes the form of the expansion of American ideals like freedom, democracy, equality of opportunity, and consumption. American neoimperialism means spreading certain consumption habits, lifestyle patterns, media orientations, electoral ambitions, and all the "good" things that people everywhere have already shown that they urgently and deeply want! Neoimperialism is cast as the latest act in a continuing drama of global human liberation (Peet 2007).

DEPENDENCY THEORY

Marxism forms the philosophical and theoretical basis for a variety of neo-Marxist theories that combine historical materialism with other critical traditions in thought. Examples include dependency and world systems theories most obviously but also neostructural notions like regulation theory, which is covered in the following section. The basic message of the dependency school draws on a theme that has run through this entire chapter, namely, that European and U.S. development was predicated on the active *under*development of the non-European world, that is, making it less developed than it had been. For dependency theorists, Europe's development was based on external destruction rather than internal innovation—brutal conquest, colonial control, and stripping non-Western societies of their people, resources, and surpluses rather than singlemindedly undertaking the rational modernization of Europe (Galeano 1973). Indeed, dependency theory prefigures poststructuralism (covered in Chapter 6) in that it brings into question the nature of European "rationality" in committing these atrocities? From just such historical processes as these came a new global geography: a European First World "center" and non-European Third World "peripheries." The relationship between center and periphery assumed, for the Brazilian geographer Teontonio Dos Santos (1970), the spatial form of dependence, in which some countries (the dominant) achieved self-sustaining economic growth while others (the dominated and dependent) grew only as a reflection of changes in the dominant countries:

[Dependency is] ... an historical condition which shapes a certain structure of the world economy such that it favors some countries to the detriment of others and limits the development possibilities of the subordinate economies ... a situation in which the economy of a certain group of countries is conditioned by the development and expansion of another economy, to which their own is subjected. (Dos Santos 1970: 226)

The incorporation of Latin America into the capitalist world economy, directly through (Spanish and Portuguese) colonial administration but more subtly through trade, asserted Dos Santos, geared the region's economies toward meeting demands from the center rather than the needs of Latin America's people themselves, even when the main economic activities in the regional economy were locally controlled. Dependence skewed the region's social structure toward a small, enormously rich, elite and a mass of poor peasants. Regional power was held by this "comprador" (collaborating, intermediary) ruling class. In terms of development, the gains made from exporting products sent to the center were used for luxurious consumption by the elite rather than for domestic investment. But real power was exercised from external centers of command in the dominant ("metropolitan") countries. Dos Santos concludes that dependence continues into the present through international ownership of the region's most dynamic sectors, multinational corporate control over technology, and huge payments of royalties, interest, and profits to corporations headquartered in New York and London.

The basic impetus behind this dependency theory derives from two main sources. In the United States a school of neo-Marxist thought centered on the socialist journal *Monthly Review* developed a theory of "monopoly capitalism," referring to the dominant form of social organization of the 20th century. Beginning in the late 19th century, this school of thought argues, large corporations increasingly took over, or outcompeted, small companies. The resulting monopolization restricted competition, and corporations accumulated large surpluses from the attendant excess profits, with the consequence that capitalist economies tended toward underconsumption and economic stagnation—as was true with the theories of imperialism mentioned earlier. Economic crises were avoided within the capitalist countries by stimulating individual consumption through advertising, while collective consumption (consumption by the society as a whole) grew through the expansion of the military–industrial complex. In the Third World, stagnation was more typical than growth. Since, in these countries, typically the bourgeoisie was "parasitic" (that is, living off and harming the workers and peasants), the ultimate solution was to break with capitalist imperialism. Paul Baran (1910–1964) and Paul Sweezy (1910–2004), leading lights of the *Monthly Review* school, found dependency to be an irrational kind of development (Baran and Sweezy 1966). Genuine development could be achieved in Third World countries, they maintained, only by withdrawing from the world capitalist system and reconstructing economy and society on a socialist basis, as Cuba and China were doing at the time.

The second main source for the dependency school was critical radical economic thinking in Latin America. The ideas of the United Nations Economic Commission for Latin America and Raul Prebisch (discussed in Chapter 3) were criticized by the Latin American left, in that the former ignored class relations. The kind of state intervention in the economy proposed by Prebisch and the ECLA, involving the protection of infant industries via tariff remedies, could end up subsidizing the profits of the local bourgeoisie, with consumers paying vastly higher prices for the subsidized commodities (at one time the tariff on refrigerators imported into Mexico was 800%!). A more radical *dependentista* (dependency) position was pieced together by such writers as Osvaldo Sunkel (1972), Celso Furtado (1963), Fernando Cardoso and Enzo Falleto (1979), and Teontonio Dos Santos (1970) and was popularized in the English-speaking world through the writings of Andre Gunder Frank.

Andre Gunder Frank (1925–2005) was a leading critic of (conventional) development economics and modernization theory. His perspective entailed a criticism of the "dual society" thesis, which stated that underdeveloped societies had a dual structure of modern and traditional sectors, each with its own characteristics and dynamic. "Underdevelopment," Frank wrote, "is not due to the survival of archaic institutions and the existence of capital shortage in regions that have remained isolated from the stream of world history. On the contrary, underdevelopment was and still is generated by the very same historical process which also generated economic development: the development of capitalism itself" (Frank 1966: 18). In this view the development of the states at the center of the capitalist world economy had the effect of underdeveloping the states of the periphery. For Frank, attributing underdevelopment to lingering traditionalism rather than the advance of capitalism was a historical and political mistake. Rather, world capitalism destroyed or transformed earlier social systems even as it came into existence, converting them into sources of its own further development (Frank 1969a). For Frank, the economic, political, social, and cultural institutions of the underdeveloped countries resulted from the penetration of capitalism rather than being original or traditional.

Frank focused on the metropole–satellite (or center–periphery) relations he found typical of Latin America. The underdevelopment of peripheral capitalist regions and people, he said, was characterized by three contradictions: the contradiction of the monopolistic expropriation of economic surplus; the contradiction of metropole–satellite polarization; and the contradiction of continuity in change. Frank drew on Marxist analyses of the class expropriation of surplus value, especially Paul Baran's (1960) version, that emphasized the potential surplus (accumulable surplus value) that could be produced if excess consumption by the middle and upper layers of society were eliminated and unproductive workers and the unemployed were put to work. Frank argued that external monopoly resulted in the foreign expropriation, and thus local unavailability, of a significant part of even the actual economic surplus produced in Latin America. So, the region was actively *under*developed (made less developed) by not producing at its potential and losing its surplus (source of investment capital, in Marxist theory) to Europe and North America. Using a case study of Chile, Frank described the pattern of surplus movement as a massive spatial expropriation system reaching into the most remote corners of the region:

> The monopoly capitalist structure and the surplus expropriation/appropriation contradiction run through the entire Chilean economy, past and present. Indeed, it is this exploitative relation which in chain-like fashion extends the link between the capitalist world and national metropolises to the regional centers (part of whose surplus they appropriate), and from these to local centers, and so on to large landowners or merchants who expropriate surplus from small peasants or tenants, and sometimes even from these latter to landless laborers exploited by them in turn. At each step along the way, the relatively few capitalists above exercise monopoly power over the many below, expropriating some or all of their economic surplus. ... Thus at each point, the international, national, and local capitalist system generates economic development for the few and underdevelopment for the many. (Frank 1969b: 7–8)

This idea of a chain of surplus transfer over space was further developed in Frank's second contradiction, whereby center and periphery become increasingly polarized as capitalism developed the one and underdeveloped the other in a single historical process. In this perspective, only a weaker, or lesser, degree of metropole–satellite relations allowed for the possibility of surplus retention and local development. These two contradictions suggested a third to Frank, namely, the continuity and ubiquity of structural underdevelopment throughout the expansion of the capitalist system—that is, surplus was continually extracted from the peripheral countries, in ever new forms, from the first days of the global capitalist system to the present day.

From this perspective, the "development of underdevelopment," Frank generated several more specific hypotheses that could be used in guiding development policy. In contrast to the world metropolis, which was satellite to no other region, the development of national and regional metropolises was limited by their dependent status—for example, local metropoles, such as Sao Paulo, Brazil, or Buenos Aires, Argentina, could only achieve a dependent form of industrialization. Real development meant separating from the global capitalist system in a more autonomous economy. Similarly, in a hypothesis directly opposed to the finding of modernization geography that development was spread through contract with the metropolis, Frank hypothesized that the satellites experienced their greatest development when ties to the metropolis were weakest—historically during wars, geographically in terms of spatial isolation. In fact, for Frank, development could occur only when the links with global capitalism had been broken. By extension, regions that had the closest ties to the metropole in the past were the most underdeveloped in the present—Frank found this confirmed by what he called the "ultra-under-development" of the sugar-exporting region of northeastern Brazil and the mining regions of Bolivia. In summary, underdevelopment in Frank's theory was not an original condition of Third World societies. Nor did it result from archaic institutions surviving in isolated regions. Nor even did it stem from Third World irrationalism. Instead, underdevelopment was generated by the development of the center. In particular, underde-velopment in the periphery resulted from the loss of surplus expropriated for investment in the center's development (Frank 1969b, 1979). Frank's analysis, together with other work emanating from the Third World, con-stituting what came to be known as dependency theory, pointed to the need for social revolution in countries experiencing the development of underdevelopment. His article on "The Development of Underdevelop-ment" published in the *Monthly Review* was seen by the U.S. government as constituting a security threat, and he was sent a letter from the U.S. Attorney General telling him that he would not be allowed reentry into the United States (Editors of *Monthly Review* 2005).

An immediately noticeable weakness in Frank's theory resided in its failure to specify the exact economic mechanisms of surplus extraction. In some cases the mechanisms of surplus extraction are obvious—for example, European, North American, or Japanese corporations owning land and factories in Latin American countries could withdraw surplus as rent or profits, or banks in New York or IFIs in Washington lend-ing capital to peripheral states could withdraw surplus as interest. But what of peasant producers owning their own land and producing cash crops for export to center markets? Here the beginning of an answer was provided by Arghiri Emmanuel (1972; see also deJanvry 1981) in the "theory of unequal exchange." Like the ECLA economists, Emmanuel argued against classical (Ricardian) trade theory, which claimed that the international division of labor and the comparative advantage system of trade brought advantages to all participants (see Chapter 2). Specifically, Emmanuel argued that trade made poor countries poorer and rich countries richer. Emmanuel assumed the perfect international mobility of capital but also the *immobility* of labor between countries—hence, wage rates persistently differed greatly among regions. Peripheral countries exported agricultural products, embodying large quantities of cheap rural labor, and imported industrial products, embodying small amounts of expensive urban labor. This led the terms of trade to favor the higher-cost products of the center while devaluing the lower-cost exports of the periphery. Peripheral countries were prevented from achieving development because they sold their goods at prices below their values (the socially necessary labor embodied in the products), while rich countries sold goods at prices above their values. For Emmanuel, unequal exchange (through trade) was a hidden mechanism of surplus extraction and a major cause of the economic stagnation in the periphery. Samir Amin (1976: 143–144) estimated the amount of surplus transferred from poor to rich countries via unequal exchange to be 1.5% of the product of the rich countries but 15% of the product of the poor countries, an amount he found "sufficient to account for the blocking of the growth of the periphery." From the perspective of the dependency theorists, the peripheral countries have borrowed back their own surplus from the rich countries to finance "development schemes." The geopolitical implications of this finding are significant, namely, that Third World countries should be "forgiven" their debts because First World countries already owe them the money. Or, pushing this conclusion further, it is the First World countries that should be seeking forgiveness!

There were other, more serious, criticisms of Frank. The Brazilian economist Fernando Cardoso (1982) found Frank's notion of the development of underdevelopment a neat play on words but not very helpful in concrete terms. In Latin America, he maintained, multinational corporations invested in modern industrialization while supposedly traditional sectors (agriculture, mining) operated in technically and organizationally sophisticated ways, and both were parts of an advanced and yet dependent capitalist development. However, he added, in countries like Argentina, Brazil and Mexico spatial and sectoral dualism emerged, composed of both advanced sectors tied to the international capitalist system and backward sectors, characterized as "internal colonies." Multinational corporations were interested in at least some prosperity for dependent countries because of the markets they provided. But the Latin American countries remained heavily dependent for technology on the United States. In contrast to Frank's universalism, Cardoso wanted to look at specific situations in particular parts of the Third World where development and dependence could be found in tandem. We might note that, on becoming president of Brazil in 1995, Cardoso adopted a neoliberal development posture that can be seen as an extension of his version of dependency.

Dependency theory was holistic in that it attempted to place a country into the larger (global) system. In its simple form, it stressed the external causes of underdevelopment rather than causes internal to a peripheral society. Emphasis was placed on economic rather than social or cultural interactions. In Frank's version the accent was on regions, spaces, and flows ("circulation") rather than class. For most theorists dependency and underdevelopment were synonymous, although Cardoso, for example, thought that at least dependent forms of capitalist development could be achieved. Finally, dependency theory was politically radical, with most adherents proclaiming the need for some kind of socialist revolution, although a purely nationalist politics (merely altering a peripheral country's relations with the world capitalist system) could also emerge from the more spatial versions of the dependency perspective.

WORLD SYSTEMS THEORY

World systems theory has obvious affinities with the dependency school in its interest in centers and peripheries. But it had antecedents too in a theory of history named after *Annales: Economies, Sociétiés, Civilisations,* a journal founded in 1929 by French historians Lucian Febvre and Marc Bloch. Dissatisfied with conventional history for being too isolated and unrealistic, the *Annales* school wanted to remake the discipline. The *Annales* historians used a comparative method, over long sweeps of time, to examine differences and similarities between societies. The French geographer Vidal de la Blache, who believed that the *genre de vie* (way of life) mediated between people and nature, deciding which of nature's possibilities came to be realized ("environmental possibilism"), was an ally of a school of historical thought that always had a strong geographic component in its regional histories, geo-histories, and studies of transportation. The main themes of the *Annales* school were social history, especially of the material conditions of working people; structural factors or relative constants; the long term as a common language for the social sciences; and, while this was not a Marxist (mode of production) school of thought, a concern with the relations among the economy, society, and civilization. Ferdnand Braudel (1902–1985), the most famous of the school's second-generation scholars, was particularly interested in structural limitations on material and economic life, the great "slopes of historical change" (those lasting centuries), regional histories, and the sudden breakup of ancient ways of life in the 19th century (Braudel 1972, 1973). This view was found to be suited to the study of the long-term history of the people of the Third World and the sudden changes thrust upon them by contact with the First World.

A more obvious connection with development theory was forged by the sociologist Immanuel Wallerstein (1930–), an English-speaking representative of the *Annales* school. Wallerstein retained the broad spatial reach and long historical time span of *Annales* scholarship by treating world history as the development of a single system. By "system," Wallerstein meant a geographic entity with a single division of labor (see Chapter 2), so that all sectors or areas were dependent on the others via interchanges of essential goods. The historical past was characterized by minisystems, spatially small societies, each with a complete division of labor and a single cultural framework, as in early agricultural, or hunting and gathering, societies. But the recent integration of the last minisystems, such as the hill tribes of Papua New Guinea or the bushmen of the Kalahari, into the capitalist world system meant that small systems no longer existed. World systems characterized by a single division of labor—yet multicultural systems—had long been dominant, in Wallerstein's view.

The outstanding example, for Wallerstein, is the capitalist world economy, in which production is for profits and products are made to be sold on the market. In such a system production is constantly expanded as long as profits can be made, and producers innovate to expand the profit margin—hence, the secret of capitalist success is the pursuit of profit. In the past, world economies held together by strong states tended to become world empires, as with China, Egypt, or Rome. Surplus was extracted from peasants by political coercion (state force). These politically dominated systems, Wallerstein thought, tended to become unstable because states (governments) ran everything. With the rise of capitalism, by contrast, power passed to the private owners of means of production and to the market, with the state guaranteeing the political conditions for capital accumulation. The capitalist world economy resisted various attempts to create world empires (for example, by Britain and the United States), and capitalism (organized economically through markets) has therefore proven to be a lasting way of regulating and coordinating global production (Wallerstein 1979, 1980, 1988).

Within the world system there are, for Wallerstein, three main economic zones: core, semiperiphery, and periphery. Countries making up the core have efficient, complex production systems and high levels of capital accumulation. Core states are administratively well organized and are militarily powerful. Peripheral countries have the opposite characteristics. The semiperiphery combines elements of both. World systems theory saw spatial relations among zones as exploitative, that is, involving the flow of surplus from periphery to core, as in dependency theory. For world systems theory most of the surplus, accumulated as capital in the core, comes from local sources (the exploitation of local workers). But adding peripheral surplus reduces the level of class and interstate conflict in the core (Chase-Dunn 1989). For the periphery, loss of surplus means that capital needed for modernization is not available. In the periphery, the system of intense labor exploitation at low wage levels shapes class relations and fosters political conflict. Semiperipheral states function to prevent political polarization in the world system while collecting surplus for transmission to the core (Shannon 1989: Chapter 2).

For Wallerstein, the capitalist world economy originated in 16th-century Europe during an era of increased agricultural production for growing urban markets. At the ultimate core of the developing world capitalist economy, in England, the Netherlands, and northern France, a combination of pastoral and arable production required high skill levels and favored free agricultural labor (yeoman farmers). The periphery of this early world system—eastern Europe and increasingly the Americas—specialized in grains, cotton, and sugar, together with bullion from mines, all activities favoring the use of coerced labor (either a kind of serfdom that Wallerstein calls "coerced cash crop labor" in eastern Europe or slavery in the Americas). In between lay a series of transitional regions, mainly former cores degenerating toward peripheral status, making high-cost industrial products, giving credit, dealing in specie, and using sharecropping in the agricultural arena (for example, northern Italy). Whereas the interests of capitalist landowners and merchants coincided in the development of the absolute monarchy and strong central state machineries in the core, ruling class interests diverged sharply in the periphery, leading to weak states. Unequal exchange in commerce was imposed by the strong core on the weak peripheries, and the surplus of the world economy was thereby appropriated by the core (Wallerstein 1974: Chapters 2 and 3). From this geo-sociological perspective, Wallerstein outlined the main stages in the history of the world capitalist economy as follows:

1. The European world economy emerged during the extended 16th century (say, 1450–1640). The crisis of feudalism posed a series of dilemmas that could only be resolved through geographic expansion of the division of labor. By the end of the period northwest Europe had established itself as core, Spain and the northern Italian cities declined into the semiperiphery, and northern Europe and Iberian America were the main peripheries of the developing world system.

2. Mercantilist struggle during the recession of 1650–1730 left England as the only surviving core state.

3. Industrial production and the demand for raw materials increased rapidly after 1760, leading to geographic expansion of frontiers in what now became truly a world system under British hegemony. Russia, previously an important external system, was incorporated into the semiperiphery while the remaining areas of Latin America, and Asia and Africa were absorbed into the periphery. This expansion enabled some former areas of the periphery (the United States and Germany) to become at first semiperipheral, and then eventually core, states. The core exchanged manufactured goods with the periphery's agricultural products. The concentrated mass of industry created an urban proletariat that became an internal threat to the stability of the core of the capitalist system—the industrial bourgeoisie eventually had to "buy off" this threat with higher wages. This development also solved the problem of what to do with the burgeoning output from the new manufacturing industries (see the later section on Fordism in this chapter).

4. World War I marked the beginning of a new stage characterized by revolutionary turmoil (the Russian Revolution ended that country's further decline toward peripheral status) and the consolidation of the capitalist world economy under the hegemony of the United States instead of Britain. After World War II, the urgent need was expanded markets, met by reconstructing western Europe, reserving Latin America for U.S. investment, and decolonizing southern Asia, the Middle East, and Africa. Since the late 1960s, a decline in U.S. political hegemony has increased the freedom of action of capitalist enterprises, now taking the form of multinational corporations.

The world system thus has structural-spatial parts (center, semiperiphery, periphery) that evolve through stages of alternating expansion and contraction. Within such a framework, Wallerstein argued, comparative analyses of the whole system and the development of its regional parts can be made. World systems theory places regional development dynamics in a global context.

REGULATION THEORY

It is often said that Marxist and neo-Marxist theories are rife with tensions: between structural imperatives and peoples' struggles to change the conditions of their lives; between the unfolding of a world system and people's actions in creating history; or between structure and agency. Resolutions of these tensions emerge as different schools of Marxist thought.

One response was the Italian Marxist Antonio Gramsci's (1891–1937) concept of "hegemony." Writing from prison during the 1920s, Gramsci compared two Marxist notions of social control: *domination,* direct physical coercion of the people by state institutions like the police, army, and law in political society; and *hegemony,* ideological control through the production of consent by unions, schools, churches, families, and so on in civil society. Civil institutions, Gramsci thought, inculcated in people an entire system of values, beliefs, and morality that he found supportive of the established order and its dominating classes. Workers identified their own good with the good of the bourgeoisie and helped to maintain the status quo rather than revolting. Hegemony is a worldview diffused through socialization into every area of daily life that, when internalized, becomes "common sense." Hegemony mystifies power relations, camouflages the causes of public issues and events, encourages fatalism and political passivity, and justifies the deprivation of the many so that a few can live well. Hegemony works to induce oppressed people to consent to their own exploitation and misery.

Along with many other theorists, Gramsci was fascinated by the development of capitalism in the United States during the early 20th century. In his concept of "American Fordism" Gramsci explored the development of a new kind of hegemonic regime in which trade unions would be subdued, workers would be offered a higher real standard of living, and the ideological legitimation of this new kind of capitalism would be embodied in cultural practices and social relations extending far beyond the workplace. More simply, Fordist capitalism might achieve institutional stability through the achievement of willing consent (keeping people happy) through mass consumption. Revolutionary political transformation, Gramsci said, was not possible without a crisis of ideological hegemony—changes in civil as well as political society. Socialist movements, Gramsci concluded, had to create "counter-hegemony" to break ideological and cultural bonds and penetrate the false world of appearances as a prelude to the making of new ideas and values conducive to human liberation (Gramsci 1971 ed.; Boggs 1976).

Using these Gramscian ideas, a neostructural, neo-Marxist French regulation school developed in France during the 1970s, 1980s, and 1990s—"regulation" meaning control and management of social systems. Unlike conventional (orthodox) economics, the French regulation school does not provide a general transhistorical account of economies or economic behavior, as when Adam Smith declared all economic actors to be inherently and eternally self-interested, or Jeremy Bentham said that all behavior may be reduced to avoiding pain and pursuing pleasure. Nor does it see the expanded reproduction of capitalist production as the natural or unproblematic consequence of rational economic behavior—indeed, it sees continued capital accumulation as a crisis-ridden improbability. Instead, the regulation school is an historically specific and yet structural analysis of the changing combinations of economic and noneconomic institutions and practices that secure temporarily and spatially specific stabilities and predictabilities in accumulation (that is, development). It sees market forces as essentially anarchic (that is, the catastrophic collision of millions of selfish actions "coordinated" by a hand that is invisible because it is not there) and emphasizes the complementary functions of other social, cultural, and political mechanisms—like collective identities, common norms, and modes of calculation—in guiding continued capital accumulation. Regulation theory developed a new set of analytical concepts with terms to express them—accumulation regimes, modes and types of regulation—that differentiate the approach from other unconventional approaches. The regulation approach also tries to relate analysis of political economy to analyses of civil society and the state, showing how these broader social formations regulate, govern, or "normalize" the conflicts in capital accumulation. This school of thought found that the overall societal framework of capitalism contained several historical and geographic variants. It divided the history of capitalism into various periods, based essentially on the prevailing labor process: manufacture, dominant in the capitalist countries between 1780 and 1870; machinofacture, dominant between 1870 and 1940; scientific management (called Taylorism after its main practitioner, Frederick Winslow Taylor (1856–1915), "father of scientific management in industry") and Fordism, beginning at the turn of the century but dominant from 1940 to the late 1970s; and flexible accumulation, or post-Fordism, beginning with the economic crises of the 1970s and expanding rapidly during the late 20th century (Dunford and Perrons 1983).

The regulation school theorizes society in terms of development models, their parts and transformations: *regimes of accumulation* (basically periods of development) describe the main production–consumption relationships; and *modes of regulation* describe the cultural habits and institutional rules related to each period of capitalist development. Regimes of capital accumulation are periods of relatively settled economic growth and profits stretching across large spaces, like countries or regions, and several decades. Regimes eventually become exhausted, fall into crisis, and are torn down as capitalism seeks to remake itself and return to periods of profit making. Capital accumulation is stabilized by modes of regulation made up from the laws, institutions, social mores, customs, and hegemonies that collectively create institutional environments for long-run profit making (Lipietz 1985, 1986, 1987; Aglietta 1979).

What the regulation school calls "Fordism" (the term originally used by Gramsci) was pioneered by Henry Ford during the immediate pre-World War I years and became generalized in the United States from the 1920s onward. Ford linked two innovations: the semiautomatic assembly line, adopted between 1910 and 1914; and the $5 eight-hour working day, inaugurated on January 5, 1914 (this was twice the prevailing wage). In terms of regime of accumulation, Fordism entails standardization of production and separation of conception, organization, and control from manual work, yielding a rapid rise in the volume of goods produced per person (that is, in labor productivity) so that the time taken to construct a Model T car fell from 12 hours in 1910 to 1.5 hours in 1913. This expansion in productivity was counterbalanced by an equally massive growth in consumption, first by well-paid wage earners in the automobile industry, later by many other sectors of the population. In the Fordist mode of regulation the competitive mechanisms of 19th-century liberal capitalism declined in favor of compulsory agreements between capital and labor (collective bargaining), the hegemony of large companies, and limited (Keynesian) state control of the overall economy. It consisted of domestic mass production with a variety of institutions and policies supporting mass consumption, including stabilizing economic policies and Keynesian demand management that generated national demand and social stability; it also included a class compromise or social contract entailing job stability and wages that could comfortably support families, leading to broadly shared prosperity—rising incomes were linked to national productivity from the late 1940s to the early 1970s. And it turned out that this provided a logic for capitalist development that worked well—incomes that have to be spent on consumption and that increase with the productivity of commodity output, are fundamentally necessary to complete the virtuous circle of mass production–mass consumption.

As Gramsci (1971 ed.) originally observed, Ford's real goal was to create a new kind of worker, thoroughly Americanized and committed to conventional morality, who would never join a union. So, in terms of the mode of regulation, the workers were well paid, but they were controlled by consumption, advertising, and mesmerization by popular culture (mass media). Fordism's massive growth in production and consumption had the long-term effect of exacerbating the environmental crisis through the mass wasting of resources used in the fabrication of trend-driven commodities made popular through the mass media (see Figure 5.2). Fordism, however, attained its chief goal of generating rapid economic growth over several decades, particularly during the postwar period.

As an intensive regime of accumulation centered on a virtuous circle linking mass production with mass consumption, Fordism was rapidly enshrined in the capitalist social formations of the center countries after

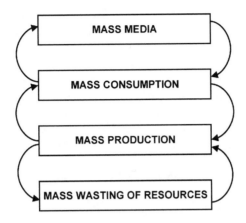

FIGURE 5.2. Fordism.

World War II, helping to produce economic growth rates typically of 4% a year. International trade was of secondary significance to the postwar Fordist model, the driving forces instead being the transformation of production processes linked to the expansion of markets internal to Fordist countries that experienced higher wages and increasing mass purchasing power. Peripheral social formations supplied labor and raw materials, with U.S. military domination assuring continued control over these resources.

What the regulation school terms a "crisis in Fordism" then occurred, possibly originating with a decrease in the growth of productivity and a fall in profitability in the Fordist countries. This led, in turn, to a more general economic crisis during the 1970s, characterized by the internationalization of production, state austerity programs, greater unemployment, and eventually a crisis of demand (that is, an underconsumption crisis). All these resulted in what the regulation school calls a new post-Fordist regime of "flexible accumulation" that has lasted from the mid-1970s to the present (Leborgne and Lipietz 1988; Piore and Sabel 1984). Instead of producing generic goods, companies increasingly produced diverse product lines aimed at specific groups of consumers and appealing to their tastes and changing fashions. Instead of investing huge amounts of money in the mass production of a single product, companies started building flexible systems of labor and machines that could respond quickly to the vagaries of the market. Modern "just-in-time manufacturing" (where parts arrive from all over the world just in time to be added to the product being assembled) is an example of flexible production. Thus, the geographer Allan

Scott (1988) argued that the typically rigid mass production processes of Fordism (that is, assembly lines turning out hundreds of thousands of exactly the same car model each year) gave way to changeable, computer-enhanced production processes, critically linked to an adaptable assortment of lowest-cost parts producers that in turn utilized flexible labor market arrangements (that is, increasingly employed nonunionized workers). The turn toward flexibility produced a new geography of Fordism: older centers of Fordist mass production, characterized by unions, rigid labor relations and governmental restrictions on producers, were avoided. The newly industrialized countries of Asia played increasingly important roles in producing manufactured goods. When flexible production began to gain a strong foothold in North America and western Europe, high technology industries were located in the suburbs of large metropolitan areas and in previously unindustrialized communities (Scott and Storper 1986).

These notions of Fordist and post-Fordist developmental systems are promises of a sophisticated neo-Marxist analysis of development. The concept of Fordism yields a sophisticated conception of development. As with Solow and the better neo-Keynesians, it emphasizes investment, technology, and growth. Unlike the neo-Keynesians, it then links greater productivity to higher worker incomes and the social construction of demand (through mass media advertizing and the like) in a virtuous circle of production and consumption. The most important point is that demand is politically, culturally, and socially created, an element missing from conventional economic theory. And production can be socially and politically designed and constructed to channel income to entirely different sets of classes. Fordist Keynesianism was the best of times for the working class under capitalism in terms of income, job security, and consumption. In brief, development managed (regulated) by states that are even remotely influenced by Keynesian social democracy can mitigate inequality and solve most problems associated with poverty. It is possible to have an economy that actually directs income toward those people who need it most rather than those who need it least. We know this because it happened for 30 years. Under Fordism (1945–1975) the working class almost got their share of the income produced by capitalist development. In contrast, under neoliberal post-Fordism all the increase in real income has gone to rich people (revisit Figure 1.1 on page 9) who, unable to spend it, have to save and invest under what is better phrased "finance capitalism." And further, much of the money invested has gone increasingly into such speculative financial vehicles as hedge funds and subprime mortgages rather than into productive ventures, helping to produce the financial crisis of 2007–2009 (Peet 2008).

CRITICISMS OF MARXIST
AND NEO-MARXIST THEORIES

Dependency theories, world systems theories, and regulation theories enjoyed wide support among critical social theorists and radical development practitioners from the 1960s through the 1980s, particularly in Latin America, India, and sub-Saharan Africa. World systems theory remains a leading source of innovative ideas and historical research, much of it published in the journal *Review*. But these theories have also come in for more than their share of criticism. Indeed, for some critics, dependency theory is so dated it can no longer be taken seriously—as one author said, dependency theory "is all but dead ... it is now a theoretical-political memory" (James 1997: 205). Economic growth in the newly industrialized countries of Latin America and East Asia during the 1970s and 1980s seemed to utterly contradict dependency theory's notion of blocked development in the periphery. Characterizing Frank and others as taking the position that capitalist development was impossible in the periphery, so that only underdevelopment was possible there (Bienefeld 1981), a number of writers (for example, Jackman 1984) showed that dependent countries can have economic growth rates higher than nondependent countries. Behind empirical inaccuracy, some critics said, lay basic errors in philosophy and theoretical methodology in neo-Marxist theory. Frank's mistake, in the view of sociologist Gabriel Palma (1978), lay in the "mechanico-formalistic" structure of his analysis, a formalism that rendered dependency theory static and unhistorical. Palma was particularly referring to dependency theory's tendency to see the internal structures of Third World countries as "mechanically determined" by their external relations with the First World. Palma wanted instead more specific studies that included the possibility of capitalist development in Latin America (see also Palma 1981).

Many later critiques followed a similar line of criticism. David Booth (1985) argued that the Marxist sociology of development (including dependency theory) reached an impasse in the 1980s related to generic difficulties in its underlying social theory. The basic problem with Marxist theory, for Booth, was its metatheoretical commitment to demonstrating that historical events were the necessary (determined) results of the objective laws of the teleological unfolding of capitalism ("teleological," conveying that the future is already contained in the dynamics of the present, that history is merely a route toward an already determined future). This commitment to necessity was expressed in development theory in two main forms:

The first operates through the way in which it is usual to conceive of the relation between the theoretical concept of the capitalist mode of production and the national or international economies, politics and social formations under analysis. The other—if anything more persistent and fundamental—involves a form of system teleology or functionalism. (Booth 1985: 773)

Booth relied on a critique by former structural Marxists Barry Hindess and Paul Hirst (1977; Cutler, Hindess, Hurst, and Hussain 1977–1978) that Marx "read off" the characteristics of social formations from the laws of motion of the capitalist mode of production—Hindess and Hirst objected to the idea that social totalities had necessary effects inscribed in their structures. In other words, the criticism is that structural Marxism sees real-world events as automatically generated by the laws of motion within capitalism. Booth found this a telling criticism of Marxist development theory as well. Either development problems were explained by their particular insertion into international capitalism, or socioeconomic processes took local forms that contributed to the wider process of capitalist accumulation. For Booth, ideas like these persisted because social scientists were seduced by notions of system teleology—for example, they wanted to discover deeper, more teleological, more functional reasons for development problems. In common with Giddens (1981) and following Hindess and Hirst (1977), Booth found this damaging to Marxism's intellectual standing. It was wrong, he said, to pretend that functional claims were explanatory—for example, Booth doubted the existence of feedback mechanisms of the type postulated by functionalism, whether Parsonian or Marxian. All this, he said, accounted for the repetitive, noncumulative character of the dependency literature, the forcing of Marxist theory along restricted lines, its failure to systematically explore urgent empirical issues. The rich complexity of reality, Booth concluded, could not be captured by the "theoretical nonsense" of the simple "laws of motion" of a system like a mode of production.

Further criticisms soon followed. Peter Vandergeest and Frederick Buttel (1988) criticized neo-Marxist theories from a Weberian perspective. Max Weber had criticized Marx for assuming that theoretical constructs, such as mode of production, were empirically valid to the point of being "real" whereas they were actually just "ideal types" (imperfect representations that stressed only some of the characteristics of a real phenomemon). Neo-Weberian Marxists instead constructed generalizations from grounded historical work and insisted on a continuing dialogue between theory and empirical evidence. For Vandergeest and Buttel, a synthesis of Weber and neo-Marxism could reconceptualize formal models as (Weberian) ideal types that might be used for a limited understanding but not a full explanation. They wished to discard some of the materialist tenets of historical materialism, like the base–superstructure metaphor, while modifying Weber, for example, replacing the notion of rational disenchantment of the world with comparative analyses of types of rationalization and derationalization. The Marxist conception of power would be broadened to include more varied kinds, while power would be reinterpreted as liberating and productive. Neo-Marxism's impoverished theory of the Third World state would be broadened to include theories of modern bureaucracy (from Weber) or reconceptualized to see the state as enabling and not just repressive—as with the social theorist Polanyi (1944). The incorporation of culture into a new neo-Weberian approach to development would look at how social groups (ethnic, class, or gender) viewed their worlds. Neo-Weberianism rendered the notion of "obstacles" to development irrelevant. For Vandergeest and Buttel (1998), development studies should deal with subjects whose behavior could not be fully understood. They preferred an agenda emphasizing empowerment and participation. In brief, they did not completely reject neo-Marxist development sociology but wished to augment it with neo-Weberian ideas.

However, the outstanding critique of neo-Marxist dependency and world systems theories came from a historian who is a Marxist. For Robert Brenner (1977, 1985), an entire line of Marxists and neo-Marxists intended to negate the optimistic model of economic advance derived from Adam Smith (that is, widening trade and a deeper division of labor bringing about economic development). But their negation ended up in a theory that was the mirror image of Smith's model. For Brenner, Frank found the dynamic of capitalist expansion to reside in the rise of a world commercial network, with growth or backwardness originating in the surplus appropriation chain. Wallerstein, Brenner continued, carried this to its logical conclusion by defining capitalism as production for profit via exchange and focusing on the expansion of the world market. With this market came a world division of labor, the development of different methods of labor control in the various specialized zones, and the creation of strong and weak states in the core and periphery. For Brenner, both analyses erred in displacing class relations from the main body of development theory. Brenner argued that the incorporation of more productive resources into an expanding world system did not determine the economic development process, nor did the transfer of surplus and the buildup of wealth in the core, nor even specialization in labor control systems. Capitalism, he said, differed from all previous societies in its systematic tendency to encourage economic development. This development is achieved through increasing labor productivity, which makes it possible for workers to produce commodities in less labor time than previously, yielding larger surpluses ("relative surplus labor," in Marx's terms). By comparison, precapitalist societies had extended "absolute labor" by lengthening the working day, gaining control over more workers, and so on. Under capitalist social relations, "free" workers could be combined with machines at the highest possible level of technology. Competition forced capitalists to innovate technologically to reduce the costs of production. Capitalist development thus derived from the class structure of the capitalist economy as a whole. This perception was ignored by Frank and Wallerstein altogether, according to Brenner. Frank's "circulationist" (rather than productionist) argument could be construed as applying only to regional autonomy (that is, development could be achieved through cutting the extent of surplus outflow). Brenner argued instead for changing the relations of production toward a class system characterized by efficiency but also equity. With the Brenner critique neo-Marxist development theory was thrown back in the direction of a more classically Marxist position centered on class rather than space.

Soon after Brenner penned these words (in the late 1970s), Marxism in its classical sense, as well as its neo-Marxist versions, came in for even more criticism as a politics, philosophy, and theory of development. The decline and eventual fall of the Soviet Union in 1989 left a political field so dominated by neoliberalism that the neoconservative thinker Francis Fukuyama (1989) could proclaim "the end of history" in the sense of an end to any socialist alternative to capitalism. The broad changes in intellectual culture that began during the early 1980s were marked generally by a retreat from radicalism. What had been taken for granted in the 1960s and 1970s became unmentionable in the 1990s. Development alternatives stemming from critical liberal dependency theory and socialist sources, notions of relative autonomy from the global system, using local productive resources to meet basic needs, the belief that the state should direct the economy toward developmental objectives—all of these were dropped from polite development discourse as irrelevant. The intellectual groundwork for this transformation in economic policy was prepared by a barrage of criticisms aimed at Marxism, the leading alternative philosophy to neoliberal theory. Historical materialism was called, among other things, economistic (the economy determines everything), functionalist (functions automatically produce human actions), totalistic (things have significance only in terms of their place within overarching structures), totalitarian (the whole taking precedence over the part justifies suppression of the individual), and teleological (history has a predetermined end).

Marxists replied that the notion of structural inevitability read into Marxism was largely a figment of the critics' own imagination. Contemporary structural Marxism derives far more from structural linguistics than functional structuralism. Far from elaborating utter structural necessities while leaving the empirical details of history and geography to be "read off" the objective laws of the motion of society, Marx's own work and the work of many Marxist theorists employ a rich complexity of structural necessity and contingent freedoms in the explanation of development—for example, the many empirical studies using the Marxian concept of articulation of modes of production (Long 1975; Post 1978; Rey 1973; Watts 1983). Historical events and geographic specificities are determined by contradictory structures and yet result also from the local specific actions of independent people (this is similar to the structure and agency formation). The dialectic between necessity and freedom lies at the heart of a materialist analysis that calls for revolutionary politics in the face of an overwhelmingly powerful global capitalist system. Non-Marxists, or very simple mechanical Marxists, have a nondialectical conception of structural determination in which structures mechanically cause things to happen, stamping out events like a machine stamps out spare parts. For some reason they read this simplicity into the whole of Marxism. Dialectical structuralism is nothing like these simple caricatures—as this chapter has abundantly demonstrated.

But what of the empirical, factual critique that the success of the NICs (South Korea, Singapore, Taiwan, Thailand, Brazil, Chile, Argentina, etc.) demonstrated that supposedly dependent countries could become developed and therefore that theories of dependency had been proven wrong by history? It is certainly true that these countries industrialized rapidly during the 1970s and 1980s, that they now have their own corporations operating on a global scale in direct competition with U.S. corporations, and that such countries are now developed in the conventional terms of income per capita whereas 40 years ago they were not. But recall Dos Santos's (1971) original definition of dependency that the development possibilities of subordinate economies are limited by the development and expansion of other economies. Since Dos Santos penned those words, globalization has made all economies dependent on the world market. Along with other countries, the NICs are vulnerable to capital flight and financial crises, as was shown repeatedly in the debt crises of the 1980s and the East Asian crisis of 1997, when Korea, Thailand, and several other "nondependent" countries had to submit to IMF restructuring to get loans (Born et al. 2003). And restructuring always means a neoliberal doctrine stressing strict limits to governmental intervention and the virtues of flexible, self-adjusting free markets. Stabilization and structural adjustment are forms of disciplining by policy discoursers emanating from the international financial institutions, the Treasury, and the investment banks in Washington, DC, and New York. At any one time the economies of 120 nation-states and the livelihoods of 2.5 billion people might be under their direct supervision. Thus, half the world's people are controlled by U.S.-dominated global governance institutions. The last three decades have not seen the end of dependency theory; rather, these years have witnessed the *intensification of dependency* in new global financial capitalist forms (Peet 2007).

SOCIALIST DEVELOPMENT IN THE USSR

Theory enables a lot to be said in a little space. But discussing development in purely theoretical terms, as we do in this book, produces an abstract atmosphere of unreality—the reader is never sure that he or she has got the main point. It also produces a view from the center, from the dominant places where theories are dreamed up. The theoretical memory can forget the practices, the ideas, and the politics of the people of the Third World. This point is discussed more in Chapter 6. For now, we merely want to mention that because Marxism, neo-Marxism, and democratic socialism are out of fashion in the two Cambridges, London, and even Paris (they were never in fashion in Washington, DC), this does not mean that the vision of a far different world of equality and social justice has disappeared elsewhere. So, let us finish this chapter with some case studies of development practice under socialism.

First, how was the Soviet economy organized (during the period 1917–1989), whose interests did it serve, and what were the outcomes in terms of the level of human development? The Soviet Union (USSR—Union of Soviet Socialist Republics) resulted from a popular revolution that overthrew the czar of Russia, ruler of the most underdeveloped country in Europe, in 1917. (The Soviet Union was invaded by the United States, Britain, France, Japan, and Canada in 1918–1919 and by Germany in 1941). After the revolution the economy of the Soviet Union was owned by the people via the Soviet state and its commissions and banks: Gosplan (State Planning Commission), Gosbank (State Bank), and Gossnab (State Commission for Materials and Equipment Supply). Starting in 1928, the economy was directed through five-year plans rather than through market forces, with overall goals for development set by the hierarchy of the Communist Party of the Soviet Union (CPSU) at meetings of the Party Congress. The Central Committee of the Communist Party and, more specifically, its leading members meeting as the Politburo set basic guidelines for planning via control figures (preliminary plan targets), major investment projects (capacity creation), and general economic policies. These guidelines were submitted as a report of the Central Committee to the Congress of the CPSU for approval. After approval, the list of priorities for the 5-year plan was processed by the

Council of Ministers, composed of industrial ministers, chairmen of state committees, and chairmen of agencies with ministerial status. This committee stood at the apex of a vast economic administration, including the state planning apparatus, the industrial ministries, the trusts (intermediate between the ministries and the enterprises), and finally the state enterprises. The Council of Ministers elaborated the Politburo plan targets and sent them to Gosplan, which gathered data on plan fulfillment. For every enterprise, the planning ministries defined the mix of economic inputs that would be used (labor, materials, machinery), a schedule for completion, and all wholesale prices and almost all retail prices. (Enterprises in the Soviet Union were more than places of work; they were responsible for a variety of social welfare functions—building and maintaining housing for their workforces, and managing health, recreational, educational, and related facilities.) The Soviet industrial effort was concentrated on the production of capital goods through the metallurgical, machine manufacture, and chemical industries—what were called group A goods, or means of production goods, with the aim of developing the productive forces to produce the rapid industrialization of the Soviet Union.

After the death of Stalin in 1953, Group B consumer goods received more emphasis in an attempt at improving the (consumptive) standard of living. Information flowed from the top downward and some goods (for example, radio and television parts) tended to be underproduced, leading to shortages and long lines at the shops, while other goods were overproduced. Heavy industry, always the focus of the Soviet economy, grew rapidly, making the Soviet Union one of the leading industrial countries in the world, enabling its high-tech sector to make steady progress, which culminated in the launching of the first satellite (Sputnik 1) into space in 1957 (much to the amazement of the U.S. State Department). After the Bolshevik Revolution of 1917, the country grew from a largely underdeveloped peasant society with minimal industry to become the second-largest industrial power in the world, as the country's share of world industrial production grew from 5.5% of global production in 1913 to 20% in 1980. The Soviet Union constructed a heavy industrial base in an underdeveloped economy without waiting for capital to accumulate and without relying on external financing. Industrialization came with better medical, health, and other social services, improving labor productivity. Campaigns were carried out against typhus, cholera, and malaria; the number of physicians increased as rapidly as facilities and training would permit; and death and infant mortality rates steadily decreased. The Soviet Union provided comprehensive healthcare to all its people as a basic human right. In 1990, the Soviet Union had a Human Development Index of 0.91, which compares with an index range of 0.95–0.99 for most western European countries and 0.88 for South Korea and Portugal. Its real GDP per capita was $6,270, higher than the best-off Latin American countries ($4,000–$5,000), but lower than western European countries ($10,000–$14,000). Life expectancy at birth was 71 years (compared with 76 years in the United States and 70 years in South Korea), the adult literacy rate was 99%, the number of doctors, scientists, and technicians was high, and there were more women than men in college-level education (UNDP 1991: 119, 174).

The planning system in the Soviet Union became cumbersome and ineffective as the economy became more complex. The volume of decisions facing planners in Moscow was overwhelming. Cumbersome procedures for bureaucratic administration did not enable the free communication and flexible response required at the enterprise level for dealing with worker alienation, innovation, customers, and suppliers. Calls for greater freedom for managers to deal directly with suppliers and customers were gaining influence among reform-minded communist cadres during the mid-1970s and 1980s. The Soviet Union did not allow democratic decision making. Party Congresses became formalistic exercises; the (relatively small) Communist party served as an elite, distant, and privileged minority government; and the people were often suppressed, at times ruthlessly. The Soviet Union was an elite society that used "communism" to control the masses. During the 1980s new thinking by younger communist *apparatchiks* (functionaries) began to emerge, culminating in Mikhail Gorbachev's assumption of the position of general secretary of the Communist party in March 1985. Gorbachev introduced programs of *glasnost* (political openness), *perestroika* (economic restructuring), and *uskoreniye* (the speeding-up of economic development), beginning in 1986. In the past, economic planners had made little effort to determine what Soviet consumers really wanted, which often resulted in severe shortages of some consumer goods and poor-quality food products often marketed under primitive conditions, such as inadequate refrigeration. The Soviet economy suffered from pervasive supply shortages aggravated by an increasingly open black market that undermined the official economy. Additionally, the costs of superpower status—for the military, space program, and subsidies to client states—could not, in the end, be supported, and the communist system rapidly faded during the late 1980s. Following the gradual dissolution of the Soviet Union during the early 1990s, all the former Soviet republics scrapped their Soviet-era systems of centralized planning and state ownership to varying degrees and with mixed results. The GNP of Russia, the primary surviving entity, is now comparable to that of such countries as Brazil and Australia, and its citizens' life expectancy at birth has dropped to 66 years (Gregory and Stuart 2001).

CUBA

Second, let us look at the organization of the Cuban economy. The "26th of July Movement," led by Fidel Castro, overthrew the government of Fulgencio Batista in 1959. Castro was sworn in as prime minister of Cuba in 1960, and became first secretary of the Communist party in 1965. After the revolution, the Cuban economy was partially nationalized. All estates over 400 hectares were nationalized and huge tracts of land owned by U.S. companies were expropriated by the state, along with such foreign-owned assets as the Texaco, Standard Oil, and Shell Oil refineries. A number of other economic measures were taken, including reducing housing rents by 50%, cutting the cost of medicine, and expanding provisions for welfare, healthcare, and education. In April 1961 at the Bay of Pigs in southwestern Cuba, a U.S.-planned and -funded invasion by armed exiles attempting to overthrow Castro's government was successfully repulsed by the Cuban army. In 1962, the United States imposed an economic, commercial, and financial embargo, undertaken with the stated aim of "bringing democracy to the Cuban people." Much later, the Helms–Burton Act of 1996 further restricted U.S. citizens from doing business with Cuba and in 1999 President Bill Clinton further expanded the trade embargo. Originally the Cuban economy had been highly dependent on the United States, which at one time provided 65% of Cuba's imports and accounted for 75% of Cuba's exports (Cole 1998: 22). In this hostile context, Castroite Cuba quickly established strong economic ties with the Soviet Union. Soviet influence led to the introduction into Cuba of centralized planning and a command economy. In 1961 the Central Planning Board, JUCEPLAN, was set up to plan and coordinate economic activity. The economy was divided into sectors, investment goals were set by state budgetary authorities, prices were fixed, and consumer goods were allocated through rationing. The initial aim of economic policy was diversification of the Cuban economy, especially by reducing its previous dependence on sugar, and the promotion of import substitution industrialization. In 1968 the "Revolutionary Offensive" brought all nonagricultural private-sector businesses under state control, but the role of the Central Planning Board was reduced and planning carried out on a more ad hoc basis. Political consciousness was used to promote economic development—a policy change that arose from the "Great Debate" of 1962–1965 over moral incentives (commitment to the aims of a revolutionary society) versus material incentives (higher wages for greater effort). The basic aim was reconciling national economic development objectives with social rather than individual gains. Ché Guevara, who as minister of industries was the main proponent of moral incentives, argued that money and material incentives should be phased out and replaced by socialist consciousness and popular participation.

While initial efforts produced a new form of social and economic organization by the mid-1960s, the economic planning system became chaotic, resulting in a shortfall in the planned 10-million-ton sugar harvest in 1970, which was taken as a symbol of failure of the new Cuban economy. Between 1970 and 1986, material incentives were reintroduced, and the Cuban economy was reorganized along Soviet lines. In 1973 the Economic Management and Planning System (SDPE), based directly on 1965 Soviet economic reforms, was introduced, resulting in significant growth in the Cuban economy during the remainder of the 1970s, in contrast to economic decline elsewhere in Latin America and the Caribbean. However, the SDPE also became increasingly inefficient and wasteful; the system's incentive structures were poorly organized and led to cynicism, a lack of work discipline, and reduced collective rights and responsibilities, problems that arose from a lack of genuine involvement and participation by workers and the people in the determination of economic development. The main response was the establishment of Poder Popular (Popular Power) in 1976 and 1977, an attempt to fuse democratic political structures with the economic system to create a sense of political and work responsibility (Cole 1998). By 1986, Cuba's income inequality index (Gini coefficient) was, laudably, among the lowest in the world. Health and education had been favorably transformed (despite the emigration during the early 1960s of most professionals, largely to the United States), and life expectancy, infant mortality, literacy, and scientific and technical education levels approached those of the leading capitalist countries—even though per capita income remained comparable to that of other underdeveloped countries.

The collapse of the Soviet bloc in 1989 was a disastrous development for Cuba. At the time, the Soviet Union accounted for 85% of Cuba's trade, and foreign trade accounted for around half of the national income. Moreover, Cuba imported two-thirds of its food, nearly all its oil, and 88% of its machinery and spare parts from Soviet bloc countries while exporting agricultural products, primarily sugar, in exchange, with an implicit subsidy (estimated relative to world market prices) for Cuba of about $5 billion per year. As a result of the ongoing communist implosion, Cuban imports fell by 70% between 1989 and 1993, and GDP fell by 50%, with a catastrophic effect on living standards. Industrial production fell to 15% of capacity, factories closed, the sugar harvest was halved in three years, public transport collapsed, oil-fired electrical plants operated only sporadically (with power cuts of up to 10 hours a day), the supply of fresh water was disrupted, agriculture was paralyzed, produce rotted in fields because of lack of transport, and tractors and mechanical harvesters broke down and could not be repaired. The quantity of food produced on the island fell by one-third, and food imports decreased by nearly one-half. Official estimates suggest that food availability per person per day dropped from 3,000 calories and 73 grams of protein in the 1980s to about 1,860 calories and 46 grams of protein by 1993—less than the amount available per person in Haiti or Bangladesh. Famine and serious malnutrition were averted only by careful monitoring of food and a continued emphasis on its equitable distribution, although this equity is beginning to erode in the face of access by only part of the population to convertible currencies from tourism, remittances and other sources.

A "Special Period in Time of Peace," declared in 1990, involved a radical restructuring of political economy, the forms of social regulation, and cultural ideological production. Many large state farms were broken up into smaller cooperatives that are self-managed and financially independent, though output goals are still decided by the ministry of agriculture. Concessions were offered to foreign investment mainly in tourism but also in nickel mining and processing, oil prospecting, steel, and transport and communications. State subsidization of enterprises was reduced, some prices increased, and taxes imposed on some economic activities. The net economic effect of the changes introduced during the Special Period was positive. The economy was saved from collapse, and since 1995 Cuba has grown more rapidly than most other Latin American countries (Susman 1998). The state subsidized, to the extent of $1 billion, the development of biotechnical and pharmaceutical industries, and it continues to set their research agendas. Most importantly, key aspects of the Cuban revolution, such as free education and health care for all, were maintained, if not increased (Dilla 1999), in the midst of increased confrontation with the United States and a tightening of the economic blockade. With legalization of the U.S. dollar's circulation in 1993, the Cuban economy experienced a split, with a centrally planned socialist industrial economy based on the peso on one side and an expanding export-oriented and partially market-based dollar service economy on the other. These economic "reforms" have led to major changes in the class structure of Cuban society (Cole 2002; Hamilton 2002).

The result of this difficult and contested socialist development process is that Cuba has a Human Development index of 0.82 (comparable to Uruguay's 0.684 reading and Mexico's 0.81 level), a life expectancy at birth of 77 years, a 97% literacy rate, and an infant mortality rate of 6 per 1,000 live births (lower than the 9 per 1,000 figure for the United States). This last favorable statistic results from Cubans' access to free healthcare for everyone and from Cuba's having the largest number of physicians (591) per 100,000 people in the world and committing 7.5% of its GDP to health expenditures, a proportion similar to Britain's

(7.7%) expenditure (UNDP 2005: 219, 238, 250). In spite of the economic disaster of the early 1990s, Cuba continues to rank among the top
5% of 125 developing countries on indicators of social development such
as life expectancy, infant and maternal mortality, adult literacy, primary
and secondary school enrollment, and many others. How has this been
possible? A general answer is that Cubans' commitment to meeting basic
needs has not wavered. Improvements in education and health as well
as the virtual elimination of absolute poverty were among the proudest
achievements of the Cuban revolution. These social gains also helped
provide legitimacy and widespread popular support to the revolutionary state. Therefore, public expenditure on health, education, and other
social programs was maintained near precrisis levels even after total state
expenditures had been cut by over 15%. Social expenditures increased
from less than one-third of GDP in the late 1980s to about two-fifths of
GDP in the 1990s. This was supplemented by popular participation at
local levels in the administration and delivery of social services.

VENEZUELA

Finally, we turn our attention to Venezuela. For the 40 years prior to
Hugo Chávez's election as president of Venezuela in 1998, two traditional parties shared power and competed for control over the country's
most important institutions, while the oil wealth of Venezuela circulated
almost exclusively within elite circles. All the while, the populace was
fed a powerful nationalist rhetoric of "sowing the oil"—everyone got a
few seeds. Nevertheless, the richest 10% of the population got 37% of
the national income, the poorest 10% got 0.9%, and 23% of the people
lived on less than $1 a day, proportions typical of most Latin American
countries. In the 1998 elections Hugo Chávez, an army officer committed
to social transformation, ran as the presidential candidate of the MVR
(Movimiento Quinta Republica), a new political "antiparty," and won
by a landslide. Chávez was seen by the marginalized majority as the "best
and only voice" against global neoliberal economic and political forces
that were arrayed against the poor. Chávez came into office committed to
strengthening the role of the state in the economy and began by ordering
the military to devise programs to combat poverty and further civic and
social development in Venezuela's urban barrios and poor rural areas.
This civilian–military program, "Plan Bolivar 2000," included road
building, housing construction, mass vaccinations, land reform, the low-
ering of infant mortality rates, the implementation of a free government-
funded healthcare system, and a system of free education up to the university level. By the end of 2001, the Chávez administration reported an

increase in primary school enrollment of one million students. The objective of the Bolivarian movement is greater participation by citizens in equitable social, economic, and political structures in a newly participatory and protagonistic democracy. To build people's capacity to practice self-determination through direct democracy, Chávez envisions a strong state role in reducing poverty and comprehensively increasing social welfare. The Chávez administration sees poverty and underdevelopment as deriving from the inequitable distribution of profits from the country's vast oil reserves. To ensure that revenues from national resources benefited everyone, the government proposed radical wealth redistribution and increased social investment, in direct contrast to neoliberal policies applied elsewhere in Latin America.

The key factor is this: Venezuela has the largest proven oil reserves in the western hemisphere (78 billion barrels) and the largest in the world (300 billion barrels) if the Orinoco tar belt is included. The Venezuelan state owns significant downstream refining and distribution facilities. In 2004, Chávez raised the royalty tax on companies working in the Orinoco belt from the 1% they had been paying to 16.6%. All the affected companies, except Exxon Mobil, acquiesced. New projects have a royalty rate of 30%. Chávez has energy agreements with China, Argentina, and India. He also wants to create an organization—Petrosur—uniting all state hydrocarbons companies in the region, with the goal of excluding the big multinational oil companies from energy development (Wilpert 2006; Weinstein 2005).

Surviving a coup attempt in 2002 of which the U.S. State Department had foreknowledge, Chávez subsequently intensified his program of fundamental social and economic transformation. Chávez expanded his land redistribution and social welfare programs by authorizing and funding "Bolivarian missions" involving massive government antipoverty initiatives, the construction of thousands of free medical clinics for the poor (which resulted in marked improvements in the infant mortality rate), the institution of educational campaigns, and the enactment of food and housing subsidies. The missions involve widespread experimentation with citizen- and worker-managed governance as well as the granting of thousands of free land titles to formerly landless poor and indigenous communities. In March 2006 a Communal Council Law allowed communities that organize themselves into councils to be given official state recognition and access to federal funds and loans for community projects, bypassing local and state governments seen as corrupt. In September 2006, the new mayor of Caracas, Juan Barreto, an ally of Chávez, ordered the forced acquisition of two golf courses within the city limits to gain land on which to build subsidized houses for 11,500 poor families (20 families can survive for a week on what it costs to maintain a square meter of golf course grass). Teodoro Petkoff, editor of the daily newspaper *Tal Cual,* and an opposition politician, said that Barreto suffered from "megalomaniacal delirium" (Romero 2006).

In his second presidency, following elections in 2000 (and after surviving a recall referendum in 2004) Chávez placed greater emphasis on alternative economic development and international trade models, much of it in the form of hemisphere-wide international aid agreements. A joint declaration signed by the presidents of Venezuela and Cuba on December 14, 2004, asserted that neoliberalism acts as "a mechanism to increase dependence and foreign domination." The presidents of the two countries, Hugo Chávez and Fidel Castro, denounced the Free Trade Area of the Americas (FTAA), proposed by the United States as the "expression of a hunger to dominate the region." The free trade agreement, they averred, would result in unprecedented levels of poverty and subordination in Latin America. Their joint declaration maintaints that, while economic integration is necessary if Latin American countries are to occupy a prominent position in the world economy, integration has to be based on cooperation, solidarity, and a common willingness to advance to a higher level of development (Joint Declaration 2004). Opposed to a uni-centered world focused on the United States and western Europe, Chávez favors a multicentered world that provides new political spaces in which people, particularly in the Third World, can organize themselves in ways they themselves determine. As an alternative to the proposed FTAA, Chávez proposed the Bolivarian Alternative for the Americas (ALBA) as Venezuela's vision for regional economic integration and social development. ALBA's key supporters (Chávez and Castro) identify its chief thrust as a "process which will assure the elimination of social inequalities, and promote quality of life and the peoples' effective participation in forging their own destiny." Chávez has articulated the following key strategic elements of alternative integration: (1) mechanisms to overcome disparities among and within nations, building equality between countries in trade negotiations and between citizens; (2) national sovereignty in setting domestic development priorities and policies, diminishing the control of foreign capital over local economies; (3) prioritizing the role of the state in providing basic services such as healthcare, housing, and education; (4) protection for agricultural production as part of cultural identities, people's relationships with nature, and critical for food security and self-sufficiency; (5) removing obstacles to access to information, knowledge, and technology; and (6) a critique of free trade as an automatic guarantor of higher levels of growth and collective well-being (Joint Declaration 2004).

The basic political-economic principle supporting these strategies is complementarity. The principle of complementarity rests on the coordination of economic activities so that countries get mutual benefit from trade relationships. Complementarity allows each trading partner to make up for what the other lacks by supplying finance, technology, and knowledge into building the other's productive capacity. Venezuela supplies Cuba with oil, and Cuba supplies Venezuela with medical doctors. Venezuela and Cuba (and subsequently Bolivia, Nicaragua, and Ecuador) identify solidarity as the "cardinal principle" by which ALBA must be guided. Integration supports domestic development so that each country is more self-sufficient and therefore more sovereign. Latin America cannot be free if countries in the region are isolated from one another (Joint Declaration 2004). Therefore, Bolivarianism is against nationalism to the detriment of other peoples, or restrictive domestic policies that inhibit the construction of regional alliances. In the discourse of ALBA, asymmetries in negotiating power between regional allies are reframed in the concepts of justice, equality, and reciprocal solidarity (Joint Declaration 2004). By creating a regional trading bloc, ALBA strengthens individual countries' negotiating positions in the global arena. Instead of countries individually entering into bilateral agreements with powerful countries, a South American/Caribbean bloc would help reduce dependence on U.S. markets and ensure that the region has greater leverage in trade and investment negotiations with the United States, Europe, and Asia (Redman 2006). In April 2006 the presidents of Venezuela, Cuba, and Bolivia signed an agreement for the creation of the Bolivarian Alternative for the Peoples of Our America (ALBA) and a Peoples' Trade Agreement. Article 5 of the agreement reads: "The countries agree to make investments of mutual interest which could take the form of public, binational, mixed or cooperative companies, joint management projects or any other form of association that they decide to establish. Priority shall be given to the initiatives which strengthen the capacity for social inclusion, resource industrialization and food security, in a framework of respect and preservation of the environment" (Peoples' Treaty 2006). With initial financing of $1 billion, the Bank of ALBA will finance economic integration and infrastructural development as well as fund social, educational, cultural, and health programs in the member countries. Unlike other IFIs, such as the World Bank or IMF, the Bank of ALBA will not impose loan conditions and will function on the consensus of all its members.

CONCLUSION: DEVELOPMENT IN CONTENTION

The ongoing struggles in Cuba and Venezuela typify "development in contention." As we explained in Chapter 1, development is the method used by a people and their institutions, predominantly the state, to pursue a better or more ideal society. Seriously intended, development entails not only "growth that raises all boats" but also economic transformation that results in income redistribution, better living standards for poor people, equal access to medical care, and other similar social objectives. In the Marxist conception, development that transforms society is necessarily accompanied by class struggle between the rich and the poor. Development means using the power of the state, backed by mass people's movements, to change society in favor of the oppressed. For Marxists, socialist democracy means control of the state and its institutions by the majority of the people. In the Third World especially, this means control by the 90% of people who are poor. But even in the First World, it means control by poor and relatively poor majorities. Development means social transformation that allows widespread freedom. The amazing thing is that so many people struggle so tenaciously for this deeply felt kind of freedom in a neoliberal world utterly opposed to it—to the point of launching invasions, coups, assassination attempts, blockades, and barrages of threatening rhetoric backed by Patriot missiles and Stealth fighter aircraft. For socialists, the struggle continues simply because they believe their cause is right.

6

Poststructuralism,
Postcolonialism, and
Postdevelopmentalism

Between the mid-1960s and early 1980s, critical thinking about development was dominated by Marxist and neo-Marxist theories. This critical thinking took systematic and structural forms. These highly generalized theories tried to position every historical event and place each social characteristic as a component of some more general overarching system, be it mode of production, world capitalist system, or global market. Explaining something meant putting it into the context of its more general system or structure. The aim was nothing less than a systematic theory of social totalities, their parts, and their developmental dynamics, with nothing left unexplained or attributed to chance, although some aspects might have to be examined empirically. Structural theories were the basis for political and social movements calling for the transformation of society through development—that is, development is a way of restructuring society. The theories behind all this can be seen as culminating triumphs of radical modern social philosophy.

Structural theories of a critical nature have always been greeted with suspicion, even antagonism, from the political right. However structural explanation and even social transformation came to be regarded with suspicion among many critical thinkers during the 1970s and early 1980s—structuralism in the sense both of societies considered as whole entities and theories as holistic explanations. Elements of this critical theorizing began to take various "*poststructural*" forms, particularly in France during the 1970s, with these philosophies spreading to Britain and the United States during the 1980s and coming into full prominence during the 1990s. The appearance of Edward Said's book *Orientalism* (1979) was a significant moment in the application of poststructural ideas to the relations between the First and Third Worlds. And from the mid-1980s onward, poststructural ideas began to appear in critical developmental studies and postdevelopmental thought.

Some apparently *post*structural thinkers actually continued to think structurally, but in new ways. For example, the French poststructural sociologist Jean Baudrillard (1929–2007) argued that societies in the late 20th century were taking new forms—a structural shift had occurred from mode of production, understood in the traditional Marxist sense (see Chapter 5), to what he called "code of production"—that is, signs and cultural codes rather than material production as the primary constituents of social life (Baudrillard 1983). For Baudrillard, we live in a "hyperreality" of simulations in which image, spectacle, and the interplay of signs (TV, text messaging, YouTube) are among the most important dimensions of life, whose symbolic logic replaces the logic of production in significance. The human experience is of a simulated reality rather than reality itself. This experience was still structural, but it represented a different interpretation emphasizing culture rather than economy.

Many other poststructural thinkers attacked structural understanding altogether rather than merely shifting its emphasis, seeing events as occuring in a far more anarchic world than structuralism posits. Theirs is a world of spontaneous events that "just happen"—discontinuities rather than continuities of history, complexity rather than structural simplicity. Whereas structuralism saw transcendent systems lending significance to the individual (event or person), many poststructualists wanted to return significance to the singular (event or person)—that is, something is not important because of its role in the larger scheme of things ... it is just important in and of itself. Whereas structuralism, in its critical forms, usually employs economic languages to criticize capitalism (understood as a class system), poststructuralism uses cultural language to criticize modernity (understood as a semiotic or sign system). Whereas structuralism saw potential for human emancipation in modern development, poststructuralism saw development as a strategy of modern power and social control. These and other markers indicated a divide in critical social thought as wide, some might say, as that between premodern (for example, mystical) and modern (for example, rational) thought—hence, the notion of a *post*modern era of thought and culture characterized by disillusionment and loss of faith in modern metanarratives (great stories) like truth, emancipation, democracy, revolution, or development (Lyotard 1984). For the postmodern theorist, it was as though the Enlightenment and its progeny had finally been laid to rest. A new era had begun ... if, that is, history even takes the form of "eras"!

THE ENLIGHTENMENT AND ITS CRITICS

The philosophies that characterize the modern Western world, from the Enlightenment thinkers of the 18th century to the scientific positivists of the 19th century and the modernization theorists of the 20th, saw human reason and rational behavior as the mainsprings of social progress. Ideas that are strenuously empirically based but also thought to be logical intervene productively between human beings and the rest of the natural world. Reasoned thinking produces science and technology as new sources of material progress and human well-being; science replaces religion as the main mode of understanding (although this never happened with any degree of completeness); happiness on earth replaces heavenly salvation as the main reason for living. Some modernists even believe that ethics can be rationalized—that is, by examining the lessons of experience, social norms, values, and morals, can be humanly reasoned by everyone rather than magically divined from the hints of God's mysterious intent. Hence, morality can be accepted as just and right by all thoughtful, responsible, and reasonable people. By synthesizing science with morality, a normative ("normative" referring to value-laden) science could act on behalf of the interests of humanity, enabling emancipation from nature and want and from superstition and ignorance. People can act rationally in all aspects of their lives. In a phrase, for the modernist, reason makes possible science that enables development on behalf of all humanity.

The philosophers of the Enlightenment considered all people to be "indefinitely perfectible." Everyone was capable of self-guidance directed solely by the light of reason—and "reason is the same for all thinking subjects, all nations, all epochs, and all cultures" (Cassirer 1951: 5, 13–14). At least that was the promise. Yet, reason, and the freedom from nature that it brought, were said to reach their highest, most developed, forms in Europe. In *Sketch for an Historical Picture of the Progress of the Human Mind* the Enlightenment philosopher Antoine-Nicolas de Condorcet (1972: 141) observed:

> Our hopes for the future condition of the human race can be subsumed under three important heads: the abolition of inequality between nations, the progress of equality within each nation, and the true perfection of mankind. Will all nations one day attain that state of civilization which the most enlightened, the freest, and the least burdened by prejudice, such as the French and the Anglo-Americans, have attained already? Will the vast gulf that separates these peoples from the slavery of nations under the rule of monarchs, from the barbarism of African tribes, from the ignorance of savages, little by little disappear? ... These

> vast lands ... need only assistance from us to become civilized [and] wait only to find brothers amongst the European nations to become their friends and pupils. (de Condorcet 1972)

Thus, an Enlightenment map of the world saw global space as divided between a center of reason, knowledge, and wisdom in western Europe and a periphery of ignorance, barbarity, and only potential reason elsewhere. The "idea of progress," which the social theorist Theodore Shanin (1997: 65) found to be the main legacy of modernity, envisaged all societies advancing "up" a route leading from diverse barbarisms to a singular European-style rationalized democracy. Europe was destined to lead the world. Europe's enlightened generosity should be demonstrated by helping others ("our pupils"). This version of Enlightenment thinking is very similar to the modernization theory discussed in Chapter 4, similar because it is the philosophical basis of modernization theory. It is more egalitarian than racism in that it says that all people are capable of rational thinking. But it also says that "we got to rationality first ... and now we can help you." And with this, postmodernists claim, democratic Enlightenment thinking turned into its opposite, oppressive rationalism, the conception of a teleologically directed history (that is, history inevitably aimed at the world victory of Western rationalism) and a predestined geography (rationalism diffusing from its Euro-American sources).

Poststructural and postmodern philosophies try to reveal the inherent flaws in this entire modern, confident, structural stream of thought. Poststructural thinking, especially in its more postmodern forms, emphasizes the other sides of modern rationality—its peasant, female, and colonized victims; its disciplinary institutions (schools, prisons, psychiatric clinics); and its sacrifice of spontaneity, emotion, and pleasure suppressed under rational control—the idea that modern people suffer by continually scrutinizing the emotional upsurge of pleasurable, free behavior through the lenses of logic, thought, and rationalized ethics (we consciously have to *try* to relax). In poststructural philosophy, modern reason is reinterpreted critically as a mode of social control that acts openly through disciplinary institutions (schools and the like), in more disguised forms through rationalized socialization (the enforcement of "responsible" behavior), and, most subtly, seditiously through rational self-discipline (limiting one's own thoughts and behavior through rational self-inspection).

In the *poststructural* view, modern philosophy's claim to universal truth is rejected as practically impossible but also dangerously motivated. The poststructural philosopher Richard Rorty (1979, 1991), criticizes modern theories of "representational truth" in which systems of symbols (statements, theories, models) accurately reflect ("mirror") real and separate structures of events. In poststructural thinking such as his, representational theories of truth can never be totally "accurate"; even at their best, they provide the perspective of a particular prejudiced thinker. In poststructural philosophy, especially the work of French philosopher Jacques Derrida (1930–2004), the relations between reality and mind are not direct, and therefore ideas cannot be objectively accurate ("truthful") but instead are linguistically mediated—that is, the play of language creates what is only taken to be "true." Derrida's notion of deconstruction was a poststructural/postmodern expression of skepticism about the possibility of telling coherent truths (Derrida 1974, 1978). "Deconstruction," in Derrida's use of the term, means reading a text (such as a theoretical statement) in such a way that weaknesses in its conceptual structure can be revealed through the inconsistencies in its analytical terms—that is, the text is shown to fail by its own criteria of logic and consistency. Derrida wanted to use deconstruction to deprive theorization of its logical authority as an attack on the certainties of what he found to be an overly arrogant, even dangerous, modernity. Hence, poststructuralism attacks the central tenets of modern progress: reason, truth, accuracy (Best and Kelner 1991). The postmodern end of poststructural theory abandons the notion of the rational unified subject in favor of a socially and linguistically decentered and fragmented subject with multiple identities. For these poststructural philosophers, too, absolute truth is impossible. Relative semitruths are the best we can do—or, more extremely, why talk of truth at all?

In particular, as Robert Young (1990: 9) points out, a special interest of French poststructural philosophy concerns the relation between the claim of the Enlightenment to speak universal truth and the ascendance of the Europeans to universal power. The new stress on this relation, Young says, had stimulated a "relentless anatomization of the collusive forms of European knowledge." Especially important is the geo-philosophical belief, buried at the heart of Western modernity, that European Enlightenment thinking *is* universal reason—for example, as we saw earlier, that classical economics, born from the prejudices of English gentlemen-scholars, is a universal economic science capable of representing all productive thinking. Added to this is the normative prescription that copying European rationality and European models (of economy, for example) is good for everyone, what all people *should* do. Hence, Derrida (1971: 213) said, "The white man takes his own mythology, Indo-European mythology, his own *logos*, that is, the *mythos* of his idiom, for the universal form of that he must still wish to call Reason." That is, Europeans take their own specific way of thinking, the mythologies of their own history, to be reason incarnate and call it science. In brief, poststructural and postmodern criticism consider "reason" to be a historical and regional form of biased, incomplete, and often mythological thought rather than a universal rationality with liberatory potential.

How does this relate to Marxism? Sometimes Marxism is seen as a utopian form of Enlightenment rationalism and sometimes as the Enlightenment's most persistent critique. On the one side, there are elements in Marxist thought that conform to Enlightenment principles—the possibility of rational thinking that is preferred over religion or mysticism, the potential of science to help all people if properly (socially, democratically) directed, development as the growth of the forces of production (and productivity) guided by rationality, to give a few instances. On the other side, there are aspects of Marxism confounding the Enlightenment, as with the notion of the dominant forms of rationalism as ideologies serving the interests of the ruling class—the "science" of economics, for instance. Both of these positions clearly have significant content. So, Marxism can be seen as modernist, but in a highly critical form—that is, sharing modernism's optimistic belief in the potential of rationality, science, and technology to bring a better life to humanity but pessimistic about the misuse of this potential in societies organized by competition and the profit motive. Most Marxists accept Enlightenment principles like reason and democracy but say they have never been realized in the radical French revolutionary tradition of the equality of all people.

As a result, critical thought in the early 21st century can be divided into critical modernism, derived from Marxism and other critical coherent political philosophies, on the one side, and critical poststructuralisms and postmodernisms, on the other. Debate between the two positions has focused particularly on the vexing question of development. Is development yet another European mechanism to control the world in the name of progress? Or is development capable of transcending its dubious origins to offer hope for poor and downtrodden peoples, in the sense of the socialist transformation of Venezuela? In the present chapter we discuss some of the contentions over these issues.

POST-ENLIGHTENMENT CRITICISMS

Modern rational thinking, with its secular beliefs and scientific attitudes, has from the beginning, and continuously since, encountered resistance. It cannot be automatically assumed that modern rationalism is so clearly the final superior form of thought that everyone who hears of it and samples its theoretical delights immediately succumbs to its logical charms. Nor should the finest product of rationality, the plentitude of modern life, with its ability to satisfy even the most trivial (consumptive) whim, be seen as satisfying to all and in every way with its seductive, sedative, selfish appeal. Even as modernist rationality unfolded, opposition was encountered from philosophers like Giovanni Battista Vico (1668–1744), who defended the irrational forces that he thought created human nature and who favored a more "common" sense rather than a thoughtfully rational sense (Vico 1984 ed.). The brilliant poet-philosopher Friedrich Nietzsche (1844–1900) believed that "truths are illusions we have forgotten are illusions" and that "truth is the kind of error without which a certain kind of being could not live" (Nietzsche 1968 ed.: 493; 1979 ed.: 84). Modern life, Nietzsche said, was compelled to found itself on the unquestioned principles of spirit, progress, and truth. Yet, the modern world brought an impoverishment of experience to the degree that people no longer could find meaning or truth (Clark 1990: 1–3). Truth in the way it had came to be thought deprived life of meaning—what we might call "truth in cleansing." Likewise, the phenomenologist Edmund Husserl (1859–1938) criticized modern rationalism's intellectual product, the realistic, empiricist, and scientific positivism of the 19th century (Husserl 1970: 5–6). Empirical science's inability to provide answers for normative evaluative (meaningful) questions, Husserl maintained, created a cultural crisis in modern life. For Husserl science as knowledge of the objectively real relegated what he called the "life-world" (the world as experienced in everyday prescientific activities) to the inferior status of a subjective appearance—less important than the "real" world uncovered by science. Instead, Husserl wanted to unearth the experiential roots of all thoughts in their original intentional contact with real phenomena—in other words, wanted phenomenology to rediscover the radical primary foundations of all knowledge because he wanted, paradoxically, to construct a new and better kind of science.

Similarly, the existential phenomenologist Martin Heidegger (1889–1976) searched for a radical foundation, not only for knowledge (as with Husserl) but also for the "qualities" of being human. Heidegger's best-known work, *Being and Time* (1962), argued that philosophy had to arise from and return to the whole existence and not come merely from a disengaged (distanced, separate) attitude of scientific knowing (that is, humans as disembodied rational consciousnesses). He saw the history of Western philosophy as one long misinterpretation of the nature of reality, which in his view was inevitable once the detached perspective of scientific theoretical reflection was adopted (that is, stepping back to get an impartial, objective view of things), for with that distancing the world went dead—that is, things lost their meaningfulness. Heidegger hoped to recover an original sense of things by setting aside the view of reality derived from abstract theorizing (phenomenologists call this "bracketing" or "putting into parenthesis") and focusing instead on the ways things showed up in the flux of everyday prereflective activities.

For Heidegger, the meaning of being was an "absence of ground," or an "abyss," in that he thought there was no *ultimate* foundation (like God's intention, or the march toward progress) for the holistic web of meaning that made up people's "being-in-the-world." In his "Letter on Humanism" Heidegger (1977b) took these arguments against modern certainty a step further. He criticized the entire Enlightenment project of emancipation as amounting to the subjection of nature to the mastery of human rational will; for Heidegger, the (ultimately insecure) modern subject manipulated an objective world, dominating nature according to the human's own (subjective) priorities. While modernists find this rational control to be beneficial to humans and (potentially!) nature, Heideggerians are highly suspicious of the entire enterprise. This fundamental critique of modern humanism passed into poststructural and postmodern thought most significantly through the writings of the brilliant French philosopher Michel Foucault (1926–1984).

POWER–TRUTH–KNOWLEDGE

Foucault shared with Nietzsche a fascination with the power–truth–knowledge complex and with Husserl and Heidegger a deeply critical attitude toward rationalism, truth, and the whole modern project. Foucault was critical of "reason"—he saw reason as saturating modern life and intruding the gaze of rationality into every nook and cranny of human existence, with science classifying and thereby regulating (controlling) all forms of experience, interpretation, and understanding. Foucault launched two kinds of attack on the philosophy of modern rational humanism. First, he said, modern reason metaphysically grounds its image of universal humanity in traits culturally specific to the Europeans—that is, reason claims to speak for everyone when, in fact, it is really speaking for the European minority in the world. Second, the values and emancipatory ideals of the European Enlightenment (autonomy, freedom, human rights, etc.) are the ideological bases for a "normalizing" discipline that imposes an "appropriate identity" on modern people—ideals are powerful ideologies. Like others, such as the Frankfurt school Marxists Max Horkheimer and Theodore Adorno, writing in their book *Dialectic of Enlightenment* (1991 ed.), Foucault believed modern rationality to be coercive rather than liberating, a force focused on controlling the minds of individuals rather than opening them to many possibilities. Foucault was a student of the structural Marxist philosopher Louis Althusser and was briefly a member of the French Communist party, but he was critical of Soviet political practice and Stalinist Marxism. So, in analyzing coercion, he employed methods different from, say, the Marxist critique of capitalist rationality as ideology, which (following Nietzsche) he called "archaeology" and "genealogy."

Foucault (1972, 1973, 1979) was particularly interested in the careful, rationalized, organized statements made by experts—what he called "discourses" to separate them from everyday conversations. In *The Archaeology of Knowledge* (1972), Foucault claimed to discover a previously unnoticed type of linguistic function, the "serious speech act," or the statement backed by validation procedures that marks it as "true" made within communities of experts (Dreyfus and Rabinow 1983: 45–47)—statements on the economy by "professional economists," for example. This "discourse" is different from a conversation in that statements made under some circumstances (a lecture, a peer-reviewed scientific article, a nonfiction book certified by other experts) are taken to be objectively true—and therefore important, worthy of respect, capable of supporting responsible action. Foucault had given up on the possibility of telling the truth—he thought discourses claimed the status of truth to gain power. Foucault was interested in the types of these serious speech acts, the regularities statements exhibited in "discursive formations," and the transformations occurring in these formations. Discursive formations, he claimed, had internal systems of rules that determined what could be said about which particular objects or events—therefore declaring some topics and some modes of talking about them to be outside the pale of serious discussion. Foucault called the setting that decided whether statements count as "real knowledge" the epistemological field, or *episteme*. So by "episteme" he meant the set of conditions in a given period that validate formalized systems of knowledge (Foucault 1973: 191). Discourses have systematic structures that can be analyzed "archaeologically" (identifying their main elements and the relations that form these into wholes) and genealogically (how discourses were formed by nondiscursive social practices, especially by institutions of power). What Foucault is basically saying is that discourses are taken to be true because their episteme is believed to be capable of separating truth from fiction.

Genealogy involves diagnosing relations of power, knowledge, discourse, and the body in modern society. Genealogy is opposed to most modern methods of inquiry in that it claims to recognize no fixed essences or underlying laws, seeks discontinuities rather than great continuities in history, avoids searching for depth, and records forgotten dimensions of the past. The genealogist finds hidden meanings, heights of truth, and depths of consciousness to be shams of the modern imagination. Instead, recalling Heidegger, genealogy's "truth" is that things (people, societies, etc.) have no essence (Foucault 1972: 142)—for example, there is no inherent "human nature," nor is there an eternal mode of human behavior, be it selfish competition or altruistic cooperation. Whenever genealogy hears of original truths, it looks for the play of power-driven wills. When talk turns to meaning, value, goodness, or virtue, the genealogist hears tales of domination and control. For the genealogist there is no conscious modern rational subject, the rational agent moving history forever forward. Instead, events come from the play of the particular forces active in any situation. History is not the progress of universal reason but, rather, humanity moving from one domination to another, but in no particular direction.

Modern discourses are founded on an appeal to truth—some statements are significant because they follow the rules set up to distinguish what is taken to be true. Yet, for Foucault, modern Western knowledge is also integrally involved in domination. For Foucault, knowledge does not detach itself from its practical empirical roots to become pure thought, subject only to the demands of reason. Rather truth, power, and knowledge operate in mutually generative ways:

> Truth is not outside of power.... Each society has its own regime of truth, its general politics of truth.... There is a combat for the truth, or at least around the truth, as long as we understand by the truth not those true things which are waiting to be discovered but rather the ensemble of rules according to which we distinguish the true from the false, and attach special effects of power to "the truth." (Foucault 1980a: 131)

For Foucault, modern power resides in the community of experts that sets up the rules for telling the truth—he had in mind not so much natural science (physics, chemistry, biology, astronomy) but rather the sciences of humanity and society (economics, political science, anthropology, sociology, geography, etc.). Foucault argued that modern "bio-power" emerged as a coherent political technology in the 17th century, when the fostering of life and the growth and care of populations became central concerns of the early modern state. The systematic empirical investigation of historical, geographic, and demographic conditions of populations led to the modern human sciences. But their aim, for Foucault, was not to enable human emancipation (through social-scientific reasoning) but rather to enable modern domination, to create docile yet productive, people, minds, and bodies (Dreyfus and Rabinow 1983). Modern science was the state's mode of social control.

In two lectures given in 1976, Foucault (1980a: 78–108) stressed certain aspects of genealogy particularly relevant to the issues of development that we are exploring here. For Foucault, thinking in terms of totalities reflected a predisposition toward theoretical unity and coherence (for example, one great theory of development), but also such thinking curtailed and caricatured local research on particular groups of people (for example, many particular ways of changing or improving societies). Instead, Foucault favored autonomous noncentralized theorizing that did not depend, for its validity, on gaining approval from the established dominant regimes of thought (for example, the World Bank). That is, he favored local knowledge, the "return of (forgotten) knowledge," the insurrection of subjugated knowledges, rediscovering blocs of historical knowledges usually disqualified as inadequate, naive, mythical, and below the required threshold of scientificity—people's knowledges that had not been "certified" as true by academicians, for instance. By resurrecting the histories of local struggles and subjugated knowledges, Foucault thought that critical discourse could discover new essential forces. Genealogy undertook this rediscovery and reconstruction of the forgotten. But such a task of reconstruction was not possible unless the "tyranny" of globalizing discourses (for example, neoliberal or neoclassical economics, modernization theories, modes of production, etc.) was first undercut, disturbed, even eliminated. Genealogies, then, were "anti-sciences," opposed not necessarily to the concepts of science but more to the effects of organized scientific discourses linked to centralized power systems—"it is really against the effects of the power of a discourse that is considered to be scientific that genealogy must wage its struggle" (Foucault 1980a: 84). By genealogy, Foucault (1980a: 83) also meant "the union of erudite knowledge and local memories which allows us to establish a historical knowledge of struggles and to make use of this knowledge tactically today"—that is, he wanted social struggles to evoke forgotten memories and employ these local knowledges in political action.

In genealogy Foucault examined anew the multiple aspects, relations, and kinds of domination. For him, the issue was not just global domination—one group of people controlling many others, center over periphery—but multiple forms of domination exercised in many different forms: power in its regional and local forms and institutions; power at levels other than conscious intention; power as something that circulated as chains and networks; power starting from infinitesimal personal relations and then colonized by ever more general mechanisms *into* forms of global domination; power exercised through the formation and accumulation of accredited knowledge; and so on. For Nietzsche and Foucault, every human interaction involves power. This is the basis of power systems. In brief, the interactions between power, knowledge, and discourse were the province of Foucault's genealogy.

The control of space was an essential constituent of the modern disciplinary technologies (Philo 1992). In modernity, space takes the form of grids (vertical and horizontal lines) with slots or positions on the grid assigned values—for example, sitting at the front of the class or living in the most desirable neighborhood. Individuals are placed in preordered disciplinary spaces, as for example military hospitals with numbered beds and wards, factories with assigned places for workers, classrooms with students' desks arranged alphabetically, suburbs ranked by socio-economic status, countries placed in tables according to GNP per capita or, in the soft version, according to the Human Development Index (see Chapter 1). Discipline "makes" individuals through this kind of distri-bution in space, by training, through hierarchical observation, through normalizing judgment, by examination, through documentation, all with help from the human (social) sciences. (Most the readers of this book are undergoing indoctrination of this type as part of being accredited as a good and worthy citizen with a degree to your name—the degree says you are knowledgeable in the right kind of way and trustworthy.) The phrase "academic discipline" is no accident: for Foucault, the acad-emy was linked with the spread of disciplinary technologies in the same matrix of power as the military–industrial complex. The academy disci-plines thought in part by breaking it into specializations, each a discur-sive formation confined by its own rules—economics, for instance. Fou-cault believed all global theories, such as modernization theory, Marxist mode of production theory, or world systems theory, to be reductionist (reducing the complexity of life to a few tendencies), universalistic (mak-ing everyone and everything follow the same rules), coercive (implying force), and even totalitarian (implying total control). He attempted to "de-totalize" history and society as wholes governed by a central essence, such as production in Marxism, world spirit in Hegelian idealism, or the march of progress in modernization theory. Foucault wanted to "de-center" the human subject as a consciousness constituting the world and instead see people as socially constructed identities. Society he understood in terms of unevenly developing discourses. Whereas modern theories of human emancipation drew on broad, essential themes to reach macropo-litical solutions—solving world poverty through Western intervention, for instance—Foucault respected differences and favored micropolitics—people being allowed to define and solve their own problems (Best and Kellner 1991; Peet 1998, 2007).

If this book is about contentious theories of development, we can do no better than Foucault to represent it!

POSTCOLONIALISM

This extreme skepticism about the Western project of reason, truth, and progress, formulated mainly in Paris (paradoxically at the center of the Enlightenment world), intersected with an increasingly sophisticated critique coming from intellectuals from the previously colonial countries, ironically often from scholars who lived in or had been partly educated in the West. These thinkers spoke from hybrid in-between positions, drawing on several traditions of thought, including Western reason and poststructural criticism, and revealing a number of conflicting experiences in a critical discourse that came to be known as postcolonialism.

Postcolonial criticism now occupies a prominent position in a number of disciplines, such as modern languages, literature, history, sociology, anthropology, and geography. In the words of the Princeton historian Gyan Prakash (1994: 1475) the idea of postcolonial criticism was to compel "a radical rethinking of knowledge and social identities authored and authorized by colonialism and Western domination." For Prakash, previous criticisms of colonialism had failed to break free from Eurocentric discourse. For example, Third World nationalism attributed agency to the subjected nation and yet staked its own claim to colonialism's order of reason and progress. Or, in another example, Marxist criticism was framed theoretically by a historical schema (modes of production) that universalized Europe's experience. The postcolonial critique, by comparison, sought to undo Europe's appropriation of "the other" (the non-European) within the realization that its own critical apparatus existed in the aftermath of colonialism. Following Derrida, it could be said that postcolonial criticism inhabited the self-same structures of Western domination that it sought to undo. More complexly, postcolonial literatures resulted from an interchange between imperial culture and the complex of indigenous cultural practices, the idea being that imperialism was, in part, resisted, eroded, and even supplanted in hybrid processes of cultural interaction (Ashcroft, Griffiths, and Tiffin 1995)

Postcolonial criticism began with the writings of the West Indian/Algerian psychoanalyst of culture Frantz Fanon (1925–1961) in his well-known book *The Wretched of the Earth* (1968), but also in the lesser-known *Black Skin, White Masks* (1986). Fanon's bitter, violent words forced European readers to rethink their experiences in relation to the history of the colonies then awakening from "the cruel stupor and abused immobility of imperial domination" (Said 1989: 223). Fanon's challenges to fixed ideas of settled identity and culturally authored definition were part of a broader convergence between the critical study of colonialism and a renewed interest in the recurring topic of subject formation—that is, how people's identities were formed (Gates 1991). Here Fanon drew from the French structural psychoanalyst Jacques Lacan (1901–1981) the idea that the ego (conscious self) was permanently schismatic (divided, split). The infant's "mirror stage" (when the child saw its behavior reflected in the imitative gestures of another, or discovered "that is me") was thought by Lacan to be deceptive, for the mirror was a decoy, producing mirages rather than images. Hence, ego construction, for Lacan, was an alienated process, and the resulting individual was permanently discordant with him- or herself (Bowie 1991). Third World intellectuals turned this into a critique of the certainty of the Western rational identity constructed by setting itself against an "inferior Third World Other." Fanon thought that the black person, the Other (not-self) for the white European, was unidentifiable and unassimilable, a confusing mirage, a hallucination rather than a confirming mirror image—whereas, he maintained, the historical and economic realities of colonialism formed the more accurate basis for a more securely defined black identity (Fanon 1986: 161). In the postcolonial literature the argument was subsequently made by Homi Bhabha (1994) that Fanon too quickly named a singular Third World "Other" to the First World "Same," but others countered that Fanon's conqueror–native relation was an accurate representation of a profound global conflict. From such differences came a number of postcolonial positions, all stressing contacts between Europe and the civilizations of the rest of the world but differing over similarity or variability in this set of experiences (among many other things).

Postcolonialism has usually been said to begin in a more organized way with the work of the "subaltern studies group" in the early 1980s—"subaltern" meaning subordinate in terms of class, caste, gender, race, and culture (Guha and Spivak 1988). One of the founders of this group, the Indian theorist Ranajit Guha (1983: 2–3), thought that elitist bias in colonial historiography denied peasants recognition as subjects of history. Acknowledging peasants as makers of rebellions, by comparison, meant attributing to them a consciousness (compare Gramsci 1971 ed.). Guha tried to identify the (recurring) elementary aspects of such a rebel consciousness as part of a "recovery of the peasant subject," his argument being that subaltern peoples acted on their own, with autonomous politics, in forms of sociality and community different from nation or class, therefore defying the conventional models of rationality used by Western historians. However, the postcolonial critic Gayatri Spivak (1987: 206–207) later saw subaltern studies' attempts at retrieving a subaltern, or peasant, consciousness as a strategic adherence to essentialist and humanistic notions, like consciousness, derived originally from the European Enlightenment. As long as such Western modernist notions of subjectivity and consciousness were left unexamined, she said, the subaltern would be recounted in what only appeared to be theoretically alternative ways (MacCabe 1987: xv).

Spivak's own alternative involved the structural notion of subject positions, in which the "subject" of a statement, for example, was not the immediate author, but instead the "author" was "a particular, vacant place that may in fact be filled by different individuals" (Foucault 1972:

95; see also Foucault 1980b: 196–197). With this Spivak sought to reinscribe the many, often contradictory, subject positions assigned by multiple colonial relations of control and insurgency. Subaltern women, for example, were subjected to three main domination systems, class, ethnicity, and gender. From this she reached the extreme conclusion that subaltern women had no coherent subject position from which to speak: "the subaltern cannot speak" (Spivak 1988: 308). Her argument was that, in straining for a voice of indigenous resistance, critics of colonialism succumbed to the romantic quest for a transparent "real" voice of the native, one which might give trustworthy evidence in the Western sense of "presence"—the sureness of knowledge gained by being on the spot. Like Bhabha, she was critical of simple "binary" (twofold) oppositions, like colonizer–colonized, and wanted to explore the heterogeneity of colonial powers. Yet, notice that Spivak herself drew on a central notion (subject positions) from the (Western) poststructural theorist Michel Foucault!

Another main source of postcolonial ideas derived from the Palestinian literary critic Edward Said's (1979: 2; 1989) concept of Orientalism: a "mode of discourse with supporting institutions, vocabulary, scholarship, imagery, doctrines, even colonial bureaucracies and colonial styles" through which European culture "produced" the Orient (politically, imaginatively) in the post-Enlightenment period. Said used Foucault's notion of discourse to look at the political and cultural dimensions of interregional power relations, arguing that binary oppositions, such as East–West, determined all interactions between Europeans and other peoples; that is, constructed notions of "the Orient" helped define a contrasting image of Europe as its spatial and cultural Other. Also, because Orientalist discourse limited thought, the Orient was not, and is not, a free subject of thought or action. In this sense Said found localities, regions, and geographic sectors, like "Orient" (East) and "Occident" (West), to be humanly "made." So we could ask, "Whose East was that?" (East of *what*?) Similar was the British theorist Benedict Anderson's (1983: 13–15) view that nationalism was a cultural artifact or, more generally, that all human groupings larger than primordial villages of face-to-face contact were "imagined communities." Subsequent work extended these "discourses on the Other" to histories of the different European conceptions ("science fictions") of "alien cultures" (McGrane 1989; Hulme 1986; Todorov 1984); such conceptions, or imaginaries, became perhaps the most significant bases of the new approach to culture and postcolonialism (Ashcroft, Griffiths, and Tiffin 1989; Bhabha 1994; Spivak 1988). In this vein we find a number of sophisticated analyses of the psychology of imperialism and colonialism, for example, critical admissions of the appeal of the idea of modernity for progressive Third World intellectuals (Nandy 1983; Sheth 1997).

For Homi Bhabha (1983a, 1983b: 19), representations of the Orient in Western discourse evidenced profound ambivalence toward "that otherness which is at once an object of dislike and derision." Colonial discourse, for Bhabha, was founded more on anxiety than arrogance, and colonial power had a conflictual structure—hence, colonial stereotyping of subject peoples was complex, ambivalent, and contradictory as a form of representation, as anxious as it was assertive. So, for example, in an analysis of mimicry, Bhabha (1984) argued that when colonized people become "European" the resemblance was both familiar and menacing to the colonists and subverted their identities rather than confirming them. The hybrid that articulated colonial and native knowledges might reverse the process of domination as repressed knowledges entered subliminally, enabling subversion, intervention, and resistance. Similarly, for Baudet (1965: vii): "The European's images of non-European man are not primarily, if at all, descriptions of real people, but rather projections of his own nostalgia and feelings of inadequacy."

Thus, the term "postcolonialism" filled a gap left by the abandonment of the phrase "Third World" within (poststructural) progressive circles—"the notion of the three worlds ... flattens heterogeneities, masks contradictions, and elides differences" (Shohat 1992: 101). Historical, literary, and psychoanalytical postcolonial work was unified around an examination of the impact of colonial discourses on subjectivity, knowledge, and power. Postcolonial writing stressed the mutuality of the colonial process. Rather than colonialism obliterating, or silencing, those distinctive colonized aspects of the culture of the oppressed survived in the hybrid cultures of postcolonial societies. What some have called "the decolonization of the imagination" involved an act of exorcism for both colonizers and colonized, while the view of the world that emerged was less cast in terms of cultural imperialism than as a global mixture (Pieterse and Parekha 1995: 1–19). Yet, the term "postcolonial," while increasingly widespread, needs to be examined and contextualized, historically, geopolitically, and culturally.

This is a complex area of writing and research. It forms one of the mainsprings of a renewed (poststructural and anti-Eurocentric) criticism of the key Western concepts of progress and development. It is part of the questioning of Western terms, like "development," that were previously assumed to be automatically good.

INTELLECTUAL DEPENDENCY THEORY

Let us add an additional dimension to these arguments. Since the colonial encounter, the political and economic hegemony of the West has been paralleled by other dependencies. These dependencies include, as we have seen, various kinds of intellectual dependence stemming from the widespread acceptance of the supposed superiority of Western rationality. In one of these dependencies, Third World intellectuals, trained in Western knowledge, have come to speak the colonizer's language (English, French) and to stress the colonizer's history and experience over their own—for example, African students studying British history for their "A-level examinations." But, more than that, the Third World is made dependent on the First World for knowledge ... about itself. This academic or intellectual dependence entails the export of raw data from the Third World to the First, where its surplus (generalized knowledge) is realized as theories and then exported back to the Third World as pearls of wisdom (Weeks 1990). The conditions of this intellectual dependency system include control of global research funds and scholarly journals by center institutions, together with the prestige accruing to those who publish in international journals or are in contact with scholars in Europe or the United States. Note that 95% of the articles published in scientific journals are written in English (Bollag 2000), and of 50 leading universities, according to *The Times* of London (the confidence to rank being exactly a part of the assumed superiority), 43 are in English-speaking countries (Halpin 2004).

Since the early 1970s, Third World scholars have made arguments about captive minds that they find to be uncritical and imitative of concepts coming from the West:

> Mental captivity ... refers to a way of thinking that is dominated by Western thought in an imitative and uncritical manner. Among the characteristics of the captive mind are the inability to be creative and raise original problems, the inability to devise original analytical methods, and alienation from the main issues of indigenous society. (Alatas 1993: 308)

In response, some Third World scholars call for the "indigenization" of social science—indeed, the indigenization of academic discourse as a whole. Social scientific indigenization goes beyond modifying Western concepts and methods to make them more suitable for non-Western contexts and problems. Indigenization refers, instead, to deriving scientific theories, concepts, and methodologies from the histories, cultures, and consciousness of non-Western rather than Western civilizations. For S. F. Alatas (1993: 310–311), the eventual aim is to develop bodies of social scientific knowledge in which theories are derived from culturally and historically specific experiences. These however would not be restricted in application to the society or civilization from which these are drawn.

He differentiates his approach from "nativism"—that is, the tendency for Western and local scholars to "go native" and reject Western science entirely. Instead, Alatas favors encountering, modifying, and combining Western theories with indigenous ideas—for him "the call to indigenization is simultaneously a call to the universalization of the social sciences" (Alatas 1993: 312; see also Amin 1989; Moghadam 1989; Pieterse and Parakha 1995).

Positions such as these are not without problems, in particular because they do not point to a convincing array of examples (but see Abdel-Malek 1981). There are interesting contrasts with poststructural arguments about the resurrection of local knowledges. While highly critical, indigenization theory does not advocate wholesale rejection of Western science, nor does it abandon notions of a common humanity, nor even universal knowledge. It does not claim that one kind of non-Western knowledge, such as Islam, is better than Western Enlightenment knowledge. Instead, it asserts that universal understanding must be based on universal experiences, interpretations, and generalizations, and not on the false "universalization" of what is purely the knowledge derived from experience and interpretations of the West. The potential for recasting visions of a better life for Third World peoples, based in a renewed, but critical, interest in local knowledges, is clearly present in this discourse.

RETHINKING DEVELOPMENT

Now we bring these highly critical notions to bear on theories of development. In the context of the growth of postcolonial studies and indigenization of knowledge, and with reference also to poststructural and postmodern criticism of social theory, the field of development studies has also undergone a significant critique and rethinking—indeed, the very notion of development has increasingly been challenged. As the Mexican social activist Gustavo Esteva (1987: 135) put it: "In Mexico, you must be either numb or very rich if you fail to notice that 'development' stinks. The damage to persons, the corruption of politics, and the degradation of nature which until recently were only implicit in 'development,' can now be seen, touched, and smelled." For former UNDP official Majid Rahnema (1997: ix), development has long been resisted at the grass-roots level by the "suffering poverty-stricken peoples" that are being "helped by development." Organizations like the Centre for the Study of Developing Societies, founded by Ranji Kothari in Delhi in 1963, and the journal *Alternatives,* started in 1975, express these frustrations in institutional and intellectual terms (Dallmeyer 1996). During the 1970s and 1980s, a movement among some liberal- and left-oriented Western practitioners began to criticize the legitimacy of development as it was then known. For instance, anthropologists reexamined their practice of producing the cultural knowledge that forms the basis for development projects. The features of an academic subculture (ethnocentrism, culturocentrism, elitism) in anthropology contributed to making development "the greatest failure of the century"; instead, they wanted "development from below" (Pitt 1976). Voluntary groups, or nongovernmental organizations (NGOs), were seen as having greater diversity, credibility, and creativity than official agencies (the World Bank, United Nations, etc.) in producing a "just development" characterized by equity, democracy, and social justice as well as economic growth (Clark 1991). Radical humanists, dissatisfied with 30 years of concerted international efforts that left, in their wake, more poverty, hunger, disease, and unemployment than were there to begin with likewise advocated local self-reliance as an alternative organizing principle (Galtung 1971), with participation advocated as research method (Gran 1983). There was a turn by academics and development practitioners toward critical self-examination that focused on their research objectives and methods.

Into this cauldron of rising self-criticism in the still critical 1970s and early 1980s came Participatory Action Research (PAR)—an attempt to form an endogenous intellectual and practical research methodology for the peoples of the Third World. In Latin America, the main critical themes of dependence and exploitation, together with countertheories of subversion, liberation theology, and reinterpretations of Marx, Gramsci, and others, were recombined with the intention of taking power rather than merely making theory. PAR was theorized as a total process of adult education, scientific research, and political action in which critical theory, situation analysis, and radical practice were seen as sources of knowledge. Summarizing experiences retrospectively from a series of participatory projects in Columbia, Mexico, and Nicaragua, Orlando Fals Borda said:

> Our objective was ... to examine and test, in a comparative and critical manner, the idea that it was possible to produce a serious analytical work based on practical knowledge of the reality of both the ordinary population and of the activists which would enrich not only the general fund of science but also the people's own knowledge and wisdom. Our idea was to take grassroots knowledge as a starting point and then to systematise and amplify it through action in collaboration with external agents of change—such as ourselves—in order to build and strengthen the power of formal and informal rural workers' organisations.... Our aim was not to carry out purely scientific or "integrated rural development" work, objectives which no longer really satisfied

us, but to fashion intellectual tools for the ordinary working class. (Fals Borda 1988: 5)

The overall political objective was to develop a more participatory, direct, and self-managed form of democracy than representational political systems. PAR defined people's power as the capacity of exploited grassroots people to articulate and systematize their own and others' knowledge so that they could become protagonists in defense of their class and in the advancement of their society.

Much of this impetus derives from the ideas of the Spanish existential philosopher José Ortega y Gasset (1883–1955), who lived in Peru during World War II. Following the philosophy of existentialism, Ortega y Gasset (1994) thought that the individual human being could not be detached from his or her circumstances (world)—"I am myself and my circumstance." Ortega y Gasset proposed a system in which life is the sum of ego and circumstance. As circumstance may be oppressive, there is a continual dialectical exchange between the person and circumstance in a drama of necessity and freedom. In this sense, freedom is being free inside a given fate. We accept fate and, within it, choose one destiny. We must therefore be active, decide, and create a "project of life." He means this in opposition to living a conventional existence in given structures by people who prefer an unconcerned and imperturbable life because they are afraid of the duty of choosing their life project. More generally, life itself is a radical reality from which all philosophical systems derive— hence, "vital reason," or "reason with life as foundation," refers to a new type of reason that constantly defends the life from which it has surged and bases knowledge on the radical reality of life, one of whose essential components is reason itself. For Ortega, it is through actual experience that people intuitively apprehend the essence of things and place their beings in wider, more fulfilling, contexts (Ferrater Mora 1956; McClintock 1971).

This version of existentialism was complemented by the sentiment expressed in Marx's (1938) statement that philosophers should change the world rather than merely explaining it. So, the notion in PAR was for scholar-activists to rise from their armchair contemplation and authentically participate in development as a real endogenous (within the community) experience. But, rather than seeing this in terms of the rebirth of the scholar, the aim was to turn the people involved into organic intellectuals without creating hierarchies. Science, PAR said, was not a fetish with a life of its own, or something that had absolute, pure value. It was simply a valid form of knowledge useful for specific purposes and based on relative rather than absolute truths. A people's science might exist as an informal endogenous process that could correct destructive tendencies in the predominant forms of science. A people's science would converge with so-called universal science to create a total paradigm (compare the concept of universalization in indigenization theory). In the PAR view, the forms and relations of knowledge production had as much, or more, value as the forms and relations of material produc- tion. Ordinary people should be able to participate in research from the beginning, deciding what the topic is, and should be involved at every step along the way. PAR preferred qualitative over quantitative analysis, yet made use of explanatory scientific schemas like cause-and-effect. Its techniques included collective research, critical recovery of history, valu- ing and applying folk culture, and the production and diffusion of new knowledge. PAR fulfilled Gramsci's objective of transforming common sense into good sense, or making critical knowledge the sum of both experiential and theoretical insights. "This is a methodology for produc- tive life and work which differs from other more academic forms in that it can be assumed and practiced autonomously by oppressed peoples who need knowledge to defend their interests and ways of life. In this way, perhaps, it will help build a better world for everybody, with justice and peace" (Fals Borda 1988: 97).

Yet, exactly as PAR was being formalized, the critique of devel- opment passed into a new phase. Majid Rahnema (1990) argued that development had once appeared as a new "authority" for nationalist, well-educated, and modernized leaders of the colonial world. But the per- sistence of problems like poverty and malnutrition led to a serious crisis of confidence among the believers. Meanwhile "field work" even in the PAR mode among the poor functioned to change the lives of idealists coming from privileged urban backgrounds. Participatory development coming from these encounters promised a new, popular, bottom-up, and endog- enous vision of development, free from colonial and techno-economistic shackles. And some experts in the most responsible international organi- zations, such as the World Bank, had begun to recognize the importance of popular participation. PAR-style development was acquiring a new, nicer face—"the face of a repentant saint, ready to amend, to work in a new fashion with the poor, and even to learn from them.... [This was] the last temptation of development" (Rahnema 1990: 201).

Rahnema noted that governments and development institutions became interested in PAR because participation was no longer perceived as a threat, was politically and economically attractive, was a good fund- raising device, and was part of a move toward the privatization of devel- opment as part of neoliberalism. There were real differences between institutional views of participation (in which local populations serve only as "extras" or "human resources") and the more radical PAR theorists, who admitted that their knowledge was irrelevant if local people did not regard it as useful and believe in full participation. Yet, Rahnema asked whether the PAR change agents, despite their undoubtedly sincere intentions, were really embarked on a learning journey into the unknown or were more concerned with finding ways of convincing the "uneducated" of the merits of their own (PAR) educated views. In the latter case, their scenario was hardly different from the conventional approach to development. The PAR activists had their own ideological conception of people's power, thought that free dialogue would persuade the "oppressed" to share their own beliefs and ideologies, attributed lack of cooperation to the people's primitive consciousness, and believed their obligation to lie in transmitting science, as the work of the world's best minds, to the "non-conscientized." For Rahnema, this nourished endless schizophrenias, like "dialogical action," self-illusions he found beginning with the Brazilian educator Paolo Friere's (1921–1997) writings, in *Pedagogy of the Oppressed* (1970) on participation and dialogue (that is, the notion that oppressed people did not yet have a critical consciousness and that progressive intellectuals needed to engage them in conscientization exercises). Rahnema saw most activists operating within a humanistic worldview in which participation was viewed as a voluntary and free exercise among responsible adults, whereas millions of people lived under terroristic repressive regimes; there were real differences between "us" and "them," and PAR-type interactions were never entirely innocent. Participation, planned in advance to serve a particular cause, for Rahnema (1990: 222), "can foster only chattering, frantic activism.... It is, ultimately, a dead tool ... inevitably bound to fall into the hands of the highest bidder on the power market. It can never serve freedom, self-discovery, or creative action."

THE POSTSTRUCTURAL
TURN IN DEVELOPMENT STUDIES

This dismissal of even the finest humanist, most committed activist research and action pushed criticism of development to new heights. During the 1980s, poststructural critiques of modern humanist endeavors, like development, together with postcolonial skepticism about the continued operation of imperialism in new "benign" forms, entered development studies and changed them forever.

Poststructural criticism brought two kinds of change to the field. First, there was a change in attitudes toward development. Progress, improvement, development—all had been assumed to be automatically good at the level of intuition. Yet, with poststructuralism, what previously had been assumed to be progressive, beneficial, and humane, was now seen as powerful, controlling, and often, if not always, detrimental. More than this, the very notions of "progress" and "beneficial" became suspect in terms not only of "beneficial for whom?" but also, more revealingly, in terms of "Who determines what 'beneficial' means?" or "Why does beneficial assume that life is progress?" To give a brief example, one contemporary critique of the effects of modern development, coming from the Austrian anarchist philosopher Ivan Illich (1926–2002), read as follows:

> We have embodied our world-view in our institutions and are now their prisoners. Factories, news media, hospitals, governments and schools produce goods and services packaged to contain our view of the world. We—the rich—conceive of progress as the expansion of these establishments. We conceive of heightened mobility as luxury and safety packaged by General Motors or Boeing. We conceive of improving the general well-being as increasing the supply of doctors and hospitals, which package health along with protracted suffering. We have come to identify our need for further learning with demand for even longer confinement to classrooms. In other words, we have packaged education with custodial care, certification for jobs, and the right to vote, and wrapped them all together with indoctrination in the Christian, liberal or communist virtues. (Illich 1997: 95)

Illich found the rational human decreasingly able to shape his or her environment because one's energies were consumed in procuring new models of the latest goods. Rich nations, he said, imposed a straightjacket of traffic jams, hospital confinements, and classrooms on poor nations and called it "development." Yet, more people, quantitatively and relatively, suffered from hunger, pain, and exposure than at the end of World War II. For Illich, underdevelopment was a kind of consciousness rather than a deficient standard of living, a reified state of mind in which mass needs were converted into demands for packaged solutions forever beyond reach of the majority. Illich instead called for counterresearch on fundamental lifestyle alternatives. For Illich, the "benefits" of the modern world, even its medical systems, education, and democracy, were far from being obvious. The direction this takes is toward total abandonment of development because it inevitably involves growth that will ultimately prove fatal. Modifying descriptions, such as "humane" or "sustainable," are rejected too as merely rehabilitating development. Instead, the economist Nicholas Georgescu-Roegen's (1995) notion of "downscaling" has been used by some environmental and antiglobalization activists. As Serge Latouche (2003: 1) says: "The main purpose of downscaling as a slogan is to mark clearly the abandonment of the insane objective of growth for growth's sake, which is driven only by unbridled search for profit for the holders of capital."

Second, there was a change in the methodology of development studies. Again, this involved reexamining what previously had been taken for granted. Development had been seen as a necessary dynamic of social life, something that occurred almost naturally in the modern world—development was to sociology what evolution was to biology. Development happened as a necessary process, in the modern understanding, unless blocked by countervailing forces that should be overcome and removed. For poststructuralists, by comparison, the term "development" was an invention, or social construction, and the concept had a discursive or cultural (rather than natural) history. From this view, economic agents acted as culturally produced identities. Economic rationalities were culturally created, took diverse forms, had distinct geographies, and produced specific forms of development as culturally embedded economic logics. As a cultural logic, development existed in two linked forms: a set of ideas, forms of behavior, and social practices operating directly in the economic world; and a discourse representing these real practices, but originating in academia, state bureaucracies, and institutions. The latter kind of development discourse did not merely represent economic practices already operating, in the sense of reflecting them in institutional thought, but also helped in forming them, directly through policy and indirectly by guiding the beliefs and ideas of economic agents—representations were part of the "culture" creating economic identities. With these poststructural realizations, discourse analysis became a crucial component of development studies. Poststructural thought, especially in the tradition of Foucault, placed new emphasis on development discourses formed in the context of cultures and framed within power relations. Hence, a new emphasis emerged: the history of ideas and discourses in the study of development.

Ideas about development—what it was, how it should be designed, who it served—were thus increasingly seen as deriving from a modernism that was suspect. The Swiss postdevelopmental theorist Gilbert Rist (1997) argued that development was the central belief in Western culture. Social beliefs, he maintained, were collective certainties continuously reproduced because of "the feeling of abandonment that wells up when one contemplates abandoning [them]" (Rist 1997: 22). The belief in development, Rist said, was deeply rooted in the Western "religion" of modernity. Rist traced development to Greek antiquity. The Greek philosophers believed that the world was marked by a succession of "ages," each age unfolding in the mode of a cycle. Aristotle theorized "nature" (which in Greek also means development) as the genesis of growing things. Reconciling this interpretation with Christian theology, St. Augustine saw God's design behind natural necessity, while the multiple Greek cycles were reduced to one, culminating in the sacrifice of Jesus Christ, opening the way, Rist postulates, to a linear view of history and development in the Western imagination.

While this particular approach positioned development deeply in Western cultural beliefs, there was a need also for explaining the use, or "deployment," of the discourse of development across global space. The geographer David Slater (1992, 1993) argued that the conceptualization of development was "enframed" by the West's geopolitical imagination. Modernization theory was a reflection of a will to spatial power, one "that sought to subordinate, contain and assimilate the Third World as other" (Slater 1993: 421). The political will fueling modernization had great difficulty accepting differences as autonomies. Thus, the "shadowy outsider" of the Third World had to be made safe through penetration and assimilation—hence the "geopolitical domestication" of global space. Slater saw modernization as passing through a series of phases: the transference of Western democratic ideals and values; the maintenance of political order and stability; and counterinsurgency. Contemporary neoliberalism, he said, bears within it a supreme belief in the universal applicability and rationality of the Western development project. Slater saw the Third World "theorizing back" via dependency, with its stress on regional specificity, autonomy of thought, and the negative impacts of the modernization process: "The dependency writers constructed and deployed a geopolitical imagination which sought to prioritize the objectives of autonomy and difference and to break the subordinating effects of metropolis–satellite relations" (Slater 1993: 430). Overall, Slater viewed the Western geopolitical imagination as a violation of other societies' rights to bring to bear their own principles of social being. Insurgent ethnic-regional identities in peripheral societies refused, challenged, and formed other forms of the geopolitical, as with struggles for the territorialization of democracy.

ENCOUNTERING DEVELOPMENT

Notions like these—the cultural embeddedness of development, its position in the Western geopolitical imagination, the deployment of development as power—led to a new fascination with the origins of the development idea in the modern mind. A new kind of poststructural critique of development emerged. Foucault's reappraisal of modern power, discourse, and knowledge was extended to Western development efforts as "uniquely efficient colonizers on behalf of central strategies of power" (DuBois 1991: 19). The pioneering ideas came from Arturo Escobar (1984–1985, 1988, 1992a, 1995), a Columbian anthropologist influenced by Foucault while both were at the University of California, Berkeley. Following Foucault, Escobar contrasted reason's project of global emancipation with the dark underside of Western domination—reasoned knowledge, using the language of emancipation, creating new systems of power in a modernized world. Development, he said, was one of these languages of power (see also Crush 1995). Under the political conditions of the Cold War from 1945 to 1989, Escobar argued, the West's scientific gaze focused anew on Asia, Africa, and Latin America. The main concepts of development were the discursive products of a geopolitical climate characterized by anticolonial struggles in Asia and Africa and growing nationalism in Latin America. But more significantly, "development" came from the rise to hegemony of the United States. In his 1949 inaugural address U.S. President Harry Truman proposed that the entire world should get a "fair democratic deal" via the intervention of a still youthful Uncle Sam eager to solve the problems of global poverty. This Truman doctrine initiated a new era in the management of world affairs by the United States. Yet, Escobar saw this doctrine as coming with a heavy price—the scrapping of ancient philosophies and the disintegration of the social institutions of two-thirds of the world's people. The Western dream of progress, he said, became a hegemonic global imagination. The Western discourse of development colonized reality so thoroughly that even opponents were obliged to phrase their critiques in developmental terms—another development, participatory development, socialist development, and so on.

Yet recently, Escobar claimed, poststructural social theories, offering accounts of how representations shaped the way reality was imagined and was thus acted upon, had been introduced by Foucault, Said, Mudimbe, Mohanty, Bhabha, and others. The poststructural account maintained the earlier Marxian theme of domination, but it extended the range of social criticism into discourse, truth, imaginary, and knowledge. Academic institutions, especially universities like Harvard or Cambridge, together with large development organizations like the World Bank, IMF, and the United States Agency for International Development (USAID), exercised power not only by controlling money flows but also by creating the dominant ideas, representations, and discourses. These "enframed" the world in terms of European theoretical categories (Mitchell 1988), captured social imaginaries, and constructed identities. Western discourses of development were deployed through the practices of planning agencies, local development institutions, and health organizations; people thought and acted through Western categories, seeing the world not as it was but through a westernized developmental gaze. In brief, reality was socially constructed in the sense of being understood and re-created through Western ideas (Figure 6.1).

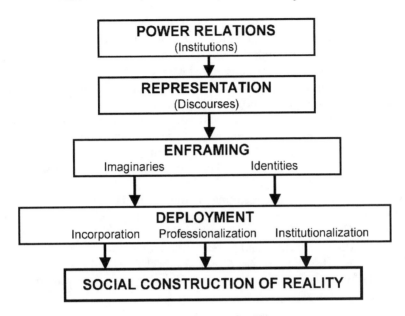

FIGURE 6.1. Escobar's model of development discourse. Data from Escobar (1995).

Escobar's creative move entailed applying poststructural and postco-lonial notions to the postwar discourse of development, paying particular attention to economic development theory and the systematic produc-tion of knowledge and power in planning, rural studies, health, nutri-tion, sustainability, women's rights, and the environment. The organizing premise of development as a postwar discourse was a belief in modern-ization through industrialization and urbanization. Its most important elements were capital formation, education in modern cultural values, and the need to create modernizing institutions at scales ranging from the international to the national and regional. Development would result from the systematization of all these elements (in a synthesis of economic growth and modernization theories—see our Chapters 2, 3, and 4). This system of thought defined the conditions under which objects, concepts, and strategies could be incorporated into development discourse—that is, "the system of relations establishes a discursive practice that sets the rules of the game: who can speak, from what points of view, with what authority, and according to what criteria of expertise" (Escobar 1995: 41). Under the hegemony of development, apparatuses of knowledge production (for example, the World Bank, planning and development agencies, etc.) established a new political economy of truth different from that of the colonial era—the comparison was with Said's Orientalism as a Western style for dominating, restructuring, and having authority over the East. A vast institutional network defined a perceptual domain, the space of development, that determined what could be said, thought, and imagined. From industrialization, through the green revolution, to integrated rural development, policies repeated the basic "truth" that development consisted in achieving conditions characteristic of the already rich societies. The development discourse defined what could be thought, practiced, even imagined, in considering the future of Third World societies: "Development can be described as an apparatus ... that links forms of knowledge about the Third World with the deployment of forms of power and intervention, resulting in the mapping and production of Third World societies.... By means of this discourse, individuals, governments and communities are seen as 'underdeveloped' (or placed under conditions in which they tend to see themselves as such), and are treated accordingly" (Escobar 1992a: 23; see also Sachs 1992).

The deployment of development, Escobar said, operated through three main strategies:

1. The progressive incorporation of problems thought of as *abnormalities* to be treated clinically—this resulted in a "field of the intervention of power."
2. The *professionalization* of development, the recasting by experts of what otherwise would be political problems into neutral "scientific" terms, the aim being a regime of truth and norms, or a "field of the control of knowledge."
3. The *institutionalization* of development, the formation of a network of new sites of power/knowledge that bound people to certain behaviors and rationalities (Escobar 1992a: 23).

In short, the three strategies entailed intersection fields of power, knowledge, and practice. For Escobar, development proceeded by defining "problems" (poverty, population growth, archaic agricultural practices) and identifying "abnormalities" (the illiterate, the malnourished, small farmers) to be observed and clinically treated. The result was the creation of a space of thought and action, a perceptual-analytical field, that limited what could be included as legitimate development issues and practices: "Development was—and continues to be for the most part—a top-down, ethnocentric, and technocratic approach, which treated people and cultures as abstract concepts, statistical figures to be moved up and down in the charts of 'progress'" (Escobar 1995: 44). Escobar saw a spatial field of power/knowledge expanding outward from the West, using development as a capturing mechanism. Within this field, networks of sites of power bound people into Western forms of thought, behavior, and practice. Development was particularly effective because it appealed to the finest ideals of the Enlightenment (often employing the most idealistic people in aid or development agencies) and to the aspirations for a better life held by poor people. Development had been "successful" to the extent that it managed and controlled populations, that it created a type of "manageable underdevelopment" far more subtly than colonialism. Escobar found this poststructural view of development as a modernist discourse different from the previous analyses of political economy, modernization, or even alternative development, all of which proposed merely modifying the current regime of development.

For Escobar all universal models, neoclassical or Marxist, denied peoples' capacities to model their own behaviors. Escobar favored, instead, autonomous peasant development strategies that opened spaces for peasants to struggle, that saw peasants not in terms of lacks but possibilities, and that modified social relations of production. As with the PAR activists, he thought that useful knowledge had to begin with people's self-understanding and build a system of communication involving peasants—"from the represented shall come that which overturns the representation" (Taussig 1987: 135). Such local constructions, he said, could be investigated via ethnographies of resistance (for example, Scott 1985) or the logics and actions of subaltern groups (Guha 1988; Comaroff and Comaroff 1991). Here local models "exist not in a pure state but in complex hybridizations with dominant models" (Escobar 1995: 96), that is, articulations between centric (dominant) texts and marginal voices—his best example was a "house model" of economy based on everyday peasant practice in Panama (Gudeman and Rivera 1992), but his own particular interest lay with the development of approaches to social movements based on theories of self-organization, complexity, and the like, an area of research nourished by work with social movements of the Colombian Pacific and, to a lesser extent, with antiglobalization movements. Rethinking development entailed two kinds of practice: making explicit the existence of a multiplicity of models of economies within the space of local constructions—the notion of "communities of modelers"; and studying the processes by which local cultural knowledges were appropriated by global forces—here radical political economy needed to be supplemented by ethnographies of development and theories of hybrid cultures. Following the poststructural philosophers Giles Deleuze and Felix Guattari (1987), Escobar believes that global capital relies not so much on the homogenization of an exterior Third World as on the consolidation of its diverse heterogenous social forms—that is, capital requires peripheral polymorphy. The global economy has to be understood as a decentered system employing manifold (symbolic, economic, political) apparatuses of capture in a process that, Escobar believes, still leaves room for localities to avoid the most exploitative mechanisms of the capitalist megamachines. Modifying political economics involves the material, but also semiotic, strengthening of local systems. While the main actors are social movements, Escobar finds also a role for interpretive social theorists in helping to form a conversational community across cultures.

Highly critical notions about development like Escobar's intersected with a profound sense of disillusionment among some progressive theorists and activists about developmental practice (for example, Edwards 1989). This produced a crisis of confidence in development studies—indeed, perhaps, a crisis in progressive thought in general. Quoting Escobar (1992a: 20):

> For some time now, it has been difficult—at times even impossible—to talk about development, protest or revolution with the same confidence and encompassing scope with which intellectuals and activists spoke about these vital matters in our most recent past. It is as if the elegant discourses of the 1960s—the high decade of both development and revolution—had been suspended, caught in mid-air as they strove toward their zenith, and, like fragile bubbles, exploded, leaving a scrambled trace of their glorious path behind.... Hesitantly perhaps, but with a persistence that has to be taken seriously, a new discourse has set in.

Brought on by critical thinking's inability to leave behind the imaginary of development, the whole project of progress was said to be sick, dying, gone. Escobar compared this situation with a powerful social movements discourse that, while unclear about its possible directions, had become a privileged arena for intellectual inquiry and political action. Escobar (1992a: 50) aimed at bridging the insights of the critiques of both development and social movements, believing:

1. Criticism of the discourse and practice of development could clear the ground for a more radical collective imagining of alternative futures.
2. Thinking about alternatives to development required a theoretical and practical transformation drawing on the practices of Third World social movements.

Escobar claimed a growing number of scholars in agreement with this prescription who, rather than searching for development alternatives, spoke about alternatives *to* development. These scholars shared a critical stance toward established science; an interest in local autonomy, culture, and knowledge; and a position defending localized, pluralistic grassroots movements. This tendency has a name: "postdevelopmentalism."

POSTDEVELOPMENTALISM

Escobar's claim that a growing body of scholars shared a similar position on postdevelopmentalism was a little ambitious. But there did come to be a set of ideas circulating in the publications of a linked group of people and practiced by alternative institutions that coexisted with some degree of ease, if not yet as a fully coherent counterdiscourse. These ideas stemmed from critics of development in Third World countries, especially in India; poststructural social theorists and a few development economists; and some political ecologists and environmentalists critical of the effects of development on nature. In *The Development Dictionary* (Sachs 1992), a manual of postdevelopmental thought, the modern age of development was proclaimed over and done with:

> The idea of development stands like a ruin in the intellectual landscape. Delusion and disappointment, failures and crimes have been the steady companions of development and they tell a common story: it did not work. Moreover, the historical conditions which catapulted the idea into prominence have vanished: development has become outdated. But above all, the hopes and desires which made the idea fly, are now exhausted: development has grown obsolete. (Sachs 1992: 1)

For the dictionary, the main development credos were historically inadequate and imaginatively sterile. Development was a blunder of planetary proportions, an enterprise to be feared not for its failure but in case it was successful. *The Development Dictionary* wanted to disable development professionals by destroying the conceptual foundations of their practices. It wanted to challenge grassroots initiatives to discard their crippling development talk.

Similarly, Serge Latouche's *In the Wake of the Affluent Society* (1993) argued that the Western dream of *la grande société* (the great society, the open society, the affluent society) promised affluence and liberty for all. Yet, these possibilities were, like film star status, achievable only by a few, while the price, measured in terms of the reduction of real solidarities, was paid by everyone. Western civilization was confronted by the dark side of progress:

> The perception that power to create is also power to destroy; that power over nature is often more imagined than real; that market

autonomy is often also an awful desolation, insecurity and simple nul-
lity—numbness in front of the TV, or Lotto, walkman, glue sniffing,
or some other virtual reality. What, in human life is truly richness and
progress? (O'Conner and Arnoux 1993: 12–13)

For Latouche, the West had become an impersonal machine, devoid of
spirit, and therefore of a master, which put humanity to its service. For
their own survival, Third World societies had to subvert this homog-
enizing movement by changing their terms of reference to escape the
disempowerment inherent in underdevelopment. For Latouche, human
practice was primarily symbolic; through the imaginary, material problems received distinctive definition and terms of resolution. Underdevelopment was primarily a cultural form of domination. Latouche saw
the West coming apart and the development myth collapsing. His main
theme was the "post-Western world," an imagined future which could
be explored via its early beginnings in the informal sectors of economies, in the practices of millions of people shipwrecked by development.
The informal sector, for Latouche, was part of a whole social context
involving neotribal peoples with residual and newly reinvented cultural
identities, peoples with metaphysical or religious beliefs, peoples whose
ensemble of daily practices were conducted under a different rationality
that appeared from the outside to be deviant or irrational—all this he
interpreted as resistances that were pregnant with another society. Latouche (1993: 26) described this vision as pushing speculation to the brink
of science fiction, and in this lay a fundamental problem with many postdevelopmental approaches.

Given that postdevelopmentalists are not just destructive cynics,
hopelessly caught in endless deconstructions, but believe in social change
and political activism, the problem became: "What do they propose?"
Based on reading *The Post-Development Reader* (Rahnema 1997), one
of the main collections of essays in this field, three positions recur:

1. *Radical pluralism*: Drawing on the ideas of Wendell Berry,
Mahatma Gandhi, Ivan Illich, Leopold Kohr, Fritz Schumacher, and others, often expressed in the journal *The Ecologist*, the true problem of
the modern age seems to lie in the unhuman scale of contemporary institutions and technologies. While people were enmeshed in global structures, they lacked the centralized power necessary for global action. To
make a difference, actions should not be grandiosely global but humbly
local. Thus, Gustavo Esteva and Madhu Suri Prakash (1997) amended
René Dubois's slogan "Think globally, act locally" to be "Think and act
locally"—that is, they believed that people could only think wisely about
things they actually knew well. Esteva and Prakesh urged support of local

initiatives by small grassroots groups—growing food, for example, in villages where collective or communal rights had priority over personal or individual rights. While local people needed outside allies to form a critical mass of political opposition, this requirement did not call for thinking globally. Indeed, the opposite was the case. They believed that people thinking and acting locally found others who shared their opposition to the global forces threatening local spaces and joined in coalitions of thinkers and activists. Every culture had a cosmo-vision, an awareness of the place and responsibilities of humans in the cosmos, but this should not be misconstrued as cosmo-power.

2. *Simple living*: "Simple living" appeared in two related versions, one ecological and the other spiritual. In the ecological argument, demands made on nature by the industrial countries (20% of the world's people consuming 80% of the energy and raw materials) had to be reduced by between 70% and 90% in a half-century. This aim would require more than just efficient resource management—it would require a "sufficiency revolution." A society in balance with nature required both intelligent rationalization of means but more importantly prudent moderation of ends (Sachs 1997). In the spiritual argument, the idea was that material pursuits should not be allowed to smother the purity of the soul or the life of the mind. Instead, the simple life should self-consciously subordinate the material to the ideal—as with Zarathustra, Buddha, Lao-Tse, Confucius, and the Old Testament (Shi 1997). So, as set out by Gandhi (1997), the simple life entailed an economics of justice, decentralization, village life, and human happiness combined with moral, spiritual growth. In both versions of the simple living idea, ecological and spiritual, there was a notion of peace and harmony coming from simpler, less materially intensive, ways of living, where satisfaction and happiness derived from spiritual sources (humanity or god) rather than consumption.

3. *Reappraising noncapitalist societies*: Here the basic idea was that life in the previous nondeveloped world had not been so bad after all: in those societies people had no cars, no Internet, and none of the consumer goods to which modern men and women are now addicted. They had no laws and no social security to protect them, no "free press," no "opposition party," no "elected leaders." But they had no less time for leisure, or, paradoxically, were no less economically "productive" for the things they most needed. And, contrary to the racist cliches in vogue, they were not always governed by cannibals and tyrants. Effective personal and collective moral obligations often took the place of legal provisions (Rahnema 1997: 379–381).

Into such societies poisonous development introduced a paraphernalia of mirages that dispossessed people of those things that had given meaning and warmth to their lives. The often hidden message of every development project was that traditional modes of thinking and practice doomed people to a subhuman condition from which nothing short of fundamental change could elicit respect from the civilized world. The main argument in favor of development was that it was a generous response to millions who asked for help. But development had little to do with the desires of the "target" populations. The hidden agenda involved geopolitical objectives. Requests for aid came from unrepresentative governments rather than the people. Thus, postdevelopmentalism was not the end of searches for new possibilities of change. Postdevelopmentalism, instead, signified that the old self-destructive, inhumane approach was over (Rahnema 1997).

In general, postdevelopmentalism rejects the way of thinking and the mode of living produced by modern development in favor of revitalized versions of nonmodern, usually non-Western, philosophies and cultures. From this view, modern Western development is destructive rather than generative, a force to be resisted rather than welcomed. In a phrase, development is precisely the problem rather than the solution.

The question remains, however, whether development can be both—problem *and* solution?

CONCLUSION: COUNTERCRITIQUE

What might we make of sweeping condemnations that seek to undermine the knowledge basis of all established notions about development, deconstruct each optimistic expression of Western reason's intervention on behalf of the oppressed people of the world, and denigrate the accomplishments of modern life? Is reason to be rejected or *re*reasoned? Is development outmoded or merely misdirected? These questions are so important that the postdevelopmental discourse must itself be deconstructed.

Poststructural and postmodern theory favor fragmentation and difference except in their own treatment of modern development theory that they portray in terms of a monolithic hegemony. Hence, for Escobar (1992a: 26), "Critiques of development by dependency theorists, for instance, still functioned within the same discursive space of development, even if seeking to attach it to a different international and class rationality." Thus, critics gather under the rubric of "modern development theory" notions regarded by their proponents as separate, different, and intensely antagonistic. A typical statement might list as one contemporary development discourse neoclassical growth theory, modernization, and radical political economy. These are said to share the following general positions:

1. A linear view of history in which the West is further along a given path of progress than Third World countries.
2. An agreement that the proximate cause of development is the exercise of human rationality, especially the application of science to production.
3. Advocacy of values like freedom, justice, and equality as experienced and defined in the West.
4. An instrumental assumption that means are separable from ends and that moral considerations apply more to ends than to means. (Banuri 1990)

Beyond a vague similarity in that all Western development discourses derive in some way from the Enlightenment, the question is whether the notion of a single developmental discourse creates a homogeneous myth that destroys differences crucial to each theory's contents, vision, and intention.

Take historical materialism as a case in point. This notion of a continuous modernist discourse sees Marx as a direct descendant of the Enlightenment. Thus, in the preface to a *Critique of Political Economy* Marx (1970 ed.) found societal transformation to be driven by development of the material productive forces that, by coming into periodic conflict with the existing relations of production, created revolutionary ruptures that moved society from one mode of production to another. What caused the development of the social forces of production? What propelled history? A rationalist version of Marxism (Cohen 1978: 150–157) finds Marx's "development thesis" resting on the proposition that humans are rational beings who use their intelligence to relieve material scarcity by expanding their productive powers—that is, increasing their ability to transform nature. In this rationalist version, Marx's theory of history can indeed be read as an elaboration of a central notion of the Enlightenment, that is, history as the progressive achievement of human reason's control over nature.

The foregoing is one reading of Marx, not the only reading, and not necessarily Marx's final position. Historical materialism was conceived as a critique of the very idea of beginning explanation with consciousness (of which rationality is a part), even in the form of an experientially based human imagination, and instead beginning social analysis with "real active life" (that is, labor and the social relations of production). Marx's (1973 ed.: 479–498) *Grundrisse* set out a version of historical materialism in which social and natural relations were the basic categories of analysis and reasoning was of multiple kinds, all depending on social relations (Lefort 1978; Giddens 1981). Marx's multilinear social relational theory does not rest easily in a supposedly singular discourse of development focused on reason as cause and stretching from the Enlightenment to the World Bank. This does not mean that Marxism does not admire the careful logical kinds of thinking that people have developed, including Western white people.

Much the same can be said about "developmentalism" as a hegemonic discourse. There may be similarities between capitalist and state authoritarian economic thought with regard to development. But developmentalism as a mode of progressive thought has long contained critical versions that stem from various oppositions to the existing forms of development, both internal to so-called developed societies and external to them, from Third World intellectuals and thinkers of all kinds. These critical developmentalisms emphasize the different trajectories of dependent societies (as with dependency theory), advocate different logics of development for different societies (as with democratic Marxism), and passionately favor the empowerment of poor people (as with PAR). Lumping together these critical notions—and the radical practices guided by them—with neoclassical economics, modernization theory, and World Bank policy into a broad, coherent "developmentalism" denies fundamental differences and denigrates the efforts of many brave theorist-activists.

This argument brings a first critical reaction to poststructuralism in general and postdevelopmentalism in particular. Poststructural discourse theory argues for the social construction of meaning, elaborating the institutional bases of discourse and emphasizing the positions from which people speak and the power relations between these positions. This conception indicates constellations of discursive positions that persist over the long term and take a multiplicity of forms. The problem is that in setting up a system of expectations about a theory, such that it may be part of a more general intellectual position, discourse analysis often denies what poststructural philosophy supposedly cherishes— that is, differences of a fundamental kind. "Discourse" then becomes a totality capable of reconciling even opposing tendencies in theorization. Indeed, there may be a kind of "discursive idealism," a process of reification in which the category "discourse" becomes an active force marshaling reluctant ideas into quasi-coherent determining wholes. Perhaps therefore we need a more discriminating critique than discourse analysis. Reconstituted Marxist theories of ideology, as with Gramsci, might do a better job—or some other conception more directly rooted in social rather than discursive relations.)

The critical point is not to make the easy claim that poststructural critics of development theory overstate their position, but to argue that the analysis of discourse, with its linking of oppositional theoretical traditions because they vaguely "share the same discursive space" (within which they oppose one another!), is prone to this kind of overgeneralization. Why? Precisely because it diverts attention away from the "international and class rationalities" and material contexts expressed in discourses, hence merging conflicting positions (PAR and the World Bank) into a single developmental discourse, or condemning modernity as a whole rather than, for example, capitalist versions of modern consumptive life. True to its word about differences, poststructural theory would instead see development as a set of conflicting discourses and practices based on positions that contradict one another. These would have a variety of potentials rather than promoting the singular copying of the experience of the West.

Let us extend this countercritique of Foucault's concepts of power and knowledge that form important parts of poststructural postdevelopmentalism. In his later (genealogical) work Foucault tried to escape from a structuralist conception of discourses as lumps of ideas determinant in history (epistemes) and tried instead to concentrate on the material conditions of discourse formation—social practices and power relations. Similarly, Foucauldian postdevelopmentalists, like Escobar, are interested in the institutions that form and disseminate development theories, models, and strategies. Yet, the power–knowledge–discourse trilogy still has its problems. It is never clear what power is with Foucault. "Power" alternates between a Nietzschean power, inherent in all human relations, and specific powers, such as those cohering in particular institutions or even individuals. If power is inherent in humans, present in all relations, then how did it get there, who put it there, and where did it come from? Here the Foucauldian refusal to look at basic causes or continuities in history may be read as an excuse for not thinking these things through. And the positive aspects of power, the ability to get things done, get short shrift, in practice, compared with the negative aspects.

Then there is the poststructural critique of modern knowledge as oppressive, disciplining, normalizing, totalizing, essentialist, truth-claiming, and knowledge thought up in the pursuit of power. These are caricatures that fail to discriminate among types of knowledge production, different motives for thinking, the interests paying for thought, the contestations between potentials, and the depositing in knowledge of competing politics. There is also the product of power and knowledge in "discourse." Discourse (not capital) has to be abandoned; postdevelopmentalism attacks the *discourse* of development. Poststructural analyses often forget, in practice, the agency behind discourse, or overgeneralize agency as "modernity" or "power." There remain even in analyses following the later Foucault strong reminders of discursive idealism. There is an overemphasis on representation and the enframing of imaginaries at the expense of practicality and action. Actually, intermediate conceptions, class, gender, and state give more exact descriptions and yield more focused analyses. Let us take the power basis of development theory as an example.

As we have seen, the contemporary notion of "development" emerged most fully as Western policymakers reassessed their positions relative to newly independent states in the Third World during the post-World War II Cold War. From the mid-1940s to the late 1950s the redefinition of foreign policy in the Cold War against communism and the notions of development aid, "humanitarian assistance," "food for peace," and so on were repeatedly linked, especially in the newly hegemonic United States—hence, the restatement of international control in American terms of the rights of man rather than European terms of "the white man's burden." While initiated by Truman, the culminating triumph of this "development of development theory" can actually to be found in the various speeches of John F. Kennedy, president of the United States between 1961 and 1963; as Sorensen (1988: 329) correctly notes, "No president before or after Kennedy has matched the depth of his empathy for the struggling peoples of Latin America, Africa and Asia, or the strength of his vow to facilitate their political and economic independence." Read a little more critically, as Derrida would perhaps have us do, and one finds that the Kennedy administration managed to contain a fierce anticommunism within the overall framework of Western humanism in a development discourse that drew consciously on the latest in social science—at that time modernization theory. Elements of Rostow's *The Stages of Economic Growth* (1960) (quoted in Sorensen 1988: 365–366) are obviously evident in Kennedy's statement that "The only real question is whether these new nations [in Africa] will look West or East—to Moscow or Washington—for sympathy, help and guidance, in their great effort to recapitulate, in a few decades, the entire history of modern Europe and America."

Thus, it quickly becomes apparent that President Kennedy's statements on the Third World may be deconstructed to reveal their intellectual sources, motives, interests, and power bases. There are excellent critical surveys by political scientists linking U.S. positions on development to broader domestic and foreign policy objectives (Higgot 1983; Gendzier 1988), although this literature largely predates the spread of poststructural notions into North American social science *and* would benefit from Foucault's or Derrida's techniques of discourse analysis. While necessary, however, the question remains whether discourse analysis is sufficient to the task. Take that culminating moment in postwar history when an idealistic young president at last expressed the finest sentiments of American generosity toward the world in the one paragraph in Kennedy's 1961 inaugural address dealing with U.S. relations with the Third World:

To those peoples in the huts and villages of half the globe struggling to break the bonds of mass misery, we pledge our best efforts to help them help themselves, for whatever period is required—not because the communists may be doing it, not because we seek their votes, but because it is right. If a free society cannot help the many who are poor, it cannot save the few who are rich. (quoted in Sorensen 1988: 12)

This speech initiated a renewed U.S. emphasis on development, using a modern rhetoric of equality, happiness, and social justice but backed as well by armed might (as with the U.S. onslaught on a popular uprising against a corrupt series of South Vietnamese regimes, the burning of not a few huts and villages in Vietnam, and the killing, delimbing, and napalming of thousands of Vietnamese women and children that the old, grainy video footage faithfully records). But Kennedy justified "helping the many who are poor" as being morally right because it "saved the few who are rich." As Foucault would say, the language of development expresses power relations. As Foucault did not say, these power relations connect the world's rich people to the world's poor. And whose side was Kennedy on? For Kennedy, scion of one of the richest families in the United States, representative of the New England liberal intelligentsia, supporter of the invasion of Cuba and military involvement in South Vietnam, development, antipoverty programs, and welfare were indeed fine philanthropic ideals, but also, at the same time, philanthropy preserved the continued possibility of wealth creation by the rich people of the world.

Yet, development, in the Kennedy statement, is not an expression of power in general, as with Foucauldian poststructuralism. "Power in general" universalizes the issue. Nor is development power employed by a specific institution, such as the U.S. State Department, as with Foucauldian institutionalism, which confines the critique. The critical analysis of development as discourse is far more revealing in terms of motive forces when it is cast not in terms of power in general, nor the power of a specific institution, but in terms intermediate between these—class, gender, ethnicity, and state, on the one hand, and their beliefs, ideals, and politics, on the other. In brief, while there is much to learn from discourse analysis, especially the serious attention given to statements and documents as symptoms of power relations, there are some real problems with it. These problems might be resolved, in part, through a dialogue between poststructuralism and Marxism, socialist feminism, and other critical traditions that employ notions of class, gender, and ethnicity and speak in the language of ideology, hegemony, and fundamental beliefs.

These methodological skirmishes touch on, yet largely avoid, the main issue—poststructuralism's negative assessment of modernism, especially its skeptical attitude toward modern projects like rationality, material progress, the emancipation of humanity, empirical truth, and the potential of science. Beginning with the critique of progress, the poststructural literature rejects Western models of development altogether; as Escobar (1992a: 27) puts it, "Rather than searching for development alternatives, [a growing number of Third World scholars] speak about alternatives *to* development, that is, a rejection of the entire paradigm." In doing so, postdevelopmentalism denies to the Third World what the First World already possesses—yet, we note that many critics of Western development live in the luxurious centers of Western modernity (Paris, New York, Geneva) and enjoy their benefits while saying that Third World people do not need them. Jean-Marie Harribey (2004: 1) says it well:

> It is politically unfair to impose equal downscaling on those who have more than enough of everything and those who lack the basic essentials. Poor people are entitled to a period of economic growth and the idea that extreme poverty is just a reflection of western values or a particular attitude is unacceptable. Schools will have to be built to end illiteracy, medical centres are needed to provide care for all and networks must be created to make clean drinking water available to all.

In postdevelopmentalism, associating any trait with the West is sufficient to condemn it without further question, as though Western people are unique in one respect only; namely, that everything we do is perverse. As with Rahnema, there are tendencies to deny that poverty originally existed in the Third World, to romanticize local alternatives *to* development, assuming a reverse snobbery in which indigenous knowledge systems are automatically superior to Western science, reveling in spiritual mysticism as though gods and goblins are as "true" as gravity. Crimes committed in the name of religion at least rival those perpetrated for the sake of reason (although we would claim that many supposedly "modern" atrocities, such as in Nazi Germany, were motivated primarily by mystical ideas—try listening to Hitler's speeches!)

Most fundamentally, the question of rationality and modern science must be debated with rigor and insight. In *The Development Dictionary* Claude Alvares (1992: 219–220) calls modern science "an epoch-specific, ethnic (Western) and culture-specific (culturally *entombed*) project, one that is a politically directed, artificially induced stream of consciousness invading and distorting, and often attempting to take over, the larger, more stable, canvas of human perceptions and experiences." Gilbert Rist (1997: 3), in a wonderfully iconoclastic argument about development, dismisses scientific realism—the view that a world exists independently of the knowing subject and can be known with accuracy—with a single overstated phrase: "As for objectivity, it is known to be a vain pursuit so long as we refuse to accept that the object is always constructed by the one who observes it." We can agree with the poststructural argument that objects assume shapes as ideas in the thinking mind through inexact representational processes while refusing to accept that this mental shaping "constructs" these objects. Realists and materialists believe, instead, that objects in the world are already "there" before being encountered in thought and shaped (inexactly) into ideas. Realist science is an as-yet-incomplete project to found belief on evidence rather than faith. We can readily admit that evidence is inadequate, sometimes misleading, and that reliance on the evidentiary is a belief. But science is a different order, a new kind of belief, that radically questions everything, even the basis of its knowledge claims ("epistemology"), rather than accepting anything as completely unknowable on the basis of faith—let it be clear that this is a response to Rist's (1997: 22) claim that Western beliefs in science and development are merely updated myths.

Science, conceived as evidence and radical questioning, may advance understanding by enabling realistic appraisals of life and its circumstances—for example, by showing that lightening is a giant electrical spark passing from positive to negative cloud particles rather than an expression of anger from the gods in heaven (and hence lightening conductors save lives, while prayer wastes time, preventing escape)—without claiming omnipotence or total knowledge. Some degree of empirical accuracy may be only the beginning of understanding, as existential philosophy argues. Accuracy may be a cultural invention of the West, as poststructural philosophy argues. But accuracy and evidence have this great difference from mystical blind faith: that they liberate the mind from its previous hallucinations about the supernatural. Science draws inspiration from a world of knowledge (as in ancient China, Egypt, and the Middle East—recall Bernal). Yet, the West has contributed something that underlies technology, productivity, and greater material certainty, namely, the possibility of founding theoretical statements on empirical "evidence"—hence, our call in Chapters 2 and 3 for the "science" of economics to be firmly grounded in historical evidence (England's real relations with Portugal, for instance, in trade theory).

We who try to base our beliefs on evidence rather than faith should look carefully at modernity's accomplishments: the fact that science has yielded enhanced productivity, enabling back-breaking labor to be performed by machines, and has permitted consumption to rise far above basic needs does create a margin of safety against natural catastrophes. A critique of development should discriminate between real advances like modern medicine, on the one hand, and the tragic misuse of scientific knowledge and technological productivity in support of frivolous consumption for a few rich people, on the other hand. Western science *has* demonstrated its positive power in improving material living standards, albeit at great environmental and social expense. Indeed, it is exactly the need for greater material security in Third World countries that empowers Western images and developmental models. Drawing on this tradition, development contains a real quest for improving the human condition. There should be a struggle to reorient developmental thought and practice rather than dismissing the entire modern developmental project as a negative power play. We need therefore more discriminating class and gender analyses that show how potentials come to be misused, restricted, exploitative, and environmentally dangerous.

We need to use the critical category of "capitalism" as the source of the perversion of the modern. A more discriminating materialist poststructural critique sees development as a discourse and system of organized practices produced under definite social relations. Social relations rather than anonymous and discontinuous epistemes guide the discovery and use of knowledge, the writing of documents, and the structuring of practices. From this perspective, the social relations that undergird discourses have to be transformed by radical politics rather than discourses merely being deconstructed—it takes more than words praising change to change the world. In this view also, development has unrealized potential, and radical analysis should be dedicated to extracting those notions from modern developmentalism that can be used to further the interests of peasants and workers rather than dismissing the entire venture.

In *Rethinking Development* (1989), Rajni Kothari argues that unfettered economic growth propelled by modern science and technology engenders a deadly arms race, a wasteful, consumption-driven civilization, and a pernicious class structure, all of which threaten democracy. The world, he says, is becoming overly dominated by a single conception of life. Yet, Kothari also warns against simplistic versions of a counterview, like reactionary antimodernism or rampant cultural relativism, that neglects the inextricable entwinement of North and South; he favors principles of both autonomy and integration. In terms of specific strategies, Kothari recommends fostering alternative lifestyles to high consumption and an ethic that discourages ostentatious living in favor of frugal limitations. In terms of the political organization of space, Kothari wants a Gandhi-style decentralization to promote a more equitable balance between urban and rural. He advocates a cultural attack on illiteracy and broad popular participation in economic production and public life (a decentralized participatory democratic structure that realizes social justice). For Kothari, the cultural and especially religious traditions of non-Western societies offer alternatives to Western scientific knowledge and the search for truth and a means of self-realization and self-control, he says, rather than a means of domination. Yet, rather than dismissing Western modernity, Kothari prefers a process of critical interaction between various civilization's traditions.

Likewise, Ashis Nandy (1987) argues for a *critical traditionalism* that tries to marshal the resources provided by inherited cultural frames for purposes of social and political transformation. For Nandy, as with Gandhi, the recollection of cultural traditions has to recognize the fissures between oppressors and oppressed while privileging the voices and categories of victims. Nandy has a general distrust of the ideas of the "winners of the world," believing that the faiths and ideals of the powerless and marginalized are the ways to freedom, compassion, and justice. In these views we find a postcolonial postdevelopmentalism open to dialogue with a critical modernism.

Finally, specifically, what of the poststructural/postmodern critique of reason (for that is the fundamental basis of this whole critical endeavor)? Here we think that poststructuralism makes a basic mistake. While claiming to despise structural, totalistic thinking as an instrument of totalitarian power, no less, poststructural thinkers see modern reason as a totality without significant internal fractures (that is, Hobbes, Locke, Smith, Marx, Ricardo, Mill, Lenin all share the same Enlightenment "space"). The case is similar with a modernity that swallows its critics. Here we find thinkers who once read Marx committing instant amnesia, while younger second- and third-generation poststructural thinkers do not even bother to open the covers of *Capital*. Were the latter to do so, they might discover a theory of ideology far more analytical than its progeny, the theory of discourse. What this theory says is: Western rationality was developed ideologically through espousing ideas that benefited the rising capitalist class and yet claimed universal good. Rationality was biased from the beginning (revisit Chapters 2 and 3 for a critique of political-economic reason); yet, this does not mean that rationality as a whole should be thrown out. It means that rationality, defined as careful, logical thinking based on provable beginning statements (for example, the earth revolves around the sun, gravity exerts downward force, humans must assure their existence by working, rich people have more power than poor people), is far preferable to its alternatives: unstructured, poetic, random, inconsistent postmodern thought (things are not caused—they just happen, history is discontinuous, power is inherent in human relations) already fast disappearing as its utter inadequacies are revealed in the crises of the 21st century. Rationality is a contested process of careful, logical ways of thinking. We should continually contest its premises and conclusions, not abandon it.

7

Feminist Theories of Development

Feminism is made up of several diverse social theories, political movements, and philosophies. Most of these adopt a critical stance toward the existing social relations, especially gendered relations. Feminist theory looks at the origins, characteristics, and forms of gender inequality in order to focus on gender politics, power relations, and sexuality. Feminism is consciously political and activist. Its politics centers on immediate issues like reproductive rights, domestic violence, maternity leave, equal pay, sexual harassment, discrimination, and sexual violence as well as such long-term issues as patriarchy, stereotyping, objectification, and oppression. Themes related to development include the inequality between genders, the disproportionate amount of work performed by women, and yet the absence of women in development policy or group decision making—in general, all of this being attributed to the subordination of women. In its early response, feminist political activism tried to create grassroots movements that crossed boundaries and brought together women of differing classes, races, cultures, religions, and regional backgrounds as a group suffering common forms of oppression. As feminism developed, this universalism came to be seen as oppressive in the sense that women from different backgrounds did not share the same experiences. In this regard especially, modern feminist theory was criticized as being predominantly associated with the views of Western middle-class academia rather than emanating from Third World intellectuals and activists. Increased emphasis was placed on differences, contradictions, and strategy rather than a unifying politics. We now have diverse feminist causes rather than a unified feminist movement.

Feminist activism and politics began as an organized movement in the latter half of the 19th century. Its first wave focused on equal contract rights and property rights for women and opposition to the ownership of married women (and their children) by their husbands. By the end of the 19th century, feminist activism concentrated primarily on gaining political power, particularly the inclusion of women in suffrage (voting rights). It was not until 1918–1928 that women finally gained the right to vote in Britain and the United States, showing the gender-biased nature of modern political democracy. The second wave of feminist activism and theory, beginning during the early 1960s and lasting through the late 1980s, expanded the feminist critique to capitalism as biased, discriminatory, and unfair. In the United States, second-wave feminism emerged from the civil rights and anti-Vietnam War movements when women, disillusioned with their second-class status even in activist student politics, began collectively to contend against discrimination. In a key book at the time, *The Feminine Mystique,* Betty Friedan (1963) observed that women were compelled to find meaning in their lives chiefly through their husbands and children, inclining them to lose their identity in that of their family. Friedan was instrumental in forming the National Organization for Women (NOW) in 1966, part of a broader social movement coalescing under the banner of "Women's Liberation." Second-wave feminists engaged in several kinds of activism, ranging from a protest against the Miss America beauty contest in 1968 to setting up consciousness-raising groups. However, differences emerged among black feminists, lesbian feminists, liberal feminists, and socialist feminists, with bell hooks, an African American feminist intellectual, arguing that the movement lacked minority voices and failed to address "the issues that divide women." The third wave of the 1990s is associated with the entry of poststructural and postmodern ideas into what had become a far more differentiated feminism. Third-wave feminism problematizes the second wave's "essentialist" definitions of femininity that often assumed a universal female identity and overemphasized the experiences of upper-middle-class white women. Third-wave theory places more emphasis on the fundamental ambiguity inherent in gendered terms and categories and usually includes queer theory and transgender politics while rejecting gender binaries. It also addresses itself to antiracism and women-of-color consciousness, womanism, postcolonial theory, critical theory, transnationalism, ecofeminism, libertarian feminism, and new feminist theory. Third-wave feminists often prefer micro- to macropolitics and include forms of gender expression and representation that are less explicitly political than their predecessors. Some theorists recognize a "postfeminist" trend beginning during the early 1990s that suggested that feminism was no longer needed. During the second and third waves, feminists interested in inequality, poverty, and gender relations produced a significant body of critical ideas on development, while issues raised by feminists became important in international agencies dealing with development problems—so much so that feminist development theory now forms a recognizable system of concepts, discourses, and practices.

This recognition of the position of women in development came not just from the efforts of feminist thinkers but also was brought about by real changes in the position of women in the global production system. The globalization of economic activity during the last third of the 20th century incorporated millions of women into the labor force. Indeed, women arguably are becoming the majority of the new global working class, pitted against global financial and industrial capital that is male-dominated. Global development pushed poor Third World women into jobs that have changed their social and economic status. There has been an increase in the number of poor households headed by women (widowed or abandoned), forcing women to undertake paid work along with their domestic responsibilities—that is, to double their total work effort. Women are entering the global labor force in record numbers, and more women work outside the household than ever before: some 1.1 billion of the world's 2.8 billion workers (40%) are women, representing a worldwide increase of nearly 200 million women in each recent decade. Unfortunately, they face higher unemployment rates and lower wages than men and therefore represent 60% of the world's 550 million working poor (International Labour Organization 2004). Of the 27 million people working worldwide in export processing zones (EPZs), some 90% are women—they usually make garments, shoes, toys, or electronic parts. Working for wages may increase women's say in the household and community, and increased communication among workers may open up the possibility for women to negotiate over their working conditions. But the feminization of employment primarily results from employers' needs for cheaper and more flexible sources of labor. This employment does not necessarily improve the well-being of the worker: it simply creates a double burden of paid and unpaid work, with employment usually occurring under poor-quality conditions. Many companies in EPZs employ young, unskilled, or semiskilled women, provide minimal training, and frequently move or restructure, leading to recurring unemployment. Women active in workers' movements, various left-wing organizations, and environmental, peace, and human rights movements are critical of this kind of global development. They look for alternatives, sometimes within development and sometimes outside of it. Critics range from those who lobby governance institutions for better economic policies founded on gender equality and social and environmental well-being to those who push for something completely different, as with good health and education, clean water and fuel, child care, and basic nutrition at a reasonable cost for the majority. Many feminists in this more critical vein join the growing resistance to the free trade and liberalization regimes of the Bretton

Woods institutions, such as women engaged in the 50 Years Is Enough campaign, End Debt, the World Social Forum, and various NGOs and women's movements (Harcourt and Escobar 2005; Miles 1996). In sum, women are on the development agenda because of their importance as well as their insistence. The question is: What positions do they occupy on that agenda?

FEMINIST EPISTEMOLOGY

To answer the question of the position of women in the development debate, we might first look at some significant arguments in feminist epistemology. ("Epistemology" basically means the theory of knowledge, especially how it is produced and how it is judged to be true or not.) Questions of feminist epistemology, many outlined for the first time during the late 1970s and early 1980s, became central foci of feminist concern by the mid- to late 1980s. Enlightenment notions of reason, progress, science, and emancipation underlie the modern development project as its foundations in modern belief. And as we have seen, the modern belief in scientific rationality came under new criticism during the last third of the 20th century from several directions, one of these being feminism. In *The Man of Reason* Genevieve Lloyd (1984) argued that the modern ideal of rationality, developed during the 17th century by Descartes, Spinoza, and other philosophers, was characterized by maleness, so that when they spoke of "human ideals" they were actually talking about "ideals of manhood." The 17th-century philosopher René Descartes, Lloyd argues, separated clear and distinct thinking (reason), which he attributed to men, from the sensuous and imaginative faculties (emotions) that he attributed to women—that is, men are rational and women emotional. Spinoza thought that emotions, in their original state as passions, were confused perceptions of reality that could be transformed into intellect only through a strong man's detached (distanced, objective) understanding of such grand questions as universality and transhistorical necessity. Then, during the Enlightenment, suggests Lloyd, passion and nonrationality were regarded somewhat more positively, as wellsprings of action. Even so, passion was either to be transcended or transformed through the medium of reason into "higher" (more masculine) rational modes of thought. Nineteenth-century romanticism, Lloyd thought, again revalued the passions but this time put women on a pedestal, leaving the man of reason intact—and thus preserving the modern dichotomy between reason and passion, men as rational and women as emotional. Poststructural feminists not only were critical of the Enlightenment notion that all problems could be solved by reason (and men) but also went on to the far more radical idea that many problems actually have their origin in (male) reason. Hence, Lloyd asserted, feminists joined in the poststructural critique of reason and its enlightened products, such as modern development.

In a parallel argument dealing with science, Sandra Harding (1986) argued that feminist criticisms had moved from positions stressing the improvement of science to ones favoring transformation of the foundations of science and the cultures that accord value to science:

> The radical feminist position holds that the epistemologies, metaphysics, ethics, and politics of the dominant forms of science are androcentric [male-centered] and mutually supportive; that despite the deeply ingrained Western cultural belief in science's intrinsic progressiveness, science today serves primarily regressive social tendencies; and that the social structure of science, many of its applications and technologies, its modes of defining research problems and designing experiments, its ways of constructing and conferring meanings are not only sexist but also racist, classist, and culturally coercive. In their analysis of how gender symbolism, the social division of labor by gender, and the construction of individual gender identity have affected the history and philosophy of science, feminist thinkers have challenged the intellectual and social orders at their very foundation. (Harding 1986: 9)

Thus, the methodologies and transcendental truths of science that had previously been taken to be humanly inclusive carried instead the marks of gender, class, race, and culture. Techniques of literary criticism, used to "read science as a text," revealed the hidden social meanings of supposedly value-neutral scientific claims and practices. Feminist epistemologies wanted to establish alternative bases that might ground the beliefs honored as scientific knowledge.

Harding outlined three sets of feminist epistemological attitudes toward science: *feminist empiricism* argued that stricter adherence to existing norms of inquiry by women scientists could correct social biases in science; *feminist standpoint theory,* originating in Hegelian and Marxist thought, argued that men's dominance resulted in partial and perverse understandings whereas women's subjugated position gave them the potential for more complete understanding; and *feminist postmodernism* challenged the universalizing assumptions of the other two positions, emphasizing the fractured identities created by modern life and the multiple nature of theorizing. Harding questioned whether feminists should give up trying to provide *one* true feminist story about reality when confronted by powerful alliances between science and sexist, racist social projects. She concluded that, while feminist epistemological notions had their own problems and contradictory tendencies, feminist criticism had already enhanced the understanding of androcentrism in science (Harding 1986: 29).

A particularly interesting variant of feminist standpoint theory was developed by the Canadian sociologist Dorothy Smith. Smith (2002) perceived a growing gap between the responsible person she was as a wife and mother and the person she was expected to be as a scholar. Ways of knowing that were relevant at home, as a wife and mother, were not recognized as a legitimate basis for knowing in the intelletual world. Women could also learn to operate in the abstract conceptual (male) mode, but this meant suppressing their experiential knowledge in favor of objectified knowing. Working "ideologically," women scholars contribute to the research that determines how the world gets framed for the people who live in it. How women's experience gets written about and reflected officially in documents differs fundamentally from women's real experiences in home and family. The new official knowledge is then used against women authoritatively, to re-order and manage them. In particular Smith was interested in official documents, or "documentary realities" more broadly, and their part in making authority and power systems: text-mediated social organization as the technology of ruling in late 20th-century capitalist societies (Smith 1990a: 209–224). In a knowledge-based society, ruling practices rely on authorized versions of knowledge routinely generated by social scientists, organization theorists, and information management scholars and consultants. People take up these ruling concepts and activate them as they go about their daily lives. Such official knowledge is routinely counted on to make organizations function smoothly. Texts transport power in ideologies and practices across sites and among people. Text-mediated ruling practices, Smith argued, subordinate local knowing, imposing ruling perspectives. Women's standpoint grounded in everyday experience offers a challenge to these ruling perspectives. "At the line of fault along which women's experience breaks away from the discourses mediated by texts ... a critical standpoint emerges" (1990a: 11). Smith asserted that women's standpoint, grounded in everyday experiences, was the starting point for a different approach to knowing fully and in a more trustworthy way. Women have the experience of being "out-of-step" in many situations. Knowing differently was the basis for changing the conditions of women's lives. This meant identifying and challenging the otherwise unquestioned, taken-for-granted, prevailing ways of knowing and acting. When people begin to see how they participate in their own and others' oppression by using the oppressor's language and tools and taking up actions that are not in their own interests, antioppressive work should be advanced (Campbell 2003). Furthering this, Smith (2002) was instrumental in forming an approach called "institutional ethnography" that emphasizes connections among sites and situations in everyday life, professional practice, and policymaking circles. These connections are accomplished primarily through "textually-mediated social organization." Smith developed the approach initially in a feminist context, calling it a method that could produce a sociology *for* (rather than *about*) women, but recognized its wider applications; theorists following Smith have looked at a number of relevant topics, including the organization of healthcare, education, and social work practice, the regulation of sexuality, police and judicial processing of violent acts against women, employment and job training, economic and social restructuring, international development regimes, planning and environmental policy, the organization of home and community life, and various kinds of activism. While the method is ethnographic (using field work to produce detailed descriptions of institutions, ethnic groups, etc.) it is more concerned with political-economic contexts than most qualitative approaches and is sensitive to the textual and discursive dimensions of social life (Devault 1999). Smith's ideas are similar to poststructural ideas derived from Foucault, but Smith disagreed with the postmodern position that "den[ies] that categories and concepts can refer to and represent a reality beyond them, indeed, that it is meaningful to speak of a reality which is not in language" (1999: 99). She found that in poststructuralist/postmodernist writings, the knowing subject, the actual person, located bodily in time and space is not there. Agency or causal efficacy, she said, is reassigned by postmodernists to discourse, language, or culture. This practice challenged the very possibility of inquiry.

Yet, even as such issues of rationality, science, text, and, by extension, modern projects like development were being raised, the entire (Western) feminist project was subjected to critique from women of color, women who were lesbians, and Third World women (Rich 1986). For Audre Lorde, a black lesbian scholar, the feminist claim that all women suffered the same oppression just because they were women lost sight of the varied tools of patriarchy and ignored how these tools were used by women themselves against women. For Lorde, differences among women should be seen as a fund of strengths—these differences were, she said, "polarities between which our creativity can spark like a dialectic" (Lorde 1981: 99). Without community there was no liberation. But community could not mean shedding differences, nor the "pathetic pretense" that differences between women did not exist. The failure of academic feminists to recognize differences as strengths was a failure to reach beyond the first patriarchal lesson—divide and conquer—which, for Lorde, had to be transformed into ... define and empower.

Lorde's notion of the power inherent in the theorization of differences was expressed with particular force by Third World women. Trinh

Minh-ha (1989) thought that differences should not be defined by the dominant sex, but neither should they be defined by the dominant (Western) culture. Under the rubric of "cartographies of struggle" Chandra Mohanty (1991a, 1991b) critically examined feminist writings that produced the "Third World woman" as a singular monolithic subject in a process that she called "discursive colonization." By this she meant the appropriation and codification of scholarship and knowledge through analytical categories that took as their primary referent feminist interests articulated in the West. For Mohanty, this discursive colonization suppressed the heterogeneity of Third World subjects. Feminist writers, she said, "discursively colonize the material and historical heterogeneities of the lives of women in the third world, thereby producing/re-presenting a composite, singular "third world woman"—an image which appears arbitrarily constructed, but nevertheless carries with it the authorizing signature of Western humanist discourse" (Mohanty 1991b: 53). Much feminist work on women in the Third World, she said, was characterized by assumptions of privilege and ethnocentric universality and was insufficiently self-conscious about the effects of Western scholarship. Analyses based on cross-culturally singular monolithic notions of patriarchy or male dominance led to a similarly reductive notion of Third World differences, a systematization of the oppression of women that she herself found to be exercising oppressive power. Mohanty found disconcerting similarities between such Western feminist positions and the project of Western humanism in general. Only because "woman" and "East" were defined as "peripheral" or "Other" could Western man represent himself as "center" or "Same." "It is not the center that determines the periphery, but the periphery that, in its boundedness, determines the center" (Mohanty 1991b: 73–74). French poststructural feminist theorists such as Julia Kristeva (1980) and Helene Cixous (1981) had deconstructed the latent anthropomorphism in Western discourse; Mohanty suggested a parallel strategy, namely, focusing on a latent ethnocentrism in feminist writing on women in the Third World.

Mohanty's statement, made from a position of feminism's Other, profoundly disrupted the prevailing mode of feminist discourse that had taken the form of competing political positions within an assumed Western and privileged realm (Western women know how to develop "them"). The notion of a singular progressive women's movement began to be questioned ... increasingly and insistently. Then, as the 1980s turned into the 1990s, the full force of the postmodern turn in philosophy and social theory also began to enter feminist theory. Postmodern feminism found modern reason to be normalizing, Western, masculine prejudice, whose "enlightenment" embodied a scientific rationalism that colonized (and therefore subjugated) alternative ways of thinking. For some, the Enlightenment and feminism had to be opposed to each other in principle. For instance, Jane Flax (1990: 42) contended that feminist theory belonged in the terrain of postmodern philosophy: "Feminist notions of the self, knowledge, and truth are too contradictory to those of the Enlightenment to be contained within its categories. The way(s) to feminist future(s) cannot lie in reviving or appropriating Enlightenment concepts of the person or knowledge." Thus, some feminist theorists began to sense that the motto of the Enlightenment "have courage to use your own reason" (this from Kant) rested on a gender-rooted sense of self and self-deception. The suspicion arose that all transcendental claims reflected and reified the experience of a few persons, mostly white male Westerners. For others, the matter was not that clear. Other feminist social theorists found greater potential in a critique of Western humanism (Johnson 1994). Christine Di Stefano (1990) argued that mainstream postmodernist theory (Derrida, Lyotard, Rorty, Foucault, etc.) had been remarkably insensitive to questions of gender in its rereadings of history, politics, and culture (that is, postmodern theory merely continued the modernist project). Perhaps most importantly, the postmodern project, if seriously adopted by feminists, would make any semblance of a united feminist politics impossible. Thus, many leftist thinkers advocated that feminists should remain skeptical about anti-Enlightenment criticisms; just as women were finally being granted the power of reason, postmodern feminists were undercutting rationality. Luce Irigaray (1985) asked: Was postmodernism the "last ruse" of patriarchy? Nancy Hartsock (1985) noted that, while postmodernism appeared to side with marginal groups, postmodernists ended up hindering them rather than helping them—that is, postmodern theories gave little political guidance at best, and at worst merely recapitulated the effects of Enlightenment theories. Such other feminist theorists as Flax and Di Stefano were ambivalent about the choice between modernism and postmodernism. However, rather than attempting to resolve this ambivalence by favoring one side over the other, Sandra Harding (1990: 86), for example, argued that "ambivalence should be much more robust and principled."—that is, she argued for a self-conscious and theoretically articulated ambivalence derived from the tensions and contradictions in the worlds inhabited by women. Harding herself, however, concluded that feminism stood on Enlightenment ground in its belief that improved theories contributed to social progress. She thought that feminist inquiry could produce less partial theories without asserting their absolute, universal, or eternal adequacy. Thus, in her view, both feminist science theorists and their feminist postmodern critics "stand with one foot in modernity and the other in the lands beyond" (Harding 1990: 100). She thought that feminism needed *both* the Enlightenment and postmodern agendas.

Located in such an "in-between position" (between the modern and postmodern), Donna Haraway (1988, 1991) argued for a feminist epistemology of objectivity that she called "situated knowledges." In this conception, objectivity was concerned with the particular and specific, with embodiment and not false visions of transcendence: "Only partial perspectives promise objective vision. ... Feminist objectivity is about limited location and situated knowledge, not about transcendence and splitting of subject and object. In this way we might become answerable for what we learn how to see" (Haraway 1991: 190). In other words objectivity is knowledge about what can be precisely known. For Haraway, feminism could theorize the grounds for trusting the vantage points of the subjugated—feminism could see from the peripheries and the depths. The positions of subjugated peoples could not be exempted from criticism, but they were to be *preferred* because they were least likely to deny the critical interpretive core of knowledge. So, the important question, for Haraway, was not *whether* to see from below but *how* to see from below. Such a preferred positioning she found to be as hostile to relativism as it was to totalization and the modern notion of a single human vision. The alternative was partial, locatable, critical knowledges, sustaining webs of political connections and conversations in epistemology (situated knowledges), whereas relativism was being nowhere and yet claiming to be everywhere (a "god-trick"). With other feminists, Haraway argued for a practice of objectivity that privileged contestation, deconstruction, construction, webbed connections, transformation, mobile positioning, and passionate detachment:

> I am arguing for politics and epistemologies of location, positioning, and situating, where partiality and not universality is the condition of being heard to make rational knowledge claims. These are claims on people's lives; the view from a body, always a complex, contradictory, structuring and structured body, versus the view from above, from nowhere, from simplicity. Only the god-trick is forbidden. (Haraway 1991: 195)

For her, the only way to find a larger vision was to be somewhere in particular. The feminist science question involved objectivity as positioned rationality. Its images were made from joining partial views and halting voices into a collective subject position that she described as a series of views from somewhere.

All this may sound intellectually interesting (if a bit obscure) but not too relevant in terms of the topics broached by this book—contentions over development. So, let us now briefly point these epistemological arguments about rationality, scientific objectivity, modernity, and truth toward issues of poverty, development, and power. Beginning with Descartes and the separation between clear and distinct thinking (male reason) and sensuous imagination (female emotions), feminist criticism raises the suspicion that all modern products of reason, like progress and development, are not universally good for everyone (as usually pretended) but instead are masculine projects, conceived by masculine minds, that are particularly good for men. In this sense, development can be seen as the *problem* for women, not the solution. Critiques of Western science by feminist epistemologists that lay the basis for alternative ways of thinking could lead also to alternative ways of developing that favor women. But the Third World feminist critique challenged this from the beginning, saying, essentially, "We are different from you in many ways—don't speak for us, and don't tell us how to develop." The postmodern feminist position on reason as colonizing scientific rationalism likewise finds development to be subtle Western coercion—"coercion" because it entraps women's optimism about the future. Other, more ambivalent, partially postmodern positions would retain development yet completely rethink it. In doing so, feminists following Harroway suggest: do not think in the grand terms of a universal development model, and do not plan development from afar in Washington or New York (the god's-eye view), but instead employ situated knowledges that listen to peoples varied experiences, particular circumstances, and varied needs and desires to construct "situated developments." For us, such issues of great importance to development are implied by feminist epistemology.

FEMINIST CRITICISMS OF DEVELOPMENT THEORY

These feminist incursions into the heart of modern epistemology, within the growth and differentiation of radical and socialist feminist thought in general, led to a critical reexamination of development theory as a masculinist enterprise. In a leading example, Catherine Scott (1995) critiqued modernization and dependency theories. She saw such conceptualizing themes as modernity, development, self-reliance, and revolution to be within a vision informed by gendered preoccupations and conceptions; these extended, she claimed, to the dominant policies and practices of international institutions and revolutionary governments alike. In modernization theory, Scott (1995: 5) argued, modernity's rational, forward-looking, male-dominated public sphere was contrasted with a feminized, backward, traditional, family-oriented private sphere. Achieving modernity was a power struggle between rational modernity and feminine traditionalism in the passage toward "maturity" (Rostow). In modernization, development required the emergence of rational industrial man, receptive to new ideas, punctual, optimistic, and universalistic, with a counterpart in the modern efficient state, with its new mechanisms of domination and power. For Scott, this universal model of modernization was based on an often idealized version of masculine modernity. In this approach, women were alternately invisible, treated paternalistically, or used as a "litmus test" for determining the degree of a country's backwardness. Modernization required self-propelled men to leave the household, abandon tradition, and assume their place among other rational men. Women and the household were conceived as parts of the past, containing a dangerous worldview that nature was unalterable and people powerless to control it. So, modernization involved the subordination of tradition, nature, and the feminine. For Scott, theories of modernization also replicated the public–private dichotomy prominent in Western thought: the private sphere and females as inferior and derivative, or merely complementary to the favored public and male sphere.

Scott also criticized dependency theory—even that opposing modernization as representing the spread of capitalism and the intensification of exploitation. Scott argued that dependency, in its U.S. version especially, did not challenge the notion of an inherently dynamic and progressive capitalism that might end the pressing requirements of material necessity. As with Marx's (early) notions about an unchanging Asia, dependency theorists saw precapitalist social formations as obstructions to the realization of autonomous development in the peripheries. Hence, dependency, Scott thought, shared modernization theory's dichotomous oppositions between the rational sphere of capitalist production and the private precapitalist realm of family reproduction, this timed within a binary logic of center and periphery. Dependency theory portrayed industrialization of the public sphere as the paradigm for economic development, with stagnant precapitalist social structures obstructing this kind of progress. Dependency theory shared with Marxism a definition of development as the mastery and transformation of nature. It too centered conceptualization of social struggles around productive activity, excluding struggles between men and women and retaining (however implicitly) notions of nature as feminine.

Scott thought that both modernization and dependency theorists could learn from such a critical rereading of their ideas. Self-criticism could lead to a reconsideration of the meaning of modernity, industrialization, work, and development. Such a rereading allowed development theory to be placed within the crisis affecting Western social theory in the sense of questioning the rational subjects of theory, such masculinist dichotomies as modern and traditional, center and periphery, First and Third Worlds, and the role of theory in maintaining the essentialist categories that made dominance possible. Scott preferred feminist standpoint theory as her theoretical and political perspective. This preference made her sensitive to the ways in which systemic power structures lives. And it has possibilities for rewriting the meaning of development in terms of people's continuing efforts to realize their aspirations (Scott 1995).

WOMEN, DEVELOPMENT, THEORY

In response to such criticisms, feminists and development activists made a series of attempts at reformulating development theory. The basic issue was this: Given that women performed most of the labor in many, if not most, Third World societies, why had they been excluded from development theory, and what differences would it make if theory was reformulated to center around gender relations and women's experiences? Placing gender relations at the center of theorization, feminist development theorists argued, reorients developmental discourse toward different topics and interests. Traditional areas of developmental concern are seen from a different vantage point. Aspects of development previously relegated to the margins become, instead, the main foci of interest; for example, Third World industrialization employed not labor (assumed to be male) but women workers, while gender relations, previously subordinated to class considerations, became essential to understanding productive activity. As a consequence new aspects of development can be brought into focus—for example, the informal and rural sectors of the economy, the reproductive sphere as a vital component of development, relations between production and reproduction, gender relations in export-oriented production, inequalities stemming from development, the products of development (needs, not whims), with the thinker going all the way from conceptualization to experience.

To make this discussion a bit more concrete, we might consider rethinking development from specific feminist positions. For example, let us take the position of the feminist standpoint theory mentioned several times already and outlined in *Money, Sex and Power* by Nancy Hartsock (1985). In Hartsock's work, standpoint theory posits a series of levels of reality, with the deeper levels including and explaining the surfaces, or only appearances, of reality. Within this ontological position, feminist standpoint theory amplifies the liberatory possibilities embodied in women's experience. The feminist standpoint is related to the working-class standpoint (that is, Marxism theorizing on behalf of the exploited) but is more thoroughgoing, particularly because women do most of the work involved in reproducing labor power. For Hartsock, the male worker's contact with nature outside the factory is mediated by women, hence the female experience is deeper. Women's experience in reproduction represents a unity with nature that goes beyond the proletarian experience of material metabolic interchange. Motherhood results in the construction of female existence centered on a complex relational nexus and focused on the woman's body. By comparison, the man's experience is characterized by a duality of the concrete versus the abstract, deriving from the separation between household and public life. Such masculine dualism marks phallocentric social theory, a system of hierarchical dualisms (abstract–concrete, mind–body, culture–nature, stasis–change, developed–underdeveloped, First World–Third World, etc.). By comparison, suggests Hartsock:

> Women's construction of self in relation to others leads in an opposite direction—towards opposition to dualisms of any sort; valuation of concrete, everyday life; a sense of variety of connectedness and continuities with other persons and with the natural world. If material life structures consciousness, women's relationally defined existence, bodily experience of boundary challenges and activity transforming both physical objects and human beings must be expected to result in a world view to which dichotomies are foreign. (Hartsock 1985: 242)

A feminist standpoint, Hartsock thought, might be based in the commonalities within women's experiences, but this is not obvious, nor is it self-evident—it needs reading out, developing, propagating. Hence, for Hartsock, women's life activity forms the basis of a specifically feminist materialism and, we might add, a specifically feminist development theory. Generalizing the human possibilities present in the life activity of women to the whole social system might raise for the first time in history "the possibility of a fully human community, a community structured by a variety of connections rather than separation and opposition" (Hartsock 1985: 247). Extending this insight, socialist feminists want to reformulate development in a way that combines, rather than separates, everyday life and the wider societal dimension, with productive activities of all kinds considered as a totality rather than split into hierarchical types (work–home), and with relations with nature placed at the heart of decisions on what and how much to produce.

We, the authors of this book, find socialist feminism of the Hartsock type to be the most convincing. But, as the preceding discussion has already shown, feminists have many different epistemologies and hold to quite different political beliefs. Thus, when it comes to feminist critical discussion of development, a variety of positions appears. Many feminist theorists of development think that the interaction between feminism and development has taken five main forms (see Figure 7.1): Women in Development (WID); Women and Development (WAD); Gender and Devel-

WID **Women in Development** Liberal Modernization Theory Restructuring Development Programs Welfare, Equity, Antipoverty, Efficiency, Empowerment	**WAD** **Women and Development** Socialist Feminism Alternative Development Dependency, Global Capitalism, Patriarchy

GAD
Gender and Development
Radical Feminism
Women's Emancipation

Capitalism, Patriarchy, Racism

WED **Women, Environment,** **and Development** Feminist Political Ecology Sustainable Development Gendered Knowledges, Rights, Politics	**PAD** **Postmodernism and Development** Postmodern Feminism Postdevelopment, Different Development Representation, Discourse, Local Knowledges

FIGURE 7.1. Forms of feminist development theory.

opment (GAD); Women, Environment, and Development (WED); and Postmodernism and Development (PAD) (Rathgeber 1990; Young 1992; Visvanathan et al. 1997). We ourselves are not too sure about the usefulness of this categorization. But it is frequently used, so we will report on it.

WOMEN IN DEVELOPMENT

Perhaps the first important statement about the position of women in development was made by Esther Boserup, a Danish agricultural economist who had previously written a seminal text called *The Conditions of Agricultural Growth* (1965), which made the case that demographic pressure (population density) promotes innovation and higher productivity in the use of land (irrigation, weeding, crop intensification, better seeds) and labor (tools, better techniques). Boserup followed up her first book with *Women's Role in Economic Development* (1970), a critique of the idea that modernization, expressed as economic efficiency and modern planning, would emancipate women in the Third World. Boserup argued, to the contrary, that the modernization process, supervised by colonial authorities imbued with Western notions of the sexual division of labor, had placed new technologies under the control of men. This arrangement marginalized women (the main food producers in agricultural societies), reducing their status and undercutting their power and income. However, while modernization was not automatically progressive, Boserup thought that more enlightened policies by national governments and international agencies might correct these earlier mistakes. As Jane Jaquette (1990: 55) observed later: "Boserup's path-breaking work defined a new arena of policymaking and marked out a new area of professional expertise. The United States and other countries that are major donors of development assistance took steps to promote the integration of women into the development process."

Boserup's revelations helped produce a new phenomenon, which was first termed "women in development," by the Women's Committee of the Washington, DC, chapter of the Society for International Development as part of a strategy calling attention to Third World women's situation (Rathgeber 1990: 490). In the United States, the Percy Amendment to the 1973 Foreign Assistance Act called for paying particular attention to projects that integrated women into the national economies of foreign countries, thereby improving their status and assisting in the development effort. An Office for Women in Development was established within USAID in 1974 (which was moved to the U.S. Bureau for Program and Policy Coordination in 1977). This office served as the nucleus for a network of researchers and practitioners in universities, research institutions (for example, the International Center for Research on Women, founded in Washington, DC, in 1976), and major foundations (the Ford Foundation chief, among them) interested in economic development. As part of this movement, the UN declared the years 1975–1985 to be the "United Nations Decade for Women." Moreover, as a result of pressure from feminist movements, virtually every development organization established programs to improve the economic and social position of women, the assumption usually being that women's problems stemmed from insufficient participation in what was otherwise assumed to be a benevolent process of economic growth. After the 1975 International Women's Year Conference in Mexico, the UN established UNIFEM (the United Nations Development Fund for Women) as a way of "reaching out to the poorest women in the world." When asked what they needed most, the predominant answer from women was income sufficient to provide for themselves and their children (Snyder 1995). The progressive, liberal idea was to increase women's participation and improve their share in resources, employment, and income in an attempt to effect dramatic improvements in living conditions. Essentially the key idea was to bring women full force into the development process (Mueller 1987).

The WID position adopted by most of these formal state and governance institutions accepted the prevailing modernization theme of the time—that development is a linear process of economic growth and that differences between modern and traditional societies resulted from lack of sufficient contacts between them. The WID approach was to integrate women into existing development projects by addressing "women's issues" like maternal mortality and setting up women-only projects and organizations that addressed practical gender needs and interests (Moser 1993). During the late 1970s several studies documented facts about women's lives, such as the amount of unpaid labor women performed, while at the same time in-depth qualitative studies explored women's roles in local communities. One such study, prepared by the UN, documented the severity of gender inequality as follows: "As a group women ... put in two thirds of the total number of working hours, they are registered as constituting one third of the total labour force and receive one tenth of the total remuneration. They own one percent of the world's material goods and their rights to ownership is often far less than those of men" (quoted in Pezzullo 1982: 15). Yet, during the United Nations decade devoted to women (1976–1985) their relative position actually worsened in terms of access to resources, work burdens, health, nutrition, and education! This lack of progress brought about the realization of the limited efficacy of an integrationist WID-type approach—integrating women into a presumed progressive system—and radicalized the study of Women and Development (WAD; Sen and Grown 1987). Formal meetings of the UN and other international organizations began to be disrupted by increasingly critical and feminist women. At the International Women's Year Conference in Mexico in 1975, and at a "mid-decade" (relative to the UN's declarations) Conference on Women in Copenhagen in 1980, fierce debates erupted over women's issues and the relevance of feminist theory. By the time of the 1985 Nairobi UN conference, Third World women, by then a clear majority of those attending, were defining the main issues, while most of the organizing and discussion occurred at alternative meetings held coincident with the official UN program. So, the Alternative Forum at Nairobi attracted 16,000 women to discuss women's conditions, the main themes being gender-based violence, the exclusion of women from control over vital resources, the feminization of poverty, and the need for more radical approaches that questioned the very structures of existing societies. Feminism in development shifted from being primarily a Western women's concern to becoming a more heterogeneous movement, with an expanded definition reflecting greater involvement by organizations and movements from Third World countries.

Caroline Moser (1993) has distinguished five variants within the WID school that reflect changes in the policies of the Western development agencies: (1) the "welfare approach" prior to 1970 focused on women's reproductive roles and related population issues, with programs initiated in such areas as birth control; Geeta Chowdry (1995) has argued that this approach illustrated WID's representation of Third World women as *zenana* (private, domestic world); (2) the "equity approach" reflected calls for equality coming from the UN Decade for Women—this met with considerable resistance from men; (3) the "antipoverty approach" focused on women entering the workforce, having access to income-generating activities, and joining the existing economic mainstream; Chowdry (1995) points out that, even so, women were still seen as occupying only the domestic private sphere, well removed from the political and economic affairs of society; (4) the "efficiency approach," which was aligned with IMF structural adjustment programs, stressed women's participation in restructured economies; and (5) the "empowerment approach" reflected Third World feminist writings, grassroots organizing, and women's need to transform laws and structures through a bottom-up approach. In all these approaches women were represented as victims.

During the late 1970s and 1980s, the WID approach came under increasing criticism. Chowdry (1995: 26) argued that WID programs, as implemented by international development agencies, originated in two modernist discourses, the colonial discourse and the liberal discourse on markets. The colonial discourse, she thought, homogenized and essentialized Third World people by using the image of the "poor woman" (as an object of pity and remorse). The liberal discourse promoted free markets, voluntary choice, and individualism, themes that Chowdry found to be disempowering to Third World women. WID basically aligned itself with liberal feminism, although it used the poor woman image to evoke sympathy and obtain funds. Many of the WID practitioners were well-educated liberal feminists, and the liberal feminist view of rationality and individual self-improvement prevailed in the approach. There was a representational emphasis in WID on "role models" or "outstanding women who have gained social recognition in the public sphere" to encourage "successful" female integration into the mainstream (Young 1993: 129). Thus, WID accepted the existing social and power structures, working within them to improve the position of women. Hence, the sexual division of labor was taken for granted as natural, without theorizing how women came to be oppressed by men. Ideological aspects of gender, unequal responsibilities between men and women, and the unequal value placed on men's and women's activities were all ignored. As an ahistorical approach, WID did not consider influences on women such as class, race, or culture. WID's exclusive focus on women, and its avoidance of gender relations, made for shallow social and economic analysis. WID avoided questioning women's subordination as part of a wider global system of capital accumulation. WID emphasized poverty and not oppression, and poverty was not seen as an outcome of male oppression over women. Hence, development strategies based on the WID position would be flawed, severely limited in their ability to bring about change. WID focused solely on the (formally) productive aspect of women's work, ignoring or dismissing reproductive activities. Mirroring moderniza- tion theory, development was seen as economic growth that could only occur in (formally) productive activities. This led to a partial analysis of women's roles and relations. For example, WID-supported activities provided income-generating opportunities for women, but there were no strategies for reducing the burden of their household tasks or improving reproductive technologies. WID adopted a nonconfrontational approach that sidestepped women's subordination and oppression. This emphasis on poverty also created a division between the demands of First World and Third World feminists as WID became involved with the needs of women "out there" in the developing world, while the feminist theorists remained part of Western culture—hence, a new kind of maternal, sor- rowful gaze on the poor woman "Other." More generally, there was a neglect of questioning the whole assumption and goal of the dominant development paradigm of modernization theory (Rathgeber 1990; Young 1993).

Postmodern feminist critics claimed that theorists and practitioners working in the WID school tended to represent Third World women con- ventionally as backward, vulnerable, and in need of help from the First World. Jane Parpart and Marianne Marchande (1995: 16) argued that the "WID discourse has generally fostered development practices that ignore difference(s), indigenous knowledge(s) and local expertise while legitimating foreign 'solutions' to women's problems in the South"— all of this fits easily with U.S. aid policies. The outstanding poststruc- tural critique of WID came from Adele Mueller (1987), using Foucault's (1980a) notions of the connections between power and knowledge, and Dorothy Smith's (1990a) ideas about the social construction of docu- mentary reality. Mueller argued that the documentary procedures used by WID programs functioned to shift control over developmental issues from Third World settings to centralized development agency headquar- ters in Washington, Ottawa, and Geneva. In WID, development was defined as a technical problem requiring sophisticated methodologies available only in the First World. Accounts of Third World women were written in policy language amenable to the ongoing textual practices of development agencies. "Integrating women into development" basically involved WID professionals learning to speak bureaucratic policy lan- guage and teaching textual practices to others. Mueller's (1987: 2) main critical finding was that "far from being a liberating force in the worldwide women's movement, Women in Development discourse is produced in and enters into the procedures of the Development institution in order to manage and otherwise rule the hierarchical divisions of the capitalist world order."

These were damning criticisms. Yet, WID did not disappear as a result of these and many other theoretical, political, and practical inadequacies, for it is ensconced in structures of power far removed from academic or theoretical critique. However, partly in response, a new paradigm opened to the left that came to be called Women *and* Development (WAD).

WOMEN AND DEVELOPMENT

The WID approach argued that women should be brought into the modernization process. The WAD perspective argued that it was precisely their link with modernization that had impoverished them. As opposed to WID's modernization theory, WAD drew much more from dependency theory and neo-Marxist approaches to underdevelopment. Questions such as the origins of patriarchy, the intensification of patriarchy with the spread of capitalism, and Engels's (1972) analysis of the rise of private property, along with the agricultural revolution and the domestication of animals, formed the deep historical background to this school of thought (Bandarage 1984; Mies 1986). Rathgeber (1990) has pointed out that the WAD perspective focused on the social relations between men and women rather than Marxism's class relations. This view finds women always playing important roles in the economies of their societies as both productive and reproductive actors. It was precisely how women and their labor had been integrated into global capitalism by the core countries that explained marginalization and oppression—as a contemporary example, women used as cheap labor for multinational corporations in export-processing zones (Visvanathan 1986, 1991, 1997).

There has long been a socialist strain to the feminism that formed around WAD. However, the relationship often takes the form of a critique of Marxism. Socialist feminists pointed to deficiencies in classical Marxism—that its analysis missed activities and relations fundamental to women's existence—yet many also continued to admire the historical materialist form of understanding and shared Marxism's liberating intent. Socialist feminists have been particularly critical of classical Marxism's emphasis on the economy and its relative silence on the question of women (Mitchell 1966). An early feminist theorist, Heidi Hartmann (1981), argued that the analytical categories of Marxism were "sex-blind" in that the causes of gender inequality (male dominance over women) were lost during structural Marxist analyses of class inequality (ruling class domination over workers). A specifically feminist socialist analysis was needed to reveal the systematic character of gender inequalities. Yet, also, most feminist analyses were insufficiently materialist and historical for Hartmann. Hence, both "Marxist analysis, particularly its historical and materialist method, and feminist analysis, especially the identification of patriarchy as a social and historical structure, must be drawn upon if we are to understand the development of western capitalist societies and the predicament of women within them" (Hartmann 1981: 3).

A main concern of socialist feminism involved retheorizing the significance of women's work. Juliet Mitchell (1966), of Cambridge University, differentiated between the several structures affecting women's condition—production, reproduction, socialization, and sexuality—with the first involving women's work in the nondomestic economic sphere and the others concerning women as wives or mothers. Each structure had different contradictions and dynamics. But all formed a unity in women's experience, with the family triptych of sexual, reproductive, and socializing functions dominant. Women performing domestic labor within the home and family created a different relation to the means of production than men. These activities fulfilled the function of the maintenance and reproduction of labor power in (contradictory) relation to production. Mariarosa Dalla Costa (1973) emphasized the quality of life and relations in domestic work as determining women's place in society regardless of circumstances of place or class. Housewives were exploited workers, whose surplus was used most immediately by their husbands as an instrument of oppression—under capitalism, Dalla Costa said, women became the slaves of wages.

In socialist feminism, as compared with Marxism, emphasis was replaced on the sexual division of labor or different types of social praxis (broadly interpreted) as the material experiential bases of physical and psychological differences between men and women. Women were constituted by the social relations they inhabited and the types of labor they performed. Beginning with the Marxist notion of production for the satisfaction of needs, socialist feminism argued that needs for bearing and raising children were as important as material needs (food, shelter) as well as needs of sexual satisfaction and emotional nurturing, all of which required (usually female) labor. Gender struggles over reproductive activity were fundamental, yet often ignored in traditional Marxist theory.

Socialist feminist theories elaborated some of the implications of this basic position. Nancy Chodorow (1978), a sociologist at the University of California, Berkeley, argued for the social construction of masculinity and femininity within the family, especially in relations with the mother. Boys grew into achievement-oriented men adapted to work outside the home; girls grew into women adapted to emotional work inside or outside the home. Relations between economy, procreation, and male dominance were conceptualized by Ann Ferguson and Nancy Folbre's (1981) notion of "sex-affective production," the historically specific sets of activities that restricted women's options and remuneration. Socialist feminists in general theorized procreative activities and public-sphere production as mutually interdependent, neither ultimately determining the other rather than the public determining the private. Public–private distinctions, socialist feminists thought, rationalized the exploitation of women. In general the idea was that women performed unpaid labor in reproducing labor power as a kind of subsidy for capital, as well as working directly for capital as employees in factories or producers of commodities. Women were the superexploited working class.

Two tendencies emerged from critical statements like these. First, there were those who wished to develop explicitly Marxian ideas in the direction of considering women and gender (Vogel 1983). Hartmann's statement that Marx and Engels were analytically sex-blind was only three-quarters true: Engels had one eye half-open. In a general statement similar to those quoted earlier (in Chapter 5) Engels said:

> According to the materialistic conception, the determining factor in history is, in the final instance, the production and reproduction of immediate life. This, again, is of a twofold character: on the one side, the production of the means of existence, of food, clothing, and shelter and the tools necessary for that production; on the other side, the production of human beings themselves, the propagation of the species. The social organization under which the people of a particular historical epoch and a particular country live is determined by both kinds of production: by the stage of the development of labor on the one hand and of the family on the other. (Engels 1972 ed.: 71–72)

Engels argued that the the position of women relative to men deteriorated with the advent of class society. In a significant elaboration of these insights, anthropologists Mona Etienne and Eleanor Leacock (1980) argued for the primary importance of social relations for understanding socioeconomic and sexual inequalities and hierarchies—the origins of all these inequalities were inextricably bound together. They developed a historical framework for considering relations between socioeconomic and sexual hierarchies by defining four broad historical types of production relations:

1. *Egalitarian relations* among most hunter-gatherer and many horticultural people. Women had autonomy, a multiplicity of economic roles, and decision-making power.

2. *Inequalities* in tribal ranking societies attributable to the growth of trade, specialization, and the reorganization of production relations. In particular, a "public" sector of the economy concerned with production for wealth accumulation and trade was differentiated from a "private" household, or lineage, sector concerned with production for subsistence and sharing. Men's responsibilities in hunting and warfare often led directly to their dominating trade and external political relations. The growth of the public sphere undermined women's previously egalitarian position.

3. *Stratified relations* in preindustrial societies. The patriarchal household became an economically independent unit. Women's work was further privatized.

4. *Exploitation* in industrial capitalist society where the subjugation of people generally was paralleled by the special subjugation of women. (Etienne and Leacock 1980: 8–16)

The main point of this historical analysis was to link modes of production (see Chapter 5) with social forms of gender relations, which helped in theorizing the transition from earlier egalitarian relations to later male domination in history. It also dispelled the myth that women have always ("naturally") been subordinated to men (see also Coontz and Henderson 1986).

Second, however, some feminists still had problems with this kind of analysis. They thought that traditional Marxist analysis was simply pointed in the direction of women in a kind of "add women and stir" formula. They believed, instead, that new analytical categories like "patriarchy" were needed. Thus, Hartmann (1981: 14) defined patriarchy as a "set of social relations between men, which have a material base, and which, though hierarchical, establish or create interdependence and solidarity among men that enable them to dominate women." Patriarchy's material base lay in men's control over women's labor power. Control was maintained by excluding women from access to essential productive resources. Here the analytical potential lay in connecting the social institutions that coerced and legitimized unequal power relations with the personal processes of psychology and consciousness through which people, especially women, accepted and rationalized their unequal positions in society.

Significant advances were therefore made by socialist feminists in broadening the Marxian conception of the material reproduction of life. The equivalent socialist feminist theories of development stressed production and reproduction as inseparable aspects of the making of existence—and therefore equally significant parts of development theory. This broader conception of development included gender relations as well as class, women's labor in the domestic and public spheres, child rearing and socialization, and the family as the particular locus of reproduction. For most of human history, productive and reproductive processes have occurred at the same time and in the same geographic location—as the barely distinguishable aspects of the social creation of a whole way of life. More recently and increasingly with "development," the various aspects of the productive–reproductive whole separated into different social and spatial spheres. These spheres were bound together by relations of inequality and dominance. The entire surplus production system came to be underwritten by the unpaid labor of women. Sophisticated ideologies legitimized this exploitative system as natural ("women have always been the weaker sex"). Development therefore was gender-determined as well as a class process. Indeed, gender and class intersected to form the specifics of the developmental process. Contradictions between parts of the life process have been a driving force in societal change. Indeed, socialist feminists find that class- and gender-dominated societies characterized by exploitation, dominance, and unequal life conditions regularly develop in biased, dangerous forms. Inequality produces catastrophe. Socialist feminists believe in entirely different forms of development predicated on transformed (egalitarian) gender relations. Socialist feminism remains committed to the Marxist notion of the historical and social creation of human nature in a process that includes gender, race, ethnicity, and other distinctions as well as class. Socialist feminism calls for reproductive democracy, including collective participatory control over family and procreative decisions, as well as collective control over commodity production (Jagger 1983: 148–163).

In this vein, the classical analysis of women in the international division of labor was presented by Maria Mies (1986). A German sociologist, Mies interpreted the historical development of the division of labor as a violent patriarchal process. By virtue of arms and warfare, a class of dominant men established an exploitative relationship with women, other classes, and other people. The rapid accumulation of wealth resulting from the globalization of exploitation produced a conception of progress in which satisfying the subsistence needs of the community appeared backward and outdated. This predatory patriarchal division of labor was based on the structural separation and subordination of men from women, local people from foreigners, that extended into the separation of men from nature. Science and technology became the main productive forces through which men could emancipate themselves from nature and from women. The colonial division of labor, exchanging raw materials for industrial products to the detriment of colonial labor, was linked to the establishment of an internal colony composed of the nuclear family and "housewifized" women. Under the new international division of labor, formed by the partial industrialization of selected Third World countries since the 1970s, the use of docile, cheap female labor (housewives rather than workers) in the Third World was linked with the manipulation of women as consumers in the First World. Hence, for Mies a feminist liberation strategy had to be aimed at the total abolition of all these relations of retrogressive "progress." Feminism called for the end of the exploitation of women and nature by men and the end of the exploitation of colonies and classes.

In particular, Mies developed a feminist conception of labor that took as its model, not the male wage earner, but the mother, for whom work was always both burden and enjoyment. For mothers, peasants, and artisans, work processes were connected with the direct production of immediate life rather than focused on things and wealth. A feminist conception of labor was oriented toward a conception of time in which work, enjoyment, and rest were interspersed. Work was a direct and sensuous interaction with nature, organic matter, and living organisms and yet was also useful and necessary for the people who did it and for those around them. For Mies, this arrangement constituted a political economy of bringing together processes of production and consumption within regions in an alternative economy that was self-sufficient.

During the early 1980s, as Third World women were calling for new theories of development that embraced feminism, related conferences were urging the empowerment of women as agents, rather than depicting them as problems, of development (Bunch and Carrillo 1990). During this period a key event was the founding of DAWN (Development Alternatives with Women for a New Era) in Bangladore, India, in 1984. DAWN is seen as essentially adhering to the WAD perspective. Grassroots organizing experiences had led the founders of DAWN to link the microlevel activities they were engaged in to macrolevel perspectives on development. As Gita Sen and Caren Grown (1987: 9–10) point out in a later study produced by DAWN:

> The experiences lived by poor women throughout the Third World in their struggles to ensure the basic survival of their families and themselves ... provide the clearest lens for an understanding of development processes. And it is *their* aspirations and struggles for a future free of the multiple oppressions of gender, race, and nation that can form the basis for the new visions and strategies that the world now needs.

Based on extensive research and debate, DAWN produced work on alternative development strategies that greatly influenced subsequent research and activism in the field. Basically the group argued that short-term ameliorative approaches to improving women's employment opportunities (of the WID type) were ineffective unless they were combined with long-term strategies to reestablish people's (and especially women's) control over economic decisions shaping their lives: "Women's voices must enter the definition of development and the making of policy choices" (Sen and Grown 1987: 82). The idea was to strengthen the voices of Third World women in an "empowerment approach" to women's development. So, at the fourth World Conference on Women, held in 1995 in Beijing, the Platform for Action highlighted the human rights of women—rights to education, food, health, greater political power, and freedom from violence (Bunch, Dutt, and Fried 1995).

Sen and Grown, in their 1987 study, argued that poor oppressed women supplied a powerful perspective for examining the effects of development programs and strategies. Oppressed women, they said, knew poverty. Yet, oppressed women's undervalued work was nevertheless vital to social reproduction. This paradoxical experience with economic growth (with hard work yielding only poverty) was largely determined by gender and class acting together. Then too the existing economic and political structures, often deriving from colonial domination, were highly inequitable between nations, classes, genders, and ethnic groups. Thus, fundamental conflicts arose between women's economic well-being and mainstream development processes. Because economic growth often ended up being detrimental to the needs of poor people, and basic needs were marginalized from the dominant production structures, survival became increasingly difficult:

> Systems of male domination ... on the one hand, deny or limit [women's] access to economic resources and political participation, and on the other hand, impose sexual divisions of labour that allocate to them the most onerous, labour-intensive, poorly rewarded tasks inside and outside the home, as well as the longest hours of work. Thus when development programmes have negative effects, these are felt more acutely by women. (Sen and Grown 1987: 26)

Women, they thought, were controlled through sexual violence. For example, public spaces were physically dominated by men, making it difficult for women to make a living in the formal ("public") sector. Modern education and mass media perpetuated sex-biased stereotypes. A series of interlinked crises (growing impoverishment, food insecurity, financial disarray, environmental degradation, demographic pressure) worsened the problem—so much so that the majority of the world's people found survival almost impossible. Rather than channeling resources into antipoverty programs and reducing the burden of gender subordination, nations militarized while donor agencies expressed hopelessness and lack of concern; the World Bank, for example, deemphasized basic needs in the 1980s, advocating that recipient governments undertake structural adjustments instead.

By comparison, an approach that originated in the perspective of poor Third World women might reorient development analysis to critical aspects of resource use and abuse; to the importance of women's labor in satisfying needs; to focusing attention on poverty and inequality; and to policies pointing to new possibilities for empowering women. The basic-needs approach of agencies like the World Bank in the 1970s had involved loans for urban sites and services, social forestry, and the support of small farmers. But the basic-needs approach had adopted a methodology of commercialization and market integration, and in the context of inequality had led to exacerbation of the very problems that it was expected to solve. While development programs used a top-down approach to project identification, planning, and implementation, the real need, asserted Sen and Grown (1987: 40–41), was for policies oriented toward meeting people's basic needs and drawing heavily on local participation. Moreover, the approach of "integrating women in development" used during the UN Decade for Women had basic flaws, not only because of the difficulties in overcoming ingrained cultural attitudes and prejudices but because of the nature of the development programs into which women were to be integrated. "Short-term, ameliorative approaches to improve women's employment opportunities are ineffective unless they are combined with long-term strategies to reestablish people's—especially women's—control over the economic decisions that shape their lives" (Sen and Grown 1987: 82). What was needed, suggested Sen and Grown, was a shift from export orientation to internal needs, reducing military expenditures, and controlling multinational corporations—in other words, structural transformation rather than mere structural adjustments.

Nevertheless, according to a critique by Eva Rathgeber (1990), WAD can be seen as neglecting social relations of gender within classes and not completely considering variations in patriarchy in different modes of production and how these impact women. The WAD approach emphasized, rather than patriarchy, women within international class structures of inequalities. When it came to the creation and implementation of development projects, critics claimed that WAD, like WID, tended to group women together without much notice being given to race, class, or ethnicity (though Sen and Grown's analysis is clearly an exception to this criticism). There was also the difficulty of changing fundamental structures (structural transformation). Kabeer (1994) argued that Marxists and dependency feminists took uncompromising (revolutionary) stands that prevented them from undertaking realistic, effective changes. Furthermore, poststructural critics saw analyses such as Sen and Grown's (1987) as universalizing the Western sexual division of labor and employing categories like "labor" and "production" rooted in the culture of capitalist modernity that were inadequate for describing "other" societies. Such concepts were abstracted from the historical experience of the European man, who repressed not just women but also "other" people (although this criticism seems to neglect the Third World woman's perspective adopted by Sen and Grown). Feminists using the Marxist paradigm had not overcome its limitations. Extending this paradigm repressed, distorted, and obscured many aspects of women's existence. Additionally, Sen and Grown were said to represent poor Third World women as too much in the thrall of feminism's own narcissistic self-image. Instead of patronizing "poor Third World women," we were best advised to learn from them, which meant appreciating the immense heterogeneity of the field. Poststructural critics also believed that First World feminists should learn to stop feeling privileged as women (Spivak 1988: 135–136). In this light, Sen and Grown's "alternative visions" were said to be mired in androcentric Western thinking in that they failed to provide a genuine alternative to mainstream development (Hirschman 1995).

GENDER AND DEVELOPMENT

The origins of the GAD perspective lie with women working in the mid-1970s at the Institute of Development Studies, University of Sussex (U.K.). This feminist group was interested in analyzing women's subordination within the development process from the vantage point of gender relations between men and women; initially it drew on Marxist analyses of social change and feminist analyses of patriarchy (Young 1993: 134). GAD differed from WID in its conceptualization of the sexual division of labor. Whereas WID tended to accept the sexual division of labor as allocating tasks between men and women, hence arguing that more value needed to be placed on the tasks done by women, GAD argued that the sexual division of labor in a society was one of connection in which men and women became dependent on each other and that therefore the allocation of tasks should be changed. DAWN's work also contributed greatly to the gender and development approach (Chowdry 1995; Rathgeber 1990).

In the GAD approach, gender relations rather than "women" became the main analytical category, while also a number of assumptions ignored by WID and WAD were explored in greater depth. For example, GAD argued that women were not a homogenous group but rather were divided by class, race, and creed. Women's roles in society could not be seen as autonomous from gender relations, and this perspective became a way of looking at the structures and processes giving rise to women's disadvantaged position, which was a function too of the globally pervasive ideology of male superiority—men had power and control over women. Young (1993: 134–135) notes that GAD was an holistic approach in which culturally specific forms of inequality and divisions occurred, and gender became interrelated with this overall socially created hierarchy. Consequently, gender had to be acknowledged as part of a wider international system. For example, capitalism used gender relations to produce a reserve of labor, while women's unpaid labor in the household was a way of creating wealth for global corporations.

When it came to developmental practice, GAD was seen as opening doors for women as social actors within wider structures of constraints:

> It is therefore necessary to analyze how these other forces (political, religious, racial and economic) intersect with and dynamize gender relations, provoking in some instances structural rather than individual responses to produce rational configurations which may be reinforcements of old forms or may be quite new ones. Alternately, individual responses may take on a momentum and massification which leads to structural change. (Young 1993: 139)

Unlike WID and WAD, GAD saw the state as an important actor promoting women's emancipation. Rathgeber (1990) has argued that GAD went further than WID or WAD in questioning underlying social, economic, and political structures, which made its recommendations difficult to implement since structural change was found to be imperative. However, Kabeer (1994) argued that GAD also opened new strategies for feminist intervention: GAD's multifarious approach distinguished between capitalism, patriarchy, and racism and also enabled feminists to identify key weak links in official policies for strategic interventions. While some saw these strategies as necessary for feminists to respond to the needs of poor women (Visvanathan, Duggan, Nissonoff, and Wiegersma 1997: 24), others argued that GAD did not get rid of its modernist tendencies while still essentializing poor women:

> The poor, vulnerable Southern woman is a powerful image, and its easy adoption by both mainstream and alternative development theorists and practitioners is understandable … Yet this very image reinforces and maintains the discourse of modernity so essential to Northern hegemony and development practices. (Parpart and Marchand 1995: 16–17)

This focus on image and discourse resulted from the influence of post-structural and postmodern ideas on the gender debate. But before we discuss postmodernism, we turn to an important offshoot of the WAD and GAD approaches that focuses more on relations among women, development, and the natural environment.

WOMEN, ENVIRONMENT, AND DEVELOPMENT

This perspective (dubbed WED for short) also began in the 1970s as feminists increasingly drew parallels between men's control over women and male control over nature, with connections made among masculine science and industrialization and assaults on the ecological health of the planet. Carolyn Merchant (1980) saw the roots of the world's environmental dilemma as emanating from the worldview developed by the founding fathers of modern science, Francis Bacon, René Descartes, and Isaac Newton, in which reality was thought of as a machine rather than a living organism. She saw the acceleration of the exploitation of human and natural resources in the name of culture and progress resulting in the death of nature as a living being. Similarly, ecofeminists interested in the contemporary Third World, such as Vandana Shiva and Maria Mies, adopted a radical feminist perspective on the exploitation of nature. Shiva argued that science and development were not universal categories but rather special projects of Western patriarchy that were killing nature (Shiva 1989). Development in the Third World superimposed the scientific and economic paradigms created by Western gender-based ideology on communities previously immersed in other cultures with entirely different relations with the natural world. As victims of the violence of patriarchal development, women resisted this "development" to protect nature and preserve their own sustenance:

> Indian women have been in the forefront of ecological struggles to conserve forests, land and water. They have challenged the western concept of nature as an object of exploitation and have protected her as Prakriti, the living force that supports life. They have challenged the western concept of economics as production of profits and capital accumulation with their own concept of economics as production of sustenance and needs satisfaction. A science that does not respect nature's needs and a development that does not respect people's needs inevitably threaten survival. (Shiva 1989: xvii)

Thus, ecological struggles simultaneously liberated nature from ceaseless exploitation and women from limitless marginalization. In an analysis of the effects of the green revolution in the Punjab region, on India's border with Pakistan, Shiva argued that the assumption of nature as a source of scarcity, with technology as the source of abundance, created ecological and cultural disruptions that ended in diseased soil, pest-infested crops, waterlogged deserts, discontented farmers, and unprecedented levels of conflict and violence.

For Diane Rocheleau, Barbara Thomas-Slayter, and Esther Wangari (1996), there were real gender differences in experiences of nature and a responsibility for the environment deriving not from biology but from social constructions of gender that varied with class, race, and place. They saw feminist scholarship on the environment taking a number of forms. Some schools of thought, such as socialist feminism, disagreed with biologically based portrayals of women as nurturer, and saw women and the environment more in terms of reproductive and productive roles in unevenly developing economies. For example, Bina Agarwal (1991) argued that women in India have been active not because of some "natural" relation with the environment (as with Shiva) but because they suffered more in gender-specific ways from environmental destruction. Feminists thus drew from cultural and political ecology's emphasis on unequal control over resources (Peet and Watts 1996) but treated gender as a critical variable in interaction with class, race, and other factors shaping processes of ecological change. Three themes were pursued in feminist political ecology: gendered knowledge, reflecting an emerging science of survival in healthy homes, workplaces, and ecosystems; gendered environmental rights, including property, resources, and space; and gendered environmental politics, particularly women's involvement in collective struggles over natural resources and environmental issues (Rocheleau, Thomas-Slayter, and Wangari 1996).

The notion of "sustainable development" became central to the WED perspective. This notion linked ideas of equity between generations, the balance between economic and environmental needs to conserve non-renewable resources, and the idea of reducing industrialization's waste and pollution. Sustainable development was seen as an opportunity for challenging the development-equals-economic-growth equation from the perspective of a feminist methodology. This meant differentiating feminism even from other alternative notions of economics and development. Thus, according to Wendy Harcourt (1994b), an alternative "real-life economics" (Ekins and Max-Neef 1992) arose that wanted to expand the notion of development to consider environmental degradation, poverty, and participation, yet still needed demystifying to disclose its sexism. In this perspective, economics in the form of mathematical models was reductionist and inadequate for expressing the ambiguities and contradictions in complex processes. Similarly, Frédérique Apffel-Marglin and Steven Marglin (1990) saw economics as part of an episteme (system of ideas and discourses) based on logic and rationality disembodied from contexts (that is, an instrumental logic of calculation); by comparison, *techne* (knowledge) was embedded in practice and gained through processes within communities. But Western civilization considers only episteme as pure knowledge. For feminists, the historical replacement of *techne* by episteme in the West and the contemporary process of replacement in the Third World undervalued women's nurturing and sustaining of the environment. Western development economics, with its devaluation of nature and failure to treat other cultures with dignity, can well afford to learn from other modes of social organization rather than always assuming its superiority (Harcourt 1994b).

POSTMODERNISM AND DEVELOPMENT

The Postmodernism and Development perspective asked whether a more accessible and politicized postmodern feminism had relevance for the problems facing women in Third World societies (Marchand and Parpart 1995). The PAD perspective criticized the GAD view as representing Third World women as "other" or, in the case of WID, using images of women as victims, sex objects, and cloistered beings. Postmodern feminists found the WID view embedded in colonial/neocolonial discourse and enshrined in the liberal discourse on markets, both of which disempowered women. Particularly appealing for PAD theorists was postmodernism's emphasis on differences, providing space for the voices of the maginalized (Hooks 1984), and disrupting the representation of women in the South as an undifferentiated "other" (Mohanty 1991a). Also the postmodern critique of the subject and its suspicion of the "truth" suggested an alliance between postmodernism and feminism based on a common critique of the modernist episteme. Postmodern critics questioned the certainty of Eurocentric development studies and criticized the silencing of local knowledges by Western expertise—all this they found relevant to the development of women.

Some of the themes arising from the encounter between feminism, postmodernism, and development included a critique of colonial and contemporary constructions of the "Third World" woman—what Apffel-Marglin and Simon (1994) call "feminist orientalism"; deconstruction of development discourses that disempowered poor women in particular; the recovery of women's knowledges and voices; the celebration of differences and multiple identities; and a focus on consultative dialogue between development practitioners and their "clients."

A good example was Jane Parpart's (1995) deconstruction of the development "expert" as a person with special technical knowledge of the modern world who can solve the problems of the developing countries. The notion of "expertise" underlying this privileged position, Parpart argued, is embedded in Western Enlightenment thought with its specialization of knowledge—for example, development economics as the "science of economic progress." Yet, many also recognized that postmodern feminism, taken to extremes, could stymie collective action among women and that the impenetrable jargon of postmodern writing was an unsurmountable obstacle for people mired in illiteracy and economic crisis (Parpart and Marchand 1995). Rather than rejecting development altogether, most postmodern feminists in this field recognized the real problems faced by poor women and the need for addressing development issues. They favored an approach "that accepts and understands difference and the power of discourse, and that fosters open, consultative dialogue [that] can empower women in the South to articulate their own needs and agendas" (Parpart and Marchand 1995: 19).

CRITIQUE: A FAILURE OF NERVE?

What distinguishes the feminist perspective on the modern development process? Development as a conscious practice, as a set of policies, alters gender relations in favor of men, shifting resources to the male sphere of control and making women more vulnerable to disasters, whether natural or social in origin. As feminist scholarship deepened, understanding the causes of these problems ranged from considering deficiencies in the distribution of material benefits, to exploring inequalities in control over productive resources, to confronting criticisms of the androcentrism of the founding Western cultural ideas about science and values. Carolyn Merchant (1980: 11) observes that feminist history turns society upside down, and at first sight feminist critiques of development appear to view the world in reverse, seeing the normal as abnormal, the praiseworthy as abhorrent, and the apparently just as unjust. In this sense, criticism from the feminist perspective tends to reverse the dominant trend, move in support of the antithesis, and see things as opposites. So, a feminist-inspired "development policy" (if that is not a contradiction in terms) would see productive labor as reproductive work.

Yet, this approach would imply mere reversal as feminism's contribution to development theory. More than this is going on beneath the ever shifting perspectives (from WID to PAD). Theoretical viewpoints derive from thinking about the experiences of particular groups of people, and these histories are far more than Western feminist reactions to male domination in the West. As feminist thought changes under the constant pressure of critique and countercritique, attempts are increasingly made to recognize, and even identify with, the quite different experiences of a world of diverse people (especially different groups of women), from experiences which, while comparable in some respects, are incomparable in many others. This incomparability means that Western women theorists cannot just reverse Western male-centeredness but rather must invent new things. More importantly, Western women's reversals are but one tradition in feminist critical thought. There is a world of different experiences waiting to be recognized, drawn upon, criticized, but also appreciated. Likewise, interventions into the development process take many forms, some of which are not only incomparable but even in opposition, one to the other, so that "global feminism" is at best a network of tolerance and at worst a barely contained squabble. This state of affairs means that "development" even as reproduction-centered improvements may take so many forms that continuity or similarity of project becomes difficult and, for some, impossible. Even the words "project" or "improvement" imply, for adherents of the PAD perspective, immersion in Western thinking, a capturing of the imagination by Western themes of progress. For others, in the WAD school for instance, immersion in Western thinking involves instead interaction between traditions, thus making anticolonial struggles (at home or in the Third World) also parts of the "Western" theme of progress. Are there emancipatory and developmental themes common to all oppressed peoples? And is it possible to synthesize differences and similarities through a dialectic that does not submerge one within the other? We think that something like this was attempted by the WAD position on feminist developmentalism. We find the criticisms of WAD overdrawn and would like this discourse to return to the agenda set forth by Sen and Grown (1987), namely, breaking down the structures that foster inequalities, reorienting production to meet the needs of the poor, combining immediate improvements with long-term strategies that establish women's control over their own decisions— themes that we raise again in our concluding chapter, which derives from a feminist socialism.

However, reading the recent literature on feminism and development, we could not help but notice the tentativeness of the ideas expressed, the tendency to repeat a few well-established themes, and the incomplete character of the conclusions that were offered. Virtually the entire discourse on women and development consists of collections of essays, most of which are case studies exemplifying general themes whose particulars are scarcely, or never, explicitly stated, so the knowledge produced is fragmentary and inconclusive. This is particularly so in coming up with concrete proposals for change—studies that cry out for proposed solutions in desperate straits suddenly end. We think that feminism is far too fractured, far too reluctant to "speak for others," too hesitant to make overarching generalizations, and too much involved in "strategy" rather than fundamental transformative politics. For us, this apparent "failure of nerve" derives from an overreaction to the criticisms presented of the early feminist ideas from Third World women. It is time to get over it!

Feminist thought, taken to the extreme, involves restructuring the imagination to think in entirely new ways. We think that feminists, regardless of nationality and class identity, need to speak on behalf of poor women everywhere. Alternative feminist conceptions about development are difficult, but not impossible, to create. It is time to raise again the fundamental issues involved in real socialist feminist alternatives. We think feminist development theorists need to regain their nerve and begin developing far more coherent arguments that advocate for others and have revolutionary implications.

Part III

CRITICAL MODERNISM

In Part I we looked at theories of development that take a conventionally uncritical view of Western modernism as the best social paradigm that has ever existed and that we can ever achieve. In Part II we looked at theories of development that are critical, in various ways, of Western modernity. Here in Part III we briefly outline an alternative to uncritical modernism and overly critical (post)modernism. We call this approach "critical modernism." We argue that critical modernism should focus on the question of development—understood as the social use of economic progress—as a central theme of our age. On the one hand, development simply as aggregate economic growth cannot continue much longer—natural constraints prevent this, and there are abundant natural signs of approaching catastrophe. On the other hand, development as material transformation for the world's hungry people is an ethical and practical necessity, just as pressing as the natural constraints on growth. Unless we can find far better systems under which a much fairer life can be led, then let nature take its revenge on a greedy species! "Development" *has* to be transformed—as a term with meaning, as a belief in better things, as a practice employing millions of altruistic people, and as the main hope for a saner world.

Let us compare critical modernism with postmodernism. Critical modernism criticizes material power relations in order to change them, while postmodernism criticizes discourses and ideas to undermine their modern certainty; critical modernism wants to transform development, while postmodernism wants to abandon it. These differences derive not only from the nature of the critique—so that postmodernism focuses on development as discourse, while critical modernism emphasizes development as a class and gendered practice—but derive also from differences about the social object that forms the target of criticism, whether modernism or capitalism. Modernism is understood mainly in discursive terms, capitalism as a system of class power. A critical modernism learns from the poststructural critique, but it is not entirely persuaded by it. The poststructural critique overemphasizes representation at the expense of practice, as though words were the main problems in life—change the word, and the world will change. As a result too many postmodern critiques end in a nihilistic never-never land, where nothing is proposed and little gets done in anything approaching real terms. Nor is critical modernism willing to abandon the political principles of an older radicalism, such as democratic Marxism or socialist feminism, especially their ideas about social control of the reproduction of existence. Most importantly, critical modernism remains modern in terms of favoring a scientific attitude toward the world, that is, requiring some kind of evidence before believing. Critical modernism focuses on a critique of capitalism as the social form taken by the modern world rather than on modernism as an overgeneralized discursive phenomenon. The idealistic aspect to this (selective) retention of the modern is that the project contains ethical intentions worthy of respect and support. The material aspect is that modernism results in benefits for large numbers of people who then live far better lives than they otherwise would. And the practical aspect is that science and democracy are now endemic to the very structure of Western meaning and will not disappear simply because postmodern theorists are tired of them (the selfsame theorists who extract a handsome income by criticizing postmodern theory—it has become a growth market for a few academics). Hence, we need to more actively focus on modernity as a form of capitalist practice guided by social relations rather than criticizing modernity as a discursive formation. We should learn to live with modernity by criticizing and changing it.

8

Critical Modernism and Democratic Development

Conventional theorists of modern capitalism concentrate their policy attention on achieving economic growth. By "growth" is meant an increase in the total volume of goods and services produced in a country. Growth, it is argued, underlies higher material standards of living. While there are several different versions—modernization theory, neoclassical economics, and neoliberalism, to name but three—the idea common to modern growth theory is that rational competitive economic behavior, coordinated through markets, drives investment that leads to technological advance and economic growth. The entrepreneurial class that organizes this process has to be well rewarded for its efforts—economic thought assumes that business people take risks in making investments in order to make money. Because such economic thought occurs in societies where people vote, the caveat has to be added that material benefits trickle down from the rich to everyone, though it may take a while. In this dominant argument, increasing inequality (the rich getting richer and investing more) "alleviates" poverty through growth. "Development" is the kindly face we place on this kind of profit-oriented endeavor wherein economic growth is recast in such terms as "millennium goals we really should try to reach," "sustainability," "social safety nets," "greater participation," "poverty reduction," or some other liberal bromide concocted to render more palatable policies that deliberately produce inequality (revisit Figure 1.1 on page 9, and look at the trend in the share of income distribution in the United States over the past 30 years). Third World countries "develop" by copying the model of modernization, competition, profit making and industrialization already proven to be effective by the modern histories of the First World countries. Thus, modernization and devel-

277

opment are captured by a single historical experience repeated eternally at the "end of history" and the "end of geography," as contemporary times are sometimes described.

Yet, it is clear from the renewed record of turmoil in the 21st century that history has not ended, that geographically based differences continue to intrude (sometimes even more violently than before), and that the currently reigning neoliberal model of developmental does not fit all circumstances. Capitalist modernization leaves 200 million people in poverty at the very heart of modernity, in the so-called advanced countries! This statistic shows the social implausibility and ethical irresponsibility of being satisfied with the existing model. After 200 years of full-steam operation, industrial capitalism leaves 2.8 billion people living in poverty (that is, on the equivalent of less than $2 a day) in the world. The existing Western-led modernization process cannot possibly continue. If "successful," normal growth under the existing consumptive model would lead within 50 years to a five- or six-fold increase in global incomes, resource use, and pollution of natural environments already strained far beyond capacity. This projected scenario shows the natural impossibility of endlessly copying the Western model: continue the process and human history will indeed end—in environmental catastrophe. Yet, such is the dominance of the prevailing neoliberal optimism that crises in the global economy lead only to purified, slightly more "liberal," versions of the same modernization approach—models with even less income redistribution, even more "incentives" (tax cuts for the already rich) are intoned as deep wisdom by "economic experts" (the high priests of conventional development theory). Meanwhile, consciences are salved by providing mosquito nets to poor Africans. Conventional thinking about modernity, growth, and development, so defined, is hopelessly, dangerously, and perversely blind to its structural deficiencies and devoid of real alternatives taken seriously in the centers of power. The future existence of the world's people depends on breaking this utterly deficient style of developmental thought.

ALTERNATIVES

Neoliberal orthodoxy must be challenged by theoretical political alternatives conceptualized by, and on behalf of, practical innovative social movements. In this book we have looked at three main alternative positions:

1. *Marxist and neo-Marxist theories* argue that modernity yields high material standards of living for a few at the expense of the

majority—inequality causes poverty—while the environment is degraded, nature destroyed, culture debased, again to satisfy the consumptive whims of the richest of the world's people. For socialists, the idea instead is to rationally control the development process through collective ownership, public control, planning, and democratic reasoning.

2. *Poststructural theory* argues that the reason, knowledge, and ideas of progress underlying the modern project are so saturated with Western power that "development" has become the source of many of the world's problems rather than their solution. The idea of postdevelopmentalism instead is to obliterate developmentalism to create room for social movements to find their own models of change.

3. *Feminist theories* find modern reason to be masculinity in logical disguise, with development practices subjugating women while feigning humanitarianism. For most feminists, the idea is to rethink the meaning and practices of development from critical gendered perspectives that value the experiences and wishes of women as well as men—with postmodern feminists advocating abandonment of the "development" rubric altogether.

All critical approaches find development, as presently understood, to be a mistake of (natural and social) global proportions. The relevant parties differ on what to do about it. Marxists want to rescue modernity from capitalism by advocating new sociopolitical formations of a socialist type. Postmodernists want to hasten the downfall of the modern project altogether through deconstructive critique. Postmodernism and feminism want to support subjugated knowledges and oppositional social movements so that people can make their own futures. In the present political and intellectual climate, dominated by neoliberalism (the market solves all problems) and neoconservatism (bring them "democracy" whether they want it or not), statements about alternative development, understood as organized collective interventions into social, cultural, and economic processes on behalf of political goals defined around social justice, have been silenced to the point almost of disappearing from memory. Yet, given the momentous problems faced still by two billion and more desperately poor people, this kind of instant amnesia is a tragedy of politics (in terms of the loss of direct engagement) and a travesty of justice (in terms of forgetting about others or losing sight of urgency in the desperate pursuit of theoretical complexity, academic reputation, or the latest exaggerated intellectual trend).

In this book we reach a different conclusion, namely, to rethink the development project rather than to discard it. We want to reconsider development in the full knowledge of the postdevelopmental and feminist critiques—indeed, using these criticisms to elaborate a more powerful, more persuasive critical yet still modernist approach. Democracy, emancipation, development, progress are fine modern principles. But they are corrupted by the social form taken by modernity—capitalism as a patriarchal class system, a type of society operated in the interests of a male elite, based on the profit motive to the exclusion of virtually everything else. The main problem with democracy is that it has never been achieved—in which society do people directly control the basic institutions and places (work, family, neighborhood) where they spend most of their lives? How can countries like the United States be "democratic" when 150,000 rich people in effect choose who will be the "serious" presidential candidates through campaign contributions, where election campaigns are waged through "sound bites" and video clips in an expensive, mass-dominated media, and where corporations spend billions of dollars each year on lobbying that they claim only gains them "access" to politicians? Likewise, the trouble with emancipation is that it applies to the privileges of the few rather the rights of the many. Emancipation means furthering the "human rights" of the already privileged. So, too, the deficiency of development lies in its limited aims (an abundance of things), the timidity of its means (copying the West), and the scope of its conception (experts plan it). And as for progress, it is little more than a cliche recounted daily in the eternally optimistic chatter of television personalities and company executives forever coming on board and moving forward. As poststructural theorists rightly claim, these modern development terms are beyond redemption if considered as statements divorced from ideas (signifiers relating only to other signifiers). But to concede "progress" to the mindlessly optimistic is to give up on an idea held by the seriously optimistic at that level of belief that still finds reasoning, science, technology, and democracy to represent real potential for a better life for all people. And while a better life, in terms of material sufficiency, may easily be denigrated by those already leading lives of abundance, it is a dream full of hope for those who have never known a secure existence. For us, "modernity" and "development" are terms that are still full of meaning.

CRITICAL MODERNISM

Critical modernist developmentalism gains insight from the Marxist, poststructural, and feminist critiques of modernity, but it emphasizes belief more in the potential, rather than the practice, of contemporary development.

Critical modernism entails a critique of capitalist power systems in socialist terms of class ownership of productive resources, in feminist terms of male dominance, and in poststructural terms of the hegemony of elite imaginaries and discourses. Yet, unlike most critiques, it converts these negative criticisms into the positives of a series of political proposals on how to change the meaning and practices of modernism. Critical modernism distrusts any elite, whether it be entrepreneurial, bureaucratic, scientific, intellectual, racial, geographic, or patriarchal. Critical modernism favors the views of oppressed peoples of all kinds— from peasant social movements, to indigenous organizations, to women organizing for reproductive rights, to working-class movements. Even so, "favoring" or "valuing" the ideas of oppressed peoples does not mean believing everything their leaders say in a kind of new-age romanticism that finds eternal wisdom glistening on the shaman's prayer. And while poor people's movements have to be seen in their own terms and contexts, critical modernism favors alliances that draw together the powers of the oppressed majority in countering what would otherwise be the overwhelming power of the exploiting minority. Critical modernism listens to what people have to say. Yet, controversially it wants to combine the popular discourses of diverse social movements with the liberating ideas of a modernism itself understood only self-critically. Critical modernism finds worth in all experiences.

But this listening applies to the Western experience of modernity as well, except that critique is all the more necessary ("we have seen the future, and we know it only partly works")—we can learn a lot from the modern experience of the West. Most importantly, critical modernism remains modern in terms of favoring a basically rational scientific attitude toward the world—that is, requiring some kind of evidence before believing rather than accepting purely on faith, as with premodern understanding, or denying any validity to evidential truth, as with much of poststructuralism. Given a choice between the "inner eye of faith" and the "outer gaze of reason," critical modernism prefers the second— except that the eye looks out critically on the world. Critical modernism believes in rationalism in terms of carefully formulated, logical, and theoretical thinking about issues of the utmost importance, like global poverty or environmental catastrophe. Logic and known experience form the bases of its theories.

The radical critique of capitalism, as a corrupt form of modernism, allows space for the retention of modernist discoveries in new forms: emancipation, democracy, reasoning, and planning as a first stream; science, technology, productivity, machines, material certainty, medicine, and hospitals as a second stream. The idealistic aspect to this (selective) retention is that the modern project contains ethical reasonings and political intentions worthy of respect and support. The material aspect is that modernism already results in benefits for large numbers of people who live far better lives than otherwise—and could do a lot more. And the practical aspect is that science and democracy are now central to the very structure of global political culture and will not disappear simply because spoiled, overindulged theorists are tired of them, yet benefit all the more by criticizing modernity (poststructural theory as a growth machine for a few, privileged academics). Hence the need for a more active, critical engagement with modernity as a form of capitalist practice guided by social relations, rather than criticizing modernity as a discursive formation. We should learn to live with modernity by criticizing and changing it!

DEMOCRATIC DEVELOPMENT

Critical modernism should focus on the question of development, understood as social, democratic control over economic progress, as a central theme of our age. Development as social transformation on behalf of the world's poor people *is* democratic in intent and effect. Equality, possibility, livelihood, removing the overwhelming might of material constraint—these are the conditions for democracy, understood as the collective freedom to make the basic decisions that determine individual and social existence. To achieve anything like this, "development" has to be transformed—as a term with meaning, as a belief in better things, as a practice employing millions of altruistic people, and as the main hope for a saner world. The will to find a better life is founded on constructive criticism of its present social forms. Criticism may be an active, creative endeavor. Society is positively transformed by showing, through criticism, what most needs changing and in which particular ways. And what most needs changing in the existing global society is an inequality that allows the privileged minority to satisfy their every consumptive desire without noticing the price while the underprivileged majority cannot satisfy even the most pressing needs, like food, shelter, and health services, because they cannot afford the prices. Development is equality, and only equality will allow democracy to occur.

What experience do we have with democratic development? The answer is, not much ... but some. For development to come from democratic reasoning, there have to be several, radically different, socioeconomic models, with free debate among their proponents and with this debate gaining broad popular participation by electorates and social movements. While utopian thinking has a role to play in outlining the great alternatives in their purest, most contrasting forms, such debate must draw on practical experience—because mistakes in thinking about development end up killing many people. Therefore, what do we know from experience about development alternatives?

Since World War II, the capitalist world has seen two main political-economic policy regimes: Keynesian democracy, predominating between 1945 and 1973; and neoliberal democracy, predominating between 1980 and the present; the years 1973–1980 represent a transitional period during which the two regimes contended for dominance. The Keynesian policy regime was characterized by interventionist states committed to achieving full employment and high incomes for everyone, using state authority to stabilize accumulation and to democratize the economic benefits. Regional differences in theoretical-interpretative and political-economic traditions informed three main variants: social democratic Keynesianism in western European countries and their former settler colonies; liberal Democratic Keynesianism in the United States; and developmental state Keynesianism in Japan and many industrializing Third World countries (Chang and Rowthorn 1995; Kohli 2004). By way of contrast, neoliberalism employs monetarist economics in the belief that such macroeconomic problems as high inflation and spiraling debt loads derive precisely from state direction on behalf of higher incomes for everyone, full employment, and free social services for all.

What happened to the global economy under these two policy regimes? The measure most commonly used by conventional economists to measure economic well-being is economic growth. Let us, for a moment, accept this measure at face value—that is, "growth is good." Economic growth in the OECD countries, the richest countries in the world, averaged 3.5% a year during the Keynesian period 1961–1980 and 2.0% a year during the neoliberal period 1981–1999. In developing countries excluding China, the corresponding figures were 3.2% and 0.7% (Pollin 2003: 133). In other words, Keynesianism vastly outperformed neoliberalism in conventional terms of growth. However, we have argued that growth just indicates whether or not development is happening. More important is income distribution. So, what happened to incomes during the two periods? In the United States, the least socially democratic country in the world, between 1947 and 1973 under the Keynesian policy regime, every income category of people experienced real income growth, with the poorest families having the highest rate of growth of all. After 1973, however, average real income not only remained stagnant, but that average reflected high income growth for the top 20% of families and a significant income decline for the poorest 20%, so that almost half of all families received lower real incomes by the mid-1990s than they had in 1973 (Leone 1995). Even under liberal Democratic Keynesianism in the United States, a lot more income went to the poorest people, while under social democratic Keynesianism in Europe this was accompanied by the extension of state-subsidized healthcare, free education, and other social services to working-class people. State intervention, for all its bureaucratic deficiencies, was good to the working class. The Fordist virtuous circle linking increased productivity to increased incomes for people who had to spend them provided a logic for growth with development. By comparison, neoliberalism, a policy regime that intends to benefit the entrepreneurial class, succeeded beyond its proponents' wildest dreams. Rich people made a lot more money. But this result broke the (Fordist–Keynesian) circle of production and consumption. Policy is capable of directing economic growth to produce entirely different development results—we know this from 50 years of economic history. A democratic debate on development should start with the historical evidence and should consider the ethics of different social models of economy. From the perspective of the historical evidence of the industrialized countries, a revitalized social democratic/developmental state model has shown that it can produce growth with equity.

Similarly, what can we learn from the experience of such socialist countries as the Soviet Union (Russia), Cuba, and Venezuela? From the experience of the Soviet Union and countries that followed its organizational model, like Cuba during the 1960s and 1970s, we see that an economy overplanned by distant elites cannot be optimally efficient. Yet, even so, the Soviet Union took the least developed country in Europe and produced not a military–industrial powerhouse but a social system that housed, fed, and kept in decent health the vast majority of its citizens (see the evidence presented in Chapter 5). Similarly, under desperate geopolitical conditions, in part attributable to a decades-long economic embargo imposed by the United States, Cuba has nonetheless managed to maintain health and welfare services that produce, in a Third World country, infant mortality rates lower than those of the world's "most advanced" country. And Venezuela represents, amazingly for the first time in history, a model of development in which the wealth from the country's vast natural resources is directed toward benefiting its poorest people—with the proven result that poverty rates have decreased sharply, literacy has become almost universal, and people who never saw a doctor in their lives now get to see a well-trained Cuban physician—for free (Wilpert 2006; Weinstein 2005). In brief, the experience of the "really existing socialism" is replete with lessons about the possibilities of alternative forms of development. We are not saying that an alternative democratic development model already exists in pure form, although Venezuela is doing its best to work out such a model in practice. We are saying that there are alternative principles, pieces of evidence, lots of experience, and millions of committed people who want nothing more than to engage in a democratic discourse on development alternatives.

ETHICS

We argue for this kind of critical modernist and radically democratic development from a number of positions, including the ethical. Ethics are principles of right and wrong, good and bad, that human beings, following their best intentions, try to exercise in their relations with others and with the natural world. Humans differ from other living beings in the fundamental sense of being conscious of existing—but also in having a conscience about the motives of our actions. That is, we make moral and ethical judgments about our intentions and behavior, and we make these judgments in relation to something greater than the particular, something long-lasting and perhaps even eternal. This relationship to wider meanings occurs at the level of belief—that is, these feelings represent principles of existence held at the emotional level so that ideas are felt in a bodily way. For the modernist, ethical principles can be derived directly from contemplating the lessons of life's experiences. Ethics can be discussed openly, without the hierarchy that inevitably comes when the priest claims special connections with the divine. Ethics can be derived far more directly in the historical terms of human experience—for example, discussing the conditions under which people are happiest or forms of life are environmentally most sustainable. In other words, when we ask how we should live and why societies develop in certain ways, the only sure guide is what we have done over long periods of time (the real eternal) and what we can learn from history, practice, and experience, all mediated through discussion.

In the case of development, however, the ethical problems of what and how much to produce are made more transparent by the obvious needs of the world's two billion poverty-stricken people. There is a disturbing tendency for poststructural discussions to see poverty in terms of the social construction of a deficient world rather than the material reality of absolute deprivation in a deficient world. This tendency is accompanied by the ethical advocacy of "convivial poverty" and the spiritual ideal of simplicity and frugality (Rahnema 1997). Support comes from such adages as: "You are poor because you look at what you do not have. See what you possess, see what you are, and you will discover that you are astonishingly rich" (Rist 1997: 294). If poverty is considered purely as a social construct, or something that has entirely different meanings depending on the cultural context, then simplicity, dignity, and the discovery of inner richness may have some validity as ethical responses. But if poverty is considered materially as the absolute lack of inputs vital to continued existence, such as not enough food (of any kind) to keep people alive—near-universal reality—then postdevelopmental ethical advocacy is a cruel hoax—it amounts to telling those about to expire that they are (astonishingly!) rich, that they should die with "dignity" rather than struggle for life (here "dignity" is the poststructural equivalent of the promise of the afterlife). But poor people are not quietly dignified—they are actively so. The poor have spoken—we only have to listen. And they want what they need: work, food, shelter, services. These are authentic needs that satisfy any ethical principle, whether of happiness or scarcity. The ethical question is not whether, but how, to provide basic needs. And the means of providing for needs is called ... development. This principle of the ethical satisfaction of urgent needs lies at the core of most social movements. While universal in its essence, it emerges in quite different forms, depending on the circumstances.

SOCIAL MOVEMENTS

Who are the actors creating the possibility of ethical approach to development? Rather than structural contradictions (such as resource deprivation and poverty) producing societal transformation directly through some kind of collective moment of ethical realization, the link between contradiction and social action occurs indirectly: contradictions provoke crises, the people affected build social movements, and these accumulate into widespread popular opposition to the existing forms of social life. The new thinking about social movements stresses the social and cultural creation of organized opposition through mediations of at least five types: (1) perceptions and interpretations may place specific adverse situations faced by people into their cultural meaning systems; (2) a sense of collective identity or commonality with others is often created through place-based or environmentally structured events; (3) deprived conditions may spur injured or aggrieved people to different levels or types of actions, ranging from sullen individual resistance to organized social movements; (4) social, cultural, and spatial linkages of many kinds between social movements can create broad-based political forces; (5) and "old" social movements, such as unions and leftist parties, can rediscover their sense of solidarity with new social movements, such as organizations advocating popular development. Recent social movement theory, often focused on the Third World, stresses the rise to prominence of new movements independent of traditional trade unions or organized political parties—for example, squatter movements and neighborhood councils, base-level communities within the Catholic church, indigenous associations, women's associations, human rights committees, youth assemblages, special-interest educational and artistic groups, coalitions for the defense of regional traditions and interests, and self-help groupings among unemployed and poor people (Evers 1985). Radical theorists find potential for direct action by the people in movements to construct a new political power base and initiate popular social change. Some of the ideas relevant here include the notion of everyday resistance (Scott 1985, 1990); de Certeau's (1984) notion that the "marginal majority" effects multiple through infinitesimal changes in power structures; social movements as cultural struggles over meaning as well as over material conditions and needs (Touraine 1981, 1988; Melucci 1988; Escobar 1992b); and the concept of politics as a discursive articulatory process (Laclau and Mouffe 1985). Putting this point more directly, the new social movements more than simply oppose deprivation: they also reinvigorate issues of culture, ideology, ethics, and ways of life.

LINKAGES

In the sense of forming linkages and joining old and new movements together, there remains a need for ethical, critical, and political principles that transcend the local so that social movements of many kinds can coalesce into regional and global oppositional movements organized around at least quasi-universal principles. An example is La Vía Campesina, representing millions of farming families belonging to 149 organizations of rural women, peasants, small- and medium-scale farmers, farmworkers, and indigenous communities in 56 countries in Africa, Asia, Europe, and the Americas. Since 1993 it has become a powerful voice of opposition to the globalization of a modern, industrial, and neoliberal model of rural development (Desmarais 2008). Why is this kind of global alliance important? Because social movements confined to the local can be obliterated in the absence of outside support (for example, the Zapatista movement in Chiapas province, Mexico, has broad support in Latin America). Local social movements often face opposition embedded in global power structures. Even local success entails changing these broader power structures, for example, changing property rights at the national level or removing international threats to common property resources. After the postmodern recognition of differences comes the critical modernist rediscovery not of sameness but of similarity. Social movements, old and new, are united in their opposition to resource deprivation, by which is meant primarily the lack of material necessities and the capacity to produce these. They are united also in their resource demands—to get back what once they had, to recover their share (or more simply to get more) so that old people can live and children survive. The dignity of the poor lies not in accepting their lot and learning to live simply with the constant possibility of death, but in the possibility too of life and resistance, silently or openly, locally and regionally, particularly and universally. Are there political principles that combine the universal with the particular? Let us propose as an answer radical democracy.

RADICAL DEMOCRACY

Radical democracy champions direct popular control over all the resources and institutions used and inhabited by people—from field to forest, factory to family, university to neighborhood, art gallery to web-site. "Democracy in everything" is favored for two essential reasons that combine the immediate with the eternal: people know best how to orga-nize and operate their own institutions; and radical democracy is neces-sary for the finest ethical human qualities to be realized, for the human to emerge as a socially responsible yet creative and free individual. Take natural circumstances, to begin with. Human beings are natural creatures bound into relations with the earth that originated them, cohabiting the environment with other organisms, dependent on the world's resources for the very possibility of continued existence. But, next addressing the social component, we are also utterly acculturated, that is, enthralled by social interaction and the constant fascination of language and expres-sion. Social interaction occurs in reproductive institutions such as the workplace, the school, the community, and even family, locales where life is made collectively and people must exist together. On the one hand, there is a structured, necessary quality to social reproduction; on the other, necessity becomes enjoyable, indeed the source of pleasure, when subject to human creativity; the one underlies the other—work can sat-isfy precisely because it is necessary. This complex of necessary yet poten-tially enjoyable tasks and relationships connects the natural environment and the reproductive locale with radical democracies. For if social repro-duction within environments is not subject to democratic control, but instead democracy is limited to the relatively superficial level of electing state representatives (under the constant barrage of media inducements), then how can it be claimed that society is, in any way, fundamentally, typically democratic? And if democracy is interpreted as liberal and rep-resentative in form rather than direct and participatory, how can it be claimed that people actually live out democracy in practice?

From just such considerations as these arises the belief that democ-racy must entail control over the basic, essential structuring activities of the life process. Democracy must be radical, reproductive, and par-ticipatory. From this alternative perspective, life-maintaining and life-expressing institutions are fundamentally characterized by cooperative effort among equal partners, equal in that all expend most of their lifetime working to satisfy needs and remaking humankind. Beyond this lies an existential locale-based equality between people living together in places, bound into networks through multiple social relations and intersecting life paths. Hence the emphasis by socialist feminism on production and reproduction as inseparable aspects of the making of existence. Hence a conception that includes gender as well as class relations, women's labor in the domestic and public spheres, child rearing and socialization, and the family, productive and reproductive processes united again under new social relations. Hence a notion of the "economic" that includes all kinds of labor, not just the part deficiently rewarded through wages. A truly democratic egalitarian society has to entail control over all of life's institutions by all its members as direct and equal participants. That is, all decisions about significant social practices must be democratically and directly made. Social and environmental relations would thus be subject to intense scrutiny by everyone directly involved. The democratic social-ist idea is to direct institutional activities through collective discussion or "reasoning"; this approach involves clarifying assumptions, collectively structuring arguments, drawing connections between actions and pos-sible consequences, evaluating the relative merits of consequences, and taking collective and individual responsibility for outcomes. In a critical modernist sense, the approach implies a conception of practical embed-ded reason, the best reasonable people can do under prevailing conditions rather than the achievement of rational perfection ("Reason"), as with the Enlightenment or Hegel's idealism. The implication for collective action seems to be that worker-member- and community-controlled institutions should be organized by democratic planning—"democratic" to ensure that popular reasoning is expressed in social activities and "planning" so that the probable consequences of actions (for the poorest people, for the environment, among other things) are known as collective decisions are made. In this, collective adherence and responsibility are gained through participation in decision making rather than through the imposition of laws—indeed, resort to laws is an admission of social dysfunctionality. When social relations, organized around these basic structural activities, are interpreted in terms of equality of contribution, when decisions are made through the active participation of all members of society, an ethi-cal system can emerge that emphasizes mutuality, in the sense of a deep responsibility to others and to the environment. In such a cooperative, egalitarian, and democratic society the possibility exists that pragmati-cally rational, compassionate decisions can be made by ethical people whose commitment to one another and to the society of which they are integral parts extends forward in history and outward in space toward all other people, toward other natural organisms, and to the world as a total system. Principles like these are worth the finest of intellectual and practical effort. In a phrase, development has to be radically reproductive and radically democratic.   *not self-interest but apply to collective good*

Let us now finally, in these last pages of an overly long book, draw these ideas together to outline a truly alternative, radically democratic, form of development. What can be extracted from developmentalism— what is worth saving? We would vouch for the idea, present even in liberal versions of development theory, of using production to satisfy needs in a *reasoned* environment, such as in planning, where the consequences of action are carefully discussed before action is taken. Specifically, that type of development means *using production to meet the needs of the poorest people.* Similarly, if we reexamine socialism—not as a monolith represented by the Soviet Union, not as a political dinosaur but as a living tradition of critical thought, as with Venezuela at the present time—what is worth saving? We would vouch for the notion of *reproductive democracy, that the people involved in an institution—the workplace, university, or family—should collectively control that institution.* Specifically, workers should not only "participate" in management or research but rather should *be* the managers and researchers. Putting the two concepts together, *democratic development means transforming the conditions of reproduction under the control of directly democratic and egalitarian social relations so that the needs of the poorest people are met.* This is an argument for a critical democratic form of development that continues to champion structure, coherence, science, reasoning, democracy in every sphere of life, and the use of productive resources to meet people's most basic needs.

We want the focal point of an alternative form of development to lie in the production of more goods to satisfy people's most desperate needs as part of a wider strategy of transforming power relations in society at large. Development for us primarily means (borrowing a term with deliberate sarcasm from the World Bank) building "economic capacity" so that material life can be improved. Yet, in our use of the term, "economic" is broadly interpreted to mean all activities employing labor organized through social relations, whether productive in the existing, restricted, sense or socially reproductive in the feminist and radical democratic senses. The model of labor comes not from the globe-trotting executive, forever scheming how to make more money, but from mothers, peasants, and artisans whose hard work every day is connected with the direct reproduction of immediate life. Work is best when it involves sensuous interaction with originally natural materials. Work is also useful and necessary for the people who do it and for those around them. Work is satisfying when its purpose of making further life possible is directly known. This means bringing together processes of production and consumption even when separated by space (Hartwick 1998). It means rediscovering the interconnectedness of life, not as a spiritual mystery but as a practical necessity.

The second word in our construction, "capacity," means not capitalist entrepreneurship, nor even just skills, but reproductive resources—that is, land, infrastructure, machines, and fertilizers devoted to increasing the production of food, housing, useful goods, and basic services like clinics, hospitals, schools, water mains, and toilets. Here we retain the notion of "economic growth" to mean not the expansion of the global economy in general—for the world already produces too much in dangerous ways—but growth of productive capacity in the hands of those people who need more so that they can live. Furthermore, means of production have to be collectively owned, directly as cooperatives, partnerships, and family enterprises, so that "development" does not continually recreate inequalities of income and power, and democratically controlled, again in direct, immediate ways, to ensure that "development" satisfies locally defined, but universally present, needs. For us, development means channeling resources directly to poor people to enhance their productivity. It does not mean channeling even more resources to the already rich in the hope that crumbs will drop from their table.

As regards critical modernism, the scientific and technical power of economic growth to underwrite development must always be maintained, but, in the greater realization of democratic socialism, scientific, technical, and economic powers need to be placed increasingly in the hands of the people, directly and cooperatively. As respects socialist feminism, development should combine rather than separate reproductive activities considered as a totality rather than allowing them to be split into hierarchical types. Regarding utopian thinking, development has to be reconceptualized as a universal liberating activity, but, with the best of materialist poststructuralism, new imaginaries of development have to spring into existance from popular discourses influenced not only by new social movements but also embracing the political ideas of the older class-based organizations and even radical reactions to the Western Enlightenment (here we find Alatas's notion of universal knowledge from universal sources persuasive). As regards poststructuralism, existing discourses of development have to be ruthlessly deconstructed to reveal conceptual and political inadequacies rooted in the utter prejudices of absolute power, but in terms of building critical modernism, development has to be seen as a project that singlemindedly employs reasoning in the processes of collective improvement. Critical developmentalism must be radical in the poststructural sense of changing the meaning of a corrupted term. But far more importantly, critical developmentalism, in the socialist sense, has to root material development in the transformation of society. Democratic development is a project highly deserving of ethical respect, political support, intellectual creativity, and practical activism. Let us work tirelessly to make its realization achievable.

References

Abdel-Malek, A. 1981. *Intellectual Creativity in Endogenous Cultures.* Tokyo: United Nations University.

Agarwal, B. 1991. *Structures of Patriarchy.* London: Zed Books.

Aglietta, M. 1979. *A Theory of Capitalist Regulation.* London: New Left Books.

Alatas, S. F. 1993. "On the Indigenization of Academic Discourse." *Alternatives* 18: 307–338.

Althusser, L. 1969. *For Marx.* Trans. B. Brewster. Harmondsworth, UK: Penguin.

Althusser, L., and E. Balibar. 1970. *Reading Capital.* London: New Left Books.

Alvares, C. 1992. "Science." In Sadis, ed. *The Development Dictionary* 219–232.

Amin, S. 1976. *Unequal Development.* New York: Monthly Review Press.

Amin, S. 1989. *Eurocentrism.* New York: Monthly Review Press.

Amsden, A. 2001. *The Rise of "The Rest"—Challenges to the West from Late-Industrialising Economies.* Oxford, UK: Oxford University Press.

Anderson, B. 1983. *Imagined Communities.* London: Verso.

Apffel-Marglin, F., and S. Marglin, eds. 1990. *Dominating Knowledges: Development, Culture and Resistance.* Oxford, UK: Clarendon Press.

Apffel-Marglin, F., and S. Simon. 1994. "Feminist Orientalism and Development." In Harcourt (1994b: 26–45).

Ashcroft B., G. Griffiths, and H. Tiffin, eds. 1989. *The Empire Writes Back: Theory and Practice in Post-Colonial Literatures.* London: Routledge.

Ashcroft, B., G. Griffiths, and H. Tiffin, eds. 1995. *The Post-Colonial Studies Reader.* London: Routledge.

Baer, W. 1972. "Import Substitution and Industrialization in Latin America: Experiences and Interpretations." *Latin American Research Review* 7: 95–122.

Bandarage, A. 1984. "Women in Development: Liberation, Marxism and Marxist Feminism." *Development and Change* 15: 495–515.

Banuri, T. 1990. "Development and the Politics of Knowledge: A Critical Interpretation of the Social Role of Modernization Theories in the Development of the Third World." In Apffel-Marglin and Marglin (1990: 29–72).

Baran, P. 1960. *The Political Economy of Growth.* New York: Monthly Review Press.

Baran, P., and P. Sweezy. 1966. *Monopoly Capital*. New York: Monthly Review Press.

Barnett, T. 1989. *Social and Economic Development*. New York: Guilford Press.

Barratt Brown, M. 1984. *Models in Political Economy*. Harmondsworth, UK: Penguin.

Baudet, H. 1965. *Paradise on Earth: Some Thoughts on European Images of Non-European Man*. New Haven, CT: Yale University Press.

Baudrillard, J. 1983. *Simulations*. New York: Semiotexte.

Bauer, P. T. 1972. *Dissent on Development*. Cambridge, MA: Harvard University Press.

Bauer, P. T. 1981. *Equality, the Third World and Economic Delusion*. London: Methuen.

Balassa, B. 1981. *The Newly Industrializing Countries in the World Economy*. New York: Pergamon Press.

Beeson, M. 2003. "Japan's reluctant reformers and the legacy of the developmental state." In A. Cheung and I. Scott (eds.), *Governance and Public Sector Reform in Post-Crisis Asia: Paradigm Shift or Business as Usual?* London: Curzon Press, 25–43.

Becker, J. 1977. *Marxian Political Economy*. Cambridge, UK: Cambridge University Press.

Bentham, J. 1996 ed. *An Introduction to the Principles of Morals and Legislation*. Oxford, UK: Clarendon Press.

Benton, T. 1984. *The Rise and Fall of Structural Marxism*. New York: St. Martin's Press.

Bernal, M. 1987. *Black Athena: The Afroasiatic Roots of Classical Civilization*. Vol. 1: *The Fabrication of Ancient Greece, 1785–1985*. New Brunswick, NJ: Rutgers University Press.

Bernal, M. 2001. *Black Athena Writes Back: Martin Bernal Responds to His Critics*. Durham, NC: Duke University Press.

Best, S., and D. Kellner, 1991. *Postmodern Theory: Critical Interrogations*. New York: Guilford Press.

Beveridge, W. 1942. *Social and Allied Services (The Beveridge Report)*. Presented to Parliament by Command of His Majesty. London: HMSO.

Bhabha, H. K. 1983a. "Difference, discrimination and the Discourse of Colonialism." In F. Barker, P. Hulme, M. Iverson, and D. Loxley (eds.), *The Politics of Theory*. Colchester, UK: University of Essex, 194–211.

Bhabha, H. K. 1983b. "The Other Question." *Screen* 24, 6: 18–35.

Bhabha, H. K. 1984. "Of Mimicry and Man: The Ambivalence of Colonial Discourse." *October* 28: 125–133.

Bhabha, H. K. 1994. *The Location of Culture*. London: Routledge.

Bienefeld, M. 1981. "Dependence and the Newly Industrializing Countries (NICs): Towards a Reappraisal." In D. Seers (ed.), *Dependency Theory: A Critical Assessment*. London: Pinter: 79–96.

Blaut, J. M. 1976. "Where Was Capitalism Born?" *Antipode* 8, 2: 1–11.

Blaut, J. M. 1989. "Colonialism and the Rise of Capitalism." *Science and Society* 53: 260–296.

Blaut, J. M. 1993. *Colonizer's Model of the World*. New York: Guilford Press.

Blaut, J. M. 1994. "Robert Brenner in the Tunnel of Time." *Antipode* 26: 351–374.

Blomstrom, M., and B. Hettne, 1984. *Development Theory in Transition*. London: Zed Books.

Boggs, C. 1976. *Gramsci's Marxism*. London: Pluto Press.

Bollag, B. 2000. "The New Latin: English Domination in Academe." *Chronicle of Higher Education International* 8 September 1.

Booth, D. 1985. "Marxism and Development Sociology: Interpreting the Impasse." *World Development* 13: 761–787.

Born, B., K. Feher, M. Feinstein, & R. Peet. 2003. *Unholy Trinity: The IMF, World Bank and WTO*. London: Zed Press.

Boserup, E. 1965. *The conditions of agricultural growth*. London: Allen and Unwin.

Boserup, E. 1970. *Women's Role in Economic Development*. London: Allen and Unwin.

Bosworth, B., and S. M. Collins. 2003. *The Empirics of Growth: An Update*. Washington, DC: Brookings Institution.

Bowden, P. J. 1971. *The Wool Trade in Tudor and Stuart England*. London: Cass.

Bowie, M. 1991. *Lacan*. Cambridge, MA: Harvard University Press.

Braudel, F. 1972. *The Mediterranean and the Mediterranean World in the Age of Phillip II*. Trans. S. Re. New York: Harper & Row.

Braudel, F. 1973. *Capitalism and Material Life, 1400–1800*. Trans. M. Kochen. New York: Harper & Row.

Brohman, J. 1996b. *Popular Development: Rethinking the Theory and Practice of Development*. Oxford, UK: Blackwell.

Brenner, R. 1977. "The Origins of Capitalist Development: A Critique of Neo-Smithian Marxism." *New Left Review* 104: 25–92.

Benner, R. 1985. "Agrarian Class Structure and Economic Development in Pre-Industrial Europe." In T. H. Aston and C. H. E. Philpin (eds.). *The Brenner Debate*. Cambridge, UK: Cambridge University Press, 10–63.

Brewer, D. C. 1926. *The Conquest of New England by the Immigrant*. New York: Putnam.

Brewer, A. 1980. *Marxist Theories of Imperialism: A Critical Survey*. London: Routledge.

Bunch, C., and R. Carillo. 1990. "Feminist Perspectives on Women in Development." In I. Tinker (ed.), *Persistent Inequalities*. Oxford, UK: Oxford University Press, 70–82.

Bunch, C., M. Dutt, and S. Fried. 1995. *Beijing 1995: A Global Referendum on the Human Rights of Women*. Rutgers, NJ: Center for Women's Global Leadership.

Caldwell, M. 1977. *The Wealth of Some Nations*. London: Zed Press.

Campbell, M. 2003. "Dorothy Smith and Knowing the World We Live In." *Journal of Sociology and Social Welfare* 30: 3–23.

Cardoso, F. 1982. "Dependency and Development in Latin America." In H. Alavi and T. Shanin (eds.), *Introduction to the Sociology of "Developing Societies."* New York: Monthly Review Press, 112–127.

Cardoso, F., and R. Faletto, 1979. *Dependency and Development*. Berkeley: University of California Press.

Cassirer, E. 1951. *The Philosophy of the Enlightenment*. Princeton, NJ: Princeton University Press.

Chang, H-J. 2002. *Kicking away the Ladder: Development Strategy in Historical Perspective*. London: Anthem Books.

Chang, H-J., and R. Rowthorn. 1995. *The Role of the State in Economic Change*. Oxford, UK: Clarendon Press.

Chase-Dunn, C. 1989. *Global Formations: Structures of the Global Economy.* Cambridge, UK: Blackwell.

Chilcote, R. H. 1984. *Theories of Development and Underdevelopment.* Boulder, CO: Westview Press.

Chodorow, N. 1978. *The Reproduction of Mothering: Psychoanalysis and the Sociology of Gender.* Berkeley: University of California.

Chowdry, G. 1995. "Engendering Development?" In Marchand and Parpart (1995: 26–41).

Cixous, H. 1981. "The Laugh of the Medusa." In S. E. Mark and I. de Courtivron (eds.), *New French Feminisms.* New York: Schocken Books.

Clark, J. B. 1888. *Capital and Its Earnings.* Monograph Vol. 3, No. 2, Publications of the American Economic Association. Baltimore: American Economic Association.

Clark, J. B. 1899. *The Distribution of Wealth: A Theory of Wages, Interests and Profits.* New York: The Macmillan Co.

Clark, J. 1991. *Democratizing Development: The Role of Voluntary Organizations.* West Hartford, CT: Kumarian Press.

Clark, M. 1990. *Nietzsche on Truth and Philosophy.* Cambridge, UK: Cambridge University Press.

Cohen, B. J. 1973. *The Question of Imperialism.* New York: Basic Books.

Cohen, G. A. 1978. *Karl Marx's Theory of History: A Defense.* Princeton, NJ: Princeton University Press.

Cohen, I. J. 1989. *Structuration Theory: Anthony Giddens and the Constitution of Social Life.* New York: St. Martins Press.

Cole, K. 1998. *Cuba: From Revolution to Development.* London: Pinter.

Cole, K. 2002. "Cuba: The Process of Socialist Development." *Latin American Perspectives* 29, 3: 40–56.

Coleman, J. C. 1971. "The Development Syndrome: Differentiation–Equality–Capacity." In L. Binder (eds.), *Crises and Sequences of Political Development.* Princeton, NJ: Princeton University Press.

Comaroff, J., and J. Comaroff. 1991. *Of Revelation and Revolution.* Chicago: University of Chicago Press.

Comte, A. 1988 ed. *Introduction to Positive Philosophy.* Indianapolis, IN: Hackett.

Coontz, S., and P. Henderson. 1986. "Property Forms, Political Power, and Female Labour in the Origins of Class and State Societies." In S. Coontz and P. Henderson (eds.), *Women's Work, Men's Property.* London: Verso.

Cortright, J. 2001. *New Growth Theory, Technology and Learning: A Practitioners Guide.* Reviews of Economic Development Literature and Practice: No. 4. Portland, OR: Impresa.

Crush, J. 1995. *Power of Development.* London: Routledge.

Culler, J. 1973. The linguistic basis of structuralism. In D. Robey (ed.), *Structuralism: An Introduction.* Oxford, UK: Clarendon Press, 20–36.

Cutler, A., B. Hindess, P. Hirst, and A. Hussain. 1977–1978. *Marx's 'Capital' and Capitalism Today* (Vol. 2). London: Routledge & Kegan Paul.

Dalla Costa, M. 1973. "Women and the Subversion of the Community." In *The Power of Women and the Subversion of the Community.* Bristol, UK: Falling Wall Press, 19–54.

Dallmeyer, F. 1996. "Global Development? Voices from Delhi." *Alternatives* 21: 259–282.

Dasgupta, A. K. 1985. *Epochs of Economic Theory*. Oxford, UK: Blackwell.

de Certeau, M. 1984. *The Practice of Everyday Life*. Berkeley: University of California Press.

de Condorcet, M. 1972. "Sketch for a Historical Picture of the Progress of the Human Mind." In L. M. Marsak (ed.), *The Enlightenment*. New York: Wiley, 131–146.

deJanvry, A. 1981. *The Agrarian Question and Reformism in Latin America*. Baltimore: Johns Hopkins University Press.

Deleuze, G., and F. Guattari, 1987. *A Thousand Plateaus*. Trans. B. Massumi. Minneapolis: University of Minnesota Press.

Derrida, J. 1981. "White Mythology." *In Margins of Philosophy*. Trans. A. Bass. Chicago: University of Chicago Press.

Derrida, J. 1974. *Of Grammatology*. Trans. G. Spivak. Baltimore: Johns Hopkins University Press.

Derrida, J. 1978. *Writing and Difference*. Trans A. Bass. Chicago: University of Chicago Press.

Derrida, J. 1981 ed. *Margins of Philosophy*. Trans. A. Bass. Chicago: University of Chicago Press.

Desmarais, A. 2008. "Peasant Resistance to Neoliberalism: La Via Campesina and Food Sovereignty." *Human Geography* 1: 74–80.

DeVault, M. 1999. "Institutional Ethnography: A Strategy for Feminist Inquiry." In M. DeVault, *Liberating Methods: Feminism and Social Research*. Philadelphia: Temple University Press, 46–54.

Dilla, H. 1999. "Comrades and Investors: The Uncertain Transition in Cuba." In L. Panitch and C. Leys (eds.), *Socialist Register 1999: Global Capitalism versus Democracy*. London: Merlin.

Di Stefano, C. 1990. "Dilemmas of Difference: Feminism, Modernity and Postmodernism." In Linda Nicholson (ed.), *Feminism/Postmodernism*. New York: Routledge, 63–82.

Domar, E. 1947 "Expansion and Employment." *American Economic Review* 37: 34–55.

Dos Santos, T. 1970. "The Structure of Dependence." *American Economic Review* 60: 231–236.

Dreyfus, H. L., and P. Rabinow. 1983. *Michel Foucault: Beyond Structuralism and Hermeneutics*. Chicago: University of Chicago Press.

DuBois, M. 1991. "The Governance of the Third World: A Foucauldian Perspective on Power Relations in Development." *Alternatives* 16: 1–30.

Dunford, M., and D. Perrons. 1983. *The Arena of Capital*. New York: St. Martins Press.

Durkheim, E. (ed.). 1983. *The Division of Labor in Society*. New York: Free Press.

Easterly, W. 2009. "Why there's no "GrowthGate": Frustration vs. Chicanery in Explaining Growth," *AidWatch*, December 10, http://aidwatchers.com/2009/12/why-there.

Eco, U. 1973. "Social Life as a Sign System." In D. Robey (ed.), *Structuralism: An Introduction*. Oxford, UK: Clarendon Press, 57–72.

Editors of *Monthly Review*. 2005. "Notes from the Editors on the Death of Andre Gunder Frank." *Monthly Review* 57, 2: 1–2.

Edwards, M. 1989. "The Irrelevance of Development Studies." *Third World Quarterly* 11: 116–135.

Eisenstadt, S. N. 1973a. *Tradition, Change and Modernity*. New York: Wiley.

Eisenstadt, S. N. 1973b. "Social Change and Development." In S. N. Eisenstadt (ed.). *Readings in Social Evolution and Development.* Oxford, UK: Pergamon Press, 3–33.

Ekins, P., and M. Max-Neef, eds. *Real-Life Economics.* London: Routledge.

Emmanuel, A. 1972. *Unequal Exchange: A Study of the Imperialism of Trade.* New York: Monthly Review Press.

Engels, F. 1972 ed. *The Origin of the Family, Private Property and the State.* New York: International Publishers.

Escobar, A. 1984–1985. "Discourse and Power in Development: Michel Foucault and the Relevance of His Work to the Third World." *Alternatives* 10: 377–400.

Escobar, A. 1988. "Power and Visibility: Development and the Invention and Management of the Third World." *Cultural Anthropology* 3: 428–443.

Escobar, A. 1992a. "Imagining a Post-Development Era? Critical Thought, Development and Social Movements." *Social Text* 31–32: 20–56.

Escobar, A. 1992b. "Culture, Economics, and Politics in Latin American Social Movements Theory and Research." In A. Escobar and S. E. Alvarez (eds.), *The Making of Social Movements in Latin America.* Boulder, CO: Westview Press, 62–85.

Escobar, A. 1995. *Encountering Development: The Making and Unmaking of the Third World.* Princeton, NJ: Princeton University Press.

Esteva, G. 1987. "Regenerating People's Spaces." *Alternatives* 12: 125–152.

Esteva, G., and M. S. Prakash, 1997. "From Global Thinking to Local Thinking." In Rahnema and Bawtree (1997; 277–289).

Etienne, M., and E. Leacock, eds. 1980. *Women and Colonization.* New York: Praeger.

Evers, T. 1985. "Identity: The Hidden Side of New Social Movements in Latin America." In D. Slater (ed.), *New Social Movements and the State in Latin America.* Amsterdam: CEDLA, 43–71.

Fals Borda, O. 1988. *Knowledge and People's Power: Lessons with Peasants in Nicaragua, Mexico and Columbia.* New York: New Horizons Press.

Fanon, F. 1968. *The Wretched of the Earth.* New York: Grove Press.

Fanon, F. 1986. *Black Skin, White Masks.* London: Pluto Press.

Ferguson, A., and N. Folbre. 1981. "The Unhappy Marriage of Patriarchy and Capitalism." In L. Sargent (ed.), *Women and Revolution.* Boston: South End Press.

Fisher, H. E. S. 1971. *The Portugal Trade: A Study of Anglo-Portuguese Commerce, 1700–1770.* London: Methuen.

Fitzgibbons, A. 1995. *Adam Smith's System of Liberty, Wealth and Virtue.* Oxford, UK: Clarendon Press.

Flax, J. 1990. Postmodernism and Gender Relations in Feminist Theory. In L. J. Nicholson (ed.), *Feminism/Postmodernism.* New York: Routledge, 39–62.

Foucault, M. 1972. *The Archaeology of Knowledge.* New York: Harper & Row.

Foucault, M. 1973. *The Order of Things.* New York: Vintage Press.

Foucault, M. 1979. *Discipline and Punish: The Birth of the Prison.* New York: Vintage Books.

Foucault, M. 1980a. *Power/Knowledge: Selected Interviews and Other Writings.* New York: Pantheon Books.

Foucault, M. 1980b. *History of Sexuality.* New York: Vintage Books.

Frank, A. 1966. "The Development of Underdevelopment." *Monthly Review* 18: 17–31.

Frank, A. G. 1969a. *Latin America: Underdevelopment or Revolution?* New York: Monthly Review Press.

Frank, A. G. 1969b. *Capitalism and Underdevelopment in Latin America.* New York: Monthly Review Press.

Frank, A. G. 1979. *Dependent Accumulation and Underdevelopment*. New York: Monthly Review Press.

Friedman, M. 1958. "Foreign Economic Aid: Means and Objectives." *Yale Review* 47: 500–516.

Friedman, M., and R. Friedman. 1979. *Free to Choose*. New York: Harcourt Brace Jovanovich.

Friedman, S. 1995. "Beyond White and Other: Relationality and Narratives of Race in Feminist Discourse." *Signs* 21: 1–49.

Friere, P. *Pedagogy of the Oppressed*. New York: Herder and Herder.

Furtado, C. 1963. *The Economic Growth of Brazil*. Berkeley: University of California Press.

G8. 2005. G8 Finance Ministers' Conclusions on Development, London, June 10–11, 2005. Available online at *www.g8.gc.ca/concl_devel-en.asp*.

Galeano, E. 1973. *Open Veins of Latin America: Five Centuries of the Pillage of a Continent*. New York: Monthly Review Press.

Galtung, J. 1971. "A Structural Theory of Imperialism." *Journal of Peace Research* 2: 81–116.

Gandhi, M. 1997. "The Quest for a Simple Life: My Idea of Swarej." In Rahnema and Bowtree (1997; 306–307).

Gates, H. L. 1991. "Critical Fanonism." *Critical Inquiry* 17: 457–470.

Gendzier, I. 1985. *Managing Political Change: Social Scientists and the Third World*. Boulder, CO: Westview Press.

Giddens, A. 1977. *Studies in Social and Political Theory*. New York: Basic Books.

Giddens, A. 1981. *A Contemporary Critique of Historical Materialism*. Berkeley: University of California Press.

Giddens, A. 1984. *The Constitution of Society; Outline of a Theory of Structuration*. Berkeley: University of California Press.

Gonce, R. A. 2003. Review of Kirzner, I., *Ludwig von Mises: The Man and His Economics*. *American Journal of Economics and Sociology* 62: 633–636.

Gould, P. 1964. "A Note on Research into the Diffusion of Development." *Journal of Modern African Studies* 2: 123–125.

Gouldner, A. 1970. *Coming Crisis of Western Sociology*. New York: Basic Books.

Georgescu-Roegen, N. 1995. *La décroissance: Entropie–Ecologie–Economie*, Paris: Sang de la terre.

Gowan, P. 1995. "Neo-Liberal Theory and Practice for Eastern Europe." *New Left Review* 213: 3–60.

Gramsci, A. 1971 ed.*Selections from the Prison Notebooks of Antonio Gramsci*. (Eds. Q. Hoare and G. N. Smith. New York: International Publishers.

Gran, G. 1983. *Development by People: Citizen Construction of a Just World*. New York: Praeger.

Granovetter, M. 1985. "Economic Action and Social Structure: The Problem of Embeddedness." *American Journal of Sociology* 91: 481–510.

Gregory, D. 1982. *Regional Transformation and Industrial Revolution: A Geography of the Yorkshire Woolen Industry*. Minneapolis: University of Minnesota Press.

Gregory, P., and R. Stuart. 2001. *Soviet and Post Soviet Economic Structure and Performance* (7th ed.). Boston: Addison Wesley.

Gress, D. 1989. "The Case against Martin Bernal." *The New Criterion*. Available online at *thenewcriterion.com:81/archive/8/dec89/gress/htm*.

Gudeman, S., and A. Rivera 1992. "Remodelling the House of Economics: Culture and Innovation." *American Ethnologist* 19: 141–154.

Guha, R. 1988. "The Prose of Counter-Insurgency." In R. Guha and G. Spivak (eds.) *Subaltern Studies* (Vol. 6). Delhi, India: Oxford University Press, 37–44.

Guha, R. 1983. *Elementary Aspects of Peasant Insurgency in Colonial India.* Delhi, India: Oxford University Press.

Guha, R., and G. Spivak, eds. 1988. *Selected Subaltern Studies.* Delhi, India: Oxford University Press.

Hagen, E. 1962. *On the Theory of Social Change.* Homewood, IL: Dorsey Press.

Hagerstrand, T. 1952. *The Propagation of Innovation Waves.* Lund: Lund Studies in Geography, Series B, No. 4.

Halpin, T. 2004. "Britain Wins Eight Places in World List of 50 Best Universities." *The Times* (London), 4 November, p. 10.

Hamilton, D. 2002. "Whither Cuban Socialism? The Changing Political Economy of the Cuban Revolution." *Latin American Perspectives,* 29, 3: 18–39.

Hamilton, P. 1983. *Talcott Parsons.* London: Tavistock.

Haney, L. H. 1949. *History of Economic Thought.* New York: Macmillan.

Haraway, D. 1988. Situated Knowledges: The Science Question in Feminism and the Privilege of Partial Perspective. *Feminist Studies* 14: 575–599.

Haraway, D. 1991. *Simians, Cyborgs and Women: The Reinvention of Nature.* New York: Routledge.

Harcourt, W. 1994a. "Negotiating Positions in the Sustainable Development Debate." In Harcourt (1994b: 11–25).

Harcourt, W. 1994b. *Feminist Perspectives on Sustainable Development.* London: Zed Books.

Harcourt, W., and A. Escobar. 2005. *Women and the Politics of Place.* New York: Kumarian Press.

Harding, S. 1986. *The Science Question in Feminism.* Ithaca, NY: Cornell University Press.

Harding, S. 1990. "Feminism, Science, and the Anti-Enlightenment Critiques." In Nicholson (ed.) (1990: 83–106).

Harribey, J-M. 2004. "Do We Really Want Development? Growth, the World's Hard Drug." *Le Monde Diplomatique,* August. Available online at *www.globalpolicy.org/socen/develop/quality/2004/04.*

Harris, N. 1986. *The End of the Third World.* Harmondsworth, UK: Penguin.

Harrison, D. 1988. *The Sociology of Modernization and Development.* London: Unwin Hyman.

Harrod, R. F. 1939. "An Essay in Dynamic Theory." *Economic Journal* 49: 14–33.

Harrod, R. 1948. *Towards a Dynamic Economics: Some Recent Developments of Economic Theory and Their Application to Policy.* London: Macmillan.

Hartmann, H. 1981. "The Unhappy Marriage of Marxism and Feminism: Towards a More Progressive Union." In L. Sargent (ed.), *Women and Revolution.* Boston: South End Press, 1–4.

Hartsock, N. 1985. *Money, Sex and Power.* Boston: Northeastern University Press.

Hartwick, E. 1998. "Geographies of Consumption: A Commodity Chain Analysis." *Society and Space* 16: 423–437.

Harvey, D. 1981. "The Spatial Fix—Hegel, Von Thunen, and Marx." *Antipode* 13, 3: 1–12.

Harvey, D. 1982. *The Limits to Capital.* Oxford, UK: Basil Blackwell.

Harvey, D. 1989. *The Condition of Post-Modernity.* Oxford, UK: Blackwell.

Harvey, D. 2005a. *The New Imperialism.* Oxford, UK: Oxford University Press.

Harvey, D. 2005b. *A Brief History of Neoliberalism.* Oxford, UK: Oxford University Press.

Hecksher, E. F. 1935. *Mercantilism* (2 vols.). London: Unwin Hyman.

Heidegger, M. 1962. *Being and Time.* Trans. John Macquarrie and Edward Robinson. New York: Harper & Row.

Heidegger, M. 1977a. *The Question Concerning Technology.* New York: Harper & Row.

Heidegger, M. 1977b. "Letter on Humanism." In D. F. Krell (ed.), *Martin Heidegger: Basic Writings.* London: Routledge & Kegan Paul, 197–242.

Hegel, G. W. F. (1967 ed.), *The Phenomenology of Mind.* New York: Harper & Row.

Higgins, B. 1968. *Economic Development: Principles, Problems and Policies.* New York: Norton.

Higgot, R. 1983. *Political Development Theory: The Contemporary Debate.* New York: St. Martin's Press.

Hindess, B., and P. Hirst. 1975. *Pre-Capitalist Modes of Production.* London: Routledge & Kegan Paul.

Hindess, B., and P. Hirst. 1977. *Mode of Production and Social Formation: An Autocritique of Pre-Capitalist Modes of Production.* London: Macmillan.

Hirschman, A. 1958. *The Strategy of Economic Development.* New Haven, CT: Yale University Press.

Hirschman, M. 1995. "Women and Development: A Critique." In Marchand and Parpert (1995: 1142–1155).

Hirsch, J. 1978. "The State Apparatus and Social Reproduction." In J. Holloway and S. Picciotto (eds.), *State and Capital: A Marxist Debate.* London: Edward Arnold, 57–107.

Hobson, J. A. 1902. *Imperialism: A Study.* London: Allen & Unwin.

Hofstadter, R. 1955. *Social Darwinism in American Thought.* Boston: Beacon Press.

Holland, M. 1998. "World Bank Book (Shh)." *The Nation* 226, 10: 4–5.

hooks, b. 1984. *Feminist Theory: From Margin to Center.* Boston: South End Press.

Horkheimer, M., and T. Adorno. 1991 ed. *Dialectic of Enlightenment.* New York: Continuum.

Hoselitz, B. 1960. *Sociological Aspects of Economic Growth.* Glencoe, IL: Free Press.

Hudson, R. A., ed. 1997. *Brazil: A Country Study.* Washington, DC: General Printing Office.

Hulme, P. 1986. *Colonial Encounters: Europe and the Native Caribbean, 1692–1797,* London: Methuen.

Hume, D. 1987 ed. *Essays: Moral, Political and Literary.* Indianapolis: University of Indiana Press.

Huntington, E. 1915. *Civilization and Climate.* New Haven, CT: Yale University Press.

Huntington, S. 1975. "Issues in Woman's Role in Economic Development Critique and Alternatives." *Journal of Marriage and the Family* 37: 1001–1012.

Huntington, S. P. 1968. *Political Order in Changing Societies* (The Henry L. Stimson Lectures Series). New Haven, CT: Yale University Press.

Huntington, S. P. 2000. "The Clash of Civilizations?" In P. O'Meara, H. D. Mehlinger, and M. Krain (eds.), *Globalization and the Challenges of a New Century.* Bloomington: Indiana University Press, 3–23.

Husserl, E. 1970. *The Crisis of European Sciences and Transcendental Phenomenology: An Introduction to Phenomenological Philosophy.* Translated with an introduction by D. Carr. Evanston, IL: Northwestern University Press.

Hutchison, T. W. 1953. *A Review of Economic Doctrines, 1870–1929.* Oxford, UK: Clarendon Press.

Illich, I. 1997. "Development as Planned Poverty." In Rahnema and Bawtree (1997: 94–102).

Ilchman, W. F., and R. C. Bhargava. 1966. "Balanced Thought and Economic Growth." *Economic Development and Cultural Change* 14: 385–399.

Inkeles, A., and D. H. Smith. 1974. *Becoming Modern: Individual Change in Six Developing Countries.* Cambridge, MA: Harvard University Press.

Innes, S. 1995. *Creating the Commonwealth: The Economic Culture of Puritan New England* New York: Norton.

Insel, A. 1993. "La Part du Don, essai d'Evaluation." In MAUSS, *Ce Que Veut Dire. Don et Interet.* Paris: Decouverte, 221–234.

International Labour Organization. "Global Employment Trends for Women, 2004." Geneva: Author.

Irigaray, L. 1985. *This Sex Which Is Not One.* Ithaca, NY: Cornell University Press.

Jackman, R. W. 1984. "Dependence on Foreign Investment and Economic Growth in the Third World." In M. A. Seligson (ed.), *The Gap between Rich and Poor: Contending Perspectives on the Political Economy of Development.* Boulder, CO: Westview Press, 211–223.

Jaquette, J. 1990. "Women and Modernization Theory: A Decade of Feminist Criticism." *World Politics* 34: 267–284.

Jagger, A. 1983. *Feminist Politics and Human Nature.* Totowa, NJ: Rowman & Littlefield.

James, P. 1997. "Postdependency? The Third World in an Era of Globalism and Late-Capitalism." *Alternatives* 22: 205–226.

Jevons, W. S. 1911. *The Theory of Political Economy.* London: Macmillan.

Johnson, C. 1982. *MITI and the Japanese Miracle: The Growth of Industry Policy, 1925–1975.* Stanford, CA: Stanford University Press.

Johnson, H. G. 1971. "The Keynesian Revolution and the Monetarist Counter-Revolution." *American Economic Review* 61: 1–14.

Johnson, E. S., and H. G. Johnson. 1978. *The Shadow of Keynes: Understanding Keynes, Cambridge and Keynesian Economics.* Oxford, UK: Blackwell.

Johnson, P. 1994. *Feminism as Radical Humanism.* Boulder, CO: Westview Press.

Johnston, D. C. 2005. "Richest Are Leaving Even the Rich Behind." *New York Times,* 5 June, pp. 1, 17.

Joint Declaration, 2004. *www.cuba.cu/gobierno/discursos/2004/ing/d141204.html.*

Kabeer, N. 1994. *Reversed Realities: Gender Hierarchies in Development Thought.* London: Verso.

Kahneman, D. 2003. " Maps of Bounded Rationality: Psychology for Behavioral Economics." *The American Economic Review,* 93: 1449–1475.

Kahneman, D., and Krueger, A. B. 2006. "Developments in the Measurement of Subjective Well-Being." *Journal of Economic Perspectives,* 20: 3–24.

Kauder, E. 1965. *A History of Marginal Utility Theory.* Princeton, NJ: Princeton University Press.

Keynes, J. M. 1936. *The General Theory of Employment, Interest and Money.* New York: Harcourt Brace.

Kiely, R. 1998. "Neo Liberalism Revised? A Critical Account of World Bank Concepts of Good Governance and Market Friendly Intervention." *Capital and Class* 64: 63–88.

Klein, N. 2007. *The Shock Doctrine: The Rise of Disaster Capitalism.* New York: Holt.

Kohli, A. 2004. *State-Directed Development: Political Power and Industrialization in the Global Periphery.* Cambridge, UK: Cambridge University Press.

Kojm, C., ed. 1984. *The Problem of International Debt.* New York: Wilson.

Kothari, R. 1989. *Rethinking Development: In Search of Humane Alternatives.* New York: New Horizons.

Kuznets, S. 1940. "Schumpeter's Business Cycles." *American Economic Review* 30: 257–271.

Kuznets, S. 1953. *Economic Change.* New York: Norton.

Krugman, P. 1995. *Development, Geography and Economic Theory.* Cambridge, MA: MIT Press.

Laclau, E., and C. Mouffe. 1985. *Hegemony and Socialist Strategy: Towards a Radical Democratic Politics.* London: Verso.

Lal, D. 1980. *A Liberal International Economic Order.* Essays in International Finance, No. 139. Princeton, NJ: Princeton University.

Lal, D. 1983. *The Poverty of Development Economics.* London: Institute of Economic Affairs.

Landes, D. 1998. *The Wealth and Poverty of Nations: Why Some Are So Rich and Some So Poor.* New York: Norton.

Lapavistsas, C. 2005. *Social Foundations of Money, Markets and Credit.* London: Routledge.

Latouche, S. 1993. *In the Wake of the Affluent Society: An Exploration of Post-Development.* London: Zed Books.

Latouche, S. 2003. "Would the West Actually Be Happier with Less?" *LeMonde Diplomatique,* 12 December: 1.

Leborgne, D., and A. Lipietz. 1988. "New Technologies, New Modes of Regulation: Some Spatial Implications." *Society and Space* 6: 263–280.

Lefkowitz, M. R. 1996. *Black Athena Revisited.* Chapel Hill: University of North Carolina Press.

Lefort, C. 1978. "Marx: From One Vision of History to Another." *Social Research* 45: 4: 372–384.

Lekachman, R. 1959. *A History of Economic Ideas.* New York: Harper & Row.

Lekachman, R. 1966. *The Age of Keynes.* New York: Random House.

Lenin, V. I. 1975 ed. *Imperialism, the Highest Stage of Capitalism.* Peking: Foreign Language Press.

Leone, R. C. 1996. Foreword in E. N. Wolf, *Top Heavy: A Study of Increasing Inequality of Wealth in America.* New York: New Press.

Lerner, D. 1958. *The Passing of Traditional Society: Modernizing the Middle East.* New York: Free Press.

Leube, K. R. 1984. "Friedrich August von Hayek: A Biographical Introduction." In F. von Hayek, *The Essence of Hayek.* Stanford, CA: Hoover Institution Press, xvii–xxxvi.

Levi-Strauss, C. 1966. *The Savage Mind.* Chicago: University of Chicago Press.

Lewis, W. D. 1955. *The Theory of Economic Growth*. Homewood, IL: Irwin.

Lipietz, A. 1985. *The Enchanted World*. London: Verso.

Lipietz, A. 1986. "New Tendencies in the International Division of Labor: Regimes of Accumulation and Modes of Reguation." In A. Scott and M. Storper (eds.), *Production, Work, Territory*. Boston: Allen & Unwin, 16–40.

Lipietz, A. 1987. *Mirages and Miracles*. London: Verso.

List, F. 1909. *The National System of Political Economy*. London: Longmans.

Little, I. M. D. 1982. *Economic Development: Theory, Policy and International Relations*. New York: Basic Books.

Lloyd, G. 1984. *Man of Reason: "Male" and "Female" in Western Philosophy*. Minneapolis: University of Minnesota Press.

Long, D. G. 1977. *Bentham on Liberty: Jeremy Bentham's Idea of Liberty in Relation to His Utilitarianism*. Toronto: University of Toronto.

Long, N. 1975. "Structural Dependency, Modes of Production and Economic Brokerage in Peru." In I. Oxaal, A. Barnett, and D. Booth (eds.), *Beyond the Sociology of Development*. London: Routledge & Kegan Paul.

Lorde, A. 1981. "The Master's Tools Will Never Dismantle the Master's House." In C. Morroga and G. Anzaldua (eds.), *The Bridge Called Me Back: Writings by Radical Women of Color*. Watertown, MA: Persaphone Press, 98–101.

Luxembourg, R. 1951 ed. *The Accumulation of Capital*. London: Routledge & Kegan Paul.

Lyotard, J-F. 1984. *The Postmodern Condition*. Minneapolis: University of Minnesota Press.

Lyons, J. 1973. "Structuralism and Linguistics." In D. Robey (ed.), *Structuralism: An Introduction*. Oxford, UK: Clarendon Press, 5–19.

MacCabe, C. 1987. "Foreword." In G. Spivak, *In Other Worlds: Essays in Cultural Politics*. New York: Methuen, ix–xix.

Malthus, T. R. 1933. *Essay on Population*. New York: Everyman.

Marchand, M. H., and J. L. Parpart, eds. 1995. *Feminism/Postmodernism/Development*. London: Routledge.

Marshall, A. 1920. *Principles of Economics*. London: Macmillan.

Marx, K. 1938 ed. *The German Ideology*. London: Lawrence & Wishart.

Marx, K. 1970 ed. "Preface." In *A Contribution to the Critique of Political Economy*. Moscow: Progress Publishers, 19–23.

Marx, K. 1973 ed. *Grundrisse: Introduction to the Critique of Political Economy*. Harmondsworth, UK: Penguin.

Marx, K. 1976 ed. *Capital* (Vol. 1). Harmondsworth, UK: Penguin.

Marx, K., and F. Engels. 1981 ed. *The German Ideology*. New York: International Publishers.

McClelland, D. C. 1961. *The Achieving Society*. Princeton, NJ: D. Van Nostrand.

McClelland, D. C., and D. G. Winter. 1971. *Motivating Economic Achievement*. New York: Free Press.

McGrane, B. 1989. *Beyond Anthropology: Society and the Other*. New York: Columbia University Press.

McNamara, R. S. 1981. *The McNamara Years at the World Bank*. Baltimore: Johns Hopkins University Press.

Macpherson, C. B. 1962 *The Political Theory of Possessive Individualism*. Oxford, UK: Clarendon Press.

Marx, K. 1973 ed. *Grundrisse: Foundations of the Critique of Political Economy.* Trans. Martin Nicolaus. Harmondsworth, UK: Penguin.

McClintock, R. 1971. *Man and His Circumstances: Ortega as Educator.* New York: Wiley.

Meier, G. 1984. *Leading Issues in Development Economics* (4th ed.). New York: Oxford University Press.

Melucci, A. 1988. "Getting Involved: Identity and Mobilization in Social Movements." In H. Kriesi, S. Tarrow, and B. Vui (eds.), *International Social Movements Research* (Vol. 1). London: JAI Press.

Merchant, C. 1980. *The Death of Nature.* San Francisco: Harper & Row.

Mies, M. 1986. *Patriarchy and Accumulation on a World Scale.* London: Zed Books.

Miles, A. 1996. *Integrative Feminisms: Building Global Visions, 1960s–1990s.* New York: Routledge.

Milanovich, B. 2007. "An Even Higher Global Inequality Than Previously Thought." World Development Discussion Paper. Available online at *siteresources.worldbank.org/INTDECINEQ/ResourcesGlobalinequality.pdf.*

Mill, J. S. 1859. *On Liberty.* London: Longman, Roberts and Green.

Mill, J. S. 1863. *Utilitarianism.* London: Parker, Son and Born.

Mill, J. S. 1909. *Principles of Political Economy.* London: Longmans.

Minh-ha, T. T. 1989. *Woman, Native, Other: Writing Postcoloniality and Feminism.* Bloomington: Indiana University Press.

Mitchell, J. 1966. "Women, the Longest Revolution." *New Left Review* 40: 11–37.

Mitchell, T. 1988. *Colonising Egypt.* Cambridge, UK: Cambridge University Press.

Moggridge, D. E. 1980. *The Collected Works of John Maynard Keynes* (2 vols.). London: Macmillan.

Mohanty, C. 1991a. "Cartographies of Struggle: Third World Women and the Politics of Feminism." In C. Mohanty, A. Russo, and L. Torres (eds.), *Third World Women and the Politics of Feminism.* Bloomington: Indiana University Press, 1–51.

Mohanty, C. 1991b. "Under Western Eyes: Feminist Scholarship and Colonial Discourses." In C. Mohanty, A. Russo, and L. Torres (eds.), *Third World Women and the Politics of Feminism.* Bloomington: Indiana University Press, 51–81.

Mommsen, W. J. 1980. *Theories of Imperialism.* Chicago: University of Chicago Press.

Moghadam, V. 1989. "Against Eurocentrism and Nativism: A Review Essay on Samir Amin's *Eurocentrism* and other Texts." *Socialism and Democracy* 9: 81–104.

Ferrater Mora, J. 1956. *Ortega y Gasset: An Outline of His Philosophy.* New Haven, CT: Yale University Press.

Martin, R., and P. Sunley. 1996. "Paul Krugman's Geographical Economics and Its Implications for Regional Development Theory: A Critical Assessment." *Economic Geography* 72: 259–292.

Moser, C. 1993. *Gender Planning and Development.* New York: Routledge.

Mueller, A. 1987. *Peasants and Professionals: The Social Organization of Women in Development Knowledge.* PhD thesis, Department of Education, University of Toronto.

Myrdal, G. 1963. *Economic Theory and Underdeveloped Regions.* New York: Harper and Row.

Myrdal, G. 1984. "Trade as a Mechanism of International Inequality." In Meier (1984: 498–503).

Nandy, A. 1983. *The Intimate Enemy: Loss and Recovery of Self under Colonialism.* Delhi, India: Oxford University Press.

Nandy, A. 1987. *Tradition, Tyranny and Utopias.* Delhi, India: Oxford University Press.

Newman, P. C. 1952. *The Development of Economic Thought.* New York: Prentice-Hall.

Nicholson, L. 1990. *Feminism/Postmodernism.* London: Routledge.

Nietzsche, F. 1968. *The Will to Power.* Trans. W. Kaufmann and R. J. Hollingdale. New York: Random House.

Nietzsche, F. 1979. *Truth and Philosophy.* Atlantic Highlands: Humanities Press.

Nurkse, R. 1953. *Problems of Capital Formation in Underdeveloped Countries.* New York: Oxford University Press.

O'Conner, M., and R. Arnoux. 1993. "Translators' Introduction." In Latouche (1993: 1–20).

Ollman, B. 1976. *Alienation: Marx's Conception of Man in Capitalist Society.* Cambridge, UK: Cambridge University Press.

Organization for European Economic Cooperation and Development, 1988. Paris: OECD.

Ortega y Gasset, J. 1994. *The Revolt of the Masses.* New York: Norton.

Palley, T. I. 2005. "From Keynesianism to Neoliberalism: Shifting Paradigms in Economics." In A. Saad-Filho and D. Johnston (eds.), *Neoliberalism: A Critical Reader.* London: Pluto Press, 20–29.

Palma, G. 1978. "Dependency: A Formal Theory of Underdevelopment or a Methodology for the Analysis of Concrete Situations of Underdevelopment?" *World Development* 6: 881–924.

Palma, G. 1981. "Dependency and Development: A Critical Overview." In D. Seers (ed.), *Dependency Theory: A Critical Assessment.* London: Pinter: 20–78.

Parpart, J. L. 1995. "Deconstructing the Development Expert." In Marchand and Parpart (1995: 221–243).

Parpart J. L., and M. H. Marchand. 1995. "Exploding the Canon: An Introduction/Conclusion." In Marchand and Parpart (1995: 1–22).

Parr, J. 1999. "Growth-Pole Strategies in Regional Economic Planning: A Retrospective View. Part 1. Origins and Advocacy." *Urban Studies* 36: 1195–1215.

Parsons, T. 1948. *The Structure of Social Action.* New York: McGraw-Hill.

Parsons, T. 1960. *Structure and Process in Modern Societies.* Glencoe, IL: Free Press.

Parsons, T. 1961. "Some Considerations on the Theory of Social Change." *Rural Sociology* 26: 219–239.

Parsons, T. 1966. *Societies: Evolutionary and Comparative Perspectives.* Englewood Cliffs, NJ: Prentice-Hall.

Parsons, T. 1971a. *The Social System.* Glencoe, IL: Free Press.

Parsons, T. 1971b. *The System of Modern Societies.* Englewood Cliffs, NJ: Prentice-Hall.

Parsons, T., and E. Shils, 1951. *Towards a General Theory of Action.* Cambridge, MA: Harvard University Press.

Parsons, T., and N. J. Smelser, 1956. *Economy and Society.* London: Routledge & Kegan Paul.

Payer, C. 1982. *The World Bank: A Critical Analysis.* New York: Monthly Review Press.

Peet, R. 1985. "The Social Origins of Environmental Determinism." *Annals of the Association of American Geographers* 75: 309–333.

Peet, R. 1998. *Modern Geographical Thought.* Oxford, UK: Blackwell.

Peet, R. 1999. "Review of David Landes, *The Wealth and Poverty of Nations.*" *Annals of the Association of American Geographers* 89: 558–560.

Peet, R. 2007. *Geography of Power: Making Global Economic Policy.* London: Zed Press.

Peet, R. 2008. "Madness and Civilization: Global Finance Capital and the Anti-Poverty Discourse." *Human Geography* 1: 82–91.

Peet, R., and M. Watts. 1996. *Liberation Ecologies.* London: Routledge.

People's Treaty 2006. Text of People's Treaty Bolivia, Cuba, Venezuela. Available online at *quest.quixote.org/node/305.*

Perroux, F. 1955. "Note sur la Notion de Pole de Croissance." *Economie Appliquée* 8: 307–320.

Pezzullo, C. 1982. *Women and Development.* Chile: UN Economic Commission for Latin America and the Caribbean.

Philo, C. 1992. "Foucault's Geography." *Society and Space* 10: 137–161.

Pieterese, J., and B. Parekha (eds.). 1995. *The Decolonization of Imagination: Culture, Knowledge and Power.* London: Zed Books.

Piketty, T., E. Hess, and E. Saez. 2006. Income Inequality in the United States: 1913–2000. Available online at *elsa.berkeley.edu/~saez.*

Piore, M., and C. Sabel, 1984. *The Second Industrial Divide.* New York: Basic Books.

Pitt, D. 1976. *Development from Below: Anthropologists and Development Situations.* The Hague, Netherlands: Mouton.

Poggi, G. 1983. *Calvinism and the Capitalist Spirit: Max Weber's Protestant Ethic.* Amherst: University of Massachusetts Press.

Polanyi, K. 1944. *The Great Transformation.* Boston: Beacon Press.

Polanyi, M. 1967. *The Tacit Dimension.* New York: Doubleday.

Polidano, C. 2000. "Measuring Public Sector Capacity." *World Development* 28: 805–822.

Pollin, R. 2003. *Contours of Descent.* London: Verso.

Post, K. 1978. *Arise Ye Starvlings.* The Hague, Netherlands: Martin Nijhoff.

Prakesh, G. 1994. "Subaltern Studies as Postcolonial Criticism." *American Historical Review* 99: 1475–1490.

Pred, A. R. 1965. "Industrialization, Initial Advantage, and American Metropolitan Growth." *Geographical Review* 55: 158–185.

Pred, A. R. 1973. *Urban Growth and the Circulation of Information: The United States System of Cities 1790–1840.* Cambridge, MA: Harvard University Press.

Prebisch, R. 1972. *International Economics and Development.* New York: Academic Press.

Rahnema, M. 1990. "Participatory Action Theory: The 'Last Temptation of Saint' Development." *Alternatives* 15: 199–226.

Rahnema, M. 1997. "Towards Post-Development: Searching for Signposts, a New Language and New Paradigms." In Rahnema and Bawtree (1997: 377–403).

Rahnema, M., with V. Bawtree, eds. 1997. *The Postdevelopment Reader.* London: Zed Books.

Rathgeber, E. M. 1990. "WID, WAD, GAD: Trends in Research and Practice." *The Journal of Developing Areas* 24: 489–502.

Redman, J. 2006. *The Bolivarian Alternative for the Americas*. MA Thesis. Clark University.

Republic of South Africa, 1996. *Growth, Employment and Redistribution: A Macroeconomic Strategy*. Johannesburg: Department of Finance, Republic of South Africa.

Rey, P. O. 1973. *Les Alliances de Classes*. Paris: Maspero.

Ricardo, D. 1911. *Principles of Political Economy and Taxation*. London: J. M. Dent.

Ricardo, D. 1951–1973. *The Works and Correspondence of David Ricardo*. (11 vols.). Ed. P. Sraffa with M. H. Dobb. Cambridge, UK: Cambridge University Press.

Rich, A. 1986. *Blood, Bread and Poetry: Selected Prose, 1979–1985*. New York: Norton.

Riddell, J. B. 1970. *The Spatial Dynamics of Modernization in Sierra Leone*. Evanston, IL: Northwestern University Press.

Rist, G. 1997. *The History of Development: From Western Origins to Global Faith*. London: Zed Books.

Ritzer, G. 1992. *Contemporary Sociological Theory*. New York: McGraw-Hill.

Roberts, P. C. 1971. "Oskar Lange's Theory of Socialist Planning." *Journal of Political Economy* 79: 562–577.

Rocheleau, D., B. Thomas-Slayter, and E. Wangari, eds. 1996. *Feminist Political Ecology: Global Issues and Local Experiences*. London: Routledge.

Roches, G. 1975. *Talcott Parsons and American Sociology*. New York: Barnes & Noble.

Rodrik, D. 2006. "Goodbye Washington Consensus, Hello Washington Confusion?" *Journal of Economic Literature* 44: 973–987.

Rogers, B. 1980. *The Domestication of Women: Discrimination in Developing Societies*. London: Tavistock.

Romer, P. M. 1992. "Two Strategies for Economic Development: Using Ideas and Producing Ideas." Proceedings of the World Bank Annual Conference on Development Economics, 1992. Supplement, *World Bank Economic Review*, 1993.

Romer, P. M. 1993. "Implementing a National Technology Strategy with Self-Organizing Industry Investment Boards." *Brookings Papers on Economic Activity* 2: 345–390.

Romero, S. 2006. "Caracas Mayor Lays Claim to Golf Links to House Poor." *The New York Times*, September 3: A3.

Rorty, R. 1979. Philosophy and the Mirror of Nature. Princeton, NJ: Princeton University Press.

Rorty, R. 1991. *Objectivity, Relativism, and Truth: Philosophical Papers*. Cambridge, UK: Cambridge University Press.

Rosenstein-Rodan, P. 1943. "Problems of Industrialization of Eastern and South-Eastern Europe." *Economic Journal* 53: 205–216.

Rossi, I. 1974. "Intellectual Antecedents of Levi-Strauss' notion of unconscious." In I. Rossi (ed.), *The Unconscious in Culture: The Structuralism of Claude Levi-Strauss*. New York: E. P. Dutton, 7–30.

Rostow, W. W. 1960. *The Stages of Economic Growth: A Non-Communist Manifesto*. Cambridge, UK: Cambridge University Press.

Roth, G., and W. Schluchter. 1979. *Max Weber's Vision of History: Ethics and Methods*. Berkeley: University of California Press.

Roussakis, E. N. 1968. *Friedrich List, the Zollverein, and the Uniting of Europe.* Bruges, Belgium: College of Europe.

Roxborough, I. 1988. "Modernization Theory Revisited: A Review Article." *Comparative Studies in Society and History* 30: 753–761.

Rudin, M. 2006. "The Science of Happiness." BBC News 24, April 30. Available online at *news.bbc.co/1/hi/programmes/happiness_formula/4783836.stm.*

Sachs, J. 1991. *The Economic Transformation of Eastern Europe: The Case of Poland.* Memphis: P. K. Seidman Foundation.

Sachs, J. 2005. *The End of Poverty: Economic Possibilities for Our Time.* Foreword by Bono. New York: Penguin Press.

Sachs, W., ed. 1992. *The Development Dictionary: A Guide to Knowledge as Power.* London: Zed Books.

Sachs, W. 1997. "The Need for the Home Perspective." In Rahnema and Bawtree (1997: 290–300).

Said, E. W. 1979. *Orientalism.* London: Routledge & Kegan Paul.

Said, E. 1989. "Representing the Colonized: Anthropology's Interlocutors." *Critical Inquiry* 15: 205–225.

Said, E. 1993. *Culture and Imperialism.* New York: Vintage.

Samuelson, P. 1980. *Economics* (11th ed.). New York: McGraw-Hill.

Samuelson, P. A. 2001. "A Ricardo–Sraffa Paradigm Comparing Gains from Trade in Inputs and Finished Goods." *Journal of Economic Literature* 39 (2001): 1204–1214.

Saussure, F. de. 1986. *Course in General Linguistics.* Trans. R. Harris. La Salle, IL: Open Court Classics.

Savage, S. 1981. *The Theories of Talcott Parsons: The Social Relations of Action.* New York: St. Martins Press.

Schluchter, W. 1981. *The Rise of Western Rationalism: Max Weber's Developmental History.* Berkeley: University of California Press.

Schultz, T. W. 1964. *Transforming Traditional Agriculture.* New Haven, CT: Yale University Press.

Schumpeter, J. 1934. *The Theory of Economic Development.* Cambridge, MA: Harvard University Press.

Schumpeter, J. 1952. *The Sociology of Imperialism.* New York: Kelley.

Scott, A., and M. Storper, eds. 1986. *Production, Work, Territory.* Boston: Allen & Unwin.

Scott, A. 1988. "Flexible Production Systems and Regional Development: The Rise of New Industrial Spaces in North America and Western Europe." *International Journal of Urban and Regional Research* 12: 171–186.

Scott, C. V. 1995. *Gender and Development: Rethinking Modernization and Dependency Theory.* Boulder, CO: Lynne Riener.

Scott, J. 1976. *The Moral Economy of the Peasant.* New Haven, CT: Yale University Press.

Scott, J. 1985. *Weapons of the Weak: Everyday Forms of Peasant Resistance.* New Haven, CT: Yale University Press.

Scott, J. 1990. *Domination and the Arts of Resistance: Hidden Transcripts.* New Haven, CT: Yale University Press.

Seers, D. 1962. "A Theory of Inflation and Growth in Under-Developed Countries Based on the Experience in Latin America." *Oxford Economic Papers* 14: 173–195.

Seers, D. 1983. *The Political Economy of Nationalism.* Oxford, UK: Oxford University Press.

Semple, E. C. 1903. *American History and Its Geographic Conditions.* Boston: Houghton Mifflin.

Semple, E. C. 1911. *Influences of Geographic Environment on the Basis of Ratzel's System of Anthropo-Geography.* New York: Russell & Russell.

Semple, R. K., H. L. Gauthier, and C. E. Youngmann. 1972. "Growth Poles in Sao Paulo, Brazil." *Annals of the Association of American Geographers* 62: 591–598.

Sen, A. K. 2000. *Development as Freedom.* New York: Anchor.

Sen, G., and C. Grown. 1987. *Development Crises and Alternative Visions.* New York: Monthly Review Press.

Shanin, T. 1997. "The Idea of Progress." In Rahnema and Bawtree (1997: 65–72).

Shannon, T. R. 1989. *An Introduction to the World-System Perspective.* Boulder, CO: Westview Press.

Sheth, D. L. 1997. "Alternatives from an Indian Grassroots Perspective." In Rahnema and Bawtree (1997: 329–335).

Shi, D. 1997. "The Searchers after the Simple Life." In Rahnema and Bawtree (1997: 308–310).

Shionoya, Y. 1997. *Schumpeter and the Idea of Social Science.* Cambridge, UK: Cambridge University Press.

Shiva, V. 1989. *Staying Alive.* London: Zed Books.

Shohat, E. 1992. "Notes on the Post-Colonial." *Social Text* 31–32: 99–113.

Sideri, S. 1970. *Trade and Power: Informal Colonialism in Anglo-Portuguese Relations.* Rotterdam, Netherlands: Rotterdam University Press.

Simon, H., and A. Newell. 1972. *Human Problem Solving.* Englewood Cliffs, NJ: Prentice-Hall.

Singer, H. 1992. "Lessons of Post-War Development Experience, 1945–1988." In S. Sharma (ed.), *Development Policy.* New York: St. Martins Press, 35–80.

Skinner, A. S. 1992. "Political Economy: Adam Smith and His Predecessors." In P. Jones and A. S. Skinner (eds.), *Adam Smith Reviewed.* Edinburgh, UK: Edinburgh University Press, 217–242.

Slater, D. 1992. "Theories of Development and Politics of the Post-Modern—Exploring a Border Zone." *Development and Change* 3: 283–319.

Slater, D. 1993. "The Geopolitical Imagination and the Enframing of Development Theory." *Transactions* (Institute of British Geographers) 18: 419–437.

Smith, A. 1937 ed. *The Wealth of Nations.* New York: Modern Library.

Smith, A. 1976 ed. *The Theory of Moral Sentiments.* Oxford, UK: Oxford University Press.

Smith, D. 1990a. *The Conceptual Practices of Power.* Boston: Northeastern University Press.

Smith, D. 1990b. *K Is Mentally Ill: The Anatomy of a Factual Account, Texts, Facts and Femininity: Exploring the Relations of Ruling.* London: Routledge.

Smith, D. 2002. "Institutional Ethnography." In T. May (ed.), *Qualitative Research in Action: An International Guide to Issues in Practice.* London: Sage, 150–161.

Smith, V. 1994. "Economics in the Laboratory." *Journal of Economic Perspectives* 8: 113–131.

Snyder, M. 1995. *Transforming Development: Women, Poverty and Politics.* London: Intermediate Technology Publications.

Soja, E. W. 1968. *The Geography of Modernization in Kenya: A Spatial Analysis of Social, Economic and Political Change.* Syracuse, NY: Syracuse University Press.

Solow, R. M. 1956. "A Contribution to the Theory of Economic Growth." *Quarterly Journal of Economics* 70: 65–94.

Solow, R. M. 1957. "Technical Change and the Aggregate Production Function." *Review of Economics and Statistics* 39: 312–320.

Solow, R. M. 1970. *Growth Theory: An Exposition.* New York: Oxford University Press.

Sorensen, T., ed. 1988. *"Let the Word Go Forth": The Speeches, Statements, and Writings of John F. Kennedy.* New York: Delacorte Press.

Spencer, H. 1882. *The Principles of Sociology.* New York: Appleton.

Spivak, G. C. 1987. *In Other Worlds: Essays in Cultural Politics.* New York: Routledge.

Spivak, G. C. 1988. "Can the Subaltern Speak?" In C. Nelson and L. Grossberg (eds.), *Marxism and the Interpretation of Culture.* Urbana: University of Illinois Press, 271–313.

Spybey, T. 1992. *Social Change, Development and Dependency.* Cambridge, UK: Polity Press.

Stiglitz, J. 2002. *Economcs.* New York: Norton.

Straussman, W. P. 1993. "Development Economics from a Chicago Perspective." In W. J. Samuels (ed.), *The Chicago School of Political Economy.* New Brunswick, NJ: Transaction Books, 277–294.

Sunkel, O. 1972. "Big Business and Dependencia." *Foreign Affairs* 50: 517–531.

Susman, P. 1998. "Cuban Socialism in Crisis: A Neoliberal Solution?" In Thomas Klak (ed.), *Globalization and Neoliberalism: The Caribbean Context.* Lanham, MD: Rowman & Littlefield, 179–208.

Szentes, T. 1976. *The Political Economy of Underdevelopment* (3rd ed.). Budapest, Hungary: Akademia Kiado.

Tabb, W. K. 2004. *Economic Governance in the Age of Globalization.* New York: Columbia University Press.

Taussig, M. 1987. *Shaminism, Colonialism and the Wild Man.* Chicago: University of Chicago Press.

Taylor, J. G. 1979. *From Modernization to Modes of Production.* London: Macmillan.

Timpanaro, S. 1975. *On Materialism.* London: New Left Books.

Todaro, M. 1971. *Development Planning: Models and Methods.* Nairobi, Kenya: Oxford University Press.

Todorov, T. 1984. *The Conquest of America: The Question of the Other.* New York: Harper & Row.

Tönnies, F. 2001. ed. *Community and Society.* Cambridge, UK: Cambridge University Press.

Touraine, A. 1981. *The Voice and the Eye.* New York: Cambridge University Press.

Touraine, A. 1988. *The Return of the Actor.* Minneapolis: University of Minnesota Press.

Toye, J. 1987. *Dilemmas of Development: Reflections on the Counter-Revolution in Development Theory and Policy.* Oxford, UK: Blackwell.

Tribe, K. 1988. "Friedrich List and the Critique of 'Cosmopolitical Economy.'" *The Manchester School* 61: 17–36.

Turgeon, L. 1996. *Bastard Keynesianism: The Evolution of Economic Thinking and Policy-Making Since World War II.* Westport, CT: Praeger.

ul Haq, M. 1995. *Reflections on Human Development.* New York: Oxford University Press.

United Nations Development Program. 1991. *Human Development Report.* New York: United Nations Development Program.

United Nations Development Program. 1998. *Human Development Report.* New York: United Nations Development Program.

United Nations Development Program. 1999. *Human Development Report.* New York: United Nations Development Program.

United Nations Development Program. 2006. *Human Development Report.* Ch. 1, 11–12.

United Nations Development Program. 2008. *Statistics of the Human Development Report.* Available online at *hdr.undp.org/en/statistics/.*

United Nations Development Program. 2008. *UN 2001 Road Map Towards Implementation of the United Nations Millennium Declaration.* Available online at *www.undp.org/mdg/basics.shtml.* New York: United Nations.

Vandergeest, P., and F. Buttel. 1988. "Marx, Weber, and Development Sociology: Beyond the Impasse." *World Development* 16: 683–695.

Vico, G. B. 1984 ed. *The New Science of Giambattista Vico.* Trans. T. G. Bergin and M. H. Fisch. Ithaca, NY: Cornell University Press.

Visvanathan, N. 1997. "Introduction to Part I." In Visvanathan et al. (1997: 17–32).

Visvanathan, N., L. Duggan, L. Nisonoff, and N. Wiegersma, eds., 1997. *The Women, Gender and Development Reader.* London: Zed Books.

Visvanathan, S. 1986. "Bhopal: The Imagination of a Disaster." *Alternatives* 11: 147–165.

Visvanathan, S. 1991. "Mrs Bruntland's Disenchanted Cosmos." *Alternatives* 16: 377–384.

Vogel, L. 1983. *Marxism and the Oppression of Women.* London: Pluto.

von Hayek, F. 1945. "The Use of Knowledge in Society." *American Economic Review* 34: 519–530.

von Hayek, F. 1984. "The Principles of a Liberal Social Order." In C. Nishiyama and K. Leube (eds.), *The Essence of Hayek.* Stanford, CA: Hoover Institution Press.

von Hayek, F. 1994 ed. *The Road to Serfdom.* Chicago: University of Chicago Press.

von Mises, L. 1912. *Theory of Money and Credit.* English translation by H. G. Batson. 1981. Indianapolis, IN: Liberty Fund.

von Mises, L. 1919. *Nation, State, and Economy.* Trans. Yeager. New York: New York University Press.

von Mises, L. 1922. *Socialism: An Economic and Sociological Analysis.* New Haven, CT: Yale University Press.

Wade, R. 1990. *Governing the Market: Economic Theory and the Role of Government in East Asian Industrialization.* Princeton, NJ: Princeton University Press.

Wallerstein, I. 1974. *The Modern World System* (Vol.1). New York: Academic Press.

Wallerstein, I. 1979. *The Capitalist World Economy.* New York: Cambridge University Press.

Wallerstein, I. 1980. *The Modern World System* (Vol. 2). New York: Academic Press.

Wallerstein, I. 1988. *The Modern World System* (Vol. 3). New York: Academic Press.

Watts, M. 1983. *Silent Violence: Food, Famine and Peasantry in Northern Nigeria.* Berkeley: University of California Press.

Weber, M. 1958 ed. *The Protestant Ethic and the Spirit of Capitalism*. New York: Charles Scribner's Sons.

Weber, M. 1978 ed. *Max Weber: Selections in Translation*. Ed. W. G. Runciman. Trans. E. Matthews. Cambridge, UK: Cambridge University Press.

Weeks, J. 1981. *Capital and Exploitation*. London: Edward Arnold.

Weeks, P. 1990. "Post-Colonial Challenges to Grand Theory." *Human Organization* 49, 3: 236–244.

Weinstein, M. 2005. "Venezuela's Hugo Chavez makes his bid for a Bolivarian revolution: Power and Interest News Report." Available online at *www.pinr.com/report.php?ac=view_printable&report_id=285&language_id=1*.

Wiarda, H. J. 1998. "Is Comparative Politics Dead? Rethinking the Field in the Post Cold War Era." *Third World Quarterly* 19: 935–949.

Williamson, J., ed. 1990. *Latin American Adjustment: How Much Has Happened?* Washington, DC: Institute for International Economics.

Williamson, J. 1997. "The Washington Consensus Revisited." In L. Emmerij (ed.), *Economic and Social Development into the XXI Century*. Washington, DC: Inter-American Development Bank, 48–61.

Williamson, O. E. 1985. *The Economic Institutions of Capitalism: Firms, Markets, Relational Contracting*. New York: Free Press.

Wilpert, G. 2006. *Changing Venezuela: The History and Policies of the Chavez Government*. London: Verso.

Wolf, E. 1982. *Europe and the People without History*. Berkeley: University of California Press.

World Bank. 1978. *World Development Report*. New York: Oxford University Press.

World Bank. 1981. *Accelerated Development in Sub-Saharan Africa: An Agenda for Action*. Washington, DC: World Bank.

World Bank. 1983. *World Development Report*. New York: Oxford University Press.

World Bank. 1984. *World Development Report*. New York: Oxford University Press.

World Bank. 1985. *World Development Report*. New York: Oxford University Press.

World Bank. 1987. *World Development Report*. New York: Oxford University Press.

World Bank. 1989. *World Development Report*. New York: Oxford University Press.

World Bank. 1990. *World Development Report*. New York: Oxford University Press.

World Bank. 1997. *World Development Report*. New York: Oxford University Press.

World Bank. 1998. *East Asia: The Road to Recovery*. Washington, DC: Author.

World Bank. 2004. *World Development Report*. New York: Oxford University Press.

World Bank. 2005. *World Development Report*. New York: Oxford University Press.

World Bank. 2007. *World Development Report*. New York: Oxford University Press.

Yergin, D., and J. Stanislaw. 1999. *The Commanding Heights: The Battle between*

Government and the Marketplace That Is Remaking the Modern World. New York: Touchstone.

Young, K. 1993. *Planning Development with Women.* New York: St. Martin's Press.

Young, R. 1990. *White Mythologies: Writing History and the West.* London: Routledge.

Zeitlin, I. M. 1972. *Capitalism and Imperialism: An Introduction to Neo-Marxian Concepts.* Chicago: Markham.

Zinn, H. 2005. *A People's History of the United States. 1492–Present.* New York: HarperCollins.

Index

Page numbers followed by an *f*, *n*, or *t* indicate figures, notes, or tables.

About the Authors

Richard Peet grew up near Liverpool, England, and received degrees from the London School of Economics (BSc), the University of British Columbia (MA), and the University of California at Berkeley (PhD). Currently, he is Professor of Geography at Clark University in Worcester, Massachusetts, where he was a founding member of the "radical geography movement" and a long-time editor of *Antipode: A Radical Journal of Geography*. Dr. Peet's interests include development, global policy regimes, power, theory and philosophy, political ecology, and the causes of financial crises. He is the author of numerous articles, book reviews, and books, including *Liberation Ecologies* (coedited with Michael Watts), *Unholy Trinity: The IMF, World Bank and WTO*, and *Geography of Power: Making Global Economic Policy*. Dr. Peet serves as editor of a new radical journal, *Human Geography*, and is working on two edited books, *New Economic Policy in India* (with Waquar Ahmed) and *Political Ecology of Global Environmental Crisis* (with Michael Watts and Paul Robbins).

Elaine Hartwick grew up in Hartford, Connecticut, and received degrees from Clark University (BA and PhD) and Boston University (MA). She has published on a variety of topics, including commodity chains, consumer politics, social theory, and development geography, with a regional specialization in Southern Africa. Currently, Dr. Hartwick serves as Associate Professor at Framingham State College in Framingham, Massachusetts, where she teaches courses in political, cultural, and regional geography and global development.